*Oracle Press*™

Oracle8*i* SQLJ Programming

Nirva Morisseau-Leroy
Martin K. Solomon
Gerald P. Momplaisir

Osborne/**McGraw-Hill**

Berkeley New York St. Louis San Francisco
Auckland Bogotá Hamburg London Madrid
Mexico City Milan Montreal New Delhi Panama City
Paris São Paulo Singapore Sydney Tokyo Toronto

Osborne/**McGraw-Hill**
2600 Tenth Street
Berkeley, California 94710
U.S.A.

For information on translations or book distributors outside the U.S.A., or to arrange bulk purchase discounts for sales promotions, premiums, or fund-raisers, please contact Osborne/**McGraw-Hill** at the above address.

Oracle8*i* SQLJ Programming

1234567890 AGM AGM 019876543210

ISBN 0-07-212160-2

Publisher Brandon A. Nordin	**Copy Editor** Gary Morris
Associate Publisher and Editor-in-Chief Scott Rogers	**Proofreader** Stefany Otis
Acquisitions Editor Jeremy Judson	**Indexer** James Minkin
Project Editor Ron Hull	**Computer Designers** Dick Schwartz Jim Kussow
Editorial Assistant Monika Faltiss	**Illustrators** Beth Young Robert Hansen
Technical Editor Dr. Bruce Horowitz	**Series Designer** Jani Beckwith

This book was composed with Corel VENTURA™ Publisher.

To my husband Axel, my children, Tara, Gina,
the journalist and Webmaster, and Alain,
and the special members of my family.

Nirva Morisseau-Leroy

To the memory of my parents, Bertha and Joseph Solomon,
and to my two precious daughters, Rachel Smith,
the South Korean radio DJ, and Michelle Solomon,
the Deerfield Beach historian.

Martin K. Solomon

To all the grandparents, single mothers, single fathers,
aunts, and uncles whose children blossom
and succeed against all odds.

Gerald P. Momplaisir

About the Authors

Nirva Morisseau-Leroy, MSCS, is an Oracle Database Administrator and Application Developer at the National Oceanic and Atmospheric Administration (NOAA) University of Miami Cooperative Institute for Marine and Atmospheric Sciences, assigned to the Hurricane Research Division (HRD) of the Atlantic Oceanographic and Meteorological Laboratory (AOML). She has over sixteen years of information systems experience as an Oracle DBA, Application Developer, and MIS director utilizing, Java, JDBC, SQLJ, SQL, Oracle PL/SQL, and UNIX C/C++. Her major areas of expertise are in users' requirements elicitation, object-oriented analysis and design, data modeling, relational and object-relational database analysis, design, implementation, and administration. She can be reached at nmorisseauleroy@data-i.com.

Dr. Martin K. Solomon is an Associate Professor of Computer Science and Engineering at Florida Atlantic University. His major areas of research include the design, implementation, and theory of database systems, computational complexity theory, and the philosophical aspects of computability. Dr. Solomon has published articles on these topics in such prestigious journals as *ACM Transactions on Database Systems, Communications of the ACM, Journal of Symbolic Logic, and British Journal for the Philosophy of Science.*

He has a strong professional interest in all aspects of the Oracle RDBMS, and is a frequent contributor to the *South Florida Oracle Users Group Newsletter*. Dr. Solomon can be reached by e-mail at: marty@cse.fau.edu.

Gerald P. Momplaisir has been working professionally in the information technology field for over thirteen years. During this time, he served in the military in technical and management capacities, and later at an NOAA environmental research laboratory where he functioned as a programmer/computer specialist—eventually ascending to Director of Computer Services. During the past eight years, he has specialized in Oracle, object-oriented systems, and internetworking technologies. His love for database systems and object-oriented technologies led him to attain a graduate degree in Computer Science after completing a thesis on the design and implementation of a financial system using a semantic (object-oriented) database and C++. A principal consultant and cofounder of Datai Inc., he currently works as a consultant, project manager, and certified trainer at midsize companies, government entities, and Fortune 500 corporations. He can be reached at gmomplaisir@data-i.com.

Contents

PART I
Basic Oracle8*i* SQLJ

v

PART III
SQLJ and Object Deployment

PART IV
Effective Use of SQLJ

PART V
Appendices

Foreword

With the rapid growth of the Internet and e-business, a new generation of enterprise applications are being built to attract and retain customers through the Internet, to market and sell them products through the Web, to tie suppliers and partners together to deliver products and services more quickly to customers, and to automate corporate business process efficiencies through self-service. This new generation of enterprise applications is being designed to fit the Internet's architecture—the application is built to comply with 100 percent Internet standards, it is deployed on highly scalable servers, and it is accessed from standard Internet browsers.

Java has emerged as the primary language for building such applications due to its power, portability, and productivity. It is the only modern, object-oriented programming language designed for the Internet. To build enterprise applications in Java, application developers needed two facilities—a highly scalable server environment in which to run Java and a simple, easy-to-program link between Java and SQL, the language in which most of the world's data is defined and stored.

Oracle recognized the emergence of the Internet Computing model and these two fundamental needs and made major strategic investments: Oracle8*i* JServer and SQLJ. To provide developers with the industry's most scalable, highly available, and high-performance Java server environment—Oracle8*i* JServer—we designed a highly specialized Java Virtual Machine directly into Oracle8*i*, our Internet database.

While complying completely with Java standards, JServer is able to support thousands of concurrent clients and scales excellently across a wide range of hardware configurations.

Oracle's other investment—SQLJ, or embedded SQL in Java—provides the simplest and most elegant way to build database applications in Java. An industry standard accepted by the ANSI/ISO standards bodies and supported by all the major database vendors, SQLJ provides a portable way to build a variety of different types of programs—database stored procedures, triggers, Enterprise JavaBeans, CORBA services, and even applets. SQLJ is designed to be simpler to use than JDBC but complement it; you can combine the two in building applications. With Oracle's comprehensive support for SQLJ, you can quickly and efficiently build applications combining Java and the Oracle database and deploy them on the Internet.

Oracle8i SQLJ Programming, by Nirva Morisseau-Leroy, Martin K. Solomon, and Gerald P. Momplaisir, is precisely the tool you need to master SQLJ programming. It begins by introducing you to why SQLJ is useful and how to get started building applications in SQLJ. It then provides a number of more detailed chapters that succinctly provide you with the necessary background to the core of SQLJ programming—including how it can be combined with SQL, PL/SQL, Java, and JDBC. Finally, as you grow in your use of SQLJ, it provides a number of superbly written advanced programming chapters that deal with such topics as server-side programming in SQLJ, combining SQLJ with the Oracle database's object-relational facilities, and distributed systems development in SQLJ involving Remote Method Invocation (RMI), CORBA Services, and Enterprise JavaBeans.

I really enjoyed the practical nature with which all the material was presented and the very rich examples on how to use SQLJ in building real applications. I am very excited about the publication of this book. I know that you will find it an indispensable guide as you learn to use SQLJ and Oracle8i JServer.

Thomas Kurian
Vice President: e-business
Oracle Corporation

Preface

"May you live in interesting times" sounds innocuous but is actually a virulent invective. The history of the computer industry is littered with victims living in interesting times who could not see the road ahead, not for want of intelligence but rather for an untimely lack of practical applicability. These predictions may sound familiar:

1943   "I think there is a world market for maybe five computers."

—Thomas Watson, Chairman of IBM

1977   "There is no reason anyone would want a computer in their home."

—Ken Olson, President, Chairman and Founder of Digital Equipment Corporation

1981   "Who in their right mind would ever need more than 640K of RAM?"

—Bill Gates, Chairman and CEO of Microsoft

But is it a curse to be living in a time when the computer industry undergoes major paradigmatic shifts with this or that company's acquisition, upon the IPO of yet another startup, or as a result of brainstorming over steaming cups of espresso (doubles, of course)? Not when the net effect is to make the tools of computing easier and more accessible to the masses. The wise prognosticator with a calculating eye on the odds thus accepts change as fundamental to the natural order:

Today   "The Internet changes everything."

—Larry Ellison,
Chairman and CEO of Oracle Corporation

The face of computing is changing with every passing clock tick. Application developers now have more tools, more powerful and scalable platforms, and a 24×7 worldwide economy ready to absorb whatever Internet and e-business solutions they can create. Equally important, the task of application development is becoming easier through the adoption of platform-independent and Internet-ready standards, making the goal of code reuse and interoperability a reality.

In particular, the Java programming language and Oracle8*i* JServer integrate seamlessly to enable application developers and database designers to harness the full potential of Internet computing. This book provides you with an in-depth understanding of the tight coupling between Java and Oracle8*i* JServer by focusing on a recent advancement in the realm of e-business applications design and implementation: SQLJ, the standard for embedding static SQL within Java programs.

The SQLJ standard provides a means by which developers can embed SQL statements directly into their Java code without having to worry about database intrinsics or data access mechanisms. Developers can drop SQL statements (DDL, DML, queries, and stored procedure calls) right into their code and delegate to SQLJ the work of communicating with the database, marshalling data, and managing result sets. SQLJ is intended to increase developer productivity without compromising application robustness or performance.

The Internet is indeed changing everything. As more and more businesses and people work and transact online, the need for new Internet computing and e-business solutions becomes insatiable. To meet this demand, application developers and database designers need to be flexible and prolific. Java and Oracle8*i* JServer significantly reduce the barriers to entry for developing robust, scalable e-business applications, thus allowing SQLJ practitioners to be proactive agents of change rather than bemused victims of it.

Sound good? Then read on!

How the Book Is Organized

For those programmers who are prone to flights of fancy, take note! This book leaves as little as possible to the imagination. The book's intent is to equip you with all of the skills and tools necessary to put SQLJ and Oracle8*i* JServer to work immediately to build Internet computing and e-business solutions.

You'll find that the book takes your hand and leads you through well-integrated and step-by-step coverage of SQLJ and the Oracle8*i* JServer, progressing through more advanced scenarios at a comfortable pace, and leaving you in a better place where you're ready to begin using your fresh SQLJ techniques in the real world.

Other facets of the book which should appeal to you include:

- Treatment of traditional relational as well as object-relational usage scenarios

- Complete, realistic programs, with line-by-line inspection

- Comprehensive deployment scenarios: client-side, server-side, client/server, and n-tier

- Demonstrations of the tight integration between SQLJ and the Oracle8*i* JServer

- A tutorial on the basics (for those new to Oracle or Java)

The book is divided into five parts that build upon each other.

Part I: Basic Oracle8i SQLJ

This introductory section leads off with a view of SQLJ from 30,000 feet, gradually descending below cloud cover to reach ground level. The basics of SQLJ syntax, tools, implementation, and deployment are covered in great detail and reinforced by comprehensive real-world sample code. By the end of this part, you should have a firm grasp of how to implement SQLJ with the Oracle8*i* JServer to modify and retrieve data from the database, as well as how to create and drop database objects. Chapters include:

- Chapter 1: Introduction to Oracle8*i* SQLJ

- Chapter 2: SQLJ Program Development

- Chapter 3: Basic SQLJ Programming

Part II: Advanced SQLJ for Relational Processing

In Part II, you'll learn to build truly robust, scalable SQLJ-based solutions by taking advantage of SQLJ's tight integration with Oracle8*i*. SQLJ joins PL/SQL (Oracle's proprietary procedural SQL language) as Oracle8*i*'s stored procedure language. This part will instruct you in the myriad ways in which to build 100 percent Java database solutions via SQLJ stored procedures and triggers. Chapters include:

- Chapter 4: Developing SQLJ Stored Procedures and Triggers

- Chapter 5: Advanced SQLJ Deployment

- Chapter 6: Advanced SQLJ Features

Part III: SQLJ and Object Deployment

Java brings application-level object oriented design and development to the masses. Oracle8*i*'s object-relational model allows object orientation to take place at the logical level as well. This part covers the object-relational features of Oracle8*i*, as well as how to interface with them via SQLJ-based methods and components. Chapters include:

- Chapter 7: Object-Relational Processing Using SQLJ

- Chapter 8: SQLJ Business and Scientific Object Deployment

Part IV: Effective Use of SQLJ

Building upon your newfound understanding of how to design, implement, and deploy your SQLJ code, this part will help you refine your solutions to be ready for prime time. Learn proven techniques to optimize your SQLJ methods and components, exploiting the robust and highly tunable Oracle8*i* platform. And if you didn't think that SQLJ was enough of a productivity boost, you'll also learn how to ease your development burden even further via Oracle tools designed expressly for Internet computing and e-business solutions. Chapters include:

- Chapter 9: SQLJ Applications—Performance Tuning

- Chapter 10: Oracle8*i* Development Tools

Part V: Appendices

For experienced Java and Oracle application developers, these appendices will be a welcome reference that you can access whenever the need arises—typically when you least expect it in the wee hours of the morning as you stare bleary-eyed at a computer screen full of code listings, wondering if it's worth the effort to swill the sludge (some might call it coffee) left warming in a pot in the kitchen. The rest of you will get a quick and dirty introduction to the mechanics of Oracle SQL, Java, JDBC, and SQLJ. Appendices include:

- Appendix A: Basic Oracle SQL

- Appendix B: Java Basics

- Appendix C: Introduction to Java Database Connectivity (JDBC)

- Appendix D: SQLJ Quick Reference Guide

Intended Audience

The traditional audience for this book will be application developers and database designers, the two groups most likely to take advantage of SQLJ in solutions (application developers) or as stored procedures and triggers (database designers). These groups also include those who aspire to the ranks of designers and implementers, including students in undergraduate and graduate programs studying The Next Best Thing in computing paradigms.

We also encourage experienced Java programmers who haven't had much database exposure to broaden their minds by wringing every last bit of information from this text. SQLJ eases the transition from monolithic, non-persistent Java programs to n-tier, database-driven e-business solutions. Take the next step in the evolution of your skills by joining the SQLJ community.

Though this book caters to programmers and database designers, we have no wish to be exclusionary. If you are familiar with the Java programming language or are willing to learn it, we hope that you'll also be interested in this book regardless of your background. You never know where your career might lead given the right opportunity and catalyst.

Internet computing's next big wave will bring us a new generation of e-business solutions. Using SQLJ as your board, and this book as your wax and sunscreen, you'll find no better battle cry than "Surf's up!"

Edward Griffin
Technical Director, Internet Servers
Alliances Partner Services
Oracle Corporation

Acknowledgments

ur book was made possible because of many people. I especially appreciate their support, advice, and feedback during the development of this project. Special thanks to Diane Spence, Senior Marketing Manager, Oracle Corporation, and the very first person to know about the book and to help me during the entire project. I would like to thank Edward O. Griffin, Technical Director, Oracle Corporation and a member of his staff, Kevin Ling, who assisted me during many months with the new release of Oracle8*i*. I would like to acknowledge the excellent technical suggestions of Luis R. Amat, Jr., Braden N. McDaniel, and Bruce M. Horowitz. Many special thanks to my coauthors, Martin K. Solomon and Gerald P. Momplaisir. Thanks to Dr. Mark D. Powell, Atmospheric Scientist, and his H*WIND team at the NOAA's Hurricane Research Division, Jeremy Judson, senior editor, Ron Hull, Gary Morris, Monika Faltiss, and Brian Wells of the Osborne/McGraw-Hill editorial staff, and the Server Technologies SQLJ Development Group, Oracle Corporation.

Nirva Morisseau-Leroy
Miami, Florida
September 1999

I would like to acknowledge the excellent technical suggestions of Bruce M. Horowitz of Telcordia Technologies, the code testing assistance of Carmine Pizzuto, the invaluable help of Ron Hull, Gary Morris, and Monika Faltiss of the Osborne/McGraw-Hill editorial staff, and the editorial leadership of Jeremy Judson. I also thank my wife Abby for her tireless typing contributions. I give special thanks to my coauthors, Nirva Morisseau-Leroy and Gerald P. Momplaisir, for being such a pleasure with whom to work.

Martin K. Solomon
Miami, Florida
September 1999

I would like to acknowledge the many people who contributed to this book. The staff of Osborne/McGraw-Hill, Jeremy Judson, Monika Faltiss, Ron Hull, and Gary Morris, who worked so hard to make this book a reality. I must thank Bruce M. Horowitz for his technical review and suggestions, and the review and comments of Luis R. Amat, Jr., Oracle Consulting. Special thanks goes to my wife Tara for providing the data for the SQL scripts of this book and her endless small contributions. Finally, I would like to express many thanks to my coauthors Nirva Morisseau-Leroy for her vision, inspiration, and tireless support of this project and "Marty" K. Solomon for his suggestions.

Gerald P. Momplaisir
Miami, Florida
September 1999

Introduction

his book focuses on the development of database applications written in SQLJ and Java. Although the application programs presented in this book were designed to run against an Oracle database 7.*x x* and later, with minimum changes, they can also be used against any SQL-based, that is, "pure" relational or object-relational database management system (DBMS).

Database Schemas

In Parts I and II of the book, you will develop SQLJ programs that manipulate a "pure" relational database, that is, a financial schema called the Purchase Order schema. The *Purchase Order* relational database schema is part of a database design presented in the *Design of a Financial Administrative System Using the Semantic Binary Model* [32]. In Part III, you will develop SQLJ programs that manipulate an object-relational database, that is, a scientific schema called the *Observation* schema. The Observation object-relational database schema is part of the scientific database design presented in the *Atmospheric Observations, Analyses, and the World Wide Web Using a Semantic Database* [34].

The Purchase Order and the Observation schemas were designed for the Atlantic Oceanographic and Meteorological Laboratory (AOML), Miami, Florida, an Environmental Research Laboratory (ERL) of the National Oceanic and Atmospheric

Administration (NOAA), part of the U.S. Department of Commerce (DOC). In particular, the Observation schema was designed for the Hurricane Research Division (HRD) at AOML and is currently being implemented by HRD as part of the H*WIND system that produces real-time surface wind analyses to National Hurricane Center's (NHC) forecasters and the FEMA Hurricane Liaison Team at NHC.

SQL Scripts to Create the Financial Purchase Order Schema

Use the following `createposchema.sql` SQL script to create the Purchase Order schema in the Oracle8*i* database:

```
-- File Name:  createposchema.sql

CREATE TABLE DEPARTMENT_LIST(
deptno          NUMBER(5),
shortname       VARCHAR2(6),
longname        VARCHAR2(20))
/
CREATE TABLE ACCOUNT_LIST (
accountno       NUMBER(5),
projectno       NUMBER(5),
deptno          NUMBER(5)),
PRIMARY KEY ( accountno )
/
CREATE TABLE EMPLOYEE_LIST(
employeeno      NUMBER(7),
deptno          NUMBER(5),
type            VARCHAR2(30),
lastname        VARCHAR2(30),
firstname       VARCHAR2(30),
phone           VARCHAR2(10))
/
CREATE TABLE CREDITCARD_LIST (
cardno              VARCHAR2(15),
employeeno          NUMBER(7),
expirationdate      DATE)
/
CREATE TABLE CHECKACCOUNT_LIST(
accountno       NUMBER(5),
employeeno      NUMBER(7))
/
```

```
CREATE TABLE VENDOR_LIST(
vendorno     NUMBER(6),
name         VARCHAR2(30),
address      VARCHAR2(20),
city         VARCHAR2(15),
state        VARCHAR2(15),
vzip         VARCHAR2(15),
country      VARCHAR2(15))
/
CREATE TABLE PROJECT_LIST (
projectno       NUMBER(5),
projectname     VARCHAR2(20),
start_date      DATE,
amt_of_funds    NUMBER,
PRIMARY KEY( projectno );
/
CREATE TABLE PURCHASE_LIST (
requestno       NUMBER(10),
employeeno      NUMBER(7),
vendorno        NUMBER(6),
purchasetype    VARCHAR2(20),
checkno         NUMBER(11),
whenpurchased   DATE)
/
CREATE TABLE LINEITEM_LIST (
requestno       NUMBER(10),
lineno          NUMBER(5),
projectno       NUMBER(5),
quantity        NUMBER(5),
unit            VARCHAR2(2),
estimatedcost   NUMBER(8,2),
actualcost      NUMBER(8,2),
description     VARCHAR2(30))
/
```

Use the following to create constraints for the Purchase Order schema:

```
-- File Name: poconstraints.sql
alter table DEPARTMENT_LIST
  ADD CONSTRAINT deptno_pk PRIMARY KEY(deptno)
  USING INDEX TABLESPACE INDX
/
ALTER TABLE ACCOUNT_LIST
  ADD CONSTRAINT projectno_pk PRIMARY KEY(projectno)
  USING INDEX TABLESPACE INDX
/
```

```
ALTER TABLE ACCOUNT_LIST
  ADD CONSTRAINT acc_deptno_fk
  FOREIGN KEY(deptno)
  REFERENCES DEPARTMENT_LIST(deptno)
  USING INDEX TABLESPACE INDX
/
ALTER TABLE EMPLOYEE_LIST
  ADD CONSTRAINT employeeno_pk PRIMARY KEY(employeeno)
  USING INDEX TABLESPACE INDX
/
ALTER TABLE EMPLOYEE_LIST
  ADD CONSTRAINT emp_deptno_fk
  FOREIGN KEY(deptno)
  REFERENCES DEPARTMENT_LIST(deptno)
  USING INDEX TABLESPACE INDX
/
ALTER TABLE CREDITCARD_LIST
  ADD CONSTRAINT cardno_pk PRIMARY KEY(cardno)
  USING INDEX TABLESPACE INDX
/
ALTER TABLE CREDITCARD_LIST
  ADD CONSTRAINT credit_employeeno_fk
  FOREIGN KEY(employeeno)
  REFERENCES EMPLOYEE_LIST(employeeno)
  USING INDEX TABLESPACE INDX
/
ALTER TABLE CHECKACCOUNT_LIST
  ADD CONSTRAINT accountno_pk PRIMARY KEY(accountno)
  USING INDEX TABLESPACE INDX
/
ALTER TABLE CHECKACCOUNT_LIST
  ADD CONSTRAINT check_employeeno_fk
  FOREIGN KEY(employeeno)
  REFERENCES EMPLOYEE_LIST(employeeno)
  USING INDEX TABLESPACE INDX
/
ALTER TABLE vendor_list
  ADD CONSTRAINT vendorno_pk PRIMARY KEY(vendorno)
  USING INDEX TABLESPACE INDX
/
ALTER TABLE Purchase_list
  ADD CONSTRAINT requestno_pk PRIMARY KEY(requestno)
  USING INDEX TABLESPACE INDX
/
```

```
ALTER TABLE LINEITEM_LIST
  ADD CONSTRAINT lineno_pk
  PRIMARY KEY(requestno,lineno,projectno)
  USING INDEX TABLESPACE INDX
/
```

Use the following to create sequences for the Purchase Order schema:

```
-- File Name: posequences.sql
CREATE SEQUENCE deptno_SEQ
  START WITH 200
  INCREMENT BY 1
/
CREATE SEQUENCE projectno_SEQ
  START WITH 300
  INCREMENT BY 1
/
CREATE SEQUENCE employeeno_SEQ
  START WITH 100
  INCREMENT BY 1
/
CREATE SEQUENCE accountno_SEQ
  START WITH 1000
  INCREMENT BY 1
/
CREATE SEQUENCE cardno_SEQ
  START WITH 311200
  INCREMENT BY 1
/
CREATE SEQUENCE vendorno_SEQ
  START WITH 400
  INCREMENT BY 1
/
CREATE SEQUENCE requestno_SEQ
  START WITH 500
  INCREMENT BY 1
/
CREATE SEQUENCE lineno_SEQ
  START WITH 1
  INCREMENT BY 1
/
```

SQL Scripts to Create the Scientific Observation Schema

Use the following createobjschema.sql SQL script to create the scientific Observation schema in the Oracle8*i* database:

```
-- File Name:  createobjschema.sql
CREATE TYPE PLATFORM_TYPE AS OBJECT(
key_id        NUMBER(8),
type          VARCHAR2(50),
description   VARCHAR2(50))
/
CREATE TABLE PLATFORM_TYPE_LIST OF PLATFORM_TYPE
/
CREATE TYPE SCIENTIST AS OBJECT(
usr_id        NUMBER(6),
lastname      VARCHAR2(20),
firstname     VARCHAR2(20),
platform_id   NUMBER,
for_platform  REF PLATFORM_TYPE)
/
CREATE TABLE SCIENTIST_LIST OF SCIENTIST
/
CREATE TYPE ATMOSEVENT AS OBJECT(
key_id          NUMBER(8),
when_t          DATE,
name            VARCHAR2(30),
type            VARCHAR2(20),
refkey          NUMBER(8),
transformed_to  REF atmosevent)
/
CREATE TABLE ATMOSEVENT_LIST OF ATMOSEVENT
/
CREATE TYPE OCEANIC_OBSERVATION AS OBJECT(
latitude_deg            NUMBER(10,4),
longitude_deg           NUMBER(10,4),
windspeed_mps           NUMBER(10,4),
adj_windspeed_mps       NUMBER(10,4),
wind_direction_deg      NUMBER(6),
pressure_mb             NUMBER(6),
air_temperature_c       NUMBER(8,2),
geohgt_m                NUMBER(8,3),
wind_gust_mps           NUMBER(10,4),
friction_velocity       NUMBER(10,4),
dew_temperature_c       NUMBER(8,2),
wet_bulb_temperature_c  NUMBER(8,2),
relative_humidity_perc  NUMBER(5,2),
```

```
sea_temperature_c        NUMBER(8,2),
sig_wave_hgt_m           NUMBER(8,3),
avg_wave_period_s        NUMBER(8,3),
mean_wave_dir_deg        NUMBER(10,4))
/
CREATE OR REPLACE TYPE OCEANIC_OBSERVATION_TYPE AS OBJECT(
obs_id          NUMBER(8),
when_t          DATE,
at_time         CHAR(8),
station_id      NUMBER(6),
produced_id     NUMBER(8),
produced_by     REF PLATFORM_TYPE,
obsobj          OCEANIC_OBSERVATION)
/
-- List of all oceanic observations by date, time, and platform type
CREATE TABLE OCEANIC_OBSERVATION_LIST OF OCEANIC_OBSERVATION_TYPE
/
-- use qc_id_seq to update QUALITY_CONTROL_EVENT qc_id
CREATE TYPE QUALITY_CONTROL_EVENT AS OBJECT(
qc_id           NUMBER(8),
when_t          DATE,
at_time         CHAR(8),
event_id        NUMBER(8),
for_event       REF atmosevent,
whom_id         NUMBER(6),
by_whom         REF scientist)
/
CREATE TABLE QC_EVENT_LIST OF QUALITY_CONTROL_EVENT
/
CREATE TYPE PASSEDOBS AS OBJECT(
obsid       NUMBER(8),
passed      CHAR(1))
/
CREATE TYPE PASSEDOBSARRAY AS TABLE OF PASSEDOBS
/
CREATE TABLE PASSED_OBSERVATION_LIST(
passed_id   NUMBER(5),
qcid        NUMBER(8),
when_t      DATE,
at_time     CHAR(8),
idobj       passedObsArray)
NESTED TABLE idobj STORE AS pobsid_list
/
ALTER TABLE POBSID_LIST
STORAGE (MINEXTENTS 1 MAXEXTENTS 20)
/
```

Use the following to create constraints for the Observation schema:

```
-- File Name: objconstraints.sql
ALTER TABLE PLATFORM_TYPE_LIST
 ADD CONSTRAINT PT_KEY_ID_PK PRIMARY KEY(KEY_ID)
 USING INDEX TABLESPACE INDX
/
ALTER TABLE SCIENTIST_LIST
 ADD CONSTRAINT SL_USR_ID_PK PRIMARY KEY(USR_ID)
 USING INDEX TABLESPACE INDX
/
ALTER TABLE ATMOSEVENT_LIST
 ADD CONSTRAINT AL_KEY_ID_PK PRIMARY KEY(KEY_ID)
 USING INDEX TABLESPACE INDX
/
ALTER TABLE OCEANIC_OBSERVATION_LIST
ADD CONSTRAINT O_OBS_ID_PK PRIMARY KEY(OBS_ID)
 USING INDEX TABLESPACE INDX
/
ALTER TABLE QC_EVENT_LIST
ADD CONSTRAINT QC_ID_PK PRIMARY KEY(QC_ID)
 USING INDEX TABLESPACE INDX
/
ALTER TABLE QC_EVENT_LIST
ADD CONSTRAINT qc_whom_id_fk
 FOREIGN KEY(whom_id)
 REFERENCES SCIENTIST_LIST(usr_id)
 ON DELETE CASCADE
/
ALTER TABLE PASSED_OBSERVATION_LIST
ADD CONSTRAINT passed_id_pk PRIMARY KEY (passed_id)
 USING INDEX TABLESPACE INDX
/
ALTER TABLE PASSED_OBSERVATION_LIST
 ADD Constraint po_qc_id_fk
 FOREIGN KEY(qcid)
 REFERENCES QC_EVENT_LIST(qc_id)
 ON DELETE CASCADE
/
ALTER TABLE PASSED_OBSERVATION_LIST
ADD CONSTRAINT passed_qcid_ukey UNIQUE(qcid)
 USING INDEX TABLESPACE INDX
/
ALTER TABLE PASSED_OBSERVATION_LIST
 MODIFY (qcid NOT NULL)
/
```

Use the following to create sequences for the Observation schema:

```
-- File Name: objsequences.sql
-- key_id sequence for PLATFORM_TYPE
CREATE SEQUENCE PT_key_SEQ
 START WITH 1
 INCREMENT BY 1
/
-- usr_id sequence for SCIENTIST
CREATE SEQUENCE USERSEQ
 START WITH 1
 INCREMENT BY 1
/
-- key_id sequence for ATMOSEVENT
CREATE SEQUENCE atm_key_seq
 START WITH 1
 INCREMENT BY 1
/
CREATE SEQUENCE OBSID_SEQ
 START WITH 1
 INCREMENT BY 1
/
-- qc_id sequence for QUALITY_CONTROL_EVENT
CREATE SEQUENCE qc_id_seq
 START WITH 1
 INCREMENT BY 1
/
-- passed_id sequence for PASSED_OBSERVATION
CREATE SEQUENCE passed_id_seq
 START WITH 1
 INCREMENT BY 1
/
```

Conventions Used in This Book

This book uses the following conventions:

- Classes are set in Courier typeface.
  Example   the standard Java class `Java.lang.*`

- Datatypes are set in Courier typeface.
  Example   the `REF CURSOR datatype`

- Filenames and extensions are lowercase and are set in Courier typeface.
  Examples   `.class` files; the `.ser` extension

- Functions and procedures are set in Courier typeface.
  Examples `InsertPurchaseOrder(); a function GetObsId()`

- SQL keywords are all capital letters and are set in Courier typeface.
  Examples `CREATE TABLE; INSERT; DELETE`

- Database table names are all capital letters and are set in Courier typeface.
  Example `PASSED_OBSERVATION`

- Java keywords in paragraphs are boldface and are set in Courier typeface.
  Example `public`

Providing Feedback to the Authors

The authors welcome your comments and suggestions on the quality and usefulness of this book. Your input is important to us. You can send comments to us via electronic mail:

- Nirva Morisseau-Leroy at nmorisseauleroy@data-i.com

- Martin K. Solomon at marty@cse.fau.edu

- Gerald P. Momplaisir at gmomplaisir@data-i.com

Retrieving Examples Online

Program source code and a glossary of terms can be found at http://www.data-i.com and http://www.osborne.com.

Programs whose source code is at the above sites are listed in a file with the same name as the source name, for instance, `SqljAppletCallsSqljSP.sqlj`.

Disclaimer

The programs presented here are not intended for use in any inherently dangerous applications. It shall be the reader's responsibility to take all appropriate fail-safe, backup, redundancy, and other measures to ensure the safe use of such applications.

PART
I

Basic Oracle8*i* SQLJ

CHAPTER
1

Introduction to
Oracle8*i* SQLJ

QLJ is a version of embedded SQL that is tightly integrated with the Java programming language, where embedded SQL is used to invoke SQL statements within "host" general-purpose programming languages such as C, C++, Java, Ada, and COBOL. In an embedded SQL program, it appears that SQL statements are directly supported as host program constructs. C and C++ can also invoke SQL statements through host language function calls via the open database connectivity (ODBC) interface. Similarly, Java programs can invoke SQL statements through the Java database connectivity (JDBC) method calls. However, as you shall see, such function call interfaces are a much lower level than the embedded SQL interfaces, in that the SQL statements in the traditional embedded SQL are passed as string arguments to functions instead of being directly coded within the host program.

Oracle8*i* is a recent release of the Oracle relational database management system (Oracle RDBMS) that heavily emphasizes the Java programming language and the development of Internet/intranet database applications. One of the important features of Oracle8*i* is the full and efficient support of SQLJ. Like with Oracle8, Oracle8*i* not only provides powerful support for relational database processing, but also supports such object-relational structures as collection types, user-defined types, and object types. In Chapter 8, you will learn about object-relational processing using SQLJ.

SQLJ consists of a set of clauses and programmatic extensions that define the interaction between SQL and Java. SQLJ is static embedded SQL for the Java programming language, that is, a SQLJ program is a Java program containing static embedded SQL statements. Note that in static embedded SQL, all the SQL statements embedded in the program are known at compile time, while in dynamic (embedded) SQL at least some SQL statements are not completely known until runtime. SQLJ complements the JDBC dynamic embedded SQL model with a static embedded SQL model, since JDBC provides a dynamic SQL interface for Java, whereas SQLJ provides a static embedded SQL interface. Thus, with the availability of SQLJ, Java programmers have two different programming interfaces between Java and SQL: JDBC and SQLJ. Programming languages such as C, C++, FORTRAN, COBOL, and Ada share essentially the same embedded SQL, whereas SQLJ has been specified for Java as a somewhat different embedded SQL standard by the ANSI standards organizations. This raises the question of why Java has its own embedded SQL, while all the other programming languages share essentially the same embedded SQL. One reason for this is that SQLJ is more tightly coupled to Java, than in other programming languages. In particular, Java classes can be used as the types for the columns in SQL tables. Also, SQLJ provides a strongly typed version of the cursor construct, called an iterator. This iterator construct is nicely integrated into the Java language, with each iterator being a Java class. Note also that, unlike SQLJ, embedded SQL for the other programming languages contains both static and dynamic SQL constructs.

In this chapter, which provides an overview of SQLJ in the Oracle8*i* environment, you will learn the following:

- The relation of the Java language to database processing on the Internet.

- The tight integration of Java and the Oracle8*i* Database Server (Oracle JServer).

- The static embedded SQL model for Java: SQLJ.

- The deployment of SQLJ in thick and thin client-side and in server-side applications.

- The other embedded SQLs such as Pro*C and PL/SQL as they compare to SQLJ.

Relation of the Java Language to Database Processing on the Internet

Java is a modern, object-oriented programming language that borrows heavily from the syntax and semantics of the C and C++ programming languages. Its initial popularity came from its capability for developing client-based applications and adding dynamic content to Web pages. Over the last several years, however, Java has matured from a programming language used to develop client-based programs, in particular Graphical User Interface (GUI) programs, to a platform for developing and deploying applications at all levels of an organization by distributing applications over networks using Internet/intranet capabilities (that is, enterprise applications).

Java facilitates the development of robust and portable programs. Like with most modern programming languages, Java is object-oriented from the ground up. This contributes to the robustness of applications developed in the language. Additionally, Java provides mechanisms that help developers produce robust code, including early (compile) checking, later dynamic (runtime) checking, and a pointer model that eliminates the possibility of overwriting memory and corrupting data. Some of Java's other features that contribute to robustness are automatic storage management (referred to as garbage collection) and type-safety. Such features make Java ideal for server-side programming, where a server crash can be quite costly in terms of time and money. Java defines both a language and a set of standard class libraries (Java packages) that ensure that applications can be constructed to run on any Java Virtual Machine (JVM) or in any other environment. The JVM is an interpreter for Java, and therefore a program that can be ported from one machine architecture to another with minimal change. The JVM is responsible for controlling the Java execution environment and obtaining resources from the computer hardware. Java programs are compiled into compact intermediate code (Java's bytecode) that has no direct correspondence to any given item of hardware. Also, the fact that Java is interpreted makes it easier for the system to perform runtime error checking, further enhancing the robustness of Java programs.

Traditional design and development strategies create monolithic systems. A monolithic system corresponds to a single application, running or executing on a single computer. Business and scientific applications are becoming far more complex than they have ever been. Therefore, their designers are turning to techniques such as distributed systems in response to the increased pressure to better manage and manipulate information. Java provides a platform and framework for developing and deploying applications for today's complex information systems. The Java language, with its component-based models, enables users to assemble, partition, and distribute application components across a network. Java's components consist of a set of platform-independent services, such as Remote Method Invocation (RMI), JavaBeans, and Enterprise JavaBeans (EJB). RMI is a standard Java facility that makes it possible to invoke Java methods remotely, whereas EJB is an architecture for developing transactional applications as distributed components in Java. See Chapter 8 for a tutorial on building RMI, EJB, and CORBA objects.

Java facilitates Internet/intranet development applications. Its virtual machine-based organization defines a highly compact set of bytecodes, which can be efficiently transported in the Internet/intranet environment. Java offers the power to unify the infrastructure of today's computing environment where mission-critical and industrial-strength servers are still heterogeneous. Distributed applications with components that need to communicate across multiple systems in a network can use Java to do so. Java supports many standard communication protocols, including TCP/IP (Transmission Control Protocol/Internet Protocol), HTTP (Hypertext Transfer Protocol), and IIOP (CORBA's Internet Interoperability Protocol).

Java applets, servlets, and applications are appearing all over the Web, bringing rich functionality to what was before a static medium. Leading hardware vendors, infrastructure providers, and software vendors provide support for building extensible applications across all tiers, as well as tools to Web-enable existing client/server applications. Leading browser platforms are building Java Virtual Machines into their systems. Database vendors, such as Oracle and Informix, are integrating Java Virtual Machines with their data servers.

Tight Integration of Java and the Oracle8*i* Database Server

Prior to the release of Oracle8*i*, Oracle application developers used PL/SQL to develop server-side applications that have tight integration with SQL data. PL/SQL is an Oracle RDBMS procedural language extension to SQL. The language integrates features such as exception handling, overloading, and a limited amount of information hiding (accomplished by declaring variables and types in a package body instead of a package specification). In addition to providing these capabilities, PL/SQL subprograms (procedures and functions) and triggers can be stored in the Oracle database server. A subprogram consists of a set of PL/SQL statements that are grouped together as a unit to perform a set of related tasks. They are created and stored in compiled form in the database. Additionally, application programmers can create PL/SQL packages. Packages provide a method of encapsulating and storing related procedures, functions, variables, and other packages constructed together as a unit in the data server. All objects are parsed, compiled, and loaded into memory once. Stored procedures and packages, because of their central location, can be called and executed by users and other database applications. These capabilities offer increased functionality, network traffic reduction, and application and system performance. See Appendix A for a tutorial on PL/SQL.

The Oracle8*i* Database Server, Oracle8*i* JServer, supports two major programming languages, Java and PL/SQL. Both languages seamlessly interoperate and complement each other in the database. SQL and PL/SQL can call Java methods. A Java stored procedure is a program written in Java to execute in the Oracle JServer. Java stored procedures can be called directly with products such as SQL*Plus or indirectly with a trigger and can be accessed from any Net8 client—OCI, PRO*, JDBC, or SQLJ. Java can also call SQL and PL/SQL, via either JDBC or SQLJ. Since the JServer provides a fully compliant implementation of the Java programming language and Virtual Machine, Java developers can develop Java programs independently of PL/SQL.

The Oracle JServer includes a Java Virtual Machine (JVM) and a Java execution environment. Since Java is an interpreted language (interpreted by the JVM) it faces a performance penalty when compared with languages like C or C++. A Java program can run very slowly, and this can be a real problem for Java applications. To address this problem, Oracle delivers the core Java class libraries (such as `java.lang`), the Aurora/ORB (Object Request Broker), and JDBC code in natively compiled form. Standard Java classes, such as `java.lang.*`, exist in shared libraries. Thus, the developer's Java code, which is loaded in the JServer, is interpreted, while the standard classes on which this code relies are fully compiled.

The JVM is embedded in the Oracle data server with native compilation and optimization and is compatible with the Java standard. The Java Virtual Machine executes Java programs on the Oracle8*i* Server. Java applets and applications can access Oracle8*i* via JDBC and/or SQLJ. The integration of the Java Virtual Machine in the data server expands Oracle's support for Java into all tiers of applications, allowing Java programs to be deployed in the client, server, or middle-tier. Using Java and Oracle8*i*, Java programmers can build and deploy server-based Java applications shared by all clients. These applications can easily be distributed across networks, providing access to Oracle data from any computer that supports Java.

Java programmers can access relational and object-relational databases via JDBC. JDBC consists of two parts: the high-level API and multiple low-level drivers for connecting to different databases. The JDBC API is a standard Java interface for connecting to relational databases from Java. It specifies Java interfaces, classes, and exceptions to support database connections, SQL Database Manipulation Language (DML) and SQL Data Definition Language (DDL) statements, processing of data result sets, database metadata, and so on. The JDBC standard was defined by Sun Microsystems. In this scenario, all Java program components such as business logic, GUI (Graphical User Interface), and JDBC drivers reside on the client side (see Figure 1-1).

Oracle8*i* is the first commercial database system to offer an integrated JVM. Oracle8*i* JServer allows programmers to manipulate data with Java and SQLJ directly in the database. The Java Virtual Machine provides a transaction server platform for distributed Java components such as Enterprise JavaBeans. Furthermore, Oracle8*i* JServer supports Java and SQLJ stored procedures, that is, Java and SQLJ logic, in the data server. These procedures can reside either in the clients or in the database and are reusable at both levels.

To ensure fast execution in the Oracle database, Java or SQLJ stored procedures have access to the same server-internal structures as SQL, and incorporate low-level compilation and optimization, which enhance application performance. Furthermore, the Java stored procedures provide better performance, because they are compiled once and stored in bytecode form in the data server. Procedure calls from Oracle JServer are quick and efficient. Browser-based, middle-tier (that is, application server) Java or CORBA clients can communicate with server-side Java/SQLJ procedures and

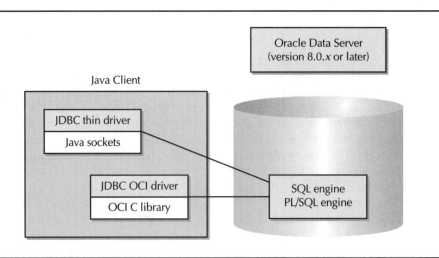

FIGURE 1-1. *JDBC API to connect to database*

EJB components via an object-based protocol such as IIOP. As explained in *Oracle8*i *Java Stored Procedures and Developer's Guide, Release 8.1.5* [39] the Oracle JServer (Figure 1-2) consists of:

■ Oracle's Aurora Java Virtual Machine, the supporting runtime environment and Java class libraries.

■ A tight integration with PL/SQL and Oracle RDBMS functionality.

■ An Object Request Broker (the Aurora/ORB) and Enterprise JavaBeans support. JServer comes with a built-in CORBA 2.0-compliant ORB (Inprise VisiBroker) and support for EJB. Programs developed in any language can communicate directly, via the Aurora/ORB, with the Oracle8*i* database through IIOP, the standard wire protocol defined by the Object Management Group (OMG), a standardization group for object-oriented systems.

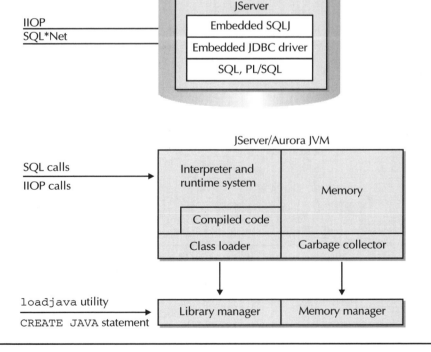

FIGURE I-2.   *Oracle JServer within Oracle8*i *Data Server*

Oracle offers client-side and server-side programming interfaces to Java developers using JDBC and SQLJ (see Figure 1-3). For client applications, Oracle

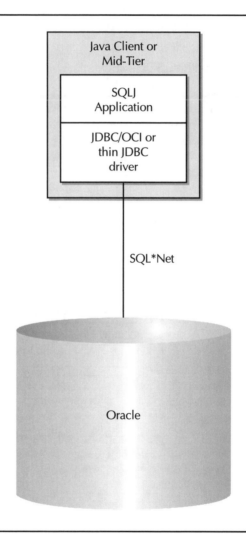

FIGURE 1-3. *SQLJ and/or JDBC to access Oracle JServer*

provides two different JDBC drivers: the JDBC-OCI, for developers writing client-server applications or Java-based middle-tier server and the JDBC-THIN for those writing Java applets. A specialized version of JDBC, JDBC-KPRB, within the database server allows Java applications that execute on the server's Java Virtual Machine to access data defined locally, that is, on the same machine and in the same process via JDBC. See Chapter 2 for SQLJ programs using Oracle JDBC-OCI, JDBC-Thin, and JDBC-KPRB drivers.

Static Embedded SQL Model for Java: SQLJ

SQL is a relational database language that is used to operate on data stored as tables in relational and object-relational database systems. While the origins of the language date from IBM's SEQUEL, the official name is SQL (pronounced S-Q-L). The ANSI/ISO standard follows this usage. SQL is an industry standard, being the most widely used relational database language. In particular, the major RDBMSs, such as Oracle, Sybase, Informix, and Microsoft SQL Server, are all based on SQL.

SQL supports statements to set up the structure of the database (DDL statements) and statements to manipulate the database (DML statements). The CREATE TABLE and CREATE VIEW are examples of DDL statements, and the INSERT, DELETE, UPDATE, and SELECT statements are the principal DML statements. See Appendix A for a tutorial on SQL.

Embedded SQL is a method for combining the computing power of host languages such as Java, C/C++, FORTRAN, COBOL, and Ada with the database processing capabilities of SQL. The term "embedded" SQL literally refers to SQL statements being placed within an application program. Most SQL statements can be placed directly in the source code of application programs, preceded by identifying tokens such as EXEC SQL or #sql. Embedded SQL is supported by most RDBMSs.

Two types of embedded SQL programs exist: dynamic and static. You will learn these concepts next.

Dynamic SQL

Unlike static embedded SQL programs, dynamic SQL programs involve the execution of at least some SQL statements that are not completely known until runtime. Such dynamic SQL statements are not directly embedded in the source program. Instead, they are stored in character strings input into, or built by, the program at runtime.

Dynamic SQL (see Figure 1-4) allows you to create general and flexible applications because the full text of the SQL statement does not have to be known at compilation time. A dynamic SQL program can contain a SQL statement that operates on a table whose name is not known until runtime. SQL statements can be built interactively with input from users having little or no knowledge of SQL.

Dynamic SQL programs can be used to implement such systems as general purpose load utilities, and query processing systems for users with no knowledge of SQL. In particular, stand-alone SQL systems such as Oracle SQL*Plus, and vendor supplied load utilities, such as Oracle SQL LOADER, are typically implemented as dynamic SQL programs.

Static Embedded SQL

In static embedded SQL programs, the SQL commands used by the application program are known at compilation time. With static embedded SQL, all data definition information, such as table definitions referenced by the SQL statements are known at compilation time. Thus, the analysis and optimization of the static embedded SQL programs can be performed at compilation time and consequently show significant speed improvement over dynamic SQL programs, where both analysis and optimization must be performed at runtime.

Overview of SQLJ

SQLJ is a new standard that has emerged as a result of a multi-vendor effort to provide support to embed static SQL in Java programs. As you have seen, a "pure" SQLJ program is static because all SQL statements must be known at compile time. However, including JDBC calls within a SQLJ program permits such a program to be dynamic, since one can compose a SQL statement as a string, and then pass that string to a JDBC method for execution. SQLJ can be used to implement stored procedures, triggers, and classes within the JServer environment, as well as being used with Enterprise JavaBeans and CORBA.

SQLJ consists of a set of clauses that extend Java programs. The language specification is a joint specification supported by leading database-tool vendors and database vendors including IBM, Compaq/Tandem, JavaSoft, Oracle, Sybase, and Informix. SQLJ provides a way to develop applications both on the client side and on the middle-tier that access databases, and on the data server using Java. SQLJ applications are portable and can communicate with databases from multiple vendors using standard JDBC drivers.

When writing a SQLJ program (source code), you write a Java program and you embed SQL statements in it following certain standard syntactic rules that govern how SQL statements can be embedded in Java source code. Then, you run a SQLJ translator to convert the SQLJ program into a standard Java program. An Oracle

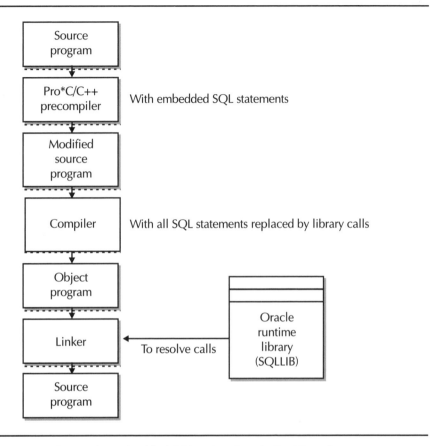

FIGURE 1-4. *Dynamic embedded SQL using Oracle Pro*C tool*

SQLJ translator is conceptually similar to other Oracle embedded SQL precompilers. A SQLJ translator performs the following tasks:

- Syntactic checking of the embedded SQL constructs.

- Java and SQL data type checking.

- Schema checking.

At translation time, the SQLJ translator replaces the embedded SQLJ statements with calls to the SQLJ runtime library, which implements the SQL operations. The result of such a translation is a Java source program that can be compiled using any Java compiler. Once the Java source is compiled, the Java executables can be run against any database.

The SQLJ runtime environment consists of a thin (that is, one containing a small amount of code) SQLJ runtime library, which is implemented in pure Java, and which in turn calls a JDBC driver targeting the appropriate database.

A SQLJ program can be executed in many environments. You can write a SQLJ program that will execute on a "thin" client, such as a Web browser or a network computer, as a client application on a workstation or PC, as part of a middle-tier application, and as a server-side application. Because of this location transparency, you can easily port SQLJ programs from location to location and from system to system. The following diagram (Figure 1-5) shows how the SQLJ translator interacts with the Java compiler and runtime system to produce a SQLJ program.

JDBC is the primary API for universal access to a wide range of relational and object-relational databases. You will now turn your attention to the basic concepts of JDBC, since an understanding of those concepts is essential for you to develop Java database applications. See Appendix C to learn more about JDBC program development.

Basic JDBC Concepts

The JDBC API, whose specification was defined by JavaSoft, is a standard data access interface developed by Sun and its partners that incorporates Java technology. It is a Java application programming interface, non vendor specific, that lets Java programs communicate with a data server. JDBC is made up of a set of Java interfaces that specify the API, and of several drivers supplied by database vendors that let Java programs connect to a database.

The JDBC API defines Java classes that represent database connections, SQL statements, result sets, and database metadata. JDBC classes are modeled after ODBC structures. These classes provide standard features. These features include: transaction management, queries, manipulation of precompiled statements with bind variables, calls to stored procedures, streaming access to long column data, access to the database dictionary, descriptions of cursors, and simultaneous connections to several databases.

Java applications that need to issue SQL statements and process the results, use the Java API to do so. The Java API is implemented via a driver manager that can support multiple drivers connecting to different databases. JDBC drivers can either be entirely written in Java, so that they can be downloaded as part of an applet, or

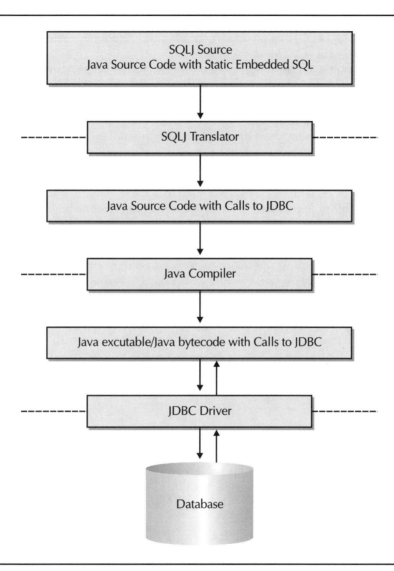

FIGURE 1-5.   *SQLJ interaction with Java compiler*

they can be implemented using methods to bridge to existing database access libraries. For example, Oracle provides two sets of JDBC drivers: JDBC-THIN for Java applets and JDBC-OCI for Java applications.

JDBC drivers fit into one of four categories (see *A Brief Overview of JDBC* [1]):

- **JDBC-ODBC bridge** provides JDBC access via most ODBC drivers. This driver is most appropriate on a corporate network, or for application server code written in Java in a three-tier architecture. ODBC binary code must be loaded on each client machine that uses this driver.

- **Native-API partly-Java technology-based driver** converts JDBC calls into calls on the client API for DBMS such as Oracle, Sybase, Informix, and DB2. This style of driver requires that some binary code be loaded on each client machine.

- **Native-API all-Java technology-based driver** translates JDBC calls into a DBMS-independent net protocol, which is then translated to a DBMS protocol by a server. This net server middleware is able to connect all of its Java clients to many different databases. This is the most flexible JDBC driver.

- **Native-protocol all-Java technology-based driver** converts JDBC calls into the network protocol used by the DBMS directly. Since many of these protocols are proprietary, the database vendors themselves will be the primary source for this style of driver. Several database vendors have these in progress.

Here is an example of a JDBC program (see Appendix C to learn more about JDBC programs):

```
import java.sql.*;
class OceanicObservation{

    public static void main(String[] args)
        throws SQLException, ClassNotFoundException {

      // Load the Oracle JDBC driver
        DriverManager.registerDriver(
                    new oracle.jdbc.driver.OracleDriver() );

      // Create an instance of the JDBC Connection class
      Connection conn;

      // Connect to the Oracle database using Oracle driver
      DriverManager.getConnection (
          "jdbc:oracle:oci8:@datai_com", "scott", "tiger");
```

```
        // Create a Statement
        Statement stmt = conn.createStatement ();

        // Select observation id from ObservationList table
        // and store the query result in a JDBC ResultSet
        ResultSet rset =
                stmt.executeQuery ("SELECT Obs_id
                                    FROM ObservationList");

        // Iterate the result
        ...
    }
}
```

Oracle provides two means by which Java database application developers can
access relational and object-relational data servers: JDBC as described previously
and SQLJ. A SQLJ program can contain both Java and SQLJ statements, as well as
JDBC calls. Next, you will learn the basic concepts of SQLJ.

Basic SQLJ Concepts

SQLJ has two major components:

■ **The SQLJ translator** A precompiler, written in pure Java, that developers
run after creating SQLJ source code. The translator produces a `.java` file
and one or more SQLJ profiles, that contain information about the SQL
operations. SQLJ then automatically invokes a Java compiler to produce
`.class` files from the `.java` file.

■ **The SQLJ runtime library** This component is invoked automatically at
runtime. The SQLJ runtime library is written in pure Java. It implements the
desired actions of the SQL operations and accesses the database using a
JDBC driver. Unlike Oracle SQLJ, non-Oracle SQLJ does not require that a
SQLJ runtime library uses a JDBC driver to access the database. The Oracle
SQLJ runtime library is a thin layer of pure Java code that runs above the
JDBC driver (Figure 1-5). An Oracle SQLJ translator translates the SQLJ
source code and generates runtime classes that act as equivalent JDBC
classes providing special SQLJ functionality.

An additional SQLJ component is the *customizer*. SQLJ automatically invokes a
customizer to tailor your SQLJ profiles for a particular database implementation and
any vendor-specific features and data types. Oracle SQLJ uses the Oracle customizer
for applications that use Oracle-specific features.

A SQLJ *profile* is a set of entries, where each entry maps to one and only one
SQL operation. Each entry specifies a corresponding SQL operation describing each

of the parameters used in executing this instruction. A profile implements the embedded SQL operations in the SQLJ executable statements. SQLJ profiles are not produced if there are no SQLJ executable statements in the SQLJ source code.

A SQLJ translator generates a profile for each *connection context* class in the application. A connection context class corresponds to a particular type of database schema to which your program connects. The SQLJ profiles are serialized Java objects. Profiles are vendor-specific; therefore, they must be customized. By default, SQLJ profile filenames end in the `.ser` extension. Optionally, profiles can be converted to `.class` files instead of `.ser` files.

SQLJ-generated profile files feature binary portability and therefore are portable across platforms. Thus a profile generated by a Java application developed on Oracle can be used as is with other kinds of databases or in other environments. For example, a profile compiled on NT against Oracle8*i* may be moved to DB2 for OS/390, *customized* and bound into a DB2 package or plan with limited modification of any source code.

This is true of generated `.class` files as well. A note of caution: The standard SQLJ translator addresses only the SQL92 (late SQL89 or early SQL92) dialect of SQL, but allows vendors' extensions beyond that. For example, Oracle SQLJ supports Oracle's SQL dialect, which contains non-SQL92 constructs. Therefore, to assure that their programs are portable, developers should avoid using SQL syntax and SQL types that are not in the standard. Vendor-specific SQL types might not be supported in all environments.

Development Tools

Oracle JDeveloper, a Windows-based visual development environment for Java programming, can be used to develop Oracle SQLJ programs. JDeveloper invokes the translator, semantics-checker, compiler, and customizer. A stand-alone SQLJ-to-Java translator can also process SQLJ. Since SQLJ runs on top of the JDBC API, a driver compliant with the database to be used must be installed in your system. The current version of SQLJ has been tested with the production release of Oracle JDBC drivers and the JDBC-ODBC available from JavaSoft. See Chapter 10 to learn more about Oracle development tools.

Basic SQLJ Features

Most SQL constructs can appear in SQLJ programs. In addition to SQL constructs, Oracle PL/SQL constructs can appear in Oracle SQLJ source code. Here is a partial list of these SQL and PL/SQL constructs:

- **SQL DML statements** such as `SELECT`, `INSERT`, `UPDATE`, and `DELETE`.
- **SQL transaction control statements** such as `COMMIT` and `ROLLBACK`.

■ **SQL DDL statements** such as CREATE TABLE and DROP TABLE.

■ **Calls to Oracle PL/SQL stored procedures, functions, and packages**
Assume a procedure named InsertPurchaseOrder() and a function GetObsId() have been created and stored in an Oracle database.

```
// Procedure call
CALL InsertPurchaseOrder ( :newOrderNbr );
VALUES ( GetObsId ( :obsId ) );   // Function call
```

■ **Session directives**.

See Chapter 4 to learn more about SQLJ calling PL/SQL procedures and functions.

SQLJ Statements
SQLJ statements can be divided into two main categories: declarations and executable statements. Each SQLJ statement starts with the token #sql.

■ **Declaration statements**   These statements are used for creating Java classes for iterators or connection contexts. A SQLJ *iterator* is similar to a JDBC result set. There are two types of SQLJ iterators: A named iterator and a positional iterator. *Connection contexts* (see Chapter 5) are used to establish database connections to different kinds of schema. A SQLJ declaration consists of the #sql token followed by the declaration of a class. See Chapter 3 for more information on SQLJ declaration.

```
// syntax: Iterator declaration
#sql <modifier> iterator Iterator_ClassName ( type declarations );


// syntax: connection context declaration
#sql <modifier> context Context_ClassName;
```

Examples of SQLJ declaration statements are:

```
// Use the SQLJ iterator called OceanObs to select data from
//a database table
// with corresponding observation id and platform type of matching
// names (obsId and fromPlatform ) and datatypes ( NUMBER and CHAR )

#sql public iterator OceanObs ( int obsId, String fromPlatform );

// Use the connection context DeclaredConnectionContext to connect to
// two different schemas residing on the same data server: localhost.
// As a result of this statement, SQLJ translator generates a public
```

```
// class DeclaredConnectionContext.

#sql public context DeclaredConnectionContext;
```

- **Executable statements** These statements are used to execute embedded SQL operations. A SQLJ clause is the executable part of a statement (everything to the right of the #sql token).

```
// Syntax: For a statement with no output, like INSERT
#sql { SQL operation };

// Syntax: For a statement with output, like SELECT
#sql result = { SQL operation };
```

Examples of SQLJ connection context declaration are:

```
// User defined connection context declaration

#sql context DeclaredConnectionContext;

// Create an instance of the following
// DeclaredConnectionContext class
// specifying an URL, username, password,
// and set the auto-commit flag.

DeclaredConnectionContext anInstanceCtx =
            new DeclaredConnectionContext
              ("jdbc:oracle:thin@localhost:1521:ORCL",
                  "username", "userpassword", boolean);

// Instances of the DeclaredConnectionContext class can be used
// to create database connections to different schemas, in this
// case: observation and besttrack

DeclaredConnectionContext observationCtx =
            new DeclaredConnectionContext
        ("jdbc:oracle:thin@localhost:1521:ORCL", "observation",
                "obspassword", false);

DeclaredConnectionContext besttrackCtx =
        new DeclaredConnectionContext
          ("jdbc:oracle:thin@localhost:1521:ORCL",
              "besttrack", "bestpassword", false);

// Explicit association of an instance of the
```

```
// connection context class, DeclaredConnectionContext
// class, with a SQLJ executable statement.

#sql [besttrackCtx] result = { SQL operation };
```

See Chapter 5 to learn more about associating an instance of a SQLJ connection context class in an executable statement.

Java Host Variables

SQLJ uses Java host expressions to pass arguments between Java source code and SQL operations. Host expressions are interspersed within the embedded SQL operations in SQLJ source code. A host expression can be any valid Java expression. A host variable is always preceded by a colon. Host expressions can represent any of the following:

- Local variables. Some host examples:

  ```
  :hostvariable, :INOUT hostvariable,
  :IN (hostvariable1+hostvariable2),
  :(hostvariable1*hostvariable2),
  :(index--), and so on
  ```

- Declared parameters

- Class attributes (such as `QualityControlActions.onOceanicObs`)

- Static or instance method calls

- Array elements

Examples of local host variables:

```
// Java variable declaration
int obsId = 11111;
String fromPlatform = "AIRCRAFT";
…

// SQLJ executable statement using host
// variables obsId and fromPlatform
#sql {UPDATE OceanicObservationList
        SET platformtype =
        :fromPlatform WHERE obs_id = :obsId};

// SQLJ executable statement calling a
// stored function and using host variables
#sql {UPDATE OceanicObservationList
        SET platform_id = :(getPlatformId (fromPlatform))
```

```
        WHERE obs_id = :obsId};

// SQLJ executable statement using many types of expressions
/*
Syntax: #sql [connctxt_exp, execctxt_exp] result_exp =
                { SQL with host expression };
*/


// SQLJ executable statements setting host variables
/*
Syntax:
#sql { SET :hostvariable = expression };
*/


// Declare a Java array of type integer
int[] generatedObsId = new int[30];

// Declare two variables: indexCtr and idNo
int idNo = 1000;
int indexCtr = 1;

// Use SQLJ statement to fill the array called generatedObsId.
// The use of the "++" suffix attached to indexCtr
// variable increments the value of this variable by 1.
// In the expression, :( idNo + indexCtr),
// the content of idNo is added to the content
// of indexCtr and the resulting value is assigned to
// the array cell indicated by indexCtr++.

#sql { SET :( generatedObsId [indexCtr++] ) = :( idNo + indexCtr) };
```

Oracle PL/SQL Blocks in SQLJ Executable Statement

PL/SQL blocks can be used within the curly braces of a SQLJ executable statement just as SQL operations can. Using PL/SQL in your SQLJ code would prevent portability to other platforms because PL/SQL is Oracle-specific.

```
/*
Syntax:
#sql { <DECLARE>  … > BEGIN   …   END; };
*/


// SQLJ executable statement setting host variables using PL/SQL block
#sql {
    BEGIN
          SET :( generatedObsId[indexCtr++] ) := :(idNo + indexCtr);
    END;
```

```
    };

// SQLJ executable statement using an Oracle anonymous PL/SQL block
// to create observation ids in the OceanicObservationList table
#sql {
    DECLARE
        incrementNo  NUMBER;
    BEGIN
        incrementNo := 1;
        WHILE incrementNo <= 100 LOOP
            INSERT INTO OceanicObservationList(obs_id)
                VALUES (2000 + incrementNo);
            incrementNo := incrementNo + 1;
        END LOOP;
    END;
    };
```

SQLJ Statement for Single-Row Query Results

SQLJ allows you to assign selected items directly to Java host expressions inside SQL syntax. This is done by using the SELECT INTO statement. The syntax is as follows:

```
/*
Syntax:
#sql { SELECT expression1,..., expressionN INTO
            :host_exp1,...,  :host_expN
        FROM datasource <optional clauses> };
*/
// SQLJ statement using SELECT .. INTO to select a single
// row from OceanicObservationList
String platformName = null;
String platformDescription = null;

// SQLJ executable statement
#sql { SELECT platform_name, platform_description
        INTO :platformName, :platformDescription
        FROM OceanicObservationList
        WHERE obs_id = 1111
    };
```

SQLJ Statement for Multiple-Row Query Results Using the SQLJ Iterator

A SQLJ iterator is a strongly typed version of a JDBC result set and is associated with an underlying database cursor (see Appendix A for a brief explanation of cursors). SQLJ iterators are used first and foremost to take query results from a SELECT statement.

```
/* Syntax for a named iterator:
#sql iterator IteratorName ( type declaration );  */

// Declare an iterator
#sql iterator OceanicObs ( int obsId, float lat,
                           float lon, String obsTime);

// Executable code
class ObservationQueryManager {
    ...
    void GetOceanicObservation () throws SQLException {
        // Declare a variable
         String platformType = "MOORED_BUOY";
        // Declare an iterator oceanicObs of type OceanicObs
        // and initialize it
        OceanicObs oceanicObs = null;
        #sql oceanicObs =
            { SELECT O.obs_id AS obsId,
               O.latitude AS lat, O.longitude AS lon,
                          O.obs_time AS obstime
               FROM OceanicObservationList O
               WHERE O.platform_type = :platformType
             };
        ...
    }
}

/* Syntax for a positional iterator:
#sql <modifier> iterator Iterator_ClassName ( type declarations ); */

// Declare a positional iterator.  Data items in the table
// must be in the same order as the iterator
#sql iterator OceanicObs ( int, float, float, String);

// Executable code
class ObservationQueryManager {
    ...
    ...
    void GetOceanicObservation () throws SQLException {

        // Declare a variable
         String platformType = "MOORED_BUOY";

        // Declare an iterator oceanicObs of type OceanicObs
        // and initialize it
        OceanicObs oceanicObs = null;

        // Execute the query and store the result in
```

```
        // the SQLJ oceanicObs iterator.
        #sql oceanicObs =
           { SELECT O.obs_id, O.latitude,
                    O.longitude, O.obs_time
             FROM OceanicObservationList O
             WHERE O.platform_type = :platformType
           };
        ...
    }
}
```

SQLJ Statement Calling Stored Procedures

SQLJ provides syntax for calling stored procedures and stored functions in the
database. These procedures and functions can be written in Java, SQLJ, or PL/SQL
(Oracle RDBMS database only), or any other language supported by the database.

```
/*  Syntax to call Java, SQLJ, PL/SQL procedure:
#sql { CALL PROC1 ( <parameter list> ) };  */
```

```
/* Syntax to call a PL/SQL function:
#sql result = { VALUES ( FUNC1 ( <parameter list> ) ) };  */
```

SQLJ Iterator as Stored Function Return: Oracle REF CURSOR

The Oracle SQLJ translator allows the use of a SQLJ iterator as a return type
for a stored function, using a REF CURSOR type in the process. The REF CURSOR
datatype is a PL/SQL cursor variable, a pointer similar to a C/C++ pointer. See the
PL/SQL User's Guide and Reference [40] to learn more about PL/SQL cursors.

Assume that a PL/SQL package, named QualityControlQueries, has been
stored in the Oracle database. Note that exception handling has been removed from
the package for the sake of clarity.

```
CREATE OR REPLACE PACKAGE QualityControlQueries AS
    TYPE observationtype IS REF CURSOR;
    FUNCTION getObservations ( p_date VARCHAR2 )
    RETURN observationtype;
END QualityCOntrolQueries;

CREATE OR REPLACE PACKAGE BODY QualityControlQueries AS
    FUNCTION getobservations ( p_date VARCHAR2 )
    RETURN observationtype IS
        v_date DATE := TO_CHAR(p_date,'MM-DD-YYYY');
        refcursor observationtype;
    BEGIN
```

```
        OPEN refcursor FOR SELECT O.obs_id, O.latitude,
                  O.longitude, O.obs_time
                  FROM OceanicObservationList O
                  WHERE O.when_t = v_date;
        RETURN refcursor;
    END getobservations;
END QualityControlQueries;
```

The following example uses a SQLJ iterator to call the function `getobservations`.

```
// SQLJ iterator declaration
#sql iterator Observations ( int obsId, float lat,
                             float lon, int obsTime );
...
Observations anObservation = null ;
...
// Get all observations for specific :aDate
#sql anObservation =
        { VALUES
          ( QualityControlQueries.getobservations ( :aDate ) )
        };
// Iterate to access each observation
while ( anObservation.next() ) {
        int obsno = anObservation.obsId();
        float latitude = anObservation.lat();
        float longitude = anObservation.lon();
        String obstimestamp = anObservation.obsTime();
}
anObservation.close();
...
```

SQLJ Versus JDBC

JDBC is a way to use dynamic SQL statements in Java programs. Java programs use JDBC to query and update tables, where details of the database object such as the column names, number of columns in the table, and table name are known only at runtime.

Many applications do not need to construct SQL statements dynamically because the SQL statements they use are fixed and static. In these cases, SQLJ can be used to embed static SQL in Java programs. In static SQL, all of the SQL statements are complete or "textually evident" in the Java program. That is, details of the database object are known at compilation time. SQLJ programs result in faster execution at runtime than dynamic SQL and provide greater opportunity for certain optimizations.

Some of the advantages that SQLJ offers over coding directly in JDBC include the following:

- Since SQLJ programs require fewer lines of code than JDBC programs, they are easier to debug.

- SQLJ can perform syntactic and semantic checking on the code, using database connections at compilation time. SQLJ clause is associated with a connection type, which represents the kind of schema where that clause will be executed.

- SQLJ provides strong type-checking (compatibility of Java and SQL expressions at translation-time) of query results and other return parameters while JDBC values are passed to and from SQL without having been checked at compilation time.

- SQLJ provides a simplified way of processing SQL statements. Instead of having to write separate method calls to bind each input parameter and retrieve each select list item, you can write one SQL statement.

- SQLJ is higher level than JDBC. In particular, SQLJ comes closer to satisfying the dual mode of use principle (See *An Introduction to Database Systems, Sixth Ed.* [15]), which asserts that embedded SQL statements should be the same as stand-alone SQL statements. In a SQLJ program, one can clearly see the SQL statements. They are not hidden in method calls as in JDBC.

SQLJ can be used to write multi-threaded applications. The SQLJ runtime supports multiple threads sharing the same connection context. However, SQLJ programs are subject to synchronization limitations imposed by the underlying JDBC driver implementation. If a JDBC driver mandates explicit synchronization of statements executed on the same JDBC connection, then a SQLJ program using that driver would require similar synchronization of SQL operations executed using the same connection context.

While connection contexts can be safely shared between threads, execution contexts should not be shared. If an execution context is shared, the results of a SQL operation performed by one thread will be visible in the other thread. If both threads are executing SQL operations, a race condition may occur in which the results of an execution in one thread are overwritten by the results of an execution in the next thread before the first thread has processed the original results. Furthermore, if a thread attempts to execute a SQL operation using an execution context that is currently being used to execute an operation in another thread, a runtime exception is raised. To avoid such problems, each thread should use a distinct execution context whenever a SQL operation is executed on a shared connection context.

See Chapter 2 to learn how to develop basic SQLJ programs and Chapters 3 to 10 to create complex SQLJ programs using the most advanced features of SQLJ.

Deployment of SQLJ in Thick and Thin Client-Side and Server-Side Applications

SQLJ code can run in several scenarios:

- Thin and thick client applications, from Java applets or Java applications.

- Server-side applications, that is, running the SQLJ translator in the data server. For example, Oracle8*i* JServer includes a SQLJ translator. Additionally, Oracle SQLJ can run against an Oracle Lite database.

See Chapter 5 to learn how to deploy SQLJ in client-side applets and applications (Java applications and applets, SQLJ applications and applets) and server-side applications (Java and SQLJ applications).

Thick Client Applications

Most Java applets on the Web today fall into the fat (or thick) Java client category (Figure 1-6). In these implementations, all components live in the client with only the persistent domain data residing on the server. Web browser users know the pain of waiting for large Java applets to download across the Internet or an intranet. The size of Java applets can make or break the success of an application. In the fat clients, referred to as one- or two-tier applications, most if not all of the application or business logic is downloaded to the client and requires no server application to service client requests. The thick client includes:

- All Graphical User Interface (GUI) widgets needed to present the application to the user.

- All controllers needed to handle user input.

- All application domain objects and logic.

- All JDBC classes to support the database access.

- All JDBC drivers (required protocols for Java programs to communicate with a database).

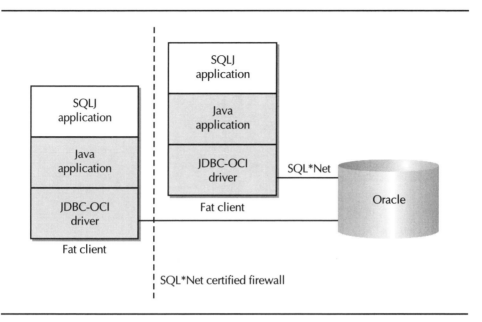

FIGURE 1-6.   *Thick SQLJ and Java clients*

Thin Client Applications

The thin client-computing concept is gaining importance. In the thin Java clients, the application must separate the presentation (GUI widgets) from the application logic. The thin client (Figure 1-7) architecture distributes as much of the design to the server leaving as little code as possible on the client. These multi-tier client/server designs limit the number of components on the client and move the application domain objects, logic, the database objects, and the database drivers to the server. In this scenario, the Java thin client networked application results in faster Java applet downloads and less client RAM. Existing distributed protocols, such as RMI (Remote Method Invocation) and CORBA/IIOP, can be used in the thin client architecture to distribute the components across a network of machines.

Server-Side Applications

At the present time, server-side SQLJ applications (Figure 1-8) can run in the Oracle8*i* data server. SQLJ code can run in the server in the form of stored procedures, stored functions, triggers, and methods (Chapter 4), as well as Enterprise JavaBeans or CORBA

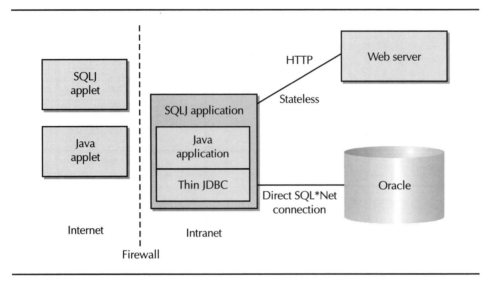

FIGURE 1-7. *Thin SQLJ client*

objects. Server-side access is done via the Oracle JDBC server-side JDBC-KPRB driver. Oracle JServer includes an embedded SQLJ translator in the Oracle8*i* Server so that SQLJ source files, for server-side use, can optionally be translated directly in the server. Loaded SQLJ source code on the server is translated and compiled by the server's embedded translator.

Server-side SQLJ source code can be translated and compiled on either a client or the Oracle server. Generated classes and resources from compilation on the client can then be loaded into the server. Client-side classes and resources can be pushed into the server via the Oracle `loadjava` utility. Server-side classes can be pulled from the server using SQL commands, SQLJ and Java client programs.

There is very little difference between coding for server-side use as opposed to client-side use. Some of the differences (as explained in *Oracle8*i *SQLJ Developer's Guide Reference* [63]) are:

- SQLJ client-side applications can establish many concurrent connections (Chapter 5). Server-side applications only have one connection.

- The connection must be to the database in which the code is running.

- The connection is implicit (does not have to be explicitly initialized, unlike on a client).

- The connection cannot be closed—any attempt to close it will be ignored.

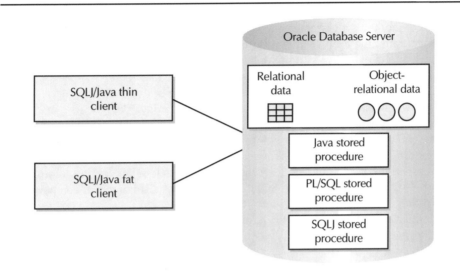

FIGURE 1-8.   *SQLJ in Oracle8i data server*

Additionally, the JDBC server-side driver does not support auto-commit.

Other Embedded SQLs such as PL/SQL and Pro*C Versus SQLJ

Oracle PL/SQL is a procedural language that extends SQL. PL/SQL stored procedures, functions, and packages allow the application programmer to develop server-side applications using static embedded SQL. One of the advantages of static embedded SQL is that the SQL statements do not change from execution to execution. The full text of the SQL statements is known at compilation time rather than at runtime. Additionally, PL/SQL allows developers to build and process a variety of SQL statements at runtime. Application programs that need to process SQL statements on the fly can use PL/SQL to do so.

Besides PL/SQL, Oracle also provides a set of programming tools called precompilers that enable you to embed dynamic SQL statements in programming languages such as C, C++, FORTRAN, COBOL, and so on. An Oracle precompiler allows you to embed SQL statements in a high-level source program. The precompiler accepts the source program as input, translates the embedded SQL statements into standard Oracle runtime library calls, and generates a modified source program that you can compile, link, and execute. Precompiling adds a step to the application development process, but it saves programmers time because the precompiler, not the programmer, translates the embedded SQL statements.

The programming tools, with the exception of PL/SQL stored procedures, can only be used in client or middle-tier database applications. SQLJ and Java are the only tools that offer the flexibility of building client-side and server-side applications. SQLJ provides a powerful way to develop both client-side and middle-tier applications that access databases from Java. Java developers can combine SQLJ programs with JDBC and use it in stored procedures, triggers, and methods within the Oracle JServer environment, as well as with EJB and CORBA. Today, leading database vendors deliver support for Java industry standards within their data server. For example, data servers such as Oracle8*i* JServer and Informix Dynamic Server include JDBC and SQLJ. These initiatives are part of the vendors' overall strategy
of providing a Java product suite that enables customers to build Java enterprise applications.

CHAPTER
2

SQLJ Program Development

he purpose of this chapter is to give you the basic information you need to write, translate, and run simple SQLJ applications. You will use three SQLJ programs as vehicles for understanding the basic components of a SQLJ program and the basic steps in the SQLJ development process. In particular, you will:

■ Use a SQLJ program that loads a table from a data file to gain an understanding of how to connect to the database using a specific JDBC driver; how to execute a standard SQL statement (other than a SELECT statement) from a SQLJ program; and how to translate, compile, and run a SQLJ program.

■ Use a SQLJ program that prints account information for accounts involving an input project to gain an understanding of how to execute a SELECT statement from a SQLJ program using a named iterator.

■ Use a modification of the preceding SQLJ program to gain an understanding of SELECT statement processing in SQLJ using positional iterators.

■ Learn about the SQLJ translation process.

■ Learn about the structure of the sqlj command line, and how to use properties files (instead of the sqlj command line) to set translator options.

Executing Non-SELECT SQL Statements from a SQLJ Program

There are two types of SQLJ statements:

■ SQLJ declarations that are used to declare connection context classes and iterator classes.

■ SQLJ executable statements that are used to execute SQL statements such as INSERT and DELETE statements that do not return results, and SQL statements such as SELECT statements that do return results.

In this section, after learning how to connect to a database, you will learn about SQLJ executable statements that do not return results. In particular, you will see a program LoadAccountList that contains such a SQLJ statement. In the sections of this chapter entitled "Executing SELECT Statements in SQLJ Programs Using Named Iterators" and "Executing SELECT Statements in SQLJ Programs Using Positional Iterators," you will learn about iterator declarations and executing SELECT statements from SQLJ programs. In Chapter 5, you will learn about connection context declarations.

Connecting to a Database

Before a SQLJ program can do anything with a database, it must first connect to the database. Probably the easiest way to connect to a database is to use the `connect()` method of the `oracle.sqlj.runtime.Oracle` class. This method creates a `DefaultContext` instance and initializes it with a specified connection URL (which indicates JDBC driver and database), Oracle username and Oracle password. SQLJ programs use either an instance of a user-declared connection context class or an instance of the `sqlj.runtime.ref.DefaultContext` class to establish a database connection. For programs that require only a single connection, it is best to use the `DefaultContext` class. The `connect()` method has several signatures, but the signature that uses a `properties` file to indicate connection URL, username, and password is the simplest to use.

In the subsequent `LoadAccountList.sqlj` program, `Oracle.connect (getClass(),"connect.properties")` passes two arguments: the `Class` object that describes the class `LoadAccountList` initiating the connection, which is returned by the `getClass()` method inherited from the Java Object class; and the name of the properties file that the program uses for the connection. Note that `getClass()`,being a nonstatic method of the application class `LoadAccountList`, cannot be called directly from a static method of `LoadAccountList`. If the `connect()` method were invoked from a static method of `LoadAccountList` (such as `main()`), `LoadAccountList.class` would be used instead of `getClass()` to return the `Class` object for `LoadAccountList`:

```
connect( LoadAccountList.class, "connect.properties" )
```

Another `connect()` signature allows you to explicitly pass connect information directly instead of using a properties file:

Listing 2-1

```
Oracle.connect
        ( "jdbc:oracle:thin:@data-i.com:1521:ORCL","scott","tiger" )
```

The first argument is the URL that identifies the JDBC driver, host machine, and database for the connection. The format of the URL depends on the JDBC driver that will read it. However, the Oracle JDBC drivers expect the following format:

```
driver:@host:port:databaseSID
```

In Listing 2-1, the JDBC driver selected is the `jdbc:oracle:thin` driver, the host machine for the database is `data-i.com`, the SQL*Net server connection port is 1521, and the SID (system identifier) of the database is ORCL. The last two arguments are the username scott and password tiger for the connection.

You can obtain a connect.properties file from your SQLJ demo directory (on UNIX, [OracleHome]/sqlj/demo, on PC Windows, [OracleHome]\sqlj\demo, where in either case [OracleHome] designates the Oracle home directory). You must then edit connect.properties so as to specify the correct URL, username, and password. The following connect.properties file has been edited to specify the URL for the JDBC Thin driver on the data-i.com system, as well as specifying the username scott, and the password tiger:

```
# The connection below uses the thin connection for
# the data-i.com server.

# Fill in the correct username and password for your login.
sqlj.url=jdbc:oracle:thin:@data-i.com:1521:ORCL
#sqlj.url=jdbc:oracle:oci8:@
#sqlj.url=jdbc:oracle:oci7:@

# Username and password here.
sqlj.user=scott
sqlj.password=tiger
```

Note that the original file contained commented lines (with #) for the three JDBC client-side drivers: JDBC Thin, JDBC OCI7 (for the Oracle7 call interface), and JDBC OCI8 (for the Oracle8 call interface). You uncomment and fill in the line for the appropriate driver (in our example, JDBC Thin), as well as filling in the appropriate username and password.

At this point, the role of the JDBC driver in SQLJ processing and the different types of Oracle8*i* JDBC drivers are discussed. First observe that the SQLJ runtime (system) accesses a database using a JDBC driver, as does the SQLJ translator, when it checks the semantics of SQLJ statements against the database structures (you will see that the runtime JDBC driver and translator JDBC driver can be different). Thus, the JDBC driver is critical for SQLJ processing.

Oracle8*i* supports three types of drivers: JDBC Thin, JDBC OCI Fat (for Oracle7 and Oracle8), and a server-side KPRB (Kernel PRogram Bundled calls) driver.

JDBC Thin is a 100 percent Java implementation that is extremely small in size. It is perfect for downloadable applications, such as applets, and in fact is the required driver for coding SQLJ applets.

The JDBC OCI Fat drivers are somewhat faster than the JDBC Thin driver since the OCI driver does a lot of its data processing in C (OCI is a call-level interface for invoking SQL from C programs). The JDBC OCI Fat driver is good for Java middle-tier applications, such as ones used with the Oracle Web Application Server.

The JDBC KPRB server is used for server-side applications such as implementing triggers, stored procedures, user-defined type methods, Enterprise JavaBeans, and CORBA objects. See Chapters 4, 7, and 8 for presentations of server-side SQLJ applications.

SQLJ Executable Statements That Do Not Return Results

A SQLJ executable statement has the syntax:

```
#sql { sqlj clause };
```

A `sqlj clause` can be an assignment clause—that is, a clause that contains a result expression because the clause delivers output (such as a clause that contains a `SELECT` statement)—or a statement clause that does not contain a result expression because it does not deliver output (such as a clause that contains an `INSERT` or `DELETE` statement). Assignment clauses are discussed in the section of this chapter entitled "Executing `SELECT` Statements from a SQLJ Program Using Named Iterators," and are treated in more detail in Chapter 3.

A statement clause can be any SQL DDL or SQL transaction control command, and any SQL DML command except a `SELECT` statement, as well as other statements to be discussed in Chapter 3. These commands can contain host variables, just like in embedded SQL (see Appendix A).

```
#sql { INSERT INTO ACCOUNT_LIST VALUES
          ( :accountno, :projectno, :departmentno) };
```

is an example from the subsequent `LoadAccountList.sqlj` program of a SQLJ executable statement containing a statement clause. The row that is inserted into `ACCOUNT_LIST` gets its values from host variables—that is, from Java variables, in this case fields from the `LoadAccountList` class. In general, a host variable can be a Java local variable, a Java declared parameter, or a Java class field. A host variable in a SQLJ clause must be preceded by a colon along with `IN` (optional-default), `OUT` (default in the `INTO` clause of the `SELECT INTO` statement), or `INOUT` depending on whether the host variable is an input variable, output variable, or both. The preceding `INSERT` statement could have been coded with `IN` explicitly specified:

```
#sql { INSERT INTO ACCOUNT_LIST VALUES
          ( :IN accountno, :IN projectno, :IN departmentno ) };
```

Note that a SQLJ clause does not terminate with a semicolon (;). Instead the semicolon (;) follows the right brace (}) of the SQLJ executable statement.

SQLJ Load Program: LoadAccountList.sqlj

The following is a SQLJ program that inserts records into the ACCOUNT_LIST table from a data file called acct_data. The source file containing this program is named LoadAccountList.sqlj. All SQLJ source files must have the extension .sqlj, and the base names of such files must be the same as the public class contained in the file (in this application, LoadAccountList), if such a public class exists. If there is no public class in a source file, the base name of the source file must be the same as the first class that is contained in the file. The LoadAccountList class uses a user-defined Java class called TokSequence, which provides convenient methods for extracting ints, doubles, and Strings from an input line. Note that the Pro*C version of LoadAccountList can be found in Appendix A as load_acctlist.pc. There are two reasons why the SQLJ version is somewhat longer than the Pro*C version. First, the Java **catch** clause, which is used in the SQLJ program to trap SQL errors and file IO errors, takes more space than an if statement testing a variable (such as SQLCODE) or testing a value returned by a function (such as fopen). Also, the lack of direct support in Java for formatted input and the decomposition of the input into a stream of tokens, forces you to implement these features yourself, using the Integer and Double wrapper classes and the StringTokenizer class.

```
/*
** Program Name:  TokSequence.java
**
** Purpose:   TokSequence.java contains the TokSequence class
**            for returning ints, doubles, and Strings from a
**            StringTokenizer object.
**
*/
/* java.util contains the StringTokenizer class, which supports
   the nextToken() method for sequentially extracting white space
   separated token strings from an input string.
*/
import java.util.*;

public class TokSequence {
  private StringTokenizer tk;
  /* TokSequence constructor initializes StringTokenizer field tk
     to StringTokenizer object for input string to be scanned.
  */
  public TokSequence( StringTokenizer tk1 ) {
    tk = tk1;
  }

  /* getInt() method extracts the next token from tk as a String,
     invokes the static Integer.valueOf() method to return an Integer
```

```
         object initialized to the integer represented by the token, and
         invokes the Integer.intValue() method on that Integer object to
         return the int value of the Integer object.
   */
  public int getInt() {
    int n = Integer.valueOf( tk.nextToken() ).intValue();
    return n;
  }

  // getDouble() method is similar to getInt(), but for doubles.
  public double getDouble() {
    double d = Double.valueOf( tk.nextToken() ).doubleValue();
    return d;
  }

  // getString() returns next token as String.
  public String getString() {
    return tk.nextToken();
  }
}

/*
** Program Name:  LoadAccountList.sqlj
**
** Purpose:  Load the ACCOUNT_LIST table from the text file acct_data.
**
*/
/* java.io contains FileReader class, for reading character files,
   and BufferedReader class that supports line-at-a-time input from
   character files.
*/
import java.io.*;

// java.util contains StringTokenizer class.
import java.util.*;

// Required SQLException class for SQL errors.
import java.sql.SQLException;

/* oracle.sqlj.runtime.Oracle class contains connect() method for
   connecting to database.
*/
import oracle.sqlj.runtime.Oracle;

// Define application class LoadAccountList.
class LoadAccountList {
  // BufferedReader class allows line-at-a-time input.
  private BufferedReader input;
```

```
/* The following three fields hold input from data file record
   (that is, line).
*/
private int accountno;
private int projectno;
private int departmentno;

/* Initialize database connection and open data file within the
   constructor of the application class.
*/
public LoadAccountList() {
  connectDB();
  openFile();
}

public static void main( String args[] ) {
  /* Invoke LoadAccountList constructor to connect to database and
     open data file.
  */
  LoadAccountList maincode = new LoadAccountList();

  /* The runLoadAccountList() method executes the main body
     of code for the application.
  */
  maincode.runLoadAccountList();
}

public void runLoadAccountList() {
  /* For each line of input in data file, read the line into String b,
     use the readRec() method to place accountno, projectno, and
     departmentno values into class fields, and insert row into
     ACCOUNT_LIST getting the row values from the class fields,
     and commit insert.
  */
  try {
    // (See Note 1.)
    for ( String b = input.readLine();
          b != null;
          b = input.readLine() ) {
      readRec(b);
      insertRow();
      commitInsert();
    }
  }

  // Catch any IO exceptions raised when reading file.
  catch( IOException e ) {
    System.err.println( "Error reading data file. \n" + e );
```

```
      closeFile();
      System.exit(1);
  }

  // Close data file.
  closeFile();
  System.out.println( "Program complete. \n" );
}

// Method to connect to database.
private void connectDB() {
  try {
    Oracle.connect( getClass(), "connect.properties" );
  }

  // Catch SQL exceptions raised when connecting to database.
  catch( SQLException e ) {
    System.err.println( "Error connecting to database. \n" + e );
    System.exit(1);
  }
}

// Method to open data file.
private void openFile() {
  try {
    // (See Note 2.)
    input = new BufferedReader( new FileReader( "acct_data" ) );
  }

  // Catch any IO exceptions raised when opening data file.
  catch( IOException e ) {
    System.err.println( "File not opened properly. \n" + e );
    System.exit(1);
  }
}

/* Method to extract accountno, projectno, departmentno from input
   string, and place them in class fields.
*/
// (See Note 3.)
private void readRec( String line ) {
  StringTokenizer tk = new StringTokenizer( line );
  TokSequence g = new TokSequence( tk );
  accountno = g.getInt();
  projectno = g.getInt();
  departmentno = g.getInt();
}
```

```
// Method to insert row into ACCOUNT_LIST table.
private void insertRow() {
  try {
    #sql {
          INSERT INTO ACCOUNT_LIST VALUES
            ( :accountno, :projectno, :departmentno )
        };
  }

  /* Catch SQL exceptions raised when inserting row into ACCOUNT_LIST
     table.
  */
  catch( SQLException e ) {
    System.err.println( accountno + projectno + departmentno +
                        " could not be inserted. \n" + e );
  }
}

// Method to commit insert.
private void commitInsert() {
  try {
    #sql {
          COMMIT WORK
        };
  }

  // Catch SQL exceptions raised when committing insert.
  catch( SQLException e ) {
    System.err.println( "commit on " + accountno +
                        " failed. \n" + e );
  }
}

// Method to close data file.
private void closeFile() {
  try {
    input.close();
  }

  // Catch IO exceptions raised when closing data file.
  catch( IOException e ) {
    System.err.println( "File not closed properly. \n" + e );
    System.exit(1);
  }
}
}
```

Notes on `LoadAccountList.sqlj`:

1. The `readLine()` method of the `BufferedReader` class returns the next line of characters from the input file as a string, if such a line exists, and returns null otherwise.

2. The `BufferedReader` class implements a buffered character input stream as a filter. By a filter, it is meant that a `BufferedReader` object must be composed with an already open input stream in our program. The `acct_data` file is opened through the `FileReader` object, and that object is specified as the argument to the `BufferedReader` constructor. The principal reason that `BufferedReader` is used in this program is that it provides the `readLine()` method for line-at-a-time input.

3. The `StringTokenizer` class is used to extract the `accountno`'s, `projectno`'s, and `departmentno`'s as strings, from the input line, and convert them into ints (in C and C++ this would be accomplished through formatted input). The `StringTokenizer` constructor takes the input line as its argument, and successive calls to `nextToken()`, from the `TokSequence.getInt()` method, returns the desired int values of `accountno`, `projectno`, and `departmentno`.

Translating and Executing the LoadAccountList.sqlj Program

In this section, you will learn how to manually translate and execute client-side SQLJ application programs. In Chapter 10, you will learn how to develop programs using the JDeveloper Integrated Development Environment (IDE). In Chapter 5, you will learn how to deploy compiled Java class files from applets and in the Oracle8*i* Server. Please note that in the subsequent discussion, it is assumed that the CLASSPATH environment variable has been set, indicating the directories in which `.class` files may be located. See Appendix D for information on setting CLASSPATH.

Of course, you must first enter `LoadAccountList.sqlj` and `TokSequence.java` using your favorite text editor.

As a first step in translating `LoadAccountList.sqlj`, you can compile `TokSequence.java` into a bytecode `TokSequence.class` file by entering

```
javac TokSequence.java
```

You can then translate `LoadAccountList.sqlj` into a Java source file by entering

```
sqlj LoadAccountList.sqlj
```

Another alternative is to use the SQLJ translator to compile both the SQLJ and Java source files:

```
sqlj TokSequence.java LoadAccountList.sqlj
```

If there are no errors in the SQLJ program, the SQLJ translation will generate a `LoadAccountList.java` file. By default, the SQLJ translator then sends this Java source file to a Java compiler, which translates this Java source file into a bytecode file, `LoadAccountList.class`. If you had set the `-compile` flag to false on the `sqlj` command line (see the section in this chapter entitled "`sqlj` Command-Line Options and Properties Files"), you would have to manually compile the Java source file by entering

```
javac LoadAccountList.java
```

You next execute the main method in the `LoadAccountList` class by entering

```
java LoadAccountList
```

You can now check that the program worked by signing on to SQL*Plus and entering

```
SELECT * FROM ACCOUNT_LIST;
```

to see if the new rows were inserted.

In a subsequent section of this chapter, you will take a closer look at the SQLJ translation process, and in the section after that you will consider the options available on the `sqlj` command line.

Executing SELECT Statements from a SQLJ Program Using Named Iterators

There are two types of declaration statements in SQLJ: iterator class declarations and connection context declarations. Connection context declarations were briefly discussed in Chapter 1, and will be discussed in more detail in Chapter 5. An *iterator* is a strongly typed version of the embedded SQL cursor (see Appendix A) and is used to receive `SELECT` statement output. There are two categories of iterators, *named iterators* and *positional iterators*. The current section deals with the former, the next section with the latter.

Named Iterator Processing

The following steps summarize named iterator processing:

- Use a SQLJ declaration to define the iterator class.

- Declare an instance of the iterator class.

- Populate the iterator instance with the output from a compatible SELECT statement in a SQLJ executable statement.

- Use the next() method of the iterator class to retrieve the next row from the iterator instance.

- Extract the column values from the current iterator row by using the iterator class accessor methods.

- Deactivate the iterator instance by invoking the close() iterator class method.

These steps are now considered in more detail.

Iterator Class Declarations

The first step in iterator processing is to define the iterator class in a SQLJ declaration. An iterator class declaration specifies a Java class that SQLJ constructs for you. The SQLJ translator replaces a SQLJ iterator declaration with a Java declaration for a class with the same name as the iterator. For example, in the subsequent SQLJ program, you will find the iterator declaration:

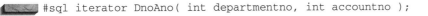

```
#sql iterator DnoAno( int departmentno, int accountno );
```

A DnoAno iterator instance can be populated by any SELECT statement whose set of SELECT list elements (that is, the expressions that follow the keyword SELECT) is a subset of the set of DnoAno attributes. That is, a DnoAno instance can be populated by any SELECT statement whose select_list consists only of the column departmentno, or only of the column accountno, or of the two columns departmentno and accountno.

The SQLJ translator will translate the SQLJ DnoAno iterator declaration into a Java declaration for a Java class DnoAno. This DnoAno Java class will contain

- A next() method that retrieves data from the iterator row by row.

- Accessor methods departmentno() and accountno() that return the values of the departmentno and accountno columns in the row currently being processed.

- A close() method that deactivates the iterator instance.

A simplified syntax for a named iterator declaration (you will see the full syntax in Chapter 3) is

```
#sql iterator iteratorname( list_of_attribute_declarations )
```

where an attribute_declaration consists of a Java type followed by an attribute name, and the elements of the list are comma separated.

SQLJ declarations—that is, iterator declarations and connection context declarations—are restricted to appear at the top level of a compilation unit (with the import statements), at the class level (with the fields, methods, and nested classes of a class), and at the nested class level (with the fields, methods, and nested classes of a nested class). SQLJ declarations cannot appear locally within a method.

Iterator Instance Declarations

After declaring an iterator class, the next step is to declare an instance variable for that iterator class. The iterator class instance is the object that will be populated by (that is, hold the output from) a SELECT statement which is consistent with the attributes in the iterator declaration. In the subsequent AcctsForProjs.sqlj program, you will find the declaration

```
DnoAno aDnoAno;
```

which declares aDnoAno as an instance variable for the DnoAno iterator class. Note that this iterator instance declaration is a Java declaration, not a SQLJ declaration. Thus, an iterator instance is a first-class Java object, which can be used in any way that any Java object can be used. For example, you can declare an array of iterators (you will see this in the next chapter), or, in fact, place an iterator in a data structure as complex as you like. Note that embedded SQL cursors are not first-class objects in the host language. Hence, SQLJ is superior to embedded SQL in this respect, suffering less of an impedance mismatch. See *An Introduction to Database Systems, Sixth Edition* [15] for a discussion of the impedance mismatch problem.

Populating an Iterator Instance with Output from a SELECT Statement

Next, you will populate the iterator instance with the output from a compatible SELECT statement in a SQLJ executable statement:

```
#sql aDnoAno = { SELECT departmentno, accountno FROM ACCOUNT_LIST
                 WHERE projectno = :projectno };
```

aDnoAno is then thought of as containing the output rows from the SELECT statement that returns account numbers and department numbers from accounts involving the project whose project number is in the host variable projectno. More precisely, when this SQLJ statement is executed, a new DnoAno object will be allocated and populated with the output rows from the SELECT statement, and the aDnoAno variable will be set to reference this new DnoAno object.

The names and the data types of the columns selected must match the names and the data types of the iterator attributes (however, for named iterators, the position of the column in the select_list is irrelevant). Note that for named iterators, you can have more attributes in the iterator attribute_list than columns in the select_list. That is, you can have attributes "left over" (we do not have that situation in our example).

The syntax of a SQLJ statement that populates an iterator instance with a SELECT statement output is

```
#sql iterator_instance = { select_statement };
```

A SQLJ executable statement has the form:

```
#sql { sqlj_clause }
```

where a sqlj_clause has the form:

```
{ sql_operation }
```

or

```
result = { sql_operation }
```

The former type sqlj_clause is called a *statement clause*. The latter type sqlj_clause is called an *assignment clause*. Therefore, you populate an iterator instance with SELECT statement output using an executable SQLJ statement containing an assignment clause. The INSERT statement in the preceding program LoadAccountList.sqlj was contained in a statement clause.

Retrieving Row and Column Values from the Iterator Instance, and Closing the Iterator Instance

Now that the iterator class instance has been populated, you can use the next() method of the iterator class to retrieve the next row from the iterator instance. The row is conceptually held in the iterator instance, from which you extract the column values using the iterator accessor methods. The next() method returns false when there are no more rows to retrieve and true otherwise. In the subsequent program AcctsForProjs.sqlj, you will extract the departmentno and accountno values by invoking aDnoAno.departmentno() and aDnoAno.accountno().

Finally, you deactivate the iterator (releasing all iterator resources) by invoking the iterator close() method—for example, aDnoAno.close().

A SQLJ Retrieval Program That Uses a Named Iterator: AcctsForProjs.sqlj

The following SQLJ program repeatedly reads a project number, and prints the department numbers and account numbers for accounts involving that project. When the program reads a -1, instead of a valid project number, it terminates. A Pro*C version of this program can be found in Appendix A as accts_for_projs.pc.

```
/*
** Program Name:  AcctsForProjs.sqlj
**
** Purpose:   Reading project numbers from standard input, one project
**            number per line, and printing the department numbers and
**            account numbers for accounts involving those projects.
**
*/
// java.io contains BufferedReader and InputStreamReader classes.
import java.io.*;

// java.util contains StringTokenizer class.
import java.util.*;

// Required SQLException class for SQL errors.
import java.sql.SQLException;

/* oracle.sqlj.runtime.Oracle class contains connect() method for
   connecting to database.
*/
import oracle.sqlj.runtime.Oracle;

/* Declare iterator class DnoAno to be consistent with the SELECT
   statement from which its instance will receive output.
*/
```

```java
// (See Note 1.)
#sql iterator DnoAno( int departmentno, int accountno );

// Define application class AcctsForProjs.
class AcctsForProjs {
  // BufferedReader class allows line-at-a-time input.
  private BufferedReader input;

  /* aDnoAno is an iterator class instance that will receive output
     from the SELECT statement.  Note that aDnoAno is declared in a
     Java declaration, not in a SQLJ declaration.
  */
  private DnoAno aDnoAno;

  /* Initialize database connection and direct System.in to a
     BufferedReader stream within application class constructor.
  */
  public AcctsForProjs() {
    connectDB();
    openInput();
  }
  public static void main( String[] args ) {
    /* Invoke AcctsForProjs constructor to connect to database and
       direct System.in to a BufferedReader stream.
    */
    AcctsForProjs maincode = new AcctsForProjs();
    /* The runAcctsForProjs() method executes the main body of code
       for the application.
    */
    maincode.runAcctsForProjs();
  }
  private void runAcctsForProjs() {
    int accountno, departmentno, projectno;
    String line;

    /* Main loop of program.  In each iteration, prompt user for,
       and read from standard input, a project number (or -1 to
       terminate), select into aDnoAno account numbers and department
       numbers for accounts involving the input project number,
       retrieve rows from aDnoAno using next() method, and retrieve
       and print fields from each row using the iterator class DnoAno
       accessor methods.
    */
    try {
      for ( ; ; ) {
        System.out.println( "Please enter a project number" +
                            " (enter a -1 to terminate) >> " );
        // Read input line.
        line = input.readLine();
```

```
    /* Invoke getProjectno() method to extract projectno from
       input line.
    */
    projectno = getProjectno( line );
    // If projectno = -1 terminate program.
    if ( projectno == -1 ) {
      System.out.println( "Bye" );
      System.exit(1);
    }

    /* Invoke select() method to populate aDnoAno with accountno's
       and departmentno's for accounts with the input projectno.
       If select() didn't detect problems with the SELECT
       statement, proceed with row processing of aDnoAno.
    */
    if ( select( projectno ) == 0 )
      /*  For each row retrieved into aDnoAno, use the accessor
          methods accountno() and departmentno() to print the
          accountno and departmentno in that row.
      */
      while ( aDnoAno.next() ) {
        System.out.println( "Account number = " +
          aDnoAno.accountno() + " Department number = " +
            aDnoAno.departmentno() );
      }
    /* Close aDnoAno so that it can be repopulated in next
       iteration of main loop.
    */
    closeIter( aDnoAno );
  }
}
/* Catch any IO exceptions raised when reading standard input
   with the readLine() method.
*/
catch( IOException e ) {
  System.err.println( "Error reading input. \n" + e );
  closeInput();
  System.exit(1);
}

// Catch any SQL exceptions raised when accessing aDnoAno.
catch( SQLException e ) {
  System.err.println
    ( "Error getting data from iterator. \n" + e );
  closeInput();
  System.exit(1);
}
}
```

```
/* Method to direct System.in to a character stream, and to direct
   that character stream to a BufferedReader stream.
*/
// (See Note 2.)
private void openInput() {
  input = new BufferedReader( new InputStreamReader( System.in ) );
}

/* Method to connect to database.  See the previous program
   LoadAccountList.sqlj.
*/
private void connectDB() {
  try {
    Oracle.connect( getClass(), "connect.properties" );
  }

  // Catch SQL exceptions raised when connecting to database.
  catch( SQLException e ) {
    System.err.println( "Error connecting to database. \n" + e );
    System.exit(1);
  }
}

/* Method to use the StringTokenizer class and TokSequence class
   from the previous LoadAccountList.sqlj example to extract projectno
   from input line.
*/
private int getProjectno( String line ) {
  StringTokenizer tk = new StringTokenizer( line );
  TokSequence g = new TokSequence( tk );
  return g.getInt();
}

/* Method to populate iterator class instance aDnoAno with output
   from SELECT statement.
*/
private int select( int projectno ) {
  try {
    #sql
      aDnoAno = { SELECT accountno, departmentno FROM ACCOUNT_LIST
                  WHERE projectno = :projectno
                };
    return 0;
  }
  // Catch SQL exceptions raised when populating aDnoAno.
  catch( SQLException e ) {
    System.err.println( "Cannot execute SELECT statement. /n" + e );
    return -1;
```

```
      }
  }
  // Method to close aDnoAno.
  private void closeIter( DnoAno aDnoAno ) {
    try {
      aDnoAno.close();
    }
    // Catch SQL exceptions raised when closing aDnoAno.
    catch( SQLException e ) {
      System.err.println
        ( "Cannot close iterator. \n" + e.toString() );
      closeInput();
      System.exit(1);
    }
  }

  // Method to close buffered stream.
  private void closeInput() {
    try {
      input.close();
    }

    // Catch IO exceptions raised when closing buffered stream.
    catch( IOException e ) {
      System.err.println
        ( "Cannot close buffered stream. \n" + e.toString() );
      System.exit(1);
    }
  }
}
```

Notes for `AcctsForProjs.sqlj`:

1. If you are concerned that the SELECT statement will return NULL values for
    the departmentno column (the accountno column is NOT NULL since
    it is the primary key of the ACCOUNT_LIST table), you should declare the
    departmentno attribute of DnoAno as being of type Integer (the Java
    wrapper class) instead of int. If you do that, aDnoAno.departmentno()
    will return NULL if the departmentno column retrieved by the SELECT
    statement was NULL. However, if you keep the int declaration, the
    SQLNullException will be raised when you try to populate aDnoAno
    with a NULL departmentno column value.

2. It is desired to read System.in a line at a time. In order to accomplish
    this, System.in (a byte stream) is directed to InputStreamReader, a

character stream, which is then directed to `BufferedReader`, a character stream that provides line-at-a-time input.

Executing SELECT Statements in SQLJ Programs Using Positional Iterators

In this section, you will consider the differences between processing positional iterators and processing named iterators, followed by a SQLJ program that illustrates positional iterators.

Differences Between Named and Positional Iterators

The following summarizes the differences between processing positional iterators and processing named iterators:

- The iterator class declaration is different. Since the correlation between the iterator attributes and a `SELECT` list is done by position, not by name, the names of the attributes are omitted from the positional iterator declarations, and only their types are listed. For example:

```
#sql iterator DnoAno2( int, int );
```

- Rows are retrieved from positional iterators using a SQLJ `FETCH` statement instead of the `next()` method. For example:

```
#sql { FETCH :aDnoAno2 INTO :accountno, :projectno };
```

This is similar to the fetching from embedded SQL cursors (see Appendix A). However, note that the positional iterator instance aDnoAno2 is prefixed with a colon (`:`), since an iterator instance is a Java variable, and is hence treated as a host variable in the `FETCH` statement.

- Since, with positional iterators, you will fetch the column values into Java host variables, there is no need for iterator accessor methods. Note that the iterator attributes are matched up with the `SELECT` list columns by position, and the number of attributes must exactly match the number of `SELECT` list columns.

- With positional iterators, end-of-data is tested using the boolean-valued `endFetch()` iterator method. Roughly speaking, `endFetch()` returns true if and only if there are no more rows to be fetched from the indicated iterator. More precisely, `endFetch()` returns true before any `FETCH` statements have been executed against the indicated iterator for the current

SELECT statement, false once a row has been successfully fetched, and then true again after the last row has been fetched.

In general, named iterators are more flexible than positional iterators, since with named iterators you don't have to worry about the position of a host variable in a FETCH statement, or a column in a SELECT list. Also, with named iterators, the number of iterator attributes must be greater than or equal to the number of SELECT list elements, but with positional iterators they must be exactly equal. On the other hand, positional iterators are processed more like embedded SQL cursors, and so some developers may be more comfortable with the positional iterators.

A SQLJ Retrieval Program That Uses a Positional Iterator: AcctsForProjs2.sqlj

The following SQLJ program has been obtained by modifying the AcctsForProjs .sqlj program from the preceding section of this chapter entitled "A SQLJ Retrieval Program That Uses a Named Iterator: AcctsForProjs.sqlj," so that a positional iterator instead of a named iterator is used. Recall that the program repeatedly reads a project number, and prints the department numbers and account numbers for accounts involving that project. When a project reads a –1 instead of a valid project number, it terminates. Observe that AcctsForProjs2.sqlj is very similar to AcctsForProjs .sqlj. The statements in AcctsForProjs2.sqlj that differ from the corresponding statements in AcctsForProjs.sqlj, by more than identifier names, are each displayed in bold.

```
/*
** Program Name:  AcctsForProjs2.sqlj
**
** Purpose:  Reading project numbers from standard input, one project
**           number per line, and printing the department numbers and
**           account numbers for accounts involving those projects.
**
*/
// java.io contains BufferedReader and InputStreamReader classes.
import java.io.*;

// java.util contains StringTokenizer class.
import java.util.*;

// Required SQLException class for SQL errors.
import java.sql.SQLException;

/* oracle.sqlj.runtime.Oracle class contains connect() method for
   connecting to database.
*/
```

```
import oracle.sqlj.runtime.Oracle;

/* Declare positional iterator class DnoAno2 to be consistent with
   the SELECT statement from which its instance will receive output.
*/
#sql iterator DnoAno2( int, int );

// Define application class AcctsForProjs2
class AcctsForProjs2 {

  // BufferedReader class allows line-at-a-time input.
  private BufferedReader input;

  /* aDnoAno2 is an iterator class instance that will receive output
     from the SELECT statement.  Note that aDnoAno2 is declared in a
     Java declaration, not in a SQLJ declaration.  Since DnoAno2 is
     a positional iterator, the DnoAno2 attributes and SELECT list
     columns will be matched up by position instead of by name.
  */
  private DnoAno2 aDnoAno2;

  /* Initialize database connection and direct System.in to a
     BufferedReader stream within application class constructor.
  */
  public AcctsForProjs2() {
    connectDB();
    openInput();
  }
  public static void main( String[] args ) {
    /* Invoke AcctsForProjs2 constructor to connect to database
       and direct System.in to a BufferedReader stream.
    */
    AcctsForProjs2 maincode = new AcctsForProjs2();

    /* The runAcctsForProjs2() method executes the main body of code
       for the application.
    */
    maincode.runAcctsForProjs2();
  }
  private void runAcctsForProjs2() {
    /* Host variables, like accountno and departmentno, that will
       be fetched into must be initialized, since the Java code
       into which the SQLJ FETCH statement is translated will not
       necessarily initialize the host variables.
    */
    int accountno = 0, departmentno = 0, projectno;
    String line;

    /* Main loop of program.  In each iteration, prompt user for,
       and read from standard input, a project number (or -1 to
```

```
      terminate), select into aDnoAno2 account numbers and department
      numbers for accounts involving the input project number, fetch
      from iterator into host variables (break out of loop if no row
      was fetched), and print values of host variables if row was
      fetched.
*/
try {
  for ( ; ; ) {
    System.out.println( "Please enter a project number" +
                        " (enter a -1 to terminate) >> " );
    // Read input line.
    line = input.readLine();
    /* Invoke getProjectno() method to extract projectno from
       input line.
    */
    projectno = getProjectno( line );
    // If projectno = -1 terminate program.
    if ( projectno == -1 ) {
      System.out.println( "Bye" );
      System.exit(1);
    }

    /* Invoke select() method to populate aDnoAno2 with
       accountno's and departmentno's for accounts with the
       input projectno.  If select() didn't detect problems
       with the SELECT statement, proceed with row processing
       of aDnoAno2.
    */
    if ( select( projectno ) == 0 )
      /*  Use FETCH statement instead of next() and accessor
          methods to extract row data from positional iterator.
      */
      for ( ; ; ) {
        #sql {
          FETCH :aDnoAno2 INTO :departmentno, :accountno
            };
        if ( aDnoAno2.endFetch() ) break;
        System.out.println( "Account number = " + accountno +
          " Department number = " + departmentno );
      }
    /* Close aDnoAno2 so that it can be repopulated in next
       iteration of main loop.
    */
    closeIter( aDnoAno2 );
  }
}
/* Catch any IO exceptions raised when reading standard input
   with the readLine() method.
```

```
      */
    catch( IOException e ) {
      System.err.println( "Error reading input. \n" + e );
      closeInput();
      System.exit(1);
    }

    // Catch any SQL exceptions raised when accessing aDnoAno2.
    catch( SQLException e ) {
      System.err.println
        ( "Error getting data from iterator. \n" + e );
      closeInput();
      System.exit(1);
    }
}
/* Method to direct System.in to a character stream, and to direct
   that character stream to a BufferedReader stream.
*/
private void openInput() {
  input = new BufferedReader( new InputStreamReader( System.in ) );
}

// Method to connect to database.
private void connectDB() {
  try {
    Oracle.connect( getClass(), "connect.properties" );
  }

 // Catch SQLExceptions raised while connecting to database.
  catch( SQLException e ) {
    System.err.println( "Error connecting to database. \n" + e );
    System.exit(1);
  }
}

  /* Method to use the StringTokenizer class and TokSequence class
     from the LoadAccountList.sqlj example to extract projectno
     from input line.
  */
  private int getProjectno( String line ) {
    StringTokenizer tk = new StringTokenizer( line );
    TokSequence g = new TokSequence( tk );
    return g.getInt();
  }

 /* Method to populate iterator class instance aDnoAno2 with output
    from SELECT statement.
*/
```

```
private int select( int projectno ) {
  try {
    #sql
      aDnoAno2 = { SELECT accountno, departmentno FROM ACCOUNT_LIST
                   WHERE projectno = :projectno
                 };
    return 0;
  }
  // Catch SQL exceptions raised when populating aDnoAno2.
  catch( SQLException e ) {
    System.err.println( "Cannot execute SELECT statement. /n" + e );
    return -1;
  }
}
// Method to close aDnoAno2.
private void closeIter( DnoAno2 aDnoAno2 ) {
  try {
    aDnoAno2.close();
  }
  // Catch SQL exceptions raised when closing aDnoAno2.
  catch( SQLException e ) {
    System.err.println
      ( "Cannot close iterator. \n" + e.toString() );
    closeInput();
    System.exit(1);
  }
}

// Method to close buffered stream.
private void closeInput() {
  try {
    input.close();
  }

  // Catch IO exceptions raised when closing buffered stream.
  catch( IOException e ) {
    System.err.println
      ( "Cannot close buffered stream. \n" + e.toString() );
    System.exit(1);
  }
}
}
```

SQLJ Translation Process

In this section, you will consider the various steps in the SQLJ translation process.

As you have seen, a SQLJ source file contains a combination of standard Java source code along with SQLJ declarations and SQLJ executable statements that contain SQL operations. This source code must be located in a file with the extension `.sqlj`. After you have entered the SQLJ source file using your favorite text editor, you run the `sqlj` command to translate the SQLJ source file into a Java source file, and to generate other output files described subsequently. The `sqlj` command runs as a script in UNIX and as an executable file in PC Windows, and invokes a Java VM (see Chapter 1), passing its arguments to the Java VM. The Java VM then invokes the SQLJ translator, which performs syntax analysis on the SQLJ source file, checking for incorrect SQLJ syntax.

The SQLJ translator next invokes the semantics checker, which checks the semantics of the executable SQLJ statements. If the online checking option was selected on the `sqlj` command line (by using the `-user` option, as discussed in the next section), the semantics checker will connect to the database and check that the usage of database objects, such as tables and stored procedures, is consistent with the structure of the corresponding objects stored in the database. If offline semantics checking was selected (by the absence of the `-user` option on the `sqlj` command line), only simple checking that doesn't require connection to the database will be performed.

The SQLJ translator then performs its code generation step by converting SQLJ executable statements into SQLJ runtime calls, and generating a separate profile for each connection class in the SQLJ source file. The results of this step are a Java source file (with the extension `.java`) that was translated from the SQLJ source, and the generated profiles. The `.java` file contains

- Any Java code from the SQLJ source file.

- Class definitions created as a result of SQLJ declarations in the SQLJ source file, such as iterator class definitions.

- A class definition for the profile-keys class that SQLJ generates and uses in conjunction with the profiles.

- A SQLJ runtime call for each SQLJ executable statement. Note that the SQLJ runtime uses the specified JDBC driver to access the database.

Each generated profile is placed, by default, in a serialized `.ser` file. However, you can specify that SQLJ converts the `.ser` files to `.class` files by setting the `-ser2class` flag on the `sqlj` command line (for example, `sqlj -ser2class LoadAccountList.sqlj`).

The information for all the SQL operations executed against a connection context class is contained in the profile for that connection context class. If there are no SQLJ executable statements in the SQLJ source file, no profiles will be generated.

As a default, the Java VM invokes the Java compiler (usually the standard javac) to compile the `.java` file generated. If you wish to suppress this compilation, you specify `-compile=false` on the `sqlj` command line. The Java compiler compiles the `.java` file into `.class` files, as usual. You will get a `.class` file for each class you defined in your SQLJ source file, as well as a `.class` file for the SQLJ-generated `profile-keys` class.

The Java VM then invokes the Oracle SQLJ customizer to customize the generated profiles in an Oracle-specific way.

For the `LoadAccountList` application in the previous section of this chapter entitled "SQLJ Load Program: `LoadAccountList.sqlj`," the SQLJ translator generates the output files `LoadAccountList.java` and `LoadAccountList_SJProfile0.ser`. In addition, the Java compiler invoked by the Java VM will generate a `LoadAccountList.class` file and a `LoadAccountList_SJProfileKeys.class` file. In general, the SQLJ translator will produce a Java file with the same base name as the SQLJ file, and at least one profile (assuming the SQLJ file contains SQLJ executable statements). A profile filename is obtained by concatenating the SQLJ base filename with `SJProfile`n, where n is a number that indicates that the context connection class for the profile was the nth one encountered in the SQLJ source file, and makes the profile filename unique. In the `LoadAccountList` application, there is only one profile corresponding to the `DefaultContextClass`, so $n=0$ is used in the profile filename: `LoadAccountListSJProfile0.ser`. Also, the SQLJ translator will generate a profile-keys class named *sqljsourcename_*`SJProfileKeys` (`LoadAccountList_SJProfileKeys` in the `LoadAccountList` application), for which the Java compiler will generate a `.class` file (`LoadAccountList_SJProfileKeys.class` in the `LoadAccountList` application). Similarly, a `.class` file will be generated for each iterator class and connection context you defined in the SQLJ source file. The base name of these files will be the same as the name of the corresponding iterator or context connection class.

When you run your application, the SQLJ runtime reads the profiles and creates "connected profiles," which incorporate database connections. The following steps are then executed each time the application accesses the database:

- The SQLJ-generated code executes methods in the profile-keys class to access the connected profile and read the relevant SQL operations, which it passes to the SQLJ runtime.

- The SQLJ runtime then invokes the JDBC driver, passing it the SQL operation for execution.

- The JDBC driver will send any data to the program that the SQL operation requires.

sqlj Command-Line Options and Properties Files

In this section you will learn how to specify options to SQLJ via the command line and via properties files. Please see Chapter 8 of *Oracle8i SQLJ Developer's Guide and Reference* [63] for more information on SQLJ options and properties files. See Appendix D of this book for a list of SQLJ options.

sqlj Command-Line Options

After learning about the structure of the `sqlj` command line, you will see examples of several important command-line options.

Structure of the sqlj Command Line

The syntax of the `sqlj` command line is

```
sqlj [ option_list ] file_list
```

`option_list` is a sequence of blank-separated SQLJ options.
`file_list` is a sequence of blank-separated `.sqlj`, `.java`, `.ser`, and `.jar` files.

In the simplest command line, one SQLJ file and no options will be passed:

```
sqlj LoadAccountList.sqlj
```

Additional SQLJ files are necessary if you wish to declare public iterator and connection context classes. Also, if you have `.sqlj` files and `.java` files that each require access to code in the others, you must enter all of them in the command line for a single execution of SQLJ. You cannot specify them for separate executions of SQLJ. `.jar` files and `.ser` files are provided as input to the profile customizer. See

Chapter 10 of *Oracle8*i *SQLJ Developer's Guide and Reference* [63] for more information on these types of files.

The general form of a SQLJ option is

```
-optionname=value
```

If an option is Boolean-valued, it is called a *flag* and can be set to true by specifying:

```
-flagname=true
```

or simply:

```
-flagname
```

The only way to set the flag to false is by specifying:

```
-flagname=false
```

A -J, -C, or -P prefix is attached to the left of an option to indicate that the option should be sent to the Java VM (-J), the Java compiler (-C), or the SQLJ profile customizer (-P). For example, in the `sqlj` command line:

```
sqlj -compile=false -ser2class -P-backup LoadAccountList.sqlj
```

you specify, using the -compile flag, that the Java compiler should not be invoked after the translation phase (-compile=false). The default setting of the -compile option is true (that is, invoke the Java compiler to generate a .class file). You specify, using the -ser2class flag, that .ser profiles should be converted to .class files. The default setting of the -ser2class option is false. You specify using the -P prefix with the -backup flag that the -backup flag should be passed to the customizer (this flag indicates that the profiles should be backed up before they are customized).

Some Important SQLJ Options

Several important SQLJ options are now discussed through examples.

```
sqlj -user=scott -password=tiger
 -url=jdbc:oracle:thin:@data-i.com:1521:ORCL LoadAccountList.sqlj
```

The specification of -user enables online semantics checking and specifies that username scott should be used when connecting to the database. If this option is not specified, no online semantics checking occurs. The -password option indicates the password to use when connecting (the password can also be indicated on the -user option: -user=scott/tiger), and the URL option indicates the JDBC driver and database to use in the connection. This URL can also be specified in the -user option:

```
-user=scott/tiger@JDBC:oracle:thin@data-i.com:1521:ORCL
```

These connection values do not have to be the same for the SQLJ translator (the values specified on the sqlj command line) as they do for SQLJ runtime (the values passed to connect methods in the SQLJ source code). For example, if you are developing in a different environment than the one in which you will deploy, the connections may be different.

```
sqlj -driver=sun.jdbc.odbc.JdbcOdbcDriver LoadAccountList.sqlj
```

The -driver option indicates the driver classes (comma separated) to register for interpreting JDBC connection URLs for online semantics checking. The default class is OracleDriver, which supports the Oracle OCI, thin, and server-side drivers.

```
sqlj -props=newprops.properties LoadAccountList.sqlj
```

indicates that SQLJ options can be found in the properties file newprops.properties that you created. Translation time properties files are discussed in the subsequent section entitled "Specifying SQLJ Options with Properties Files."

```
sqlj -help
sqlj -help-long
```

In order to receive help in using the sqlj command-line options, you execute the sqlj command with no options or files specified, or with only -help specified, to give you a synopsis of the most frequently used SQLJ options and a listing of the additional -help flag settings available. -help-long gives a complete list of SQLJ options information.

```
sqlj -linemap LoadAccountList.sqlj
```

Specifying -linemap (that is, -linemap=true) causes runtime Java error messages to be labeled with SQLJ source line numbers instead of Java source line numbers. Thus, the error will be related to code that you wrote, instead of code that was generated by the SQLJ translator. The default value for this flag is false, that is, line numbers refer to generated .java source.

Specifying SQLJ Options with Properties Files

In this section, you will see that instead of using the command line to specify options to the SQLJ translator, Java compiler, and SQLJ profile customizer, you can use *properties files*. However, you cannot use properties files to set the following SQLJ options, flags and prefixes: -classpath, -help, -help-long, -help-alias, -C-help, -P-help, -J, -n, -passes, -props, -version, -version-long, -vm. Also, properties files can only be used with client-side applications, as there is a different mechanism for specifying options to SQLJ in the server.

First, you will learn about the structure of a properties file. Then you will consider the order in which options are set. In particular, you will consider the processing of sqlj.properties files.

Structure of Properties Files

Option settings in a properties file are placed one per line, and lines with SQLJ options, compiler options, and customizer options can be interspersed, since they are parsed by the SQLJ front end and handled appropriately. Each option has the form:

```
target.optionname=value
```

where target is sqlj, compile, or profile, and optionname is the name of the option being set. For example:

```
sqlj.linemap=true
```

A flag can be enabled by entering it without a setting. For example:

```
sqlj.linemap
```

As you have seen, the SQLJ props option indicates the properties file to be used for the translation:

```
sqlj -props=myprops.properties LoadAccountList.sqlj
```

Please consider the following properties file myprops.properties:

```
sqlj.user=scott
sqlj.password=tiger
sqlj.url=jdbc:oracle:@data-i.com:1521:ORCL
sqlj.linemap
```

`myprops.properties` specifies the username, password, and URL needed to connect to the database for the purpose of online semantics checking; and that line numbers in error messages should refer to SQLJ source and not Java source.

Default sqlj.properties Files and the Order of Setting Options

Before discussing default properties files, the SQLJ_OPTIONS environment variable is introduced. Any option that can be set on the `sqlj` command line can alternatively be set using the SQLJ_OPTIONS variable. SQLJ inserts the SQLJ_OPTIONS settings, in order, at the beginning of the `sqlj` command line, before any other command-line setting. For example, using your operating system's specific method for setting environment variables, SQLJ_OPTIONS can be set to:

```
-linemap=true -compile=false
```

These options will then be automatically inserted at the beginning of any subsequently executed `sqlj` command line.

Even if you specified a properties file in a `-props` option, the SQLJ front end still searches for files named `sqlj.properties`, the default properties files. The following indicates the order in which SQLJ takes option settings, where each step overrides settings from the previous steps, and the options on the `sqlj` command line are set from left to right.

- Set default settings for options.

- Set settings for options found in the `sqlj.properties` file in the Java home directory (if such a properties file exists).

- Set settings for options found in the `sqlj.properties` file in the user home directory (if such a properties file exists).

- Set settings for options found in the `sqlj.properties` file in the current directory (if such a properties file exists).

- Extract settings for options in the SQLJ_OPTIONS environment variable, inserting them at the beginning of the `sqlj` command line, and set those settings.

- Extract settings for properties file set in `-props` option, and place those settings on the command line where `-props` appears.

- Set option settings found on the command line, with latter settings overriding earlier settings.

A sample `sqlj.properties` file can be found in your SQLJ demo directory `[OracleHome]/sqlj/demo`, with sample option lines commented out. You can then edit this file to appropriately remove the comment symbols and enter desired option values. An example of such an edited `sqlj.properties` file is

```
###
### Settings to establish a database connection for online checking
###

### turn on checking by uncommenting user
### or specifying the -user option on the command line
sqlj.user=scott
sqlj.password=tiger

### add additional drivers here
#sqlj.driver=oracle.jdbc.driver.OracleDriver<,driver2...>

### Oracle JDBC-OCI7 URL
#sqlj.url=jdbc:oracle:oci7:@

### Oracle JDBC-OCI8 URL
#sqlj.url=jdbc:oracle:oci8:@

### Oracle JDBC-Thin URL
#sqlj.url=jdbc:oracle:thin:@<host>:<port>:<oracle_sid>
sqlj.url=jdbc:oracle:thin:@data-i.com:1521:ORCL
```

The preceding `sqlj.properties` file specifies username, password, and URL for the semantics-checking database connection.

In this chapter, you examined SQLJ programs that illustrated how to connect to the database and execute non-SELECT and SELECT SQL commands from your SQLJ program. You also considered the SQLJ translation process, and how to influence that process through the SQLJ command line and through properties files. In Chapter 3, you will encounter an extensive treatment of the different types of SQLJ statements that can be embedded in your SQLJ program. In particular, you will consider how host expressions and result expressions can be used in your executable SQLJ statements.

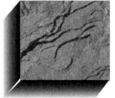

CHAPTER
3

Basic SQLJ
Programming

here are two types of SQLJ statements: SQLJ declarations and SQLJ executable statements. Also, there are two types of SQLJ declarations: connection context declarations and iterator declarations. Further, there are two types of executable SQLJ statements: statements that return values and thus contain result expressions to hold those values, and statements that do not contain result expressions. Therefore, it appears that SQLJ follows the Noah's Ark "two by two" model.

In Chapter 5, connection context declarations are discussed. In Chapter 6, iterator conversion executable SQLJ statements, which convert a JDBC result set to an iterator, are discussed, along with other JDBC interoperability features. In this chapter, you will learn about the other SQLJ statements. In particular, you will encounter:

- Executable SQLJ statements without result expressions: SQLJ DDL and SQLJ non-`SELECT` DML commands.

- Executable SQLJ statements without result expressions: SQLJ transaction control commands.

- Executable SQLJ statements without result expressions: anonymous PL/SQL blocks and stored procedure calls.

- Executable SQLJ statements without result expressions: `SET`, `FETCH`, and `SELECT INTO` statements.

- Executable SQLJ statements with result expressions: SQLJ `SELECT` statements.

- Executable SQLJ statements with result expressions: stored function calls.

- Evaluation of host expressions and result expressions at runtime.

- JDBC and SQLJ exception classes.

- Other useful JDBC and SQLJ classes.

A SQLJ executable statement can appear anyplace a Java block statement can appear, namely, within method definitions and static initialization blocks. The syntax of a SQLJ executable statement depends on whether or not the statement involves a result expression. The syntax of a SQLJ executable statement that does not contain a result expression is

```
#sql { sql_operation }
```

The syntax of an executable statement that contains a result expression is

```
#sql result_expression = { sql_operation }
```

In either case, a *SQLJ clause* is the executable part of a statement (that is, everything to the right of the #sql token). A SQLJ clause that does not contain a result expression is called a *statement clause*. A SQLJ clause that does contain a result expression is called an *assignment clause*. A result expression can be any legal Java expression that is assignable.

A statement clause can consist of any SQL command except a SELECT statement. In particular, a statement clause can consist of any SQL DDL command, any SQL transaction control command, or any SQL DML command except a SELECT statement. In addition, a statement clause can consist of the following SQLJ-specific statements: a SELECT INTO statement, a FETCH statement, a stored procedure call, and an anonymous PL/SQL block.

An assignment clause can consist of a query clause (that is, a SQLJ SELECT statement) that selects data into a SQLJ iterator, a stored function call, or an iterator conversion clause.

In this chapter, you will learn about all of these statement clauses and assignment clauses, except the iterator conversion clause.

Executable SQLJ Statements without Result Expressions: SQLJ DDL and Non-SELECT DML Commands

In this section, you will examine the structure of SQLJ DDL and non-SELECT SQLJ DML commands. In particular, you will see how host expressions—that is, Java expressions—can be incorporated into DML commands.

SQLJ DDL Commands

A SQLJ DDL command is a SQLJ statement that consists of a SQL DDL command. A SQL DDL command is used to set up the structure of the database (see Appendix A). All SQL DDL commands start with one of the keywords CREATE, DROP, or ALTER. A SQLJ statement clause can consist of any DDL command. Such statement clauses are particularly simple since they cannot contain Java expressions—that is, host expressions. You will see in the subsequent section "SQLJ DML Commands" that host expressions can appear anywhere in a SQLJ DML command that an expression can appear, as well as in the target lists of FETCH and SELECT INTO statements, and in other places also.

An example of a SQLJ CREATE TABLE statement is

```
#sql { CREATE TABLE ACCOUNT_LIST (
         accountno    number( 5 ),
```

```
            projectno     number( 5 ),
            departmentno number( 5 ),
            PRIMARY KEY  ( accountno ),
            FOREIGN KEY  ( projectno )     REFERENCES PROJECT_LIST,
            FOREIGN KEY  ( departmentno ) REFERENCES DEPARTMENT_LIST )
      };
```

SQLJ DML Commands

A SQLJ DML command is a SQLJ statement that consists of a SQL DML command. A SQL DML command is used to manipulate the database (see Appendix A). The SQL DML commands are the INSERT, DELETE, UPDATE, and SELECT statements. Unlike the SQLJ DDL commands, the SQLJ DML commands can contain host expressions. These SQLJ host expressions are discussed next.

SQLJ Host Expressions

SQLJ uses Java host expressions to pass arguments between SQLJ DML commands, SELECT INTO statements, FETCH statements, PL/SQL blocks, SET statements, SELECT statements, stored procedure calls, stored function calls, and the Java code that surrounds these statements.

The simplest kind of host expression consists of only a non-dotted Java identifier. This is called a *host variable*, which you encountered in Chapter 2. In general, any valid Java expression can be used as a host expression. These include expressions that contain fields, class variables, Java method calls, array elements, and arithmetic expressions. Any Java variable whose type is SQL convertible (see Appendix D for a table correlating SQL and Java types), and that is legal in the Java scope where the SQLJ executable statement appears, can be used in a host expression. Host expressions, like the host variables described in Chapter 2, can have mode IN, OUT, or INOUT.

The syntax for a host variable is

```
:[ mode ] host_variable
```

The syntax for a host expression that is more complicated than a host variable requires parentheses:

```
:[ mode ] ( host_expression )
```

Note that a white space is required after the mode for the host variable, but not for the host expressions that involve parentheses. An outer set of parentheses is needed around a host expression that is not a host variable, even if the expression starts with a parenthesis. For example:

```
:( ( a + b ) * c )
```

is legal, whereas:

```
:( a + b ) * c
```

is not legal.

The modes are IN, OUT, and INOUT. IN designates that the value of the host expression will be used (that is, read) by the SQLJ statement that contains it, but will not be changed by that statement. OUT designates that the value of the host expression can be changed by the SQLJ statement that contains it, but will not be used by that statement. INOUT designates that the value of the host expression will be used and can be changed by the SQLJ statement. An OUT or INOUT host expression must be an l-value, that is, an expression that can appear on the left-hand side of a Java assignment statement. Thus, the expression x + y, where x and y are, say, int variables, cannot be used as an OUT or INOUT host expression, since x + y cannot appear on the left-hand side of a Java assignment statement.

The default mode is OUT for host expressions in the into_list of a FETCH statement, the into_list of a SELECT INTO statement, and the assignment host expression of a SET statement. The default mode is IN for all other host expressions.

NOTE
In Oracle SQLJ, the same host variable can appear multiple times in the same SQLJ statement. However, you must not use this feature if you expect your SQLJ program to be portable to non-Oracle platforms.

Finally, consider the different parts of SQLJ DML statements where a host expression can appear. In an INSERT VALUES statement, a host expression can appear in a value position, as is illustrated by the program LoadAccountList2 .sqlj that you will see next. In an INSERT SELECT statement, a host expression can appear anyplace in the select_list and in the WHERE clause that an expression can appear. For example, consider the following SQLJ statement, where all the NEW_ACCOUNTS rows will be inserted into the ACCOUNT_LIST table that involve the department whose department number is in the :departmentno host variable.

```
#sql { INSERT INTO ACCOUNT_LIST
         SELECT accountno, projectno, :departmentno
           FROM NEW_ACCOUNTS WHERE departmentno = :departmentno
     };
```

In a DELETE statement, a host expression can appear anyplace in the WHERE clause that an expression can appear:

```
#sql { DELETE FROM ACCOUNT_LIST WHERE accountno = :oldaccountno };
```

In an UPDATE statement, a host expression can appear anywhere in the SET and WHERE clauses that an expression can:

```
#sql { UPDATE ACCOUNT_LIST
          SET departmentno = :newdepartmentno
            WHERE accountno = :acc
      };
```

You will next consider a SQLJ program that contains more complicated host expressions.

A SQLJ Load Program That Contains an Insert Statement with Host Expressions: LoadAccountList2.sqlj

In this section you will see a modification of the LoadAccountList.sqlj program from Chapter 2 that contains an INSERT statement with host expressions that involve subscripted array elements and method calls.

Recall that the LoadAccountList.sqlj program loads the ACCOUNT_LIST table from a data file called acct_data by reading each line from the acct_data file, extracting the account number, project number, and department number from that line, and inserting into the ACCOUNT_LIST table the row constructed from this information. In LoadAccountList2.sqlj, all the data from the acct_data file is first read into an array of AccountRec records called accountRecs. Then, each row from that array is inserted into the ACCOUNT_LIST table. The insert is accomplished by the following INSERT statement that gets its values from the accountRecs array using the accessor methods from the AccountRec class:

```
#sql { INSERT INTO ACCOUNT_LIST VALUES (
          :( accountRecs[i].getAccountno() ),
          :( accountRecs[i].getProjectno() ),
          :( accountRecs[i].getDepartmentno() ),
      };
```

A possible performance benefit can be obtained in LoadAccountList2 .sqlj, as compared to LoadAccountList.sqlj, by performing all the sequential reads on the file acct_data closer together in time.

```
/*
** Program Name:  AccountRec.java
**
** Purpose:  The accountRecs array in the LoadAccountList2.sqlj
**           program is an array of objects of class AccountRec.
**           The AccountRec class is defined here.
**
*/
```

```
public class AccountRec {
  private int accountno;
  private int departmentno;
  private int projectno;

  /* The AccountRec constructor is used to initialize the AccountRec
     instance with an account number (iaccountno), department number
     (idepartmentno), and project number (iprojectno).
  */
  public AccountRec
    ( int iaccountno, int iprojectno, int idepartmentno ) {
      accountno = iaccountno;
      departmentno = idepartmentno;
      projectno = iprojectno;
  }

  /* Since the accountno, departmentno, and projectno fields are
     private, accessor methods getAccountno(), getDepartmentno(),
     and getProjectno() are provided to return those respective
     field values.
  */
  public int getAccountno() {
    return accountno;
  }
  public int getDepartmentno() {
    return departmentno;
  }
  public int getProjectno() {
    return projectno;
  }
}


/*
** Program Name:  LoadAccountList2.sqlj
**
** Purpose:  Load the ACCOUNT_LIST table from the text file acct_data.
**
*/
/* java.io contains FileReader class, for reading character files,
   and BufferedReader class that supports line-at-a-time input from
   character files.
*/
import java.io.*;

// java.util contains StringTokenizer class.
import java.util.*;
```

```
// Required SQLException class for SQL errors.
import java.sql.SQLException;

/* oracle.sqlj.runtime.Oracle class contains connect() method for
   connecting to database.
*/
import oracle.sqlj.runtime.Oracle;

// Define application class.
class LoadAccountList2 {

   // BufferedReader class allows line-at-a-time input.
   private BufferedReader input;

   /* nrecs will be the number of records in the accountRecs array.
      nrecs is initialized to 0 and will be incremented every time
      a line is read from acct_data.
   */
   private int nrecs = 0;

   // accountRecs is an array of account records.
   private AccountRec[] accountRecs;
   public static void main( String args[] ) {

      /* Invoke LoadAccountList2 constructor to connect to database,
         open data file, and create accountRecs instance.
      */
      LoadAccountList2 maincode = new LoadAccountList2( 100 );

      /* The runLoadAccountList2() method executes main body of code
         for the application.
      */
      maincode.runLoadAccountList2();
   }

   /* Initialize database connection, open data file within the
      constructor of the application class, and create accountRecs
      instance.  Note that LoadAccountList2.sqlj takes an int argument
      that indicates the maximum number of ACCOUNT_LIST records that
      will be loaded, and hence specifies the dimension of the
      accountRecs array.
   */
   public LoadAccountList2( int maxrecs ) {
      connectDB();
      openFile();

      /* Note that only space for the AccountRec references will be
         allocated here.  No space will be allocated for the records
```

```java
        being referenced.
   */
   accountRecs = new AccountRec[ maxrecs ];
}
public void runLoadAccountList2() {
   /* The readArray() method reads the data from the acct_data file
      into the accountRecs array.  The insertRows() method inserts
      the data from the accountRecs array into the ACCOUNT_LIST
      table.  The commitInsert() method commits the inserts executed
      in insertRows().
   */
   readArray();
   insertRows();
   commitInserts();

   // Close data file.
   closeFile();
   System.out.println( "Program complete. \n" );
}

// Method to connect to database.
private void connectDB() {
  try {
    Oracle.connect( getClass(), "connect.properties" );
  }

    // Catch SQL exceptions raised when connecting to database.
    catch( SQLException e ) {
      System.err.println( "Error connecting to database. \n" + e );
      System.exit(1);
    }
  }

  // Method to open data file.
  private void openFile() {
    try {
      input = new BufferedReader( new FileReader( "acct_data" ) );
    }

    // Catch any IO exceptions raised when opening data file.
    catch( IOException e ) {
      System.err.println( "File not opened properly. \n" + e );
      System.exit(1);
    }
  }
/* Method to read data from acct_data file into the accountRecs
   array.
*/
private void readArray() {
```

```
try {

    /* For each input line read with the readLine() method, until
       the readLine() method returns null (indicating end of data),
       or until there are no more remaining slots in accountRecs.
       The readRec() method is used to place the data from the
       input line into the next row of the accountRecs array.
    */
    for ( String b = input.readLine();
          b != null; b = input.readLine() ) {
      if ( nrecs == accountRecs.length ) {

        /* If there are no more remaining slots in the accountRecs
           array, print an error message, close the data file, and
           terminate the program.
        */
        System.err.println( "Too many records." );
        closeFile();
        System.exit(1);
      }
      readRec(b);
    }
}

// Catch IO exceptions raised when reading file.
catch( IOException e ) {
    System.err.println( "Error reading data file. \n" + e );
    closeFile();
    System.exit(1);
}
}

/* Method to extract accountno, projectno, departmentno from
   input string, and place that data in AccountRec row.
*/
private void readRec( String line ) {
  StringTokenizer tk = new StringTokenizer( line );
  TokSequence g = new TokSequence( tk );

  /* The following statement accomplishes three tasks.  First,
     the getInt() method is employed to extract the account
     number, project number, and department number from the
     tokenized input string.  Then, a new AccountRec instance
     is created, and the values delivered by getInt() are used
     to initialize that AccountRec instance.  Finally, the next
     row of the accountRecs array is set to reference the newly
     created and initialized AccountRec instance.
  */
```

```
      accountRecs[ nrecs++ ] =
            new AccountRec( g.getInt(), g.getInt(), g.getInt() );
}

/* Method to insert the data from each row of the accountRecs array
   into the ACCOUNT_LIST table.
*/
private void insertRows() {
  for ( int i = 0; i < nrecs; i++ )
    /* insertRow(i) inserts the data from the i-th row of the
       accountRecs array into the ACCOUNT_LIST table.
    */
    insertRow(i);
  }
}
// Method to insert row into ACCOUNT_LIST table.
private void insertRow( int i ) {
  try {
    // (See Note 1.)
    /* Since the fields of the AccountRec class are private,
       the accessor methods getAccountno(), getProjectno(), and
       getDepartmentno() are needed to obtain the respective
       account number, project number, and department number
       values for insertion.
    */
    #sql {
          INSERT INTO ACCOUNT_LIST VALUES (
                :( accountRecs[i].getAccountno() ),
                :( accountRecs[i].getProjectno() ),
                :( accountRecs[i].getDepartmentno() )
            )
        };
  }

  /* Catch SQL exceptions raised when inserting row into
     ACCOUNT_LIST table.
  */
  catch( SQLException e ) {
    System.err.println
      ( "Account " + accountRecs[i].getAccountno()
            + " could not be inserted. \n" + e );
  }
}

// Method to commit inserts.
private void commitInserts() {
  try {
```

```
      #sql {
        COMMIT WORK
            };
    }

    // Catch SQL exceptions raised when committing insert.
    catch( SQLException e ) {
      System.err.println( "Commit on " +
                          accountRecs[nrecs].getAccountno() +
                          " failed. \n" + e );
    }
  }

  // Method to close data file.
  private void closeFile() {
    try {
      input.close();
    }

    // Catch IO exceptions when closing data file.
    catch( IOException e ) {
      System.err.println( "File not closed properly. \n" + e );
      System.exit(1);
    }
  }
}
```

Note for `LoadAccountList2.sqlj`:

    1. Instead of using complicated host expressions in the `INSERT` statement, you could have first assigned the host expressions to simple variables, and then placed those host variables in the `INSERT` statement:

```
int accountno    = accountRecs[i].getAccountno(),
    projectno    = accountRecs[i].getProjectno(),
    departmentno = accountRecs[i].getDepartmentno();
#sql { INSERT INTO ACCOUNT_LIST VALUES
        ( :accountno, :projectno, :departmentno )
      };
```

This illustrates the general point that a SQLJ clause that involves complicated host expressions can always be rewritten as a SQLJ clause involving only simple Java variables, as long as extra assignment statements are placed before the SQLJ statement containing that clause (for `IN` expressions), after that statement (for `OUT` expressions), or before and after that statement (for `INOUT` expressions).

Executable **SQLJ** Statements without Result Expressions: **SQLJ** Transaction Control Commands

A *SQLJ transaction control command* is a SQLJ statement that consists of a SQL transaction control command. A *transaction* is a sequence of SQL statements that the DBMS server treats as a single unit. In case of a system crash, a transaction will either be rerun to completion or it will be completely undone. When several transactions (from different programs) are concurrently executing, their effect on the database, at least theoretically, is such that they each appear to be executing in isolation from each other—that is, they do not appear to be executing concurrently, but instead it seems as if one transaction finishes before another begins.

A SQLJ program is divided into transactions in the following way. A transaction begins with the first executable SQLJ statement after the execution of a connection to the database, a commit, or a rollback. A transaction ends with the explicit or implicit execution of a commit or a rollback. Executing a commit makes permanent all changes made to the database in the current transaction. Executing a rollback cancels all changes to the database made in the current transaction. A commit can be accomplished by explicitly executing a COMMIT statement:

```
#sql { COMMIT };
```

or

```
#sql { COMMIT WORK };
```

or it can be executed automatically, as indicated in the following.

In Oracle, all DDL commands are automatically and immediately committed. Thus, the execution of a DDL command terminates the current transaction. In addition, you can specify that all INSERT, DELETE, and UPDATE statements be automatically and immediately committed, by enabling the auto-commit flag. You will learn how to enable auto-commit in the subsequent section "auto-commit."

A rollback occurs when a ROLLBACK statement is explicitly executed:

```
#sql { ROLLBACK };
```

or

```
#sql { ROLLBACK WORK };
```

or when a program terminates without having a transaction committed.

NOTE
If you have enabled `auto-commit`, *you cannot*
execute any explicit `COMMIT` *or* `ROLLBACK` *statements.*

You will next learn about:

■ `auto-commit.`

■ The `SET TRANSACTION` statement.

auto-commit

You can enable `auto-commit` (which is disabled by default) either when you
define a SQLJ connection, or by using the `setAutoCommit()` method on an
existing connection object. For example, you can enable `auto-commit` by using
the `connect()` method of the `oracle.sqlj.runtime.Oracle` class with the
signature that takes `URL(String)`, `username(String)`, `password(String)`,
and `auto-commit` flag `(boolean)`:

```
Oracle.connect(
  "JDBC:oracle:thin:@snook.cse.fau.edu:1521:v815","scott","tiger",true)
```

Although there is typically no reason to do so, you can change the
`auto-commit` flag setting for an existing connection for which you have a
connection context instance by first invoking the `getConnection()` method of
that instance to return the underlying JDBC connection object for the instance. Then
you invoke the `setAutoCommit()` method of that JDBC connection object:

```
mycontext.getConnection().setAutoCommit(true)
```

The advantage of enabling `auto-commit` is that you do not have to explicitly
code `COMMIT` statements.
The disadvantages are

■ You cannot rollback changes.

■ Since a separate `COMMIT` will be executed for each `INSERT`, `DELETE`, and
`UPDATE` statement, as soon as they are executed, you will suffer a loss of
runtime performance due to this increased "`COMMIT` overhead."

NOTE
You cannot enable `auto-commit` *in server*
applications.

SET TRANSACTION Statement

The SQL-92 standard includes a SET TRANSACTION statement to allow an increase in concurrency of transactions, the downside being that these transactions may interfere with each other.

Oracle SQLJ supports a version of the SET TRANSACTION statement. The SQLJ SET TRANSACTION statement has the following syntax:

```
#sql {
  SET TRANSACTION [ access_mode ] [ , ]
    [ ISOLATION LEVEL isolation_level ]
    };
```

A SET TRANSACTION statement must specify an access_mode, or an isolation_level, or both. If it specifies both, the isolation_level can be specified before or after the access_mode. The SET TRANSACTION statement, if it appears, must be the first statement in a transaction. Note that unlike other Oracle tools such as SQL*Plus, Oracle SQLJ allows both the access mode and the isolation level to be set in a single SET TRANSACTION statement.

The two access_mode settings are read only and read write. read write is the default setting and allows INSERT, DELETE, and UPDATE statements, as well as SELECT statements, to be executed. The read only setting does not allow INSERT, DELETE, UPDATE, or SELECT FOR UPDATE statements to be executed in the transaction. However, DDL commands are allowed in Oracle. The only DML command allowed is the SELECT statement.

Specifying the read only setting guarantees that the transaction will enjoy transaction-level consistency instead of statement-level consistency. By this it is meant that all queries in the current transaction will only see changes made by other transactions that were committed before the current transaction began. This can be very convenient for reports that contain more than one query, involving the same tables, which are running at the same time that other users are updating those tables.

The isolation_level settings are serializable and read committed. serializable is the default setting in the SQL-92 standard, and will guarantee that concurrently executing transactions will not interfere with each other—that is, that it appears as if one will finish before another one begins. This is the appropriate setting for most applications.

Concurrent transactions are regulated in Oracle by locking rows and (in the case of the SQL lock table command) locking entire tables. Locking a unit—say, a row—means that the server reserves the row for a particular transaction, and it won't let any other transaction access that row until the lock is released (SELECT statements only lock out INSERT, DELETE, and UPDATE statements; INSERT,

DELETE, and UPDATE statements lock out SELECT statements as well). Serializability is enforced by the server holding all locks until the entire transaction completes.

The read committed setting for a transaction is the default setting in Oracle, and it guarantees that an uncommitted change made by another transaction will not be read by the current transaction. However, two types of interference between other concurrent transactions with the current transaction will be allowed with this setting, namely, nonrepeatable reads and phantom reads. Because of this, a transaction running under the read committed setting does not really satisfy the theoretical definition of a transaction given, for example, in *Transaction Processing: Concepts and Techniques* [20], or the definition given previously in this chapter.

A nonrepeatable read in the current transaction occurs when the current transaction reads a record once, and then reads the same record again, only to encounter different data. This can happen when the Oracle server releases the lock that the current transaction has on the record as soon as the statement that is reading the record completes, instead of holding the lock until the entire transaction completes. Thus, two different locks are held on the record for the current transaction at two different points in time. This allows another transaction to update the record in between those two points in time.

read committed is enforced by only holding locks for the duration of a SQL statement, not for the duration of the whole transaction.

The nonrepeatable read interference is allowed in order to gain runtime performance (the updating transaction will not be held up until the entire reading transaction completes).

The phantom read phenomenon is similar to the nonrepeatable read phenomenon, but deals with sets of records returned by SELECT statements instead of field values of individual records. The phantom read phenomenon occurs when a transaction executes the same SELECT statement twice but encounters new "phantom records" the second time.

You are referred to *Transaction Processing: Concepts and Techniques* [20] for an excellent treatment of transaction processing in general. The *Oracle8i SQL Reference Manual* [28] offers more information on the SET TRANSACTION command.

An example of a SET TRANSACTION command, which declares a transaction to be read only, and disallows nonrepeatable and phantom reads is

```
#sql { SET TRANSACTION read only, ISOLATION LEVEL serializable };
```

Executable SQLJ Statements without Result Expressions: Anonymous PL/SQL Blocks and Stored Procedure Calls

In this section, you will consider invoking the following from SQLJ programs:

- Anonymous PL/SQL blocks.

- Stored procedures.

Anonymous PL/SQL Blocks

A PL/SQL block can appear within the curly braces of a SQLJ executable statement, in the same manner that a SQL DDL, DML, or transaction control command can. Note that the final end of the PL/SQL block must have a terminating semicolon. For example, consider the following PL/SQL block that inserts some rows into the ACCOUNT_LIST table:

```
#sql {
  begin
     INSERT INTO ACCOUNT_LIST VALUES ( 10000, 20000, 30000 );
     INSERT INTO ACCOUNT_LIST VALUES ( 40000, 50000, 60000 );
     INSERT INTO ACCOUNT_LIST VALUES ( 70000, 80000, 90000 );
  end;
     };
```

Such an embedded PL/SQL block can contain host expressions. If it does, those host expressions are evaluated before the PL/SQL block is executed, in the order that they appear. For example, consider the SQLJ code fragment:

```
int z, x = 0;
#sql {
  begin
     :OUT x := 5;
     :OUT z := :x;
  end;
     };
System.out.println( "x = " + x + " z = " + z );
```

In the PL/SQL assignment statement :OUT z := :x, 0, not 5, is substituted for the IN host variable :x, since :x is evaluated (and is replaced by its value) before the PL/SQL block is executed, hence before :x is set to 5. Therefore the value of z that is printed is 0, whereas the value of x that is printed is 5. Also, note that you must explicitly declare the modes for :x (in the first assignment statement) and :z to be OUT because the default mode for host expressions in PL/SQL blocks is IN. This PL/SQL default mode IN situation includes host expressions on the left-hand side of PL/SQL assignment statements (such as in the previous code fragment) and host expressions in the INTO clauses of SELECT INTO and FETCH statements (unlike SELECT INTO and FETCH statements that are not contained in PL/SQL blocks, but appear directly in SQLJ clauses, in which case the host expressions in the INTO clauses have default mode OUT). Thus, PL/SQL assignment statements, SELECT INTO statements, and FETCH statements provide examples of where the default mode of host expressions is inappropriate, and the desired mode must be explicitly declared. So you have

```
#sql {
  begin
    SELECT COUNT(*) INTO :OUT x FROM ACCOUNT_LIST;
  end;
      };
```

but

```
#sql { SELECT COUNT(*) INTO :x FROM ACCOUNT_LIST };
```

In both cases x will be assigned the count value, but in the PL/SQL block x must be explicitly declared to be of mode OUT.

An advantage of embedding a PL/SQL block in your SQLJ program, instead of embedding the SQL statements from the block individually, is that all those SQL statements will be sent to the server in one call, thus saving time.

Stored Procedure Calls

A stored procedure is a procedure that has been stored in the database with a command such as the Oracle SQL CREATE PROCEDURE statement (see Appendix A). Stored procedures can be coded in PL/SQL, Java, or any other language that the DBMS allows. In Chapter 4, you will learn about coding stored procedures in SQLJ. In this section, you will consider stored procedures coded in PL/SQL. In any case, the syntax for a SQLJ stored procedure call is

```
#sql { call procedure_name [ ( parameter_list ) ] };
```

`procedure_name` is the name of the procedure, which can optionally take a list of parameters. If the procedure does not have any parameters, this can be indicated by omitting the parentheses, or by having empty parentheses:

```
#sql { call hit };
```

or

```
#sql { call hit() };
```

However, only the former method is compatible with Oracle7.

Consider the PL/SQL procedure `deleteacct` that deletes an account, specified by an account number, from the `ACCOUNT_LIST` table. This procedure is stored in the database by executing the following `CREATE PROCEDURE` statement in, say, SQL*Plus:

```
CREATE PROCEDURE
    deleteacct( acctno ACCOUNT_LIST.accountno%type,
                worked out Boolean ) as
  x integer;
  begin
    /* Check if account record exists. */
    /* When selecting into a PL/SQL variable (like x), the PL/SQL
       variable is not prefixed with a ":"
    */
    SELECT COUNT(*) INTO x FROM ACCOUNT_LIST
      WHERE accountno = acctno;
    /* If it doesn't exist, set worked to false and return. */
    if x = 0 then worked := false;
      return;
    end if;
    /* If it does exist, delete the account, commit the delete,
       and set worked to true.
    */
    DELETE FROM ACCOUNT_LIST WHERE accountno = acctno;
    COMMIT WORK;
    worked := true;
  end deleteacct;
```

You can then invoke this procedure from a SQLJ program:

```
#sql { call deleteacct( :accountno, :OUT status ) };
```

Here, you use host variables to pass in the account number of the account to be deleted, and to receive the Boolean status of the deletion. Recall that PL/SQL supports modes in, out, and in out for subprogram parameters, just as SQLJ supports modes IN, OUT, and INOUT for host expressions. If you are using host expressions in the procedure call, the mode of the host expression must be the same as the mode of the corresponding formal parameter in the procedure. Also, of course, the types of the host expressions must be compatible with the types of the corresponding formal parameters in the procedure.

As an alternative to the preceding procedure call syntax, you can optionally use JPublisher to create a Java wrapper for a stored procedure, and subsequently invoke the Java wrapper as you would any other Java method.

In any case, the ability to invoke stored subprograms from your SQLJ programs allows you to conveniently reuse code that already exists, instead of having to recode it again.

Executable SQLJ Statements without Result Expressions: SET, FETCH, and SELECT INTO Statements

In this section you will consider the three types of SQLJ statements that can contain host expressions with default mode OUT:

- The SET statement.
- The FETCH statement.
- The SELECT INTO statement.

SET Statement

The SET statement is used to compute the value of an expression and assign that value to a host expression. The syntax for the SET statement is

```
#sql { set :host_expression = expression };
```

The host_expression has default mode OUT and must be a Java l-value. Do not try to specify an IN or INOUT mode for the host_expression. That will result in a translation-time error. The SET clause is equivalent to a PL/SQL block clause:

```
#sql {
  begin
    :OUT host_expression := expression;
  end;
    }
```

Thus, the expression to the right of the = in a SET statement can contain anything that is legal in an expression that is located in a PL/SQL block without a declare section. In particular, the expression can contain several stored function calls. In fact, the major application of the SET statement is to easily perform such a computation in one SQLJ statement. Without the SET statement, you would either have to invoke a PL/SQL block, or you would have to invoke several SQLJ statements, each statement capturing one of the stored function values. Stored function call statements are discussed in a subsequent section of this chapter.

In Appendix A there is a PL/SQL package emppak that contains a function insertemp that inserts an employee record into the EMPLOYEE_LIST table, returning true on success and false on failure. If instead insertemp returned 0 on success, and 1 on failure, the following SQLJ SET statement could use this function to insert three employee records, counting the number of inserts that failed:

```
#sql {
      SET :nfailed =
  emppak.insert( 1000, 'Jones', 'Joe',   '(305)999-9999', 1050 ) +
  emppak.insert( 2000, 'Smith', 'Damon', '(212)999-9999', 1050 ) +
  emppak.insert( 3000, 'Cohen', 'Naomi', '(212)888-8888', 1050 )
    };
```

SELECT INTO Statement

The SELECT INTO statement, which is also supported in PL/SQL and embedded SQL, is used to retrieve a single row from the database, and place data from that row in host expressions. The syntax for the SELECT INTO statement is the same as the syntax for a SELECT statement with the addition of a list_of_host_expressions following the select_list of the SELECT statement. The number of elements in the list_of_host_expressions must be the same as the number of elements in the select_list. The default mode for the host expressions in the list_of_host_expressions is OUT. An attempt to specify the mode as IN or INOUT will result in a translator error. A SELECT INTO statement that returns more than one row will result in an execution-time error. A SELECT INTO statement that computes the number of ACCOUNT_LIST records for the project whose number is in the host variable pno is

```
#sql {
      SELECT COUNT(*) INTO :num_of_accts FROM ACCOUNT_LIST
        WHERE projectno = :pno
    };
```

NOTE
Host variables in the WHERE clause of a SELECT INTO statement have default mode IN.

FETCH Statement

The FETCH statement is used to retrieve a row from a positional iterator instance. The syntax for a FETCH statement is

```
FETCH iterator_host_expression INTO list_of_host_expressions
```

where iterator_host_expression references an iterator instance, and has default mode IN. The host_expressions in the list_of_host_expressions have default mode OUT. An attempt to designate modes IN or INOUT for the latter host_expressions will generate a translator error. The number of elements in the list_of_host_expressions must be the same as the number of attributes in the positional iterator attributes, and the host_expressions in the list and the iterator attributes are matched up by position. Note that the host_expressions in the list must be initialized or you will get a Java compiler error indicating that they may never get assigned (the FETCH statement will only assign values if a row was fetched). An example of a FETCH statement, taken from the AcctsForProjs2.sqlj program in Chapter 2, is

```
#sql { FETCH :aDnoAno2 INTO :accountno, :projectno };
```

where that program had the declarations:

```
#sql iterator DnoAno2( int, int );
     DnoAno2 aDnoAno2;
     int accountno, projectno;
```

Executable SQLJ Statements with Result Expressions: SELECT Statements

The processing of multi-row SELECT statements in SQLJ requires a strongly typed version of a cursor called an iterator, as seen in Chapter 2. In this section, you will learn additional information about iterators. Specifically, you will consider:

- The full syntax of iterator declarations (except for connection expressions).

- The full syntax of query clauses (except for connection expressions).

- A SQLJ retrieval program AcctsForProjs3.sqlj that illustrates result expressions

- Populating iterators with nested cursor output.

■ Support for `ref cursor` types in SQLJ

Note that connection expressions will be discussed in Chapter 5.

Syntax of Iterator Declarations

As you saw in Chapter 2, there are two types of iterators: named and positional. Named iterator declarations will be considered first, and then positional iterators.

Named Iterator Declarations

The syntax for named iterator declarations is

```
#sql [ modifiers ] iterator iterator_class_name [ implements_clause ]
    [ with_clause ] ( type_name_list );
```

`modifiers` is a sequence of Java class modifiers such as **public**, **private**, **protected**, and **static**. `iterator_class_name` is the name of the iterator class being defined, and the `type_name_list` is the list of iterator attribute names and types with which any `SELECT` statement that populates the iterator instance must be compatible. Before examining the `implements_clause` and `with_clause`, an example illustrating modifiers is given:

```
#sql public iterator DnoAno3( int departmentno, int accountno );
```

This declaration is similar to the one that appears in the `AcctsForProjs.sqlj` program in Chapter 2. However, in that program the **public** modifier was absent. With the **public** modifier present, SQLJ will generate DnoAno3 as a **public** class. Since DnoAno3 is defined as a **public** class, the iterator declaration for it should be contained in its own SQLJ file, and translated and compiled before any program that uses it. This is in conformance with the Java practice of putting a **public** class declaration in its own source file.

A `SELECT` statement that populates an iterator must have its `select_list` elements match up with the iterator attributes by name. If a `select_list` element is not a column name, or has a name that differs from the name of the desired iterator attribute with which it should match up, a column alias can be assigned to the `select_list` element so as to give the `select_list` element the proper name. For example:

```
DnoAno3 dx;
#sql dx =
  { SELECT ano AS accountno, dno AS departmentno
```

```
        FROM OLD_ACCOUNTS WHERE pno = 55555
  };
```

Here the OLD_ACCOUNTS table has column names ano, dno, and pno for account number, department number, and project number, respectively. Thus, accountno and departmentno are assigned as column aliases to ano and dno, causing the select_list to match up by name with the attributes of DnoAno3.

The implements_clause and the with_clause are now considered. The implements_clause lists Java interfaces that the iterator class will implement. Recall that a Java interface is like a class except that none of its methods have bodies—that is, they are abstract—and the interface does not contain any non-final fields. A class *implements* an interface if it contains fully coded methods with the same names and signatures as the interface methods. Thus, if an iterator class implements an interface, the set of interface methods must be a subset of the set of methods that the translator will generate for the iterator class. For the most part, you have an iterator class implement a user-defined interface if you wish to hide some of the iterator methods from some applications. In that case, you have the applications access the iterator instance through the interface. For example, suppose you wish to hide the departmentno() accessor method from certain applications. You can code an interface, Ano, that only contains an accountno() method, have DnoAno3 implement that interface, and only expose Ano to the applications:

```
/*
** Program Name:   InterfaceExample.sqlj
**
** Purpose:   Illustrate the use of iterator class implements clause
**            to accomplish hiding.
**
*/
// Required SQLException class for SQL errors.
import java.sql.SQLException;

/* oracle.sqlj.runtime.Oracle class contains connect() method for
   connecting to database.
*/
import oracle.sqlj.runtime.Oracle;

/* Interface Ano will be used to hide the departmentno field from
   the main() method.
*/
/* All the iterator methods that main needs must be declared in the
   interface.
*/
/* Since the SQLJ generated iterator methods accountno(), next(),
   and close() throws SQLException, the corresponding interface
```

```
    methods must do the same.
*/
interface Ano {
  int accountno() throws SQLException;
  boolean next() throws SQLException;
  void close() throws SQLException;
}

// Declare the iterator class.
#sql iterator DnoAno3 implements Ano
  ( int departmentno, int accountno );

// Define application class InterfaceExample.
/* Quick and dirty example where methods throw exceptions (that is,
   propagate them back to the calling method) instead of catching
   them (one or the other has to be done since SQLException is a
   checked exception class).
*/
public class InterfaceExample {
  public static void main( String[] args ) throws SQLException {

      // Invoke InterfaceExample constructor to connect to database.
      InterfaceExample e = new InterfaceExample();

      /* Invoke getIterInst() method to create iterator instance and
         return it as interface instance. Note that the departmentno()
         accessor method is inaccessible for ax.
      */
      Ano ax = e.getIterInst();

      // Retrieve row from iterator.
      ax.next();

      /* Use accountno() accessor method to retrieve account number
         from row, and then print that account number.
      */
      System.out.println( "Account number = " + ax.accountno() );

      // Close iterator.
      ax.close();
  }

  // Initialize database connection within constructor.
  public InterfaceExample() throws SQLException {
    Oracle.connect( getClass(), "connect.properties" );
  }

  /* This method populates iterator instance and returns it as
     interface instance, hiding the departmentno() accessor method
     from the calling method.
```

```
*/
public Ano getIterInst() throws SQLException {
  DnoAno3 dx;
  #sql dx = { SELECT departmentno, accountno FROM ACCOUNT_LIST };
  return( (Ano) dx );
}
}
```

Also, you can specify that your iterator class implements special SQLJ predefined interfaces, such as the `sqlj.runtime.ForUpdate` interface (which will be discussed shortly). In this situation, SQLJ will generate the appropriate methods in the iterator class to implement the interface methods.

The `with_clause` enables you to define and initialize constants that will be included in the definition of the generated iterator class. These constants are **public static final**. In standard SQLJ, there is a predefined set of constants, mostly involving cursor state options, that can be defined in a `with_clause`, and these are the only constants that can be so defined. However, in Oracle SQLJ, any constant can be defined. Furthermore, all of the predefined constants have no meaning in Oracle SQLJ, at the time of this writing. The syntax for the `with_clause` is

```
with var1 = value1, var2 = value2, ..., varn = valuen
```

where the `vari`'s are the constant names, and `valuei` is the value for constant `vari`.

An example of an iterator declaration containing a `with_clause` is

```
#sql public iterator DnoAno4 implements Oracle.runtime.ForUpdate
    with ( updateColumns = "departmentno, accountno" );
```

The value of an `updateColumns` constant is a String literal that contains a comma-separated list of column names indicating the columns that can be updated by a subsequent UPDATE command containing a `where_current_of` clause for the iterator. For example, consider:

```
DnoAno4 dx;
#sql dx =
  { SELECT accountno, departmentno FROM ACCOUNT_LIST
      FOR UPDATE OF accountno, departmentno
  };
dx.next();
UPDATE ACCOUNT_LIST SET departmentno = 5555, accountno = 6666
  WHERE CURRENT OF dx;
```

This would update the `departmentno and accountno` fields in the current row retrieved from the iterator with the `next()` method. Unfortunately, Oracle SQLJ does not currently support such a `where_current_of` clause.

An iterator class declaration that contains a `with_clause` specifying `updateColumns` must also have an `implements_clause` that specifies `oracle.runtime.ForUpdate`.

The other predefined constants in the SQLJ standard, also not yet supported by Oracle SQLJ, are

- **Returnability** (values: true/false) specifies whether an iterator can return JDBC result sets from a stored procedure call.

- **Holdability** (values: true/false) specifies whether iterator position will be held after a `COMMIT` is executed.

- **Sensitivity** (values: sensitive, asensitive, insensitive) specifies whether an open iterator is guaranteed to be insensitive to the changes made by other SQL statements in the same transaction, whether it is guaranteed to be sensitive to the changes made by other SQL statements made in the same transaction, or whether there are no guarantees either way (asensitive).

The syntax of the positional iterator declaration is

```
#sql modifiers iterator iterator_class_name
     [ implements_clause ] [ with_clause ] ( type_list )
```

The only difference between the positional iterator declaration and the named iterator declaration is that the former contains a `type_list`—that is, a list of types—while the latter contains `type_name_list` that is a list of attribute names and types. This is because when a `SELECT` statement populates a positional iterator instance, the elements of its `select_list` are matched up with the iterator attributes by position, whereas when the `SELECT` statement populates a named iterator, the elements of its `select_list` are matched up with the iterator attributes by name. The following positional iterator declaration appeared in the `AcctsForProjs.sqlj` program from Chapter 2:

```
#sql iterator DnoAno2( int, int );
```

Syntax of Query Clauses

The syntax of a SQLJ executable statement that contains a query clause is

```
#sql result_expression = { select_statement };
```

The `result_expression` can be any Java expression that is an l-value and that references an iterator instance. For example, the subsequent program `AcctsForProjs3.sqlj` contains the following statement:

```
#sql DnoAno3s[i] =
    { SELECT accountno, departmentno FROM ACCOUNT_LIST
        WHERE projectno = :( projectnos[i] )
    };
```

Here you see a result expression that is an array element, as well as a host expression that is an array element. In a query clause `SELECT` statement, host expressions can appear anyplace that SQL expressions can appear.

You will next see a program `AcctsForProjs3.sqlj` that illustrates query clauses with result expressions that are more complicated than simple Java variables.

A SQLJ Retrieval Program: AcctsForProjs3.sqlj

This program is a modification of the program `AcctsForProjs.sqlj` from Chapter 2. `AcctsForProjs.sqlj` inputs project numbers, one at a time, and prints the account numbers and department numbers for accounts that involve the indicated projects. In `AcctsForProjs3.sqlj`, all the project numbers are first input into an array. Then, for each project number, a separate iterator instance in an array of iterator instances is populated with the department numbers and account numbers for accounts that involve the project. Finally, the rows are retrieved and printed from the iterator instances, one iterator instance at a time.

The advantage of this program over `AcctsForProjs.sqlj` is that there are no delays between the inputting of project numbers, which is particularly convenient when standard output has been redirected to a file, and therefore interspersed output cannot be seen immediately anyway.

```
/*
** Program Name:  AcctsForProjs3.sqlj
**
** Purpose:  Reading project numbers from standard input, one project
**           number per line, and printing the department numbers and
**           account numbers for accounts involving those projects.
**
*/
// java.io contains BufferedReader and InputStreamReader classes.
import java.io.*;

// java.util contains StringTokenizer class.
import java.util.*;

// Required SQLException class for SQL errors.
```

```
import java.sql.SQLException;

/* oracle.sqlj.runtime.Oracle class contains connect() method for
   connecting to database.
*/
import oracle.sqlj.runtime.Oracle;

/* Declare iterator class DnoAno3 to be consistent with the SELECT
   statement from which its instance will receive output.
*/
#sql iterator DnoAno3( int departmentno, int accountno );

// Define application class AcctsForProjs3
class AcctsForProjs3 {

   // BufferedReader class allows line-at-a-time input.
   private BufferedReader input;

   /* DnoAno3s is an array of iterator class instances. Each element
      of DnoAno3s will reference an iterator instance associated with
      a projectno.
      (See Note 1.)
   */
   private DnoAno3[] DnoAno3s;

   /* The array projectnos will hold the project numbers that the user
      will supply.  Such an array is needed in this program, since the
      project numbers will be read in before they are processed.
   */
   private int projectnos[];

   /* nprojs is the number of projects that have been read in.  nprojs
      is initialized to 0, and is incremented by one when a new project
      has been read.
   */
   private int nprojs = 0;
   public static void main( String[] args ) {

      /* Invoke AcctsForProjs3 constructor to connect to database,
         direct System.in to a BufferedReader stream, assign an int[]
         instance to projectnos having slots for 10 ints, and assign
         a DnoAno3[] instance to DnoAno3s having slots for ten
         references to DnoAno3 iterator instances.
      */
      AcctsForProjs3 maincode = new AcctsForProjs3( 10 );

      /* The runAcctsForProjs3() method executes the main body of code
         for the application.
      */
```

```
    maincode.runAcctsForProjs3();
 }

 /* Initialize database connection, direct System.in to a
    BufferedReader stream, and assign array instances to
    projectnos and DnoAno3s having maxprojs elements, within
    application class constructor.
 */
 public AcctsForProjs3( int maxprojs ) {
   connectDB();
   openInput();
   projectnos = new int[ maxprojs ];
   DnoAno3s = new DnoAno3[ maxprojs ];
 }
 private void runAcctsForProjs3() {

   /* Invoke inputProjnos() method to input the project numbers
      into the projectnos array.  Invoke populateIters() method to
      populate the elements of the DnoAno3s array with the SELECT
      statement outputs for the corresponding project numbers.
      Invoke fetchIters() method to retrieve and print the output
      sets from each of the iterator instances that were populated
      by the populateIters() method.  Invoke closeInput() method to
      close buffered stream.
   */
   inputProjnos();
   populateIters();
   fetchIters();
   closeInput();
 }

 // Method to connect to database.
 private void connectDB() {
   try {
     Oracle.connect( getClass(), "connect.properties" );
   }
   //Catch SQL exceptions raised when connecting to database.
   catch( SQLException e ) {
     System.err.println( "Error connecting to database. \n" + e );
     System.exit(1);
   }
 }

 /* Method to direct System.in to a character stream, and to direct
    that character stream to a BufferedReader stream.
 */
 private void openInput() {
   input = new BufferedReader( new InputStreamReader( System.in ) );
 }

 // Method to input project numbers into projectnos array.
```

```
private void inputProjnos() {
  try {
    int projectno;
    String line;
    for ( ; ; ) {
      System.out.println( "Please enter a project number" +
                          " (enter a -1 to terminate) >> " );
      // Read input line.
      line = input.readLine();

      /* Invoke getProjectno() method to extract projectno
         from input line.
      */
      projectno = getProjectno( line );

      // If projectno = -1 return to runAcctsForProjs3() method.
      if ( projectno == -1 ) { break;
                             }

      /* Place new project number in the nprojs-th slot of
         projectnos array, and increment nprojs.
      */
      projectnos[ nprojs++ ] = projectno;
    }
  }

  /* Catch any IO exceptions raised when reading standard input
     with the readLine() method.
  */
  catch( IOException e ) {
    System.err.println( "Error reading input. \n" + e );
    closeInput();
    System.exit(1);
  }
}

/* Method to use the StringTokenizer class and get class from the
   previous ACCOUNT_LIST example to extract projectno from input
   line.
*/
private int getProjectno( String line ) {
  StringTokenizer tk = new StringTokenizer( line );
  TokSequence g = new TokSequence( tk );
  return g.getInt();
}

/*  Method to populate each of the nprojs iterator elements of
    DnoAno3s with the select output for the corresponding project
    number.
*/
```

```
private void populateIters() {
  for ( int i = 0; i < nprojs; i++ ) {
    /* Invoke select() method to populate DnoAno3s[i] with
       accountno's and departmentno's for accounts with the input
       projectno.  If select() detected problems with the SELECT
       statement, set projectnos[i] to -1 so DnoAno3s[i] can be
       skipped in subsequent processing.
    */
    if ( select(i) != 0 ) projectnos[i] = -1;
  }
}

/* Method to populate iterator class instance DnoAno3s[i] with
   output from SELECT statement for i-th project number.
*/
private int select( int i ) {
  try {
    #sql
      DnoAno3s[i] = { SELECT accountno, departmentno
                      FROM ACCOUNT_LIST
                        WHERE projectno = :( projectnos[i] )
                    };
    return 0;
  }
  // Catch SQL exceptions raised when populating DnoAno3s[i].
  catch( SQLException e ) {
    System.err.println( "Cannot execute select statement. /n" + e );
    return -1;
  }
}

/* Method to fetch and print the output from each of the nprojs
   iterator elements of DnoAno3s.
*/
private void fetchIters() {
  try {
    for ( int i = 0; i < nprojs; i++ ) {
      /* For each row retrieved into DnoAno3s[i], use the accessor
         methods accountno() and departmentno() to print the
         accountno and departmentno in that row.
      */
      while ( DnoAno3s[i].next() ) {
        System.out.println
          ( "Account number = " + DnoAno3s[i].accountno()
          + " Department number = " + DnoAno3s[i].departmentno() );
      }
```

```
        /* Close DnoAno3s[i] so that it can be repopulated in next
           iteration of main loop.
        */
        closeIter( DnoAno3s[i] );
      }
    }
    // Catch any SQL exceptions raised when accessing DnoAno3s[i].
    catch( SQLException e ) {
      System.err.println
        ( "Error getting data from iterator. \n" + e );
      closeInput();
      System.exit(1);
    }
  }

// Method to close iterator.
private void closeIter( DnoAno3 x ) {
  try {
    x.close();
  }

  // Catch SQL exceptions raised when closing iterator.
  catch( SQLException e ) {
    System.err.println
      ( "Cannot close iterator. \n" + e.toString() );
    System.exit(1);
  }
}

// Method to close buffered stream.
private void closeInput() {
  try {
    input.close();
  }

  // Catch I/O exceptions raised when closing buffered stream.
  catch( IOException e ) {
    System.err.println
      ( "Cannot close buffered stream. \n" + e.toString() );
    System.exit(1);
  }
}
}
```

Note for `AcctsForProjs3.sqlj`:

   1. An advantage of iterators being bona fide Java constructs is that you can
   have an array of iterator instances.

Populating Iterators with Nested Cursor Output

The material covered in this section is specific to Oracle, and is not part of the SQLJ standard. In Oracle8, a *nested cursor* designates a set of rows that can appear in the `select_list` of a `SELECT` statement. For example:

```
SELECT projectno, cursor
  ( SELECT accountno FROM ACCOUNT_LIST
     WHERE PROJECT_LIST.projectno = ACCOUNT_LIST.projectno )
  FROM PROJECT_LIST
```

This `SELECT` statement prints the project number of each project followed by the set of account numbers of accounts that involve that project. Sample output obtained by executing this `SELECT` statement in SQL*Plus for a `PROJECT_LIST` table that contains three projects (with project numbers 10000, 20000, and 30000), and an `ACCOUNT_LIST` table that contains accounts 1 and 2 for project 10000, accounts 3 and 4 for project 20000, and no accounts for project 30000 is

```
PROJECTNO  CURSOR(SELECTACCOUNT
---------- --------------------
     10000 CURSOR STATEMENT : 2

CURSOR STATEMENT : 2

 ACCOUNTNO
----------
         1
         2

     20000 CURSOR STATEMENT : 2

CURSOR STATEMENT : 2

 ACCOUNTNO
----------
         3
         4

     30000 CURSOR STATEMENT : 2

CURSOR STATEMENT : 2

no rows selected
```

The nested cursor method allows the account numbers for each project to be separately delivered.

In this section you will learn two ways to retrieve nested cursor data in SQLJ using iterators:

- Selecting a nested cursor into an iterator.

- Populating a nested iterator with a nested cursor.

Selecting a Nested Cursor into an Iterator

A SELECT INTO statement that contains a nested cursor in its select_list can contain an iterator instance in its into_clause. The following program NestedCursorExample.sqlj, which prints the name of project 10000 followed by the set of account numbers of accounts that involve project 10000, contains such a SELECT INTO statement.

```
/*
**
** File Name:  AnosForPnos.sqlj
**
** Purpose:  If an instance of an iterator class will be used in a
**           host expression, that iterator class must be declared
**           public, and hence have its declaration be contained in
**           its own file.  An AnosForPnos instance will hold a set
**           of account numbers.
**
*/
#sql public iterator AnosForPnos( int acountno );


/*
** Program Name:  NestedCursorExample.sqlj
**
** Purpose:  To illustrate selecting nested cursor output into
**           an iterator.
**
*/
// Required SQLException class for SQL errors.
import java.sql.SQLException;

/* oracle.sqlj.runtime.Oracle class contains connect() method for
   connecting to database.
*/
import oracle.sqlj.runtime.Oracle;

// Define application class NestedCursorExample.
```

```
public class NestedCursorExample {

  /* SQLExceptions, like all checked exceptions, must be caught
     or thrown (that is, propagated back to the calling method).
  */
  public static void main( String[] args ) throws SQLException {

    // Invoke NestedCursorExample constructor to connect to database.
    NestedCursorExample maincode = new NestedCursorExample();

    /* The runNestedCursorExample() method executes the main body
       of code for the example.
    */
    maincode.runNestedCursorExample();
  }

  // Initialize database connection within constructor.
  public NestedCursorExample() throws SQLException {
    Oracle.connect( getClass(), "connect.properties" );
  }
  private void runNestedCursorExample() throws SQLException {
    /* Declare iterator variable anAnosForPnos that will be
       populated by SELECT INTO statement.
    */
    AnosForPnos anAnosForPnos;
    String projectName;

    /* Select project name into projectName variable and nested cursor
       output (namely, the account numbers for accounts that involve
       project 10000) into anAnosForPnos.  Of course, anAnosForPnos is
       a host variable here.
    */
    #sql {
      SELECT projectName, cursor
        ( SELECT accountno FROM ACCOUNT_LIST
            WHERE PROJECT_LIST.projectno = ACCOUNT_LIST.projectno )
              INTO :projectName, :anAnosForPnos
                FROM PROJECT_LIST WHERE projectno = 10000
          };
    System.out.println( "Project Name = " + projectName );
    System.out.println( "Accounts for project 10000 is = " );

    /* Retrieve rows from the anAnosForPnos iterator, and print the
       account numbers in those rows using the accessor method
       accountno().
    */
    while ( anAnosForPnos.next() ) {
```

```
        System.out.println( anAnosForPnos.accountno() );
    }

    // Close iterator.
    anAnosForPnos.close();
  }
}
```

Populating a Nested Iterator with a Nested Cursor

A *nested iterator* is an iterator that is an attribute of another iterator. Iterators that contain nested iterators as attributes can be populated by SELECT statements that contain nested cursors, with the output from the nested cursor going to the nested iterator. For example, consider the following program NestedCursorExample2.sqlj that contains such a nested iterator. NestedCursorExample2.sqlj prints each project number, followed by the account numbers of accounts that involve that project. The same output, in a different format, was produced by the stand-alone SQL statement at the beginning of "Populating Iterators with Nested Cursor Output."

The corresponding sample output from NestedCursorExample2.sqlj is

```
Project number = 10000
Account numbers =
1
2
----
Project number = 20000
Account numbers =
3
4
----
Project number = 30000
Account numbers =
----

/*
** Program Name: NestedCursorExample2.sqlj
**
** Purpose:   Illustrate nested iterators.
**
*/
// Required SQLException class for SQL errors.
import java.sql.SQLException;

/* oracle.sqlj.runtime.Oracle class contains connect() method for
```

```
    connecting to database.
*/
import oracle.sqlj.runtime.Oracle;

/* Declare named iterator class PnoAno so that a PnoAno instance will
   hold a set of rows consisting of a project number and a set of
   account numbers.  The set of account numbers will be held in the
   nested iterator anos. A nested iterator class, such as
   AnosForPnos, must be a public class.
*/
#sql iterator PnoAno( int projectno, AnosForPnos anos );
public class NestedCursorExample2 {
  public static void main( String[] args ) throws SQLException {

    // Invoke NestedCursorExample2 constructor to connect to database.
    NestedCursorExample2 maincode = new NestedCursorExample2();

   /* The runNestedCursorExample2() method executes main body of
      code for example.
    */
    maincode.runNestedCursorExample2();
  }

  // Define application class NestedCursorExample2.
  public NestedCursorExample2() throws SQLException {

    // Initialize database connection within constructor.
    Oracle.connect( getClass(), "connect.properties" );
  }
  public void runNestedCursorExample2() throws SQLException {

    // Declare "outer" iterator variable aPnoAno.
    PnoAno aPnoAno;

    /* Populate aPnoAno with SELECT statement output.  The SELECT
       statement returns, for each project, the project number of
       that project and the set of account numbers of accounts which
       involve that project.  The nested cursor output from the SELECT
       statement goes to the nested iterator anos in aPnoAno.
       (See Note 1.)
    */
    #sql aPnoAno =
       { SELECT projectno, cursor
           ( SELECT accountno FROM ACCOUNT_LIST
```

```
                 WHERE PROJECT_LIST.projectno = ACCOUNT_LIST.projectno )
             AS anos
               FROM PROJECT_LIST
      };

    // Retrieve rows from aPnoAno using next() method.
    while ( aPnoAno.next() ) {
      /* Retrieve project number from aPnoAno row using projectno()
         accessor method, and print the project number.
       */
      System.out.println
        ( "Project number = " + aPnoAno.projectno() );
      /* Retrieve nested iterator output from aPnoAno row using
         anos() accessor method, and populate AnosForPnos instance
         variable anAnosForPnos with that output.
       */
      AnosForPnos anAnosForPnos = aPnoAno.anos();
      System.out.println( "Account numbers = " );

      // Retrieve rows from anAnosForPnos using next() method.
      while ( anAnosForPnos.next() ) {

        /* Retrieve account number from anAnosForPnos row using
           accountno() accessor method, and print account number.
         */
        System.out.println( anAnosForPnos.accountno() );
      }

      // Close anAnosForPnos iterator.
      anAnosForPnos.close();
      System.out.println( "----" );
    }
    // Close aPnoAno iterator.
    aPnoAno.close()
  }
}
```

Note for `NestedCursorExample2.sqlj`:

1. The column alias anos is required in the SELECT statement so that the nested cursor column matches up by name with the anos attribute of aPnoAno.

For illustrative purposes, the next program `NestedCursorExample3.sqlj` is a variation of the preceding program where the outer iterator is a positional iterator but the nested iterator is a named iterator.

```
/*
** Program Name: NestedCursorExample3.sqlj
**
** Purpose:   Illustrate a named iterator nested within a positional
**            iterator.
**
*/
// Required SQLException class for SQL errors.
import java.sql.SQLException;

/* oracle.sqlj.runtime.Oracle class contains connect() method for
   connecting to database.
*/
import oracle.sqlj.runtime.Oracle;

/* Declare positional iterator class PnoAno2 so that its instances
   can hold the same type of data as iterator PnoAno instances held
   in the preceding program NestedCursorExample2.sqlj.  Note the
   nested iterator in PnoAno2 is of type AnosForPnos, and hence is
   a named iterator.
*/
#sql iterator PnoAno2( int, AnosForPnos );

// Define application class NestedCursorExample3.
public class NestedCursorExample3 {
  public static void main( String[] args ) throws SQLException {

    // Invoke NestedCursorExample3 constructor to connect to database.
    NestedCursorExample3 maincode = new NestedCursorExample3();

    /* The runNestedCursorExample3() method executes main body
       of code for example.
    */
    maincode.runNestedCursorExample3();
  }
  public NestedCursorExample3() throws SQLException {

    // Initialize database connection within constructor.
    Oracle.connect( getClass(), "connect.properties" );
  }
```

```
public void runNestedCursorExample3() throws SQLException {

  // Declare outer positional iterator variable aPnoAno.
  PnoAno2 aPnoAno;

  /* Populate aPnoAno with SELECT statement output.  The
     nested cursor output from the SELECT statement goes to
     the nested named iterator in aPnoAno.
     (See Note 1.)
  */
  #sql aPnoAno =
     { SELECT projectno, cursor
         ( SELECT accountno FROM ACCOUNT_LIST
             WHERE PROJECT_LIST.projectno = ACCOUNT_LIST.projectno )
         FROM PROJECT_LIST
     };

  // Loop to process outer iterator rows.
  for ( ; ; ) {
    /* Variables to be fetched into must be initialized.
       anAnosForPnos is initialized to null since it is
       a class instance.
    */
    int projectno = 0;
    AnosForPnos anAnosForPnos = null;

    /* Fetch from positional iterator into host variables.
       Named iterator instance anAnosForPnos will hold output
       from nested iterator.
    */
    #sql { FETCH :aPnoAno INTO :projectno, :anAnosForPnos };

    // If at end of data, terminate program.
    if ( aPnoAno.endFetch() ) break;

    /* Otherwise, print project number and set of account numbers
       that was fetched.
    */
    System.out.println( "Project number = " + projectno );
    System.out.println( "Account numbers = " );

    /* Retrieve rows from iterator instance anAnosForPnos using
       next() method.
    */
```

```
    while ( anAnosForPnos.next() ) {

      /* Use accountno() accessor method to retrieve account
         number from row, and print that account number.
      */
      System.out.println( anAnosForPnos.accountno() );
    }

    // Close iterator anAnosForPnos.
    anAnosForPnos.close();
    System.out.println( "----" );
  }
  // Close iterator aPnoAno.
  aPnoAno.close();
  }
}
```

Note for `NestedCursorExample3.sqlj`:

1. Note that, unlike the `SELECT` statement in the preceding program `NestedCursorExample2.sqlj`, a column alias is not needed here because the `SELECT` columns and positional iterator attributes are matched up by position and not by name.

Support for ref cursor Types in SQLJ

See the *PL/SLQ User's Guide and Reference* [40] for detailed information on ref cursors. A *ref cursor variable* is a variable that references a cursor. A `ref cursor` variable can be dynamically attached to different `SELECT` statements in a PL/SQL block at runtime, using the PL/SQL `open for` statement. This attachment of a `ref cursor` variable to a `SELECT` statement must be accomplished in PL/SQL. However, iterator variables can receive their output sets from `ref cursor` variables. There are, in fact, four ways that a SQLJ iterator variable can be attached to the output set of a `ref cursor` variable. These include the iterator instance being

- An `OUT` host expression in a PL/SQL block.

- The actual parameter passed to an `OUT` formal parameter of a PL/SQL procedure or function.

■ An OUT host expression in the INTO clause of a SQLJ SELECT INTO or FETCH INTO clause. You have already seen this in the preceding section, since nested cursors are actually implicit ref cursors.

■ The result expression in a SQLJ stored function call. You will consider this case in the subsequent section on stored function calls.

Examples of the first two ways that an iterator variable can be attached to ref cursor output are illustrated in the following program, RefCursorExample.sqlj, which prints project numbers from the ACCOUNT_LIST table.

```
/*
** Program Name: curpak.sql
**
** Purpose:   Package curpak contains the definition of the specific
**            ref cursor type to be used in procedure pnoscur, and
**            also contains that procedure pnoscur.  All ref cursor
**            variables must be declared to be of a specific named
**            type that was defined by a PL/SQL type statement.
**
*/
CREATE PACKAGE curpak AS
  type pcur is ref cursor;
  procedure pnoscur( p out pcur );
end curpak;
/

CREATE PACKAGE BODY curpak AS

  /* The parameter p must be declared to be of mode OUT so that the
     iterator that will be passed to p can be changed.
  */
  procedure pnoscur( p out pcur ) is
  begin

    /* The PL/SQL open for statement attaches a SELECT statement to
       a ref cursor variable, executes the query, and identifies the
       result set.
    */
    open p for SELECT projectno FROM ACCOUNT_LIST;
  end;
end curpak;
/
```

```
/*
** Program Name:  Pnos.sqlj
**
** Purpose:  If an instance of an iterator class will be used in a
**           host expression, that iterator class must be declared
**           public, and hence have its declaration be contained in
**           its own file.  A Pnos instance will hold a set of project
**           numbers.
**
*/
#sql public iterator Pnos( int projectno );



/*
** Program Name: RefCursorExample.sqlj
**
** Purpose:  To retrieve the set of project numbers from the
**           ACCOUNT_LIST table in two ways: using an embedded
**           PL/SQL block containing an open for statement, and
**           using a stored procedure containing an open for
**           statement.
**
*/
// Required SQLException class for SQL errors.
import java.sql.SQLException;

/* oracle.sqlj.runtime.Oracle class contains connect() method for
   connecting to database.
*/
import oracle.sqlj.runtime.Oracle;

// Define application class RefCursorExample.
public class RefCursorExample {
  public static void main( String[] args ) throws SQLException {

    // Invoke constructor to connect to database.
    RefCursorExample maincode = new RefCursorExample();

    /* The runRefCursorExample() method executes the main body
       of code for the example.
    */
    maincode.runRefCursorExample();
  }
  // Initialize database connection within constructor.
  public RefCursorExample() throws SQLException {
    Oracle.connect( getClass(), "connect.properties" );
  }
```

```
public void runRefCursorExample() throws SQLException {

  /* Declare px to be an array of references to Pnos iterators,
     and assign an array with two slots to px.
  */
  Pnos[] px = new Pnos[2];

  /* Execute a PL/SQL block that opens a ref cursor for the set
     of project numbers in the ACCOUNT_LIST table, and populates
     px[0] with the result set from that ref cursor.  px[0] is an
     OUT host variable expression here, so that its value can be
     changed by the PL/SQL block, that is, so that it can reference
     the appropriate result set.
  */
  #sql {
    begin
      open :OUT ( px[0] ) for SELECT projectno FROM ACCOUNT_LIST;
    end;
      };

  /* Another way to get the same output is to call the procedure
     pnoscur stored in the package curpak, passing the OUT host
     expression, :OUT px[1] as a parameter to pnoscur.  Note that
     the mode of the host expression must match the mode of the
     pnoscur parameter.
  */
  #sql {
    CALL curpak.pnoscur( :OUT ( px[1] ) )
      };

  /* A for loop is used to retrieve the data from px[0] and px[1]
     (the output for both will be the same).
  */
  for ( int i = 0; i < 2; i++ ) {
    // Use the next() method to retrieve the next row from px[i].
    while ( px[i].next() ) {

      /* Use the projectno() accessor method to retrieve the project
         number from the row, and then print that project number.
      */
      System.out.println( px[i].projectno() );
    }
    // Close the px[i] iterator.
    px[i].close();
    System.out.println( "----" );
  }
  }
}
```

Executable SQLJ Statements with Result Expressions: Stored Function Calls

The syntax for a stored function call embedded in a SQLJ program is

```
#sql result_expression =
    { values ( function_name ( parameter_list ) ) };
```

Note that the outer parentheses around the function call are optional in Oracle SQLJ. The `result_expression` can be any Java l-value expression that is compatible with the return type of the function. The syntax and semantics of the `parameter_list` is the same as those described for stored procedure calls. The following SQLJ executable statement calls the function `insertemp` from the package `emppak` (described in a previous section of this chapter, "SET Statement"), which inserts a row into the `EMPLOYEE_LIST` table using the data passed as its arguments. `insertemp` returns 0 if the insert was successful, and 1 otherwise:

```
int status;
#sql { status = values( emppak.insertemp
          ( 1000, 'Smith', 'Joe', '(999)999-9999', '1050' ) )
      };
```

If the stored function does not take any arguments, you can use either empty parentheses, `function_name()`, or no parentheses, `function_name`. However, use no parentheses if you wish your code to be compatible with Oracle7.

If a stored function returns a `ref cursor` type, you can assign the return value of the stored function to an iterator.

For example, suppose that the PL/SQL package `curpak` coded in the preceding section contains the following function:

```
function dfunc return pcur is
p pcur;
begin
  open p for SELECT projectno FROM ACCOUNT_LIST;
  return  p;
end;
```

Then, the following code fragment would assign the output set from `p` to the iterator instance `px`:

```
#sql iterator Pno( int projectno );
Pno px;
#sql px = { values( curpak.dfunc ) };
```

Evaluation of Host Expressions and Result Expressions at Runtime

Since Java expressions (such as ++x) can have side effects, the order in which these expressions, in particular host and result expressions, are evaluated can affect their values. The following indicates the order in which host and result expressions in a SQLJ statement are evaluated:

- Result expressions are evaluated before host expressions.

- Host expressions are evaluated from left to right in the order they appear in the SQLJ clause. Each host expression is evaluated only once, and saved.

- IN and INOUT host expressions are passed to SQL, and the SQL statement or PL/SQL block is executed.

- After execution of the statement or PL/SQL block, the OUT and INOUT host expressions are assigned values in order from left to right as they appear in the statement or PL/SQL block.

- If there is a result expression, it is assigned a value last.

NOTE
Host expressions in PL/SQL blocks are evaluated before the block is sent to be executed, and each host expression in a PL/SQL block is evaluated exactly once. See the example given in the earlier section "Anonymous PL/SQL Blocks."

JDBC and SQLJ Exception Classes

In this section, you will consider the SQLException classes and its subclasses, and how to extract information from those classes. The SQLException class was defined for JDBC, and is a subclass of the Java Exception class. You have already seen that printing a SQLException object will print an error message identifying the error that caused the exception to be raised.

SQLException also contains two methods that can provide additional information: getSQLState() and getErrorcode(). The exact information provided by these two methods depends on where the exception was raised. If the exception was raised from Oracle SQLJ runtime, getSQLState() returns a five-digit string containing the SQLState—that is, a string identifying the error according to X/Open standard conventions. If the exception was raised by the

Oracle server, getErrorCode() returns the xxxxx portion of the ORA-xxxxx error code. In all other cases, the methods do not return anything of use.

Useful subclasses of SQLException are SQLNullException and SQLWarning. sqlj.runtime.NullException is a SQLJ exception that is raised when a null value might be returned to a Java primitive variable. java.sql.SQLWarning is raised when a warning condition, instead of an error, has occurred.

You can print the message that goes along with these exceptions by printing the exception object, as you do with SQLException objects. Also, you should place the catch blocks for the subclass exceptions before the SQLException catch, so that they will be handled first, carrying out special operations appropriate to the subclass type of exception.

Other Useful JDBC and SQLJ Classes

You may need java.sql classes besides SQLException such as java.sql.ResultSet (if you are using Java ResultSets instead of, or in addition to, iterators).

You have already used java.sqlj.runtime.Oracle that contains the connect() method. Other sqlj.runtime classes you may need are in the sqlj.runtime.ref package (the sqlj.runtime.ref.DefaultContext class, to be discussed in Chapter 5, is defined in this package). Some important runtime classes that are directly in the sqlj.runtime package are sqlj.runtime.AsciiStream and sqlj.runtime.BinaryStream (these are SQLJ Stream classes that will be discussed in Chapter 6), sqlj.runtime.ResultSetIterator (also to be discussed in Chapter 6 along with other topics regarding the interoperability of JDBC and SQLJ), and sqlj.runtime.ExecutionContext (to be discussed in Chapter 5).

In this chapter, you examined the different types of SQLJ executable statements. In particular, you considered stored function calls and procedure calls. In the next chapter, you will learn how to code stored procedures and functions in SQLJ, instead of in PL/SQL, as well as how to code database triggers in SQLJ.

PART
II

Advanced SQLJ for Relational Processing

CHAPTER
4

Developing SQLJ Stored Programs and Triggers

tored subprograms are procedures and functions that are either directly stored in the database with the SQL `CREATE PROCEDURE` and `CREATE FUNCTION` statements, or are stored in the database by being contained in PL/SQL packages and user-defined object types that are stored in the database. In Chapter 3, you saw that stored procedures and functions could be invoked from SQLJ programs. The stored subprogram examples in Chapter 3 were all coded in PL/SQL. In this chapter, you will learn how to code stored procedures and functions in SQLJ. Such stored subprograms can be used in exactly the same way as the stored subprograms implemented in PL/SQL: they can be invoked from SQL statements as well as from PL/SQL blocks, and can be contained in PL/SQL packages as well as being members of user-defined SQL object types. Also, just as is the case for PL/SQL subprograms, SQLJ stored procedures (that is, SQLJ methods that return void) can be invoked from SQL*Plus, Pro*C, database triggers, and SQLJ statement clauses using the SQL `CALL` statement, and SQLJ stored functions (that is, SQLJ methods that have a non-void return type) can be invoked directly from SQL DML commands as well as from SQLJ assignment clauses, and, using the SQL `CALL` statement, from SQL*Plus and Pro*C.

In this chapter, you will consider

- The development of SQLJ stored subprograms on the client side.

- Creating SQL stored subprogram wrappers in PL/SQL packages.

- The invocation of SQLJ stored subprograms from SQL statements and PL/SQL blocks in various environments.

- The loading and translation of SQLJ source in the server.

- Dropping Java schema objects with the `dropjava` utility.

- Advantages and disadvantages of implementing stored subprograms in SQLJ vs. implementing them in PL/SQL.

In Chapter 7, you will see how SQLJ stored subprograms can be members of user-defined object types. In Chapter 8, you will consider the invocation of stored subprograms from CORBA objects and Enterprise JavaBeans.

Development of SQLJ Stored Programs on the Client Side

There are two approaches to developing SQLJ stored subprograms. One approach is to translate and compile the SQLJ source on the client side, and then load the generated class and resource files into the server. The other approach is to load the

SQLJ source into the server, and then translate and compile it using the server-side translator. The former approach is probably the best, since the client-side translator has better support for option setting and error processing, and that approach is the subject of the current section. Specifically, in this section you will consider

- SQLJ coding considerations for server-side applications.
- `EmpInsert.sqlj`: an example server-side application.
- Translating SQLJ source files on the client side.
- Loading classes and resources into the server.
- Checking that schema objects have been loaded in the server.
- Creating a top-level SQL wrapper for a stored subprogram.
- `FuncTest.sqlj`: a simple application that invokes a stored subprogram.
- Summary of development steps.

-

Coding Considerations for Server-Side Applications

Since stored subprograms run in the Oracle8*i* server, when implementing a SQLJ subprogram you have to take into account the differences between writing code that will execute on the client side and writing code that will execute on the server side. Fortunately, there are only the following small number of differences to consider:

- You must set the JDBC driver in your `connect.properties` file to be the server-side Oracle JDBC KPRB driver.
- You only have one database connection, namely to the database in which the code is running. That connection is implicit. You do not explicitly connect to the database (that is, you will not have an explicit call to a method like `connect()`).
- This connection cannot be closed. Any attempt to close it will be ignored, but no error will be generated.
- Since the SQLJ runtime packages are directly available in the server, you do not include `import` statements for them. Therefore, `import` statements for classes such as `oracle.sqlj.runtime.Oracle` are not needed.

■ You must be very careful about closing iterators when you are done with them, because the KPRB driver does not release cursors for an iterator until the iterator is closed. The cursors will persist across calls to the stored subprogram. If you do not close your iterators, you could run out of available cursors, causing your subprogram to fail.

■ The KPRB driver does not support auto-commit. You must therefore explicitly commit all your updates, either in the stored subprogram or the client that invokes the stored subprogram.

Note that any public static method, including main(), in a Java class can be used to define a stored subprogram, and that such a method can invoke any other accessible method in the same class, or in another accessible class that is stored in the server.

The default output device in the Oracle8*i* Java VM is the current trace file. If you wish to redirect your output to the screen, you have two alternatives. One alternative is to execute the PL/SQL dbms_output.put_line procedure from your SQLJ subprogram code, which will direct your output to the dbms_output buffer. Such a call must be preceded by a call to dbms_output.enable, which will enable your program to place output into the buffer. A client program can then read this output from the buffer by first calling dbms_output.enable, and then calling the dbms_output.get_line procedure to read a line of output from the buffer. The other alternative for getting output from a stored subprogram is to invoke, in the stored subprogram, the PL/SQL procedure dbms_java.set_output, which will direct subsequent Java output (from methods such as System.out.println) to the dbms_output buffer. This invocation must be followed by a call to dbms_output.enable. The client program can then read this output from the dbms_output buffer using dbms_output.get_line, just as in the first alternative. Both these alternatives will be illustrated with the subsequent program EmpInsert.sqlj.

Observe that the first method must also be used in any SQLJ program (client-side or server-side) to get the output from an embedded PL/SQL block that contains a call to dbms_output.put_line, since the call to dbms_output.put_line will not directly send output to the screen when invoked from SQLJ. You must precede the call to dbms_output.put_line in the PL/SQL block with a call to dbms_output.enable, so that the output will go to the dbms_output buffer. The information must then be read in the SQLJ program from the buffer using dbms_output.get_line:

```
#sql { begin
          /* The enable procedure accepts as its parameter
             the desired size of the buffer.
             enable must be called before you output to (the
             situation we have here) or input from the buffer.
          */
```

```
        dbms_output.enable( 500 );
        dbms_output.put_line( 'Hello' );
      end;
    }
String x;
int status;

/* The enable procedure must be called before you output to
   or input from (the situation we have here) the buffer.
*/
#sql { CALL dbms_output.enable( 500 ) };

/* The get_line procedure accepts two OUT parameters: the string to
   hold the input line, and the integer variable that is set to 0 if
   the line was successfully read, and is set to 1 otherwise.
*/
#sql { CALL dbms_output.get_line( :OUT x, :OUT status ) } ;
System.out.println( x );
```

EmpInsert.sqlj: An Example of a Server-Side Application

The following program `EmpInsert.sqlj` contains a method `insertEmp()` that will insert a new employee record into the `EMPLOYEE_LIST` table. The method `insertEmp()` will return 1 if the record could be inserted and 0 otherwise, as well as printing an error message in the latter case. A PL/SQL function `insertemp` that is similar to `insertEmp()` appears in the section "PL/SQL Subprograms" of Appendix A. `EmpInsert.sqlj` is written with the preceding coding considerations in mind, since it is intended to subsequently use the `insertEmp()` method to define a stored function. In particular, the `connect.properties` file is not explicitly referenced in the program.

```
/*
** Program Name:  EmpInsert.sqlj
**
** Purpose:  Define a method insertemp() to insert a record into
**           EMPLOYEE_LIST table, returning 0 on success and 1 on
**           failure.
**
*/
/*  There is no need to import oracle.sqlj.runtime.Oracle, since
    the connect() method of oracle.sqlj.runtime.Oracle will not be
    invoked, and all runtime classes are directly available anyway.
*/
import java.sql.SQLException;
```

```
public class EmpInsert {
  public static int insertEmp( int empno, String lastname,
                               String firstname, String phone,
                               int departmentno ) {

    int x;
    try {
      #sql { INSERT INTO EMPLOYEE_LIST VALUES( :empno, :lastname,
                                               :firstname, :phone,
                                               :departmentno )
          };

      /* Return 0 if insert was successful, that is, SQLException
         wasn't raised.
      */
      return 0;
    }

    // Handle SQLException raised during insert.
    catch( SQLException e ) {
      try {

        /* Enable access to dbms_output buffer, and print error
           message in buffer.
        */
        #sql { CALL dbms_output.enable( 500 )
            };
        #sql { CALL dbms_output.put_line( :( "Insert failed. " + e ) )
            };
        // (See Note 1.)

        // Since exception was raised during insert, return 1.
        return 1;
      }

      // If exception was raised during calls, return 1.
      catch( SQLException ex ) {
        return 1;
      }
    }
  }
}

# File Name:  connect.properties
# The connection below uses the KPRB connection
# for the data-i.com server.
#
# If you wish to test the program on the client side first,
```

```
# use a different connect.properties file for testing that
# specifies a client-side JDBC driver.
#
# Fill in the correct username and password for your login.
sqlj.url=jdbc:oracle:kprb:@data-i.com:1521:ORCL
#sqlj.url=jdbc:oracle:oci8:@
#sqlj.url=jdbc:oracle:oci7:@

# User name and password here
sqlj.user=scott
sqlj.password=tiger
```

Note for `EmpInsert.sqlj`:

1. If you wish to implement the second alternative for redirecting output to the
`dbms_output` buffer, you would replace the lines of code:

```
#sql { CALL dbms_output.enable( 500 ) };
#sql { CALL dbms_output.put_line( :( "Insert failed. " + e ) )
    };
```

with

```
/* The set_output procedure accepts as its parameter
   the desired buffer size.
*/
#sql { CALL dbms_java.set_output( 500 ) };
#sql { CALL dbms_output.enable( 500 ) };
System.out.println( "Insert failed. " + e );
```

However, the calling code would remain the same.

Translating SQLJ Source Files on the Client Side

It simplifies naming considerations if the generated profiles are stored as `.class`
files instead of `.ser` files. The `-ser2class` option of the translator will accomplish
this. Thus, the following command can be used to translate and compile the
preceding `EmpInsert.sqlj` program:

```
sqlj -ser2class EmpInsert.sqlj
```

Loading Classes and Resources into the Server

The Oracle client-side utility `loadjava` is used to convert `.class` files into
database library units, called *Java class schema objects*, that are stored in the server,

and to convert `.ser` files (if any) into similar units, called *resource schema objects*, that are also stored in the server. A distinct schema object is created for each `.class` file and each `.ser` file. See the section "SQLJ Translation Process" in Chapter 2 for information on files generated by the SQLJ translator.

On the `loadjava` command line, you can specify each `.class` or `.ser` file separately, or you can first combine them into a `.jar` (Java archive) file and then just specify that `.jar` file on the `loadjava` command line.

If you submit to `loadjava` all your `.class` and `.ser` files as a `.jar` file, make sure that `jar` does not compress your files, since `loadjava` does not support compressed files. Passing a 0 option to `jar` will suppress compression. The following command line creates an uncompressed file called `EmpInsert.jar` for all the output files from the translation of `EmpInsert.sqlj` (note that there are no `.ser` files due to the use of the `sqlj -ser2class` option):

```
jar -cvf0 EmpInsert.jar EmpInsert.class
   EmpInsert-SJProfileKeys.class EmpInsert-SJProfile0.class
```

This can be expressed more succinctly as:

```
jar -cvf0 EmpInsert.jar EmpInsert*.class
```

Note that:

- The c option creates a new and empty archive, the v option generates verbose output on `stderr`, and the f option indicates that the archive is to be placed in a file (the next argument) instead of on standard output.

- You could not use the succinct "wildcard" version of the `loadjava` command line if you had other files, unrelated to the desired class output, that start with "`EmpInsert.`"

Next, you will consider the `loadjava` command line to load the `.class` files for `EmpInsert.sqlj` into the server as class schema objects. The default driver for `loadjava` is the JDBC OCI8 driver, which does not require a URL in the `-user` option setting. However, suppose instead that you desired the JDBC thin driver, which does require a URL. This can be specified by using the `-thin` option and indicating a URL on the `-user` option:

```
loadjava -resolve -verbose -thin -user scott/tiger@data-i.com:1521:ORCL
EmpInsert.jar
```

The `-resolve` option directs `loadjava` to immediately resolve class references, instead of later when the subprogram is first executed. The `-verbose` option prints a step-by-step report on the `loadjava` command execution.

If you instead prefer the default OCI8 driver, you execute

```
loadjava -user scott/tiger EmpInsert.jar
```

Checking That Schema Objects Have Been Loaded in the Server

From SQL*Plus, you can query the `user_objects` view to determine if `loadjava` successfully loaded your schema objects. In order to do this, you need to know how schema objects are named. There are two types of schema objects produced: class objects and resource objects (if you specified the `-ser2class` option to `sqlj`, only class objects are produced, simplifying naming). The class schema object *full name* is produced by taking the class name, fully qualified with its package path, and substituting slashes (`/`) for dots (`.`). So, if a fully qualified class name is `A.B.C.D.EmpInsert`, the full name of the corresponding schema object would be `A/B/C/D/EmpInsert`.

The naming scheme for resource objects (that is, schema objects for `.ser` files) is somewhat more complicated, providing a reason for converting all `.ser` files to `.class` files with the `sqlj -ser2class` option. However, if the `loadjava` or `jar` command, on which the `.ser` file is specified, is executed from the directory specified by the `sqlj -d` option (that is, the top-level directory in which `.class` and `.ser` files are to be placed), and if that directory is in your `CLASSPATH`, then the full name of the `.ser` file is the `.ser` filename (including the .ser extension), prefixed with the package path for the corresponding application class. For example, the full name of the `.ser` file for the class `A.B.C.D.EmpInsert` would be `A/B/C/D/EmpInsert-SJProfile0.ser`.

If the full name of a schema object exceeds 31 characters, or contains illegal characters, a *short name* is generated for the schema object, and the schema object is loaded under that name. However, when querying the `user_objects` view, you do not need to know if the full name or short name is used, because the `dbms_java.shortname` function will take a long name as its argument and return a short name, if there is one for the object, or the full name if there isn't a short name. Thus,

```
SELECT object_name FROM USER_OBJECTS
    WHERE object_name = dbms_java.shortname( 'A/B/C/D/EmpInsert' );
```

will tell you if a schema object were loaded for `A.B.C.D.EmpInsert`, whether or not a short name was used for loading that schema object.

Creating a Top-Level SQL Wrapper for a Stored Subprogram

The final step in the development of a SQLJ subprogram is to create a SQL wrapper for the stored subprogram. It is this wrapper that makes the SQLJ subprogram appear that it is written in PL/SQL, and is used in invoking the subprogram from SQL statements and PL/SQL blocks. In this section, you will learn how to create a "top-level" wrapper (that is, one that is not contained in another unit such as a PL/SQL package) by using the SQL `CREATE PROCEDURE` and `CREATE FUNCTION` statements. In a subsequent section, you will learn how to create wrappers as part of PL/SQL packages. In Chapter 7, you will learn how to create wrappers as part of object type definitions.

Oracle8*i* provides new syntax options for the SQL `CREATE PROCEDURE` and `CREATE FUNCTION` statements (see Appendix A for the original syntax). These options allow you to associate the stored subprogram you are creating with a Java method in a Java class that you have already loaded into the server with the `loadjava` utility (that is, to create a SQL wrapper for your Java method). In such `CREATE` commands, you specify the parameter types and return type (if you are creating a stored function) of the stored subprogram, as well as the argument types and return type (if non-void) of the corresponding Java method. The stored subprogram parameter types must be SQL types, and must be compatible (see Appendix D) with the Java types of the corresponding (by position) arguments of the Java method. The SQL return type of a stored function must be compatible with the Java return type of the Java method. The Java method can return void (indicated by an absent return clause for the Java method) if and only if a stored procedure is being created.

For example, the following `CREATE FUNCTION` statement creates a wrapper for the `EmpInsert.insertEmp()` Java method previously considered:

```
CREATE FUNCTION insertemp( employeeno number, lastname varchar2,
    firstname varchar2, phone varchar2, departmentno number )
  return number AS
  LANGUAGE java
  NAME 'EmpInsert.insertEmp
    ( int, java.lang.String, java.lang.String, java.lang.String, int )
  return int';
```

This statement creates a stored function named `insertemp` having the indicated SQL return type and the indicated parameters. The stored function corresponds to a method written in Java having the fully qualified name `EmpInsert.insertEmp`. Note that the fully qualified specification must be given of any Java type (such as String) that is defined in a Java package.

Notice also that there are two obvious differences between the `CREATE FUNCTION` given here and the `CREATE FUNCTION` for the PL/SQL version of `insertemp` given in Appendix A:

- The `insertemp` here returns number, whereas the `insertemp` in Appendix A returns boolean. You could not declare the `insertemp` here to return boolean, even if you were willing to have the `EmpInsert.insertEmp()` Java method return boolean. The reason is that PL/SQL subprograms can have PL/SQL types (which include SQL types and some other types) for their parameter and return types, whereas SQLJ stored subprograms must have SQL types for their parameter and return types. Since boolean is a PL/SQL type, but not a SQL type, it can be a return type for a PL/SQL stored function, but not for a SQLJ stored function. If you recoded the Java method `EmpInsert.insertEmp` to return boolean, and then coded your `CREATE FUNCTION` so that `insertemp` returned boolean, you would still get an inconsistent data type error message any time you tried to call `insertemp`, even from SQLJ.

- The Appendix A version of the `CREATE FUNCTION` used the `%type` attributes to define the parameters of `insertemp`, whereas the version given here uses the explicit types `number` and `varchar2`. Although neither PL/SQL nor SQLJ stored subprograms can use explicit constrained types as parameter and return types, PL/SQL subprogram parameter and return types can be specified using the `%type` attribute for a table field that is of a constrained type. If you used such a `%type` attribute when you defined your SQLJ subprogram, you would get a "Can't have constrained type" error message when you execute your `CREATE FUNCTION` statement.

The stored function `insertemp` can be invoked from a SQLJ program via the following SQLJ executable statement that contains an assignment clause:

```
int x;
#sql x = { VALUES
          ( insertemp ( 10000, 'Smith', 'John',
                        '(999)999-9999', 20000 ) )
        };
```

If you wish the calling program to read the output deposited by `insertemp` in the `dbms_output` buffer, you would follow the `#sql` statement with:

```
int status;
String z;
#sql { CALL dbms_output.enable( 500 ) };
#sql { CALL dbms_output.get_line( :OUT z, :OUT status ) };
if ( status == 0 ) System.out.println( z );
```

The subsequent section of this chapter, "FuncTest.sqlj: A Simple Application That Invokes a Stored Subprogram," contains a fully coded, simple SQLJ program that invokes the `insertemp` stored function.

The syntax of the CREATE FUNCTION and CREATE PROCEDURE statements for defining SQL wrappers for Java methods is given by the *Oracle8i Java Stored Procedures Developer's Guide* [39, p. 3-10]:

```
CREATE
{ PROCEDURE procedure_name [ ( param[, param]... ) ]
  | FUNCTION function_name [ ( param[, param]... ) ] RETURN sql_type }
  [ AUTHID { DEFINER | CURRENT_USER } ]
  [ PARALLEL_ENABLE ]
  [ DETERMINISTIC ]
  { IS | AS } LANGUAGE JAVA
  NAME 'method_fullname (java_type_fullname[, java_type_fullname ]...)
    [ return java_type_fullname ]';
```

where `param` stands for:

```
parameter_name [ in | out | in out ] sql_type
```

Note that:

- Constraints, such as the maximum number of digits in a `number` type, or maximum length of a `varchar2`, cannot be specified for subprogram parameters. This is also the case for any PL/SQL subprogram formal parameter.

  The stored subprogram parameter list element `param` can contain the PL/SQL modes `in`, `out`, and `in out`. If a parameter has mode `out` or `in out`, the corresponding argument of the Java method must be an array. The final value of the zero-th element of that array will be propagated back to the caller. However, the caller does not pass in an array to such a stored subprogram. For example, the method `setOne` in the following class `ExampleOut` sets its argument to one:

  ```
  //Program Name:  ExampleOut.sqlj
  public class ExampleOut {
    public static void setOne( int[] x ) {
      x[0] = 1;
    }
  }
  ```

  The following creates a wrapper for the method (after the class has been compiled and loaded into the server):

```
CREATE PROCEDURE setone ( x out  number ) AS
  LANGUAGE java
    NAME 'ExampleOut.setOne( int[] )';
```

`setone` can be invoked from the following SQLJ fragment:

```
int y = 5;
#sql { CALL setone( :OUT y ) };
System.out.println( y );
```

The above `println` will print 1, not 5.

A restriction you should note is that stored functions with `in out` and `out` parameters cannot be invoked from SQL DML commands.

■ The `authid` clause indicates whether the stored subprogram executes with the privileges of its `definer` or its `invoker`. The default is the `invoker`.

■ The `parallel_enable` option allows a stored function to be used in slave sessions of parallel DML evaluations.

■ The `deterministic` hint instructs the optimizer that the value returned by a stored function depends only on the values of its arguments. The optimizer can therefore store and reuse the results of past function calls.

■ The `method_fullname` must be fully qualified with the name of the class containing the method, and the complete package path for the class—for example, `A.B.C.D.classname.methodname`.

Except when the Java method is the `main` method of the class, the subprogram parameters and the method arguments must be in one-to-one correspondence. The `String[]` argument of `main` can be mapped to multiple `char` and `varchar2` subprogram parameters:

```
class Example {
  public static void main( String[] args ) {
    ...
  }
}
CREATE PROCEDURE nothing ( x1 varchar2,
                           x2 varchar2,
                           x3 varchar2,
                           x4 varchar2 ) AS
  LANGUAGE java
  NAME 'Example.main( java.lang.String[] )'
```

- If the Java method does not have any arguments, an empty parameter list (f()) is coded for it in the name clause. However, the procedure or function call would contain no parameter list at all (f).

- Semantic errors in the CREATE PROCEDURE and CREATE FUNCTION statements are not reported until the procedure or function is invoked. Thus, if there was a type mismatch between the type of a procedure parameter and the corresponding Java method argument, it would not be reported when you executed the CREATE PROCEDURE statement, but when you first tried to invoke the procedure.

FuncTest.sqlj: A Simple Application That Invokes a Stored Subprogram

```
/*
** Program Name:  FuncTest.sqlj
**
** Purpose:  Test the insertemp stored function, and report the error
**           message placed by insertemp in the dbms_output buffer in
**           the case that the insert failed.
**
*/
import java.sql.SQLException;
import oracle.sqlj.runtime.Oracle;
public class FuncTest {

  // Initialize database connection within FuncTest constructor.
  public FuncTest() {
    try {
      Oracle.connect( getClass(), "connect.properties" );
    }
    catch( SQLException e ) {
      System.out.println( "Connection failed. " + e );
      System.exit(1);
    }
  }
  public static void main( String[] args ) {

    // Invoke FuncTest constructor to connect to database.
    FuncTest f = new FuncTest();
    int error, output;
    String errmess;

    /* Invoke insertemp to insert record.  Store return code in
       error variable.
```

```
      */
      try {
        #sql error = { VALUES( insertemp ( 1946, 'Jones', 'Joe',
                                           '(999)999-9999', 10000 ) )
                     };
      }
      // Handle SQLException raised during function call.
      catch( SQLException e ) {
        System.out.println( "Error in call to FuncTest. " + e );
        System.exit(1);
      }
      // If no error, commit insert.
      try {
        if ( error == 0 ) {
          #sql { COMMIT WORK };
          System.out.println( "Example complete." );
        }
      }
      // Handle SQLException raised during commit.
      catch( SQLException e ) {
          System.out.println( "Error in commit. " + e );
          System.exit(1);
        }
      /* Otherwise, enable access to dbms_output buffer, read message
         from dbms_output buffer using get_line procedure, and print
         the message.
      */
      else try {
        #sql { CALL dbms_output.enable( 500 )
             };
        #sql { CALL dbms_output.get_line
                 ( :out errmess, :out output )
             };
        if ( output == 1 ) { System.out.println( "Insert failed." ); }
          else { System.out.println( errmess ); }

          // Disable access to dbms_output buffer.
          #sql { CALL dbms_output.disable };
        }
        // Handle SQLException raised during buffer read.
        catch( SQLException e ) {
          System.out.println( "Error in reading buffer. " + e );
          System.exit(1);
        }
    }
  }
```

Summary of Development Steps

In this section, the previously given development steps for client-side stored subprogram development are summarized, using the `insertemp` example.

- Create the SQLJ source file, `EmpInsert.sqlj`, for the class `EmpInsert`, which contains the method `insertEmp` that will be "converted" into a stored subprogram.

  Translate and compile the SQLJ source file `EmpInsert.sqlj`, specifying that generated `.ser` files be converted to `.class` files:

  ```
  sqlj -ser2class EmpInsert.sqlj
  ```

- Combine the `.class` files generated in the previous step into a `.jar` file:

  ```
  jar -cvf0 EmpInsert.jar EmpInsert*.class
  ```

- Load the `.class` files contained in the `.jar` file `EmpInsert.jar` into the Oracle8*i* server:

  ```
  loadjava -thin -resolve -verbose
   -user scott/tiger@data-i.com:1521:ORCL
  ```

- Check in SQL*Plus that server schema objects were created for the classes loaded in the previous step:

  ```
  SELECT object_name FROM USER_OBJECTS
    WHERE object_name = dbms_java.shortname( 'EmpInsert' );
  ```

- Create a wrapper in SQL*Plus for the stored subprogram :

  ```
  CREATE FUNCTION insertemp( employeeno number, lastname varchar2,
                  firstname varchar2, phone varchar2, departmentno
  )
    return number AS
    LANGUAGE java
    NAME 'EmpInsert.inesertEmp( int, java.lang.String,
  java.lang.String,
                                  java.lang.String, int )
      return number';
  /
  ```

- Invoke the stored subprogram `insertemp`:

  ```
  int x;
  #sql x = { VALUES( insertemp ( 10000, 'Jones', 'John',
                                '(999)999-9999', 20000 ) ) };
  ```

Creating SQL Stored Subprogram Wrappers in PL/SQL Packages

As described in Appendix A, a PL/SQL package consists of a package specification, which contains (among other things) the specifications of subprograms that are available for use by clients of the package, and a package body that contains (among other things) the implementation (specification and body) of each subprogram declared in the package specification. Such an implementation can consist of a SQL wrapper for a SQLJ stored subprogram, instead of a fully coded PL/SQL subprogram.

For example, consider the following package emppak2, where the CREATE PACKAGE and the CREATE PACKAGE BODY statements for emppak2 are each contained in their own SQL*Plus script, which is similar to the package emppak from Appendix A.

```
/*
** Program Name:  emppak2.sql
**
** Purpose:  Define a package specification for PL/SQL package
**           emppak2.  emppak2 contains deleteemp procedure
**           and insertemp function to, respectively, delete and
**           insert employee records in the EMPLOYEE_LIST table.
**
*/
CREATE PACKAGE emppak2 is
procedure deleteemp( empno number );
function insertemp( empno        number,
                    lastname     varchar2,
                    firstname    varchar2,
                    phone        varchar2,
                    departmentno number )
  return number;
end emppak2;
/

/*
** Program Name:  emppak2body.sql
**
** Purpose:  Implement emppak2.deleteemp and emppak2.insertemp
**           by providing wrappers for the Java methods
**           EmpPak2.deleteEmp() and EmpPak2.insertEmp(),
**           respectively.
**
*/
CREATE PACKAGE BODY emppak2 is
```

```
// Wrapper for EmpPak2.deleteEmp().
/* Remember to use unconstrained type for deletetemp
   parameter type.
*/
procedure deleteemp( empno number ) AS
  LANGUAGE java
  NAME 'EmpPak2.deleteEmp( int )';

// Wrapper for EmpPak2.insertEmp().
/* Remember to use only unconstrained types for insertemp
   parameter types and return type.
*/
function insertemp ( empno        number,
                     lastname     varchar2,
                     firstname    varchar2,
                     phone        varchar2,
                     departmentno number )
  return number AS
  LANGUAGE java

  // Remember to give full name for Java String type.
  NAME 'EmpPak2.insertEmp( int, java.lang.String,
                           java.lang.String,
                           java.lang.String, int )
       return int';
end emppak2;
/
```

If you wish, you could create your subprogram wrappers in your package specification, which can eliminate the need for a package body. This is illustrated by the SQL*Plus script emppak3.sql.

```
/*
** Program Name:  emppak3.sql
**
** Purpose:   Provide wrappers for the Java methods EmpPak2.deleteEmp()
**            and EmpPak2.insertEmp() in the package specification,
**            eliminating the need for a package body.
**
*/
CREATE PACKAGE emppak3 AS

// Wrapper for EmpPak2.deleteEmp.
procedure deleteemp (empno number) AS
  LANGUAGE java
  NAME 'EmpPak2.deleteEmp(int)';
```

```
// Wrapper for EmpPak2.insertEmp.
function insertemp ( empno           number,
                     lastname        varchar2,
                     firstname       varchar2,
                     phone           varchar2,
                     departmentno    number )
   return number AS
   LANGUAGE java
   NAME 'EmpPak2.insertEmp ( int, java.lang.String,
                                  java.lang.String,
                                  java.lang.String, int )
           return int';
end emppak3;
/
```

The stored subprograms defined in emppak2 can be invoked by qualifying the subprogram names with the package name emppak2.

```
#sql { CALL emppak2.deleteemp( 10000 ) };
```

The methods for emppak2 come from the following Java class EmpPak2:

```
/*
** Program Name:   EmpPak2.sqlj
**
** Purpose:   Provide SQLJ methods to implement the subprograms
**            emppak2.deleteemp and emppak2.insertemp.
**
*/
import java.sql.SQLException;
public class EmpPak2 {

  // Method to implement emppak2.insertemp.
  public static int insertEmp( int empno, String lastname,
                               String firstname, String phone,
                               int departmentno ) {
     int x;
     try {
       /* Check for duplicate employee number.  Return 1 if a
          duplicate exists.
       */
       #sql { SELECT COUNT(*) INTO :x
                FROM EMPLOYEE_LIST
                  WHERE employeeno = :empno
              };
       if (x != 0) return 1;
```

```
        /* Otherwise, insert employee record, commit insert,
           and return 0.
        */
        #sql { INSERT INTO EMPLOYEE_LIST VALUES
               ( :empno, :lastname, :firstname, :phone, :departmentno )
             };
        #sql { COMMIT WORK };
        return 0;
      }
      /* Return 1 if exception was raised by insert or commit
         statement.
      */
      catch( SQLException e ) {
        return 1;
      }
    }
    /* Method to implement emppak2.deleteemp.  Method deleteemp()
       reports errors by propagating SQLException.
    */
    public static void deleteEmp( int empno ) throws SQLException {
      int x;

      // Check if employee record exists.
      #sql { SELECT COUNT(*) INTO :x FROM EMPLOYEE_LIST
             WHERE employeeno = :empno
           };
      /* If it doesn't exist, throw a SQLException, terminating
         the procedure.
      */
      /* When procedure deleteemp is invoked, SQLException explicitly
         thrown by deleteemp, as well as SQLExceptions thrown by SQL
         statements within deleteemp, will all get converted into
         "Uncaught Java exception" error.
      */
      /* If deleteemp procedure is invoked from SQLJ, any such thrown
         exceptions will get converted into the SQLException for
         uncaught Java exceptions.
         (See Note 1.)
      */
      if ( x == 0 ) throws SQLException;
        // If it does exist, delete employee, and commit the delete.
        #sql { DELETE FROM EMPLOYEE_LIST
               WHERE employeeno = :empno
             };
        #sql { COMMIT WORK } ;
    }
}
```

Note for `EmpPak2.sqlj`:

1. `Emppak2.deleteemp` propagates the `SQLException` to its invoker,
   generating a "Java call terminated by uncaught Java exception" error
   (Oracle error 29532) in the invoker. In fact, any uncaught exception thrown
   by a Java stored subprogram generates that error in the invoker, whether the
   subprogram was invoked from PL/SQL, SQL*Plus, Pro*C, or SQLJ. If
   the subprogram was invoked from SQLJ, any uncaught exception, even a
   user-defined exception, is propagated to the invoker as a `SQLException`
   for Oracle error 29532. This makes it more difficult in the invoker to
   distinguish between different exceptions thrown by an invoked SQLJ stored
   subprogram.

The following program `PakTest.sqlj` illustrates the invocation of
`emppak2.insertemp` and `emppak2.deleteemp` from a SQLJ program:

```
/*
** Program Name:   PakTest.sqlj
**
** Purpose:   Sample invocation of emppak2.insertemp
**            and emppak2.deleteemp.
**
*/
import java.sql.SQLException;
import oracle.sqlj.runtime.Oracle;
class PakTest {

  /* Initialize database connection from the PakTest constructor.
  public PakTest() {
    try {
      Oracle.connect ( getClass(), "connect.properties" );
    }
    catch ( SQLException e ) {
      System.out.println (" Cannot connect, " + e );
      System.exit(1);
    }
  }
  public static void main( String[] args ) {
    int status;

    // Invoke PakTest constructor so as to connect to database.
    PakTest t = new PakTest();

    /* Invoke stored function emppak2.insertemp.  The variable
       status gets the return code from this invocation.
    */
```

```
      try {
      #sql status = {
        VALUES( emppak2.insertemp( 50000, 'Smith', 'Ann',
                                  '(999)999-9999', 10000 ) )
                      };
      }
      /* Insert failed because of SQLException thrown by SQL
         statements in insertemp.
      */
      catch( SQLException e ) {
        System.out.println( "Can't hire employee, " + e );
        System.exit(1);
      }
      /* Insert failed because employeeno was already in the
         EMPLOYEE_LIST table.
      */
      if (status == 1) {
        System.out.println
          ( "Can't hire employee, employee already on board." );
        System.exit(1);
      }
      System.out.println( "Hiring complete." );

      // Invoke stored subprogram emppak2.deleteemp.
      try {
        #sql { CALL emppak2.deleteemp( 2000 ) };
        System.out.println( "Firing complete." );
      }

      /* Delete failed either because of SQLExceptions thrown by SQL
         statements within emppak2.deleteemp, or by SQLException
         explicitly thrown because the employeeno was not in the
         EMPLOYEE_LIST table.
         (See Note 1.)
      */
      catch( SQLException e ) {
        System.out.println( "Can't fire employee, " + e );
      }
    }
  }
```

Note for `PakTest.sqlj`:

1. It follows from the note for the program `EmpPak2.sqlj` that, even if you throw an exception other than `SQLException` when `employeeno` is not in the `EMPLOYEE_LIST` table, that exception would still get converted to the `SQLException` for "Java call terminated by uncaught Java exception." This caveat makes it harder in the invoker to distinguish between a "non-existing employee" error and an error generated by the execution of one of the SQL statements in the `EmpPak2.deleteEmp()` method.

The Invocation of SQLJ Stored Subprograms from SQL Statements and PL/SQL Blocks

In this section, you will learn how to invoke stored subprograms from SQL statements and PL/SQL blocks, in the SQL*Plus, Pro*C, and SQLJ environments, as well as from database triggers.

You will consider these topics in the following order:

- Invocation of stored subprograms from PL/SQL blocks.

- Invocation of stored functions from SQL DML commands.

- Invocation of stored procedures from SQLJ, SQL*Plus, Pro*C, and database triggers using the SQL `CALL` statement.

- Invocation of stored functions from SQL*Plus and Pro*C using the SQL `CALL` statement.

- Invocation of stored functions from SQLJ using assignment clauses.

You will see that the nice thing about SQLJ stored subprograms is that, because of the SQL wrappers, their invocation is exactly the same as the invocation of PL/SQL stored subprograms. You can say that stored subprogram usage is independent of the language in which the subprogram is written (subject to a few restrictions on SQLJ stored subprograms that are discussed in the last section of this chapter).

Invocation of Stored Subprograms from PL/SQL Blocks

Since SQLJ stored subprograms are invoked exactly the same way as PL/SQL stored subprograms, SQLJ stored functions and procedures can appear the same way in a PL/SQL block as can any PL/SQL function and procedure. For example, the following PL/SQL block invokes the subprograms from the emppak2 package:

```
begin
   emppak2.deleteemp( 10000 );
   if emppak2.insertemp( 70000, 'Jones', 'Joe',
                          '(999)999-9999', 10000 ) = 1
     then dbms_output.put_line( 'Insert rejected.' );
   end if;
   exception
     when others then
       dbms_output.put_line( 'Record not deleted.' );
end;
```

Note that PL/SQL blocks can be executed from SQL*Plus, Pro*C, SQLJ, and database triggers. Thus, SQLJ stored subprograms can be indirectly invoked in all these environments by being invoked from PL/SQL blocks that are being executed in these environments.

Invocation of Stored Functions from SQL DML Commands

A stored function can be invoked from anyplace in a SQL INSERT, DELETE, UPDATE, or SELECT statement that an expression of the same type as the function return type can appear. In particular, stored functions can be invoked from the select_list and where_clause of a SELECT statement. For example, suppose a stored function projamt takes a project number as its parameter and returns the amount of money invested in the project with that project number. projamt appears in the select_list and where_clause of the following SELECT statement, which prints the project number and project amount for each project that has an amount greater than $100,000:

```
SELECT projectno, projamt( projectno )
   FROM PROJECT_LIST WHERE projamt( projectno ) > 100000
```

SQL DML statements that invoke stored functions can be executed from SQL*Plus, Pro*C, PL/SQL blocks, SQLJ, and database triggers.

Note that you cannot invoke a stored function from a SQL DML command if:

■ The DML command is a `SELECT` statement and the function modifies any tables.

■ The DML command is an `INSERT`, `DELETE`, or `UPDATE` statement, and the function queries or modifies tables that are modified by the statement.

■ The function executes transaction control or DML commands.

These rules are intended to control harmful side effects. Violation of these rules generates a runtime error when the DDL command is parsed.

Invocation of Stored Procedures Using the SQL CALL Statement

You have already seen in Chapter 3 how to execute PL/SQL stored procedures from SQLJ programs using the SQL `CALL` statement. By the principle of independence from the implementation language of stored subprogram invocation, these PL/SQL stored procedures may as well have been SQLJ stored procedures. The usage is exactly the same. For example, you have seen that the procedure `emppak2.deleteemp` can be invoked from a SQLJ program as:

```
#sql { CALL emppak2.deleteemp ( 80000 ) };
```

Also, being a bona fide SQL statement, the `CALL` statement can be invoked from SQL*Plus and Pro*C (although not from PL/SQL).

You will now consider the invocation of stored procedures from:

■ SQL*Plus.

■ Database triggers.

■ Pro*C.

Invocation of Stored Procedures from SQL*Plus Using the SQL CALL Statement

Calling stored procedures from SQL*Plus is essentially the same as calling them from SQLJ. The following invocation of `emppak2.deleteemp` (see "Creating SQL

Stored Subprogram Wrappers in PL/SQL Packages" earlier in this chapter) from SQL*Plus illustrates this sameness. Note that this invocation causes an error to be generated, in the case that the delete failed, indicating that an uncaught Java exception was thrown in the procedure.

```
SQLPLUS> CALL emppak2.deleteemp( 20000 );
```

Invoking the SQL CALL Statement from Database Triggers

A database trigger consists of an action (that is, a block of code) that is stored in the database and is fired (that is, automatically executed) whenever an event occurs (that is, the execution of a DELETE, INSERT, UPDATE, or DDL command on a specified table) and a specified condition is satisfied. Triggers are very useful for propagating updates on one table into related data in other tables. In particular, triggers can be used to enforce the consistency of the database.

Database triggers are created with the SQL CREATE TRIGGER statement. Prior to the release of Oracle8*i*, the action in an Oracle database trigger had to be a PL/SQL block. In Oracle8*i*, the action can be either a PL/SQL block or a stored procedure call. See the *Oracle8i SQL Reference Manual* [28] for the full syntax of the CREATE TRIGGER statement.

The following SQL CREATE TRIGGER statement (to be executed in, say, SQL*Plus) implements the SQL-92 SET NULL referential action for the EMPLOYEE_LIST table. Recall from Appendix A that the referential integrity rule states that no foreign key can reference a non-existing record. The EMPLOYEE_LIST table contains the departmentno field as a foreign key that references the DEPARTMENT_LIST table. The default way (as described in Appendix A) of enforcing the referential integrity rule for deletes and updates on the referenced table (here, the DEPARTMENT_LIST table) is to prevent such commands from executing that would violate referential integrity. This is called NO ACTION in the SQL-92 standard. There are three other *referential* actions (that is, means of enforcing referential integrity for deletes and updates on the referenced table) in the SQL-92 standard: CASCADE, SET NULL, and SET DEFAULT. Oracle supports the CASCADE action as an option on the CREATE TABLE and ALTER TABLE statements, but does not support the SET DEFAULT or SET NULL actions. The SET NULL referential action indicates that when a DELETE or UPDATE statement is executed on the referenced table, the foreign key values on all matching records in the referencing table are set to NULL. So the SET NULL referential action applied to the EMPLOYEE_LIST table would cause the deletion of a department from the

DEPARTMENT_LIST table to force each employee in that department to have their departmentno field set to NULL.

```
CREATE TRIGGER setnulldept
   BEFORE DELETE OR UPDATE OF departmentno
      on DEPARTMENT_LIST
         FOR EACH ROW
begin
   if deleting or :old.departmentno != :new.departmentno
      then UPDATE EMPLOYEE_LIST
         SET departmentno = NULL
            WHERE departmentno = :old.departmentno;
   end if;
end;
/
```

Note that:

- The CREATE TRIGGER statement specifies the *name* of the trigger (setnulldept), the *time* that the trigger is to be fired (before, as opposed to after, the delete or update on the row is complete), the *event* that will fire the trigger (either a delete on DEPARTMENT_LIST or an update of the departmentno field of DEPARTMENT_LIST), the *granularity* of the trigger (the trigger will be fired once for each row affected by the DELETE or UPDATE command, as opposed to being fired once for the entire DELETE or UPDATE statement), and the action of the trigger (the indicated PL/SQL block).

- The deleted row is referenced by the *correlation variable* :old.

- The row before the update is referenced by :old. The row after the update is referenced by the *correlation variable* :new.

- The predefined PL/SQL Boolean functions, *deleting* and *updating*, indicate whether the triggering event was the execution of a DELETE or an UPDATE statement. If the delete and update cases are to be handled somewhat differently, these functions are quite convenient. For example, in the setnulldept trigger, the matching departmentno in EMPLOYEE_LIST will be set to NULL in the update case only if the updated departmentno field in DEPARTMENT_LIST has a different value than the original value, whereas it will be unconditionally set to NULL in the delete case.

- This trigger does not contain the optional `when_clause`, which specifies a condition that must be satisfied in order for the trigger to be fired. Thus, this trigger will be unconditionally fired whenever the indicated delete and update are executed.

Now suppose that you wish to implement the trigger action by a SQLJ stored procedure call. One way to do this is to invoke the procedure from the PL/SQL block. However, the new CREATE TRIGGER statement syntax in Oracle8*i* allows you to bypass the PL/SQL block entirely:

```
CREATE TRIGGER setnulldeptd
  BEFORE DELETE ON DEPARTMENT_LIST
    FOR EACH ROW
      CALL setnulltrig( 0, :old.departmentno, 0 )
/
```

Here, `setnulltrig` is a stored procedure that corresponds to the method `Trig.setNullTrig()` in the program `Trig.sqlj`.

```
/*
** Program Name:  Trig.sqlj
**
** Purpose:  The class Trig contains the method setNullTrig() that
**           will be used to define the trigger procedure setnulltrig.
**
*/
import java.sql.SQLException;
public class Trig {
  // For the method setNullTrig():
  /* The argument dmlcommand indicates whether the event that fired
     the trigger was a delete statement (dmlcommand == 0) or an update
     statement (dmlcommand == 1).
     The argument olddepartmentno is the number of the department
     that was deleted (if the firing event was a delete statement)
     or the departmentno before the update (if the firing event was
     an update statement).
     The argument newdepartmentno is zero (if the firing event was
     a delete statement) or the departmentno after the update (if
     the firing event was an update statement).
  */
  /* Need throws clause because the raise_application_error call
     will raise a SQLException.
  */
  public static void setNullTrig( int dmlcommand,
    int olddepartmentno, int newdepartmentno )
  throws SQLException {
```

```
    /* If the firing event was a delete or the firing event was
       an update that actually changed the department number to
       something different, set the departmentno field in all
       matching EMPLOYEE_LIST records to NULL.
    */
    if ( dmlcommand == 0 || olddepartmentno != newdepartmentno ) {
      try {
        #sql { UPDATE EMPLOYEE_LIST SET departmentno = NULL
                WHERE departmentno = :olddepartmentno
             };
      }
      /* If a SQLException was raised in the update command, call
         the raise_application_procedure passing in an error number
         of -20100 and an error message 'Referential integrity
         action failed'.
         (See Note 1.)
      */
      catch( SQLException e ) {
        #sql { CALL raise_application_error
                ( -20100, 'Referential integrity action failed.' )
             };
      }
    }
  }
}
```

Note for `Trig.sqlj`:

1. The `raise_application_error` call will terminate the trigger,
    roll back the effects of the DML command that caused that trigger to be
    fired, and report to the client program an error code and error message.
    If the client was coded in PL/SQL or Pro*C, the error code can be
    obtained from the `SQLCODE` variable, and the error message can be
    obtained in PL/SQL from the `sqlerrm` variable, and in Pro*C from the
    `sqlca.sqlerrm.sqlerrmc` variable. If the client was coded in SQLJ,
    the error code can be obtained by invoking the `SQLException` instance
    method `getErrorCode()`, and the error message can be obtained by
    invoking the `SQLException` instance method `getMessage()`.
    Unfortunately, for all these clients, if the stored subprogram was
    coded in SQLJ instead of PL/SQL, the error code will be for the generic
    "Java call terminated by uncaught Java exception" (–29532 in PL/SQL and
    Pro*C, 29532 in SQLJ), instead of the error code (such as –20100) that
    was passed as a parameter into the `raise_application_error`

procedure. Thus, even if a SQLJ stored subprogram contains several calls to `raise_application_error` corresponding to different errors, passing in different error codes to help the client trap these errors, the client will always get back the same error code. This caveat is an instance of the exception problem pointed out in the note to the program `EmpPak2.sqlj`, in "Creating SQL Stored Subprogram Wrappers in PL/SQL Packages" earlier in this chapter. However, the error code number and message passed into `raise_application_error` will be part of the error message (along with the "Java call terminated by uncaught Java exception" message) that is passed back to the client, which is why the `raise_application_error` call is present in this method.

After loading the `Trig` class into the server, you can create the following wrapper for the `setnulltrig()` method in SQL*Plus:

```
CREATE PROCEDURE setnulltrig( dmlcommand number,
    olddepartmentno number, newdepartmentno number ) AS
  LANGUAGE java
  NAME 'Trig.setNullTrig( int, int, int )';
/
```

A similar trigger, using the same stored procedure, `setNullTrig`, can be defined for the update case. Unfortunately, if you are implementing the action as a stored procedure call and if you want the two cases to be handled somewhat differently by the action, you cannot define the same trigger for both delete and update. This is because Oracle will not allow you to invoke the deleting and updating predicates in the stored procedure call. Thus, the following is illegal, even if `setNullTrig` was coded in PL/SQL so that the first parameter could be boolean:

```
CREATE TRIGGER setnulldeptu
  BEFORE DELETE OR UPDATE OF departmentno ON DEPARTMENT_LIST
    FOR EACH ROW
    // Illegal:
    CALL setNullTrig( DELETING, :old.departmentno, :new.departmentno )
/
```

Here is the (legal) separate update trigger:

```
CREATE TRIGGER setnulldeptu
  BEFORE UPDATE OF departmentno ON DEPARTMENT_LIST
    FOR EACH ROW
      CALL setnulltrig( 1, :old.departmentno, :new.departmentno )
/
```

As you may have observed from the preceding examples, in the `CALL` format of the `CREATE TRIGGER` statement you do not place a semicolon (`;`) after the stored procedure call.

Note that whenever a feature, such as the `CASCADE` referential action, is available as a declarative option of a SQL statement, you are better off using that declarative option, instead of implementing the feature yourself as a trigger. The trigger will complicate your system, is riskier than the declarative feature, and will probably underperform the declarative feature. Please see the *Oracle8i Application Developer's Guide—Fundamentals* [42] for information on the proper use of database triggers.

Invocation of Stored Procedures from Pro*C Using the SQL CALL Statement

The SQL `CALL` statement also provides the mechanism for directly invoking stored subprograms from Pro*C.

The following `exec sql` statement will invoke the `deleteemp` stored program that is contained in the PL/SQL package `emppak2`:

```
exec sql CALL emppak2.deleteemp( :empno );
```

The C host variable `empno` is passed as a parameter to `emppak2.deleteemp`. This host variable must be declared in the declare section for the Pro*C program:

```
exec sql begin declare section;
   int empno;
exec sql end declare section;
```

Invocation of Stored Functions from SQL*Plus and Pro*C Using the SQL CALL Statement

There are two formats for the SQL `CALL` statement: one for calling stored procedures and one for calling stored functions. The format for calling stored functions contains an `into_clause` (such a `CALL` statement will be referred to as a `CALL INTO` statement) indicating the host variable in which to place the value returned by the function. Note that the `CALL INTO` statement is illegal in SQLJ programs (assignment clauses are used to call stored functions), and both forms of the `CALL` statement are illegal in PL/SQL.

You will now consider the usage of the `CALL INTO` statement in SQL*Plus and Pro*C.

Invocation of Stored Functions from SQL*Plus Using the SQL CALL Statement

The function `insertemp` from the earlier section "Coding Considerations for Server-Side Applications" is used in the following example. Note that you must first declare a SQL*Plus bind variable to receive the output from the function:

```
SQLPLUS> set serveroutput on
SQLPLUS> variable n number
SQLPLUS> CALL insertemp( 10000, 'Jones', 'Joe',
          '(999)999-9999', 20000 ) INTO :n;
SQLPLUS> print n
```

The `serveroutput` flag is turned on so that the output from `emppak2.insertemp` that was directed to the `dbms_output` buffer can be printed. Unlike SQLJ and Pro*C, it is not necessary in SQL*Plus to call `dbms_output.enable` or `dbms_output.get_line` to enable and extract the buffer contents for printing. Also, if a PL/SQL block containing a call to `emppak2.insertemp` were submitted to SQL*Plus, in order to print the output from `emppak2.insertemp`, it would suffice to `set serveroutput on` in SQL*Plus before executing the PL/SQL block:

```
set serveroutput on
declare
n integer;
begin
  n := emppak2.insertemp( 30000, 'Cohen', 'Naomi',
                          '(999)999-9999', 10000 );
  dbms_output.put_line( n );
end;
/
```

Invocation of Stored Functions from Pro*C Using the SQL CALL Statement

Calling a stored function from Pro*C is identical to calling a stored procedure from Pro*C, except that the CALL INTO statement is used:

```
exec sql begin declare section;
   int employeeno, departmentno, status, n;
   varchar2 last[40], first[40], phone[20], s[100];
exec sql end declare section;
exec sql CALL insertemp( :employeeno, :last, :first,
                         :phone, :departmentno ) INTO :n;
if (n == 1) {
  exec sql CALL dbms_output.enable( 500 );
  exec sql CALL dbms_output.get_line( :s, :status );
  if ( status == 0 ) printf( "%s\n", s);
}
```

Note that like SQLJ, but unlike SQL*Plus, the client must enable access to the `dbms_output` buffer, and then `get_line` from it, in order to display the information that `emppak2.insertemp` wrote into the buffer.

Invocation of Stored Functions from SQLJ Using Assignment Clauses

This was already discussed in Chapter 3. For example, the following SQLJ code fragment invokes the stored function `emppak2.insertemp`:

```
int x;
#sql x = { VALUES( emppak2.insertemp( :employeeno, :last, :first,
                                       :phone, :departmentno )
       };
```

The Loading and Translation of SQLJ Source Files in the Oracle8*i* Server

Since the client SQLJ translator supports many more options, and the option setting and error processing are more convenient for the client translator, it is recommended that the SQLJ source for stored subprograms be translated and compiled using the client SQLJ translator instead of the server translator. However, for completeness, this section provides a discussion of the usage of the server SQLJ translator. In this approach, you will load your SQLJ source into the server, and have the embedded SQLJ translator in the Oracle8*i* Java VM process your source.

The `loadjava` utility is used to load, translate, and compile your SQLJ source:

```
loadjava -resolve -thin -user scott/tiger@data-i.com:1521:ORCL
  EmpInsert.sqlj
```

The `loadjava` command without the `-resolve` option will merely load the SQLJ source into the server, creating a source schema object for it, which is analogous to the class schema objects and resource schema objects created when `.class` and `.ser` files (respectively) are loaded into the server. The source will then be implicitly translated, compiled, and customized the first time an attempt is made to use a class that is contained in the source. However, the `-resolve` option causes

- The embedded SQLJ translator to automatically translate, compile, and customize the SQLJ source.

- Any translation or compilation error messages to be output to your screen.

- The resolution of external references in each generated class.

Classes are loaded into the server when the source is loaded, and the resources are loaded into the server when the source is translated. Thus, a separate `loadjava` execution for these steps is not necessary.

The remaining step in the creation of the stored subprogram—namely, the creation of top-level or packaged SQL wrappers for the subprogram—is done exactly as described when the source was translated by the client-side translator in "Creating a Top-Level SQL Wrapper for a Stored Subprogram" and "Creating SQL Stored Subprogram Wrappers in PL/SQL Packages," earlier in this chapter. Note that:

- Once you load classes and resources from a source file, you cannot subsequently reload the classes and resources directly unless you first use the `dropjava` command to drop the SQLJ source. See "The `dropjava` Utility" later in this chapter for more information.

- You can put multiple SQLJ source files into an uncompressed `.jar` file, and submit that `.jar` file to `loadjava`.

You will now learn about:

- Options supported in the server translator.

- Setting options for the server translator.

- Generated output from the server translator and `loadjava`.

- Error output from the server translator.

Options Supported in the SQLJ Server Translator

Only the following options are supported by the server translator: `encoding`, `online`, and `debug`.

- The `encoding` option specifies that NLS encodings, such as SJIS, be applied to your `.sqlj` and `.java` source files and your `.java` generated files, when they are loaded in the server. See p. 8-27 of the *Oracle8i SQLJ Developer's Guide and Reference* [63], and Appendix D of this book, for information about the encoding option.

- Setting the `online` flag to true (the default value) enables online semantics checking. Setting it to false specifies offline checking. See "SQLJ Translator Process" in Chapter 2 for some information on semantics checking.

- The debug option is equivalent to the javac -g option, and directs debugging information to be output when the SQLJ source is compiled.

Setting Options for the Server Translator

Since there is no command line and no properties files for the server translator, options are held in a table called java$options. Options are queried and entered into this table through subprograms in the package dbms_java:

- get_compiler_option is a function that returns the setting for the indicated option in the indicated source.

```
CALL dbms_java.get_compiler_option( 'EmpInsert', 'online') INTO :x;
```

- set_compiler_option is a procedure that sets the indicated option to the indicated value in the indicated source.

```
CALL dbms_java.set_compiler_option( 'EmpInsert', 'online', 'false' );
```

- reset_compiler_option is a procedure that resets the indicated option to its default value in the indicated source.

```
CALL dbms_java.reset_compiler_option( 'EmpInsert', 'online' );
```

Generated Output from the Server Translator and loadjava

In addition to the class and resource schema objects already discussed for loadjava when the source is translated and compiled on the client, a source schema object is generated for the SQLJ source. The full name of this source schema object is obtained from the fully qualified package path of the first class defined in the source, with slash (/) used instead of dot (.).

For example, if classname is in package x.y.z, and is the first class defined in its source, the source schema object would be called: s/y/z/classname.

Error Output from the SQLJ Server Translator

SQLJ errors are directed into the USER_ERRORS table of the user schema. A SELECT statement that returns the text field of this table will report the message for an error:

```
SELECT text FROM USER_ERRORS;
```

The dropjava Utility

The `dropjava` utility is the inverse of the `loadjava` utility; it is used to remove class, resource, and source schema objects from the Oracle8*i* server. You can identify the schema objects to be dropped by listing the `.sqlj`, `.class`, `.ser`, and `.jar` files that generated them, or you can list the schema object names (full names) directly. It is probably simpler to list the filenames, so that the `dropjava` commands resemble the `loadjava` commands that created the schema objects. For example, to remove the schema objects loaded for the `EmpInsert.sqlj` file, when it was translated and compiled on the client side, you would enter

```
dropjava -thin -user scott/tiger@data-i.com:1521:ORCL EmpInsert.jar
```

You should drop schema objects for dependent classes before the classes on which they depend.

Note that if you reload a class that is already loaded, and the new version differs from the version that is already loaded, the new version will automatically replace the already loaded version. Thus, in that case, dropping the already loaded version is unnecessary.

Advantages and Disadvantages of Implementing Stored Subprograms in SQLJ Versus Implementing Them in PL/SQL

In this chapter, you learned how to implement stored subprograms in SQLJ, and how to invoke stored subprograms from SQL and PL/SQL, in SQLJ, SQL*Plus, Pro*C, and database triggers. Note that such stored subprograms can also be coded in pure Java. In fact, the SQLJ stored subprogram is just a special case of the Java stored subprogram. You are referred to the *Oracle8i Java Stored Procedures Developer's Guide* [39] for information on implementing Java stored subprograms, in general, and to Chapter 11 of the *Oracle8i SQLJ Developer's Guide and Reference* [63] for information on implementing SQLJ stored subprograms, in particular.

At this point, it is desirable to say a few words about the relative advantages of implementing a stored subprogram in SQLJ vs. PL/SQL.

The individual non-SQL statements are probably executed more efficiently in Java than in PL/SQL. However, the SQL call overhead is higher for SQLJ than it is for PL/SQL.

It is clearly more convenient to develop a SQLJ subprogram than a PL/SQL subprogram. There are more development tools (IDEs, and so on) available for Java than for PL/SQL. Also, when you code in SQLJ, you reap the well-known benefits of developing your subprograms in a full-scale object-oriented programming language (see, for example, the Introduction to *Java with Object-Oriented Programming and World Wide Web Applications* [62]).

Subprograms implemented in PL/SQL cannot be ported to other database systems, since PL/SQL is proprietary to Oracle. However, standardization of SQLJ should ensure portability across many different database management systems.

If your application consists largely of Java programs, then implementing your stored subprograms in SQLJ instead of PL/SQL will reduce the overall complexity of your system by reducing the number of languages used in the implementation. However, if your subprogram will be mostly called from PL/SQL, there are advantages to be gained by implementing the subprogram in PL/SQL. For one thing, as you have seen in "Creating a Top-Level SQL Wrapper for a Stored Subprogram" earlier in this chapter, PL/SQL subprograms can use PL/SQL parameter and return types, whereas SQLJ subprograms must use only SQL types. Thus, a PL/SQL function can return a boolean, but a SQLJ subprogram cannot. More precisely, a PL/SQL function returning a boolean can be successfully invoked from a PL/SQL block, whereas a SQLJ function that returns a boolean cannot be successfully invoked from any environment, not even from SQLJ: an incompatible types error message is generated when the function is invoked. Note that a PL/SQL function returning a boolean cannot be invoked from SQLJ. The preceding error message will be generated.

Another advantage of coding your subprograms in PL/SQL is that the `raise_application_error` procedure can be used to conveniently report errors back to the caller, whether the caller is implemented in PL/SQL, Pro*C, or SQLJ. Unfortunately, as was pointed out in the section "Invoking the SQL `CALL` Statement from Database Triggers," `raise_application_error` does not have a very useful behavior when called from a SQLJ stored subprogram. The error code returned to the caller is the code for the generic "Java call terminated by uncaught Java exception," instead of the error code that the subprogram passed to `raise_application_error`. This caveat greatly reduces the usefulness of `raise_application_error` in trapping different errors in the client program that were generated in the subprogram, and it is expected that the caveat will be removed in a subsequent release of Oracle8*i*.

Another point in favor of PL/SQL is that SQL is more seamlessly integrated into PL/SQL than into SQLJ. This causes SQLJ to suffer more from the impedance mismatch problem than PL/SQL. For example, the following PL/SQL loop from the section "PL/SQL Block" of Appendix A presents a more natural way of processing SELECT statement output than does the iterator construct:

```
for i in ( SELECT departmentno FROM DEPARTMENT_LIST )
  loop
    SELECT COUNT( DISTINCT projectno ) INTO nprojsd
      FROM ACCOUNT_LIST
        WHERE departmentno = i.departmentno;
    if nprojs = nprojsd
      then dbms_output.put_line( i.departmentno );
    end if;
  end loop;
```

However, as was remarked in the section "Iterator Instance Declarations" of Chapter 2, the iterator construct is certainly more tightly coupled to Java than is the cursor construct to embedded SQL host languages, causing the cursor to generate more impedance mismatch on the host language side than does the iterator.

A situation where it is preferable to code your subprogram in SQLJ is when you decide to move certain already existing client code, implemented in SQLJ, into the Oracle8*i* server as stored subprograms. If you also code your subprograms in SQLJ, you will get away with making at most minor coding changes, as opposed to the situation in which you code the subprograms "from scratch" in PL/SQL.

In Chapter 5, you will see an example of migrating client-side code into the Oracle8*i* server, and invoking stored subprograms in advanced scenarios, such as invoking them from applets. You will also learn about connection contexts and execution contexts in that chapter.

CHAPTER
5

Advanced SQLJ
Deployment

 SQLJ program connects to a database via an instance of a connection class, a Java class that is defined by the declaration of a SQLJ connection context. Instances of this class allow a SQLJ program to establish a single connection or multiple connections to a single database server. Additionally, these instances can be used by a program to connect to several databases located on different servers.

In the previous chapters, you learned the basic features of SQLJ and some of its advanced features. In this chapter, you will learn how to use these features and deploy SQLJ in many complex scenarios, specifically how to:

■ Use a SQLJ connection context to establish database connections

■ Use the SQLJ `DefaultContext` class to connect to databases

■ Manage multiple database connections with SQLJ

■ Deploy SQLJ in an application: SQLJ application

■ Deploy SQLJ in a thick client: SQLJ thick client

■ Deploy SQLJ in an application server: SQLJ middle tier

■ Deploy SQLJ in a thin client: SQLJ thin client

■ Deploy SQLJ in a Java application: Java application

■ Deploy SQLJ in a Java applet: Java applet

■ Deploy SQLJ in an applet: SQLJ applet

■ Deploy SQLJ in an Oracle8*i* data server: SQLJ stored procedure

Using SQLJ Connection Context for Database Connections

SQLJ programs can use the following types of class instances to establish a database connection (see Appendix C for a discussion on the concept of a class versus an instance of a class):

■ The instances of a declared connection context class

■ The instances of the `sqlj.runtime.ref.DefaultContext` class

First, you will learn how to declare a SQLJ context class, and then you will develop SQLJ programs to implement your declared SQLJ context class. The basic SQLJ connection context declaration uses the following syntax:

```
#sql <modifiers> context Context_Classname;
```

SQLJ *modifiers* can be any standard Java class modifiers such as **public**, **private**, **protected**, **static**, and **final**. The SQLJ modifier rules correspond to the Java modifier rules. See Appendix B for a tutorial on Java.

The following is an example of a declared SQLJ connection context class using a Java modifier:

```
#sql public context LocalHostConnectionContext;
```

As a result of this statement, the SQLJ Translator creates a Java **public** `LocalHostConnectionContext` class. A SQLJ program that specifies this class can use its instances to establish database connections to schemas stored in a data server. If you are writing Java programs and you wish to use the instance of a declared SQLJ connection context class, you should define the SQLJ connection context class in a separate file. The `javac` compiler provided with the Sun JDK requires that each public class be defined in a separate file. For example, specify the declared SQLJ connection context class, the `LocalHostConnectionContext` class, in a separate file called `LocalHostConnectionContext.sqlj`.

When you declare a connection context class, you can also specify one or more interfaces to be implemented by the generated class:

```
#sql <modifiers> context Context_Classname
        implements InterfaceClass1,..., InterfaceClassN;
```

The **implements** clause, the portion **implements** `InterfaceClass1,...,` `InterfaceClassN`, derives one class from a Java interface. Each part of the **implements** clause for the connection context, the `InterfaceClass1,...,` `InterfaceClassN`, must be a user-defined Java interface. However, in addition to a user-defined interface, a SQLJ iterator that uses the **implements** clause in its declaration can also implement the SQLJ interface `sqlj.runtime.ForUpdate`. The SQLJ **implements** clause corresponds to the Java **implements** clause (see Appendix B for the definition and examples of the Java **implements** clause).

SQLJ programs can connect to a database either at application runtime or at translation time. This feature provides semantics checking at different levels. Semantics checking at translation time is very useful because it allows you to discover program errors at translation time, thus helping you avoid generating errors at runtime.

During semantics checking, the SQLJ *translator* connects to the specified schema via the connection context class and performs two specific tasks:

■ It examines the construct of each SQLJ statement specified by an instance of the connection context class and checks its SQL operations such as SELECT, UPDATE, INSERT, DELETE, etc. Schema object definitions (tables, views, stored procedures, and so on) also undergo semantics checking.

■ It verifies that the objects referred in the SQL operations match the objects in the specified schema. In other words, the schema objects referred in the SQL operations must also exist in the database.

NOTE
You can use a schema example—that is, a test schema—instead of a production schema, as long as they each have the same schema object definitions.

The SQLJ **with** clause allows you to declare a SQLJ connection context class with a list of constants:

```
#sql <modifiers> context Context_Classname
     with (variable1=value1,..., variableN=valueN);
```

The constants from the **with** clause are included in the generated connection class and are always defined as Java **public static final** constants, and, as such, cannot be changed. These constants, however, can be initialized. Note that the concept of the **with** clause, **with** (variable1=value1,...,variableN= valueN), is unique to SQLJ. There is no Java clause that corresponds to the SQLJ **with** clause.

There is a predefined set of standard SQLJ constants that can be defined within a **with** clause. The SQLJ standard constants involve cursor states and can only take particular values (see Chapter 3 for a discussion of the SQLJ cursor). Note that the definitions of constants other than the SQLJ standard constants are vendor specific and might not be portable from one database to another. In fact, the SQLJ translator will generate error warnings when translating a SQLJ program that specifies nonstandard SQLJ constants.

SQLJ allows you to place both the **implements** clause and the **with** clause in the declaration of a SQLJ connection context class, but the **implements** clause must precede the **with** clause:

```
#sql <modifiers> context Context_Classname
          implements InterfaceClassi ( i = 1,...,N)
     with (aSqljStandardConstant=…);
```

NOTE
*See Chapter 3 and Appendix D to learn more
about the SQLJ* **implements** *clause.*

Instances of a declared connection context class or of the `DefaultContext`
class can be associated with an instance of the `ExecutionContext` class. Next,
you will learn about this class and its relation to the `ConnectionContext` class.

Relation of the Execution Context to the Connection Context in the SQLJ Executable Statement

In a SQLJ program, all statements that are used for database access are in SQLJ
clauses. An executable statement is a SQLJ clause that contains a SQL operation.
Remember that SQLJ executable statements are used to execute embedded SQL
operations (see Chapters 1 and 3). Also note that SQLJ executable statements can
only execute embedded SQL operations that are supported by the JDBC driver that
a SQLJ program uses. Thankfully, JDBC drivers support most SQL operations (DML,
DDL, and transaction control statements).

A SQLJ executable statement consists of a `#sql` token followed by a SQLJ clause:

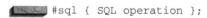

```
#sql { SQL operation };
```

A SQLJ operation is always associated with an instance of the
`ExecutionContext` class. An execution context is an instance of the `sqlj.`
`runtime.ExecutionContext` class. If you do not associate an execution
context object explicitly with your SQLJ clause, SQLJ will implicitly associate
the default instance of this class with the clause.

An execution context provides a context in which SQL clauses are executed.
More importantly, the `ExecutionContext` class contains methods that can help you
control the execution of your SQL operations. The available methods (see Appendix D)
are categorized as status methods, control methods, and cancellation methods. You
use the status methods to get the results of the most recent SQL operation, the control
methods to modify the semantics of future SQL operations, and the cancellation
methods to cancel or terminate operations in situations where multiple SQL operations
are occurring on the same underlying connection object (see Chapter 6).

Each SQLJ executable statement requires a connection context instance, declared
either implicitly or explicitly. The connection context is an optional expression and is
delimited by square brackets. An instance of this class indicates the location of the
data server where the SQL operation will execute:

```
#sql [aConnectionContextInstance] { SQL operation };
```

For example, the following SQLJ clause executes a SELECT statement at the database located on data-i.com (see the SingleDefaultContext SQLJ application in the "Using the SQLJ DefaultContext Class" section of this chapter).

Listing 5-1

```
#sql [dataiConnCtx] lineItems =
    { SELECT requestno, projectno, quantity, unit,
        estimatedcost, actualcost, description
      FROM LINEITEM_LIST
      ORDER BY requestno };
```

In the SQLJ executable statement in Listing 5-1, the explicit connection context instance, dataiConnCtx, is associated with the SQLJ clause. Note that each connection context object implicitly has its own execution context instance. Since no explicit instance of the ExecutionContext class is associated with the SQLJ operation, consequently, SQLJ associates a default instance of the ExecutionContext class to this clause.

The execution context is an optional expression and, like the connection context, is delimited by square brackets:

```
#sql [anExecutionContextInstance] { SQL operation };
```

Listing 5-2 demonstrates the explicit association of an instance of the ExecutionContext class with the SQLJ clause. The connection context instance, dataiConnCtx, specifies the data server on which to perform the SQL operation.

Listing 5-2

```
// First import the ExecutableContext class.
import sqlj.runtime.ExecutionContext;

// Create an instance of the above class using
// the constructor of the ExecutionContext class
ExecutionContext anExecutionContext = new ExecutionContext();

// Associate the instance to a SQLJ executable statement.
#sql [dataiConntCtx,anExecutionContext] lineItems =
    { SELECT requestno, projectno, quantity, unit,
        estimatedcost, actualcost, description
      FROM LINEITEM_LIST
      ORDER BY requestno };
```

See the listing of the MultiDeclaredConnectionCtx.sqlj application in the "Managing Multiple Database Connections with SQLJ" section of this chapter for an example of how to use instances of the `ExecutionContext` class and its methods in a SQLJ program.

In the next section, you will use instances of the SQLJ `DefaultContext` class to connect to databases. Remember that instances of this class are used to create single or multiple connections to a single database.

Using the SQLJ DefaultContext Class

If you need to establish a single database connection to a specific schema type, you can use the `getConnection()` method of the `DefaultContext` class to do so. When you construct the `DefaultContext` object, you specify the database URL, username, and password:

```
// Declaration of two DefaultContext instances
DefaultContext aDefaultContext1;
DefaultContext aDefaultContext2;

// Assignment of both instances to databases located at
// data-i.com and haiti respectively
aDefaultContext1 = getConnection
        ("jdbc:oracle:thin:@data-i.com:1521:ORCL",
                "scott","tiger",boolean value);
aDefaultConnection2 = getConnection
        ("jdbc:oracle:thin:@haiti:1521:ORCL",
                "scott","tiger",boolean value);
```

Note that SQLJ programs that use instances of the `DefaultContext` class must import the `sqlj.runtime.ref.DefaultContext` class or the whole `sqlj.runtime.ref.*` package. See the listing of the `SingleDefaultContext.sqlj` application for an example of how to implement a `DefaultContext` instance:

```
/*                          (See Note 1.)
    ** Program Name:        SingleDefaultContext.sqlj
    **
    ** Purpose:
    ** SQLJ application that implements a single SQLJ default
    ** context to connect to one database server. Also,
    ** this program uses a named SQLJ iterator to query a
    ** relational database table in Oracle8i and
    ** the Oracle.connect() method to set the DefaultContext
    ** instance.
    ** Required classes: none
    **
    */
    // Required SQLJ classes for any SQLJ program
```

```
import sqlj.runtime.*;            // (See Note 2.)
import sqlj.runtime.ref.*;

// Required Java classes for any application
// that needs to access a database
import java.sql.*;

// Required Oracle classes for Oracle database
import oracle.sql.*;
import oracle.sqlj.runtime.Oracle;
import oracle.jdbc.driver.*;

public class SingleDefaultContext {
      // Declare a named SQLJ iterator: LineItemIterator()
      // This iterator will access data from dataiConnCtx
      #sql public iterator LineItemIterator   // (See Note 3.)
         (int requestno, int projectno, float quantity,
          String unit, float estimatedcost,
           float actualcost, String description);

      // Declare one protected static variable of type
      // DefaultContext. Variables must be static.
      // This is a Java requirement.
    protected static DefaultContext dataiConnCtx;// (See Note 4.)

      // Constructor
      public SingleDefaultContext () {
          try {
            // Instantiate Default Context for the specific host
            // (See Note 5.)
                dataiConnCtx = Oracle.getConnection
                    ("jdbc:oracle:thin:@data-i.com:1521:ORCL",
                            "scott","tiger",false);
          } // end try
          catch (SQLException ex) {         // (See Note 6.)
             System.err.println("Error from dataiConnCtx   "
                            +"SingleDefaultContext: "  +ex);
             String sqlMessage = ex.getMessage();
             System.err.println("SQL Message: " + sqlMessage);
          } // end catch
      }  // end constructor

    // Main entry point
    public static void main(String[] args) throws SQLException {

        // Instantiate SingleDefaultContext constructor
        // to create one connection context of type
        // DefaultContext
```

```
        SingleDefaultContext app = new SingleDefaultContext();

        // Stop execution if we cannot connect.
        if   (dataiConnCtx == null) {
            System.out.println("I cannot connect to "
                    + "the database - Stop execution.");
            System.exit(1);
        }
        try {
          // Run the application (See Note 7.)
          app.runSingleDefaultContext(dataiConnCtx);
        }  // end try
        catch (SQLException ex) {
            System.err.println("Error running "
                +"runSingleDefaultContext: " + ex);
            String sqlMessage = ex.getMessage();
            System.err.println("SQL Message: " + sqlMessage);
        }  // end catch
}  // end main()

void runSingleDefaultContext(DefaultContext dataiConnCtx)
        throws SQLException {

    //  Set DefaultContext to dataiConnCtx   (See Note 8.)
    DefaultContext.setDefaultContext(dataiConnCtx);

    /* Instantiate the named SQLJ iterator
       and initialize it to null.    */
    LineItemIterator lineItems = null;       // (See Note 9.)

    /* obtain all lineItems info from the default context */
    #sql [dataiConnCtx] lineItems =        // (See Note 10.)
        { SELECT requestno, projectno, quantity, unit,
                estimatedcost, actualcost, description
          FROM LINEITEM_LIST
          ORDER BY requestno };

    /* Use iterator methods to get the values from
       the table columns. (See Notes 11 and 12.) */
    while (lineItems.next()) {
        System.out.println("Request No: " +
                    lineItems.requestno() );
        System.out.println("Project No: " +
                    lineItems.projectno() );
        System.out.println("Quantity: " +
                    lineItems.quantity() );
        System.out.println("Unit: " +
                    lineItems.unit() );
```

```
                    System.out.println("Estimated Cost: " +
                            lineItems.estimatedcost() );
                    System.out.println("Actual Cost: " +
                            lineItems.actualcost() );
                    System.out.println("Description: " +
                            lineItems.description() );
            } // End while
            // Close the iterator
            lineItems.close();    // (See Note 13.)
        } // End of runSingleDefaultContext()
} // End SingleDefaultContent class
```

Notes on `SingleDefaultContext.sqlj` application:

1. Program documentation. This section is optional but is highly recommended.

2. These statements import the SQLJ, JDBC, and Oracle packages that are used by SQLJ.

3. This iterator declaration clause declares a named iterator, `LineItemIterator`, which is used to select rows from the `LINEITEM_LIST` table. When you specify an iterator in the SQLJ application, SQLJ generates a class named `LineItemIterator`. You must then ensure that `LineItemIterator` is a valid Java class name that is unique within its scope.

4. This statement creates a `DefaultContext` instance named `dataiConnCtx`.

5. This statement uses the Oracle thin driver to set up a connection to the Oracle database at URL address `data-i.com`, listening on port 1521 (default port number for Oracle database), using ORCL as the Oracle SID. The connection will be established using "`scott`" and "`tiger`" as the username and password, respectively, and the `autoCommit` feature will be set to off.

6. These statements allow you to catch any raised exceptions and to print a corresponding sql error message.

7. This statement invokes the method `runSingleDefaultContext()` while specifying a `DefaultContext` instance as its parameter.

8. This statement sets up the instance `dataiConnCtx` to be the default for the SQLJ execution statement that will select the rows from the `LINEITEM_LIST` table.

9. This statement declares `lineItems` as an instance of the named iterator `LineItemIterator` class and initializes it to null.

10. This assignment clause executes the SELECT statement, constructs an iterator object that contains the result table for the SELECT statement, and assigns the iterator object to variable lineItems. Note that an execution context instance is associated implicitly with this SQL operation. Also, because the application is using a default connection, it is not necessary to specify a connection context instance. For example, the following statement would have selected the data from the LINEITEM_LIST table located at dataiConnCtx even though the context instance is not specified.

```
#sql lineItems =
    { SELECT requestno, projectno, quantity, unit,
            estimatedcost, actualcost, description
      FROM LINEITEM_LIST
      ORDER BY requestno
    };
```

11. The next() method, which belongs to the generated class, LineItemsIterator, advances the iterator to successive rows in the SQLJ result set. This method is similar to the next() method for the Java JDBC ResultSet. The next() method returns a value of true when a next row is available or a value of false when all table rows have been fetched from the iterator.

12. The accessor methods lineItems.requestno(), lineItems. projectno(), lineItems.quantity(), lineItems.unit(), lineItems.estimatedcost(), lineItems.actualcost(), and lineItems.description() retrieve the values of the table columns from the current row of the result table.

13. The close() method, which also belongs to the generated class, LineItemIterator, closes the iterator and frees any database resources being held by the iterator.

SQLJ programs can use the connect() method from the oracle.sqlj. runtime.Oracle class to set the value of the DefaultContext object. This class provides two basic methods: the getConnection() and the connect() methods. The getConnection() method is used to create a new database connection and return a handle to it in the form of a connection context instance. The getConnection() method is used when you wish to create multiple connection context instances, explicitly. The connect() method is similar to the getConnection() method in that it creates a new database connection. Also, note that the connect() method, additionally, installs the new connection as the static default context. The latter function can only be used with Oracle databases because the SQLJ program needs to import an Oracle-specific class to use the connect() method. If you need to access non-Oracle databases, you should use an instance either of a declared connection context class or of the `sqlj.runtime.ref.DefaultContext` class to establish database connections.

Both methods, the `getConnection()` and the `Oracle.connect()`, have several overloaded signatures that allow you to pass the URL, username, and password as parameters to the methods. You may also set these parameters indirectly via the `connect.properties` file provided by Oracle. If you wish to use a `connect.properties` file, you must import `oracle.sqlj.runtime.Oracle` class, and then edit the properties file appropriately and package it with your application. See Chapter 2 for a discussion on the Oracle `connect.properties` file. The following is an example of a properties file:

```
#  File Name:       connect.properties
# Users should uncomment one of the following URLs or add their own.
#sqlj.url=jdbc:oracle:thin:@localhost:1521:orcl
#sqlj.url=jdbc:oracle:oci8:@
#sqlj.url=jdbc:oracle:oci7:@
# User name and password here
sqlj.user=scott
sqlj.password=tiger
```

See the `UsingSqljDefaultContext.sqlj` and the `SqljClientAccessJavaStoredProc.sqlj` for examples on how to use the `Oracle.connect()` method with a properties file. See Chapter 2 to learn more about the `Oracle.connect()` method with a properties file and the `UsingSqljDefaultContext` SQLJ application in the "Using the SQLJ `DefaultContext` Class" section of this chapter. Here is the syntax:

```
// The Oracle.connect() method using a properties file.
Oracle.connect(class_name.class, "connect.properties");

// class_name.class can be replaced with getClass
Oracle.connect(getClass(), "connect.properties");
```

Note that if a default connection has been set, the `Oracle.connect()` method will not reset it. You may, however, use the `setDefaultMethod()` of the `DefaultContext` class in order to override a default connection that has been previously set. The following is a list of the various `Oracle.connect()` overloaded signatures and their input parameters (see the *Oracle8i SQLJ Developer's Guide and Reference* [63] for a complete listing for both methods, the `getConnection()` and the `connect()`):

```
// The method declaration followed by its parameter list
public static DefaultContext connect ( list of parameters )
                 throws SQLException
```

- URL (String), username (String), password (String).

- URL (String), username (String), password (String), auto-commit flag (boolean).

- URL (String), `java.util.Properties` object containing properties for the connection.

- URL (String), `java.util.Properties` object, auto-commit flag (boolean).

- URL (String) fully specifying the connection, including username and password.

- URL (String), auto-commit flag (boolean).

- `java.lang.Class` object for class used to load properties file, name of properties file (String).

- `java.lang.Class` object, name of properties file (String), auto-commit flag (boolean).

- `java.lang.Class` object, name of properties file (String), username (String), password (String).

- `java.lang.Class` object, name of properties file (String), username (String), password (String), auto-commit flag (boolean).

- JDBC connection object.

- SQLJ connection context object.

The following SQLJ applications use the `Oracle.connect()` method associated with a `connect.properties` file to create database connections:

- The `UsingSqljDefaultContext.sqlj` application uses the following syntax:

  ```
  Oracle.connect(getClass(), "connect.properties");
  ```

- The `SqljAppletCallsSqljSP.sqlj` applet (see the "Deploying SQLJ in an Oracle8*i* Data Server" section of this chapter) uses the following syntax:

  ```
  Oracle.connect(class_name.class(), "connect.properties");
  ```

Furthermore, the SQLJ applet uses the `ConnectionManager` Java class to create a `DefaultContext` database connection.

```
/*
** Program Name:        UsingSqljDefaultContext.sqlj
*/
// Required SQLJ classes for any SQLJ program
import sqlj.runtime.*;
import sqlj.runtime.ref.*;

// Required Java classes for any application
// that needs to access a database
import java.sql.*;

// Required Oracle classes for Oracle database
import oracle.sql.*;
import oracle.sqlj.runtime.Oracle;
import oracle.jdbc.driver.*;

public class UsingSqljDefaultContext {

      // Declare a named SQLJ iterator. LineItemIterator()
      #sql public iterator LineItemIterator
         (int requestno, int projectno, float quantity, String unit,
          float estimatedcost, float actualcost, String description);

      // Constructor
      public UsingSqljDefaultContext () {
        try {
             // set the default connection to the URL, user,
             // and password specified in your
             // connect.properties file (See Note 1.)
               Oracle.connect(getClass(), "connect.properties");
         } // end of try
         catch (Exception ex) {
           System.err.println("Error from constructor "
                           + "UsingSqljDefaultContext: " + ex);
         } // end of catch
       }   // end constructor
    // main entry
    public static void main(String[] args) throws SQLException {

        // Instantiate UsingSqljDefaultContext
        UsingSqljDefaultContext app = new UsingSqljDefaultContext();

        // Cannot connect to database, stop program execution.
        // (See Note 2.)
        if (DefaultContext.getDefaultContext() == null ) {
            System.out.println("I cannot connect to the database "
```

```
                                           + "-- Stop Execution.");
                System.exit(1);
        }
        try {
            // Run the application
            app.runUsingSqljDefaultContext();
        }  // end try
        catch (SQLException ex) {
            System.err.println("Error running " +
                    runUsingSqljDefaultContext: " + ex);
            String sqlMessage = ex.getMessage();
            System.err.println("SQL Message: " + sqlMessage);
        }  // end catch
    }  // end main

    void runUsingSqljDefaultContext() throws SQLException {
        LineItemIterator lineItems = null;
        #sql lineItems =
                { SELECT requestno, projectno, quantity, unit,
                      estimatedcost, actualcost, description
                  FROM LINEITEM_LIST
                  ORDER BY requestno };
...
...
//  The remaining SQLJ source code is the same as the
//  SingleDefaultContext.sqlj
```

Notes on the `UsingSqljDefaultContext.sqlj` application:

1. This statement uses the `Oracle.connect()` method to set an instance of the `DefaultContext` class. The method installs the new connection as the static default context. The database connection uses the parameters listed in the properties file: the JDBC driver, the URL, the listener port, the Oracle SID, the username, and the user password.

2. This statement retrieves the default connection that the `connect()` method had previously installed. Use the `connect()` method when you need to create a single connection context, implicitly.

Managing Multiple Database Connections with SQLJ

Recall that instances of the `DefaultContext` class are typically used for single or multiple connections to a single database. SQLJ, also, supports connecting to multiple databases within the same program at the same time. You can create multiple instances of the DefaultContext class to connect to databases located at different sites.

The MultiDefaultCtx.sqlj application uses two DefaultContext objects to access two databases located on data-i.com and haiti servers. In the case where the application needs to create multiple connections to different types of database schemas, you should use connection context declarations (see the "Using SQLJ Connection Context for Database Connections" section of this chapter) to define your own connection context classes so that SQLJ can do more rigorous semantics checking of your code.

The FireWallMultiDefaultCtx.sqlj application demonstrates making multiple database connections to an Internet data server and an intranet data server (see listing at www.osborne.com). This SQLJ application creates two instances of the DefaultContext class to replicate platform data from an Oracle database (version 8.0.4) located outside of a firewall (on the Internet) to an Oracle8*i* database located inside of that firewall (in an Intranet). (See the "How Firewalls Work" section in the *Oracle8*i *JDBC Developer's Guide*, A64685-1[38]):

```
/*
** Program Name:        MultiDefaultCtx.sqlj
**
** Purpose:             SQLJ application that implements
** two sqlj default context to connect to two databases located
** on two different Oracle servers. Also, this program uses
** a named SQLJ iterator to query a relational database table.
*/

// Required SQLJ classes for any SQLJ program
import sqlj.runtime.*;
import sqlj.runtime.ref.*;

// Required Java classes for any application that needs to
// access a database
import java.sql.*;
// Required Oracle classes for Oracle database
import oracle.sql.*;
import oracle.sqlj.runtime.Oracle;
import oracle.jdbc.driver.*;

public class MultiDefaultCtx {

    // This iterator will access data from data-i.com
    #sql public iterator LineItemIterator (int requestno,
        int projectno, float quantity,String unit,
            float estimatedcost,float actualcost,String description);

    // PlatformIter() will access haiti
```

```
#sql public iterator PlatformIter (int aPlatformId, String aType,
                                   String aDesc);

// Declare two protected static variables of type DefaultContext
// Variables must be static. Java requirement.
protected static DefaultContext dataiConnCtx;  // (See Note 1.)
protected static DefaultContext haitiConnCtx;
// Constructor
public MultiDefaultCtx () {

    try {
        // Instantiate Default Context for each host
        // (See Note 2.)
          dataiConnCtx = Oracle.getConnection
            ("jdbc:oracle:thin:@data-i.com:1521:ORCL",
                 "scott","tiger",false);
        haitiConnCtx = Oracle.getConnection
            ("jdbc:oracle:thin:@haiti:1521:ORCL",
                            "scott","tiger",false);
    } // end try
    catch (Exception ex) {
             System.err.println("Error from " +
                   "haitiConnCtx/dataiConnCtx " +
                   "MultiDefaultCtx: " + ex);
    } // end catch

 }  // end constructor

public static void main(String[] args) throws SQLException {

    // Instantiate MultiDefaultCtx constructor to create
    // two connection contexts of type DefaultContext.
    MultiDefaultCtx app = new MultiDefaultCtx();

    // We cannot connect to the database, stop program execution.
    if   (dataiConnCtx == null) {
        System.out.println("I cannot connect to the " +
            "data-i.com database - Stop execution.");
        System.exit(1);
     } // end if
    if   (haitiConnCtx == null) {
        System.out.println("I cannot connect to the " +
         "haiti database  - Stop execution.");
        System.exit(0);
     } // end if

    try {
    // Run the application (See Note 3.)
```

```
                app.runMultiDefaultCtx(haitiConnCtx, dataiConnCtx);
            } // end try
        catch (SQLException ex) {
            System.err.println("Error running" +
                    " runMultiDefaultCtx: " + ex);
            String sqlMessage = ex.getMessage();
            System.err.println("SQL Message: " + sqlMessage);
        }   // end catch

    }   // end main

    void runMultiDefaultCtx(DefaultContext haitiCtx,
                DefaultContext dataiCtx  )  throws SQLException {

        /*      ** Set DefaultContext to haitiCtx       */
        DefaultContext.setDefaultContext(haitiCtx);   // (See Note 4.)

        LineItemIterator lineItems = null;
        #sql [haitiCtx] lineItems =     // (See Note 5.)
            { SELECT requestno,projectno,quantity,
                  unit,estimatedcost,actualcost,description
                FROM LINEITEM_LIST
                ORDER BY requestno };

        while (lineItems.next()) {
            System.out.println("Request No: " + lineItems.requestno() );
            System.out.println("Project No: " + lineItems.projectno() );
            System.out.println("Quantity: " + lineItems.quantity() );
            System.out.println("Unit: " + lineItems.unit() );
            System.out.println("Estimated Cost: " +
                    lineItems.estimatedcost() );
            System.out.println("Actual Cost: " +
                    lineItems.actualcost() );
            System.out.println("Description: " +
                    lineItems.description() );
        };   // end while

        // Close iterator
        lineItems.close();

        /* ** Set DefaultContext to dataiCtx    */
        DefaultContext.setDefaultContext(dataiCtx); // (See Note 6.)
        PlatformIter platform = null;    // (See Note 7.)

        #sql [dataiCtx] platform =       // (See Note 8.)
            { SELECT P.key_id AS aPlatformId,
```

```
        P.type AS aType,P.description AS aDesc
        FROM PLATFORM_TYPE_LIST P };

    while (platform.next()) {
     System.out.println("Platform id: " + platform.aPlatformId() );
     System.out.println("Type: " + platform.aType() );
     System.out.println("Description: " + platform.aDesc() );
     }  // end while
     // Close iterator
     platform.close();

  }   // End runMultiDefaultCtx()
}  // End MultiDefaultCtx class
```

Notes on `MultiDefaultCtx.sqlj` application:

1. This statement and the one that follows it create two `DefaultContext`
    instances named `dataiConnCtx` and `haitiConnCtx` respectively.

2. These statements use the `getConnection()` and the Oracle thin driver to
    set up connections to two databases located on `data-i.com` and `haiti`
    respectively. The `getConnection()` method is used when multiple or
    explicitly passed connection contexts are required.

3. This statement invokes the method `runMultiDefaultCtx()` while
    specifying two `DefaultContext` instances as its parameters.

4. This statement sets up the instance `haitiCtx` as the default for the SQLJ
    execution statement that will select the rows from the `LINEITEM_LIST`
    table located at URL address: `haiti`. The static `setDefaultContext()`
    method of the `DefaultContext` class sets a specific database connection
    as the default connection. Use this method when an application needs to
    perform several SQL operations on a specified database. There is no need
    to specify a connection class instance for a SQL operation in this case.
    For example, the SQLJ clause in Listing 5-3 executes a `SELECT` on the
    `LINEITEM_LIST` table located on `haiti` and uses an explicit connection
    context instance called `haitiCtx`, whereas in Listing 5-4, the SQLJ clause
    uses an implicit connection context instance to perform the same SQL
    operation.

Listing 5-3

```
// SQLJ iterator instance using explicitly a DefaultContext instance
#sql [haitiCtx] lineItems =
```

```
   { SELECT requestno, projectno, quantity, unit,
            estimatedcost, actualcost, description
     FROM LINEITEM_LIST
     ORDER BY requestno
   };
```

Listing 5-4

```
// SQLJ iterator instance using implicitly a DefaultContext instance
// after calling the setDefaultContext() method.
#sql lineItems =
{ SELECT requestno, projectno, quantity, unit, estimatedcost,
     actualcost, description
  FROM LINEITEM_LIST
  ORDER BY requestno };
```

5. This assignment clause executes a SELECT statement, constructs an iterator object that contains the result table for the SELECT statement, and assigns the iterator object to the lineItem variables. The iterator accesses the table located on haiti.

6. This statement sets up the instance dataiCtx as the default for the SQLJ execution statement that will select the rows from the PLATFORM_TYPE_LIST table located at URL address data-i.com.

7. This statement creates an instance of the iterator PlatformIter class and initializes it.

8. This iterator instance accesses a table located on data-i.com.

Next, you will use a user-defined SQLJ declared connection context class to connect to a single database as well as to several databases located at different remote sites. Recall the SQLJ syntax in the "Using SQLJ Connection Context for Database Connections" section of this chapter:

```
#sql <modifiers> context Context_Classname;
```

Because a connection context class implements the sqlj.runtime. ConnectionContext interface, it must implement all of its methods. See *Oracle8i SQLJ Developer's Guide and Reference Release 8.1.5* [63]:

■ close (boolean CLOSE_CONNECTION/KEEP_CONNECTION)
Use this method to close a connection and release all resources.

- `getConnection()` This method returns the underlying JDBC Connection object for this connection context instance.

- `getExecutionContext()` A method that returns the default `ExecutionContext` instance for this connection context instance.

In addition to these methods, each declared connection context class defines its own methods:

- `getDefaultContext()` This is a static method that returns the default connection context instance for a given connection context class.

- `SetDefaultContext` (the specified connection context object) This is a static method that defines the default context instance for a given connection context object.

The SQLJ translator generates a Java class for the user-defined connection context class in the `MultiDeclaredConnectionCtx.sqlj` application:

```
// A declared SQLJ connection context class
#sql context DeclaredConnectionContext;
```

Listing 5-5 shows a list of the methods that the SQLJ translator generates for the user-defined `DeclaredConnectionContext` class. Method implementations are omitted for the sake of clarity.

Listing 5-5

```
class DeclaredConnectionContext
        extends sqlj.runtime.ref.ConnectionContextImpl
            implements sqlj.runtime.ConnectionContext {

    public DeclaredConnectionContext(java.sql.Connection conn)
        throws java.sql.SQLException;

    public DeclaredConnectionContext(java.lang.String url,
                java.lang.String user, java.lang.String password,
                boolean autoCommit) throws java.sql.SQLException;

    public DeclaredConnectionContext(java.lang.String url,
            java.util.Properties info, boolean autoCommit)
                    throws java.sql.SQLException;

    public DeclaredConnectionContext(java.lang.String url,
```

```
                  boolean autoCommit) throws java.sql.SQLException;

   public DeclaredConnectionContext
              (sqlj.runtime.ConnectionContext other)
                 throws java.sql.SQLException;

   public static DeclaredConnectionContext getDefaultContext();

   public static void setDefaultContext
              (DeclaredConnectionContext ctx);

   private static DeclaredConnectionContext defaultContext = null;

   public static java.lang.Object getProfileKey
              ( sqlj.runtime.profile.Loader loader,
              java.lang.String profileName )
                  throws java.sql.SQLException;

  private static final sqlj.runtime.ref.ProfileGroup profiles =
                      new sqlj.runtime.ref.ProfileGroup();

  public static sqlj.runtime.profile.Profile
              getProfile(java.lang.Object profileKey);
}
```

The following SQLJ application, `MultiDeclaredConnectionCtx.sqlj`, associates explicitly an instance of the `ExecutionContext` class to each connection context instance.

```
/* ** Program Name:        MultiDeclaredConnectionCtx.sqlj
** Purpose:           SQLJ application that implements
** two instances of a declared SQLJ connection context class to
** connect to two databases located on two different Oracle servers:
*/
// Required SQLJ classes for any SQLJ program
import sqlj.runtime.*;
import sqlj.runtime.ref.*;

// Required SQLJ class to use instances of the ExecutionContext class
import sqlj.runtime.ExecutionContext;   // (See Note 1.)

// Required Java classes for any application that needs
// to access a database
import java.sql.*;

// Required Oracle classes for Oracle database
import oracle.sql.*;
import oracle.sqlj.runtime.Oracle;
```

```
import oracle.jdbc.driver.*;

// Import the user-defined SQLJ connection context class
// import DeclaredConnectionContext;
#sql context DeclaredConnectionContext;  // (See Note 2.)

public class MultiDeclaredConnectionCtx {

    // Declare a named SQLJ iterator. LineItemIterator()
    // This iterator will access data from haiti
    #sql public iterator LineItemIterator (int requestno,
        int projectno,float quantity,String unit,float estimatedcost,
          float actualcost,String description);

    // PlatformIter() will access data-i.com
    #sql public iterator PlatformIter (int aPlatformId, String aType,
                                        String aDesc);
    // Constructor
    public MultiDeclaredConnectionCtx () {
    }  // end constructor

    public static void main(String[] args) throws SQLException {

        /* If you are using an Oracle JDBC driver and call the
        standard Oracle.connect() method to create a default
        connection, then SQLJ handles this automatically.
        Oracle.connect() registers the
        oracle.jdbc.driver.OracleDriver class. */
        //(See Note 3.)
        DriverManager.registerDriver
                (new oracle.jdbc.driver.OracleDriver());

        MultiDeclaredConnectionCtx app =
            new MultiDeclaredConnectionCtx();
        // (See Note 4.)
        DeclaredConnectionContext haitiConnCtx =
          new DeclaredConnectionContext("jdbc:oracle:thin:" +
          "@haiti:1521:ORCL","scott","tiger",false);

        // Stop program execution if we cannot
        // connect to the database
        if  ( haitiConnCtx == null ) {
            System.out.println("I cannot connect to the database "
                    + " - Stop execution");
            System.exit(1);
        }  // end if

        // Create an instance of an ExecutionContext class for haiti
```

```
        ExecutionContext haitiExecCtx =
                        new ExecutionContext(); // (See Note 5.)

        try {           // Run the application
         app.runMultiDeclaredConnCtxHaiti(haitiConnCtx,haitiExecCtx);
         } // end try
         catch (SQLException ex) {
            System.err.println("Error running "
                        + "runMultiDeclaredConnCtxHaiti: " + ex);
            String sqlMessage = ex.getMessage();
            System.err.println("SQL Message: " + sqlMessage);
         } // end catch

        // Instantiate a connection to second host
        DeclaredConnectionContext dataiConnCtx =
           new DeclaredConnectionContext("jdbc:oracle:thin:" +
                  "@data-i.com:1521:ORCL",
                        "scott","tiger",false); // (See Note 6.)

        if (dataiConnCtx == null ) {
            System.out.println("I cannot connect to the database "
                        + " - Stop execution");
            System.exit(1);
        } // end if

        // Create an instance of an ExecutionContext
        // class for data-i.com
        ExecutionContext dataiExecCtx =
                        new ExecutionContext();    // (See Note 7.)

    try { // Run the application
        app.runMultiDeclaredConnCtxDatai(dataiConnCtx,dataiExecCtx);
    } // end try
    catch (SQLException ex) {
        System.err.println("Error running "
                    + "runMultiDeclaredConnCtxDatai: " + ex);
        String sqlMessage = ex.getMessage();
        System.err.println("SQL Message: " + sqlMessage);
    } // end catch
     // Close the database connection
     haitiConnCtx.close();  // (See Note 8.)
     dataiConnCtx.close();

 } // end main

public void runMultiDeclaredConnCtxHaiti
        (DeclaredConnectionContext haitiCtx,
         ExecutionContext haitiExCtx )  throws SQLException {

   LineItemIterator lineItems = null;
```

```
        #sql [haitiCtx, haitiExCtx] lineItems =     // (See Note 9.)
            { SELECT requestno,projectno,quantity,unit,
                    estimatedcost,actualcost,description
              FROM LINEITEM_LIST
              ORDER BY requestno };

      while (lineItems.next()) {
          System.out.println("Request No: " +
                    lineItems.requestno() );
          System.out.println("Project No: " +
                    lineItems.projectno() );
          System.out.println("Quantity: " +
                    lineItems.quantity() );
          System.out.println("Unit: " +
                    lineItems.unit() );
          System.out.println("Estimated Cost: " +
                    lineItems.estimatedcost() );
          System.out.println("Actual Cost: " +
                    lineItems.actualcost() );
          System.out.println("Description: " +
                    lineItems.description() );
      }  // end while
      // Close iterator
      lineItems.close();

}  // End runMultiDeclaredConnCtxHaiti()

public void runMultiDeclaredConnCtxDatai
        ( DeclaredConnectionContext dataiCtx,
            ExecutionContext dataiExCtx ) throws SQLException {
      PlatformIter platform = null;
  #sql [dataiCtx,dataiExCtx] platform =
      { SELECT P.key_id AS aPlatformId,P.type AS aType,
              P.description AS aDesc
        FROM PLATFORM_TYPE_LIST P };

    while (platform.next()) {
        System.out.println("Platform id: " +
                platform.aPlatformId() );
        System.out.println("Type: " +
                platform.aType() );
        System.out.println("Description: " +
                platform.aDesc() );
    }  // End while loop

    // Close iterator
    platform.close();

}  // End runMultiDeclaredConnCtxDatai()
}
```

Notes on `MultiDeclaredConnectionCtx.sqlj` application.

1. This class is required if you wish to create explicitly instances of the `ExecutionContext` class.

2. This statement creates a declared connection context class.

3. This statement registers the Oracle JDBC driver. If you are using an Oracle JDBC driver and you call the standard `Oracle.connect()` method to create a default connection, this method registers the `oracle.jdbc.driver.OracleDriver` class automatically for you. If you are using an Oracle JDBC driver but do not use `Oracle.connect()`, then you must manually register the `OracleDriver` class. In the event that you are using a non-Oracle JDBC driver, you must register this driver prior to creating an instance of the connection context class. Failure to register the JDBC driver generates the following error at runtime: driver not available.

4. This statement creates an instance of a declared connection context class named `haitiConnCtx` and uses one of the constructors generated by the SQLJ translator to connect to the database on `haiti` (see Listing 5-5 for a listing of the generated Java class and its methods).

5. This statement creates an instance of the ExecutionContext class named `haitiExecCtx`. The instance is associated explicitly with the `haitiConnCtx` instance. A SQL operation will use both instances to execute a query on the `LINEITEM_LIST` table located on `haiti`.

6. This statement creates an instance of a declared connection context class named `dataiConnCtx` and uses one of the constructors generated by the SQLJ translator to connect to the database on `data-i.com`.

7. This statement creates an instance of the ExecutionContext class named `dataiExecCtx`. A SQLJ executable statement uses both instances, the `dataiConnCtx` and the `dataiExecCtx`, to execute a query on the `PLATFORM_TYPE_LIST` table located on `data-i.com`.

8. This statement and the one that follows it closes the database connections to the data servers located on `haiti` and `data-i.com`, respectively. The `close()` method releases all resources used in maintaining this connection and closes any open connected profiles. So it's important that you close all the connection context instances.

9. This assignment clause executes the `SELECT` statement, constructs an iterator object that contains the result table for the `SELECT` statement, and assigns the iterator object to variable `lineItems`. This iterator accesses

the table located on `haiti`. The SQLJ executable statement uses explicitly an instance of connection context and an instance of execution context. With this construct, SQLJ does more rigorous semantics checking of your code. Furthermore, developers have better control over SQL operations that are being executed on a particular server.

Deploying a SQLJ Application

A SQLJ application is a Java application with static embedded SQL statements. SQLJ applications are stand-alone programs that run independently of any browser. Recall from Chapter 1 that when you compile SQLJ source code, the SQLJ translator converts the program into a standard Java program. A SQLJ application then behaves like a regular Java application. A Java program can be called a Java application if there is a `main()` method entry point in the source code (see Appendix B).

The `main()` method in SQLJ, similarly in Java, controls the flow of the program, allocates whatever resources are needed, and runs any other methods that provide the functionality for the SQLJ application just as it does in plain Java.

NOTE
The SQLJ programs listed in the previous sections are all SQLJ applications.

Deploying a SQLJ Thick Client

Typically, a thick SQLJ application would include the following:

- All domain objects and logic to manipulate the database, such as DML, DDL, and transaction control statements

- SQLJ classes to support the database access

- Imported JDBC drivers

The decision to design a thick SQLJ client program over a thin SQLJ client depends not only on the application requirements but also on the availability of hardware resources. Resources are typically scarce in small information technology (IT) shops. For example, at the Atlantic Oceanographic & Meteorological Laboratory (AOML) in Miami, one of the Environmental Research Laboratories (ERL) of the National Oceanic and Atmospheric Administration (NOAA), where many of the SQLJ programs for this book were designed and implemented, the limited resources, initially, imposed the design of SQLJ/Java thick clients versus thin clients. With the release of Oracle8*i* JServer, the design strategy has changed so that more database logic will be removed from the thick client and moved to the Oracle data server, freeing the client from database processing that can be done more efficiently by the server. Another advantage of removing database processing from the client is the reduction of network traffic. Consequently, SQLJ client programs gain performance. See the "Deploying SQLJ in an Oracle8*i* Data Server" section of this chapter to learn how to move database logic into the Oracle8*i* data server.

Several design strategies and techniques exist that can help in reducing database processing in SQLJ clients. One of them is the distributed system (see Chapter 1). Next, you will learn how to distribute application logic between a client and an application server (middle tier).

Deploying SQLJ in an Application Server (Middle Tier)

Conventional two-tier systems (see Figure 5-1) put most database operations and business logic in the client tier. This is often due to the limited hardware resources and the constraints of current tools. A significant amount of code along with having to speak to a database puts a burden on a client. In an effort to reduce the client's size, database and hardware vendors have introduced the three-tier or middle-tier model commonly referred to as an application server model. The middle-tier model is a logical layer (often, a physical layer) between a client and a database (see Figure 5-2).

In a three-tier system, the client program communicates with the middle tier and the middle tier communicates with the database. Given this scenario, the application server is the only entity that talks to the database. Moving some of the code to an application server reduces the SQLJ thick client-side code. For example, most, if not all, of the DML, DDL, and transaction control statements, and the JDBC driver could be placed in the middle-tier server. In fact, you can move entire SQLJ applications to the application server, thereby freeing the client, now a thin client, from database processing code.

Deploying a SQLJ Thin Client

The advantages of the industry's trend toward smaller Java programs are twofold:

- The applications are small, and they can be downloaded much faster.

- Java applications are a good fit for the Internet, where bandwidth is limited.

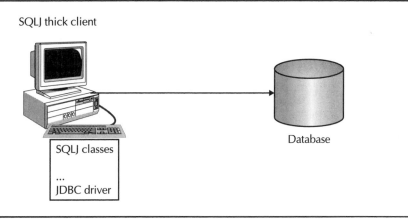

SQLJ thick client

SQLJ classes

...

JDBC driver

Database

FIGURE 5-1. *Conventional two-tier system*

NOTE
See the `SqljAppletCallsSqljSP.sqlj`
applet at the end of the chapter for an example
of SQLJ thin client.

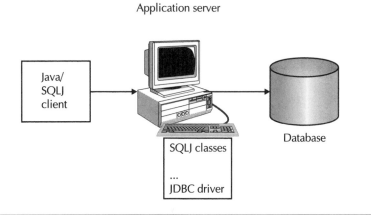

Application server

Java/
SQLJ
client

SQLJ classes

...

JDBC driver

Database

FIGURE 5-2. *SQLJ logic in the application server*

Deploying SQLJ in a Java Application

Java applications can call Java methods from other Java classes. In a similar manner, Java programs can also call SQLJ methods. To call SQLJ methods from a Java source:

 1. Create a stand-alone SQLJ application.

 2. Compile the SQLJ application using the SQLJ Translator.

 3. Run the SQLJ application.

 4. Write the Java application. Call the SQLJ method as you would call a Java method. For example,

```
sqljProc.addLineItem (aRequestno, aQuantity, aProjectNo,
            aUnit, anEstimatedcost, anActualcost, aDescription);
```

where `sqljProc` is an instance of the SQLJ `PIManager` class followed by the SQLJ `addLineItem()` method of the class.

 5. Compile the Java application.

 6. Run the Java application.

Note that all program source code (SQLJ and Java code) should be placed in the same directory. The following examples illustrate the preceding steps:

Step 1   Create the SQLJ application: `PIManager.sqlj`.

```
/* Program Name:    PIManager.sqlj
**
*/
// Required SQLJ classes
import sqlj.runtime.*;
import sqlj.runtime.ref.*;

// Required Java classes
import java.sql.*;

// Required Oracle classes
import oracle.sql.*;
import oracle.sqlj.runtime.Oracle;
import oracle.jdbc.driver.*;

// A java utility class that creates a JDBC connection
import ConnectionManager;  // (See Note 1.)

public class PIManager {

    // Constructor to establish database connection
```

```
    public  PIManager () {
        try {  // Establish a Connection
            ConnectionManager.initContext();   // (See Note 2.)
        }
        catch (Exception ex) {
           System.err.println("Unable to connect "
                  + "ConnectionManager : " + ex);
        }
    }  // End Constructor

    public static void main (String argv[])
                      throws SQLException  { // Main entry

        PIManager sqljApp = new PIManager();    // (See Note 3.)

        // cannot connect to the database, stop program execution.
        if  (DefaultContext.getDefaultContext() == null ) {
            System.out.println("I cannot connect to the database "
                            + "-- Stop Execution.");
            System.exit(1);
        }

        // Create host variables
        int aRequestno = 501;   // (See Note 4.)
        int aQuantity = 20;
        int aProjectNo = 300;
        String aUnit = "04";
        double anEstimatedcost = 10000;
        double anActualcost = 7000;
        String aDescription = "FAU-Consulting";

        // Call the SQLJ method (See Note 5.)
        sqljApp.addLineItem (aRequestno,aQuantity,aProjectNo,
            aUnit, anEstimatedcost, anActualcost, aDescription);
    } // End Main

    public static void addLineItem (  // (See Note 6.)
          int aRequestno,int aQuantity,int aProjectNo, String aUnit,
          double anEstimatedcost, double anActualcost,
           String aDescription ) throws SQLException {

        int aLineNo = 0;
        #sql {SELECT lineno_seq.NEXTVAL
             INTO :aLineNo FROM DUAL };  // (See Note 7.)

          if   (aLineNo > 0) {
               try {
                  #sql {
                        INSERT INTO LINEITEM_LIST     // (See Note 8.)
                       ( requestno,lineno,projectno,quantity, unit,
```

```
                    estimatedcost, actualcost, description )
                    VALUES
                    (
                      :IN aRequestno,:IN aLineNo,
                      :IN aProjectNo,
                      :IN aQuantity,:IN aUnit,
                      :IN anEstimatedcost,
                      :IN anActualcost,
                      :IN aDescription
                    )
                 };
            } // End of try
            catch (SQLException er) {
                   System.err.println(er.getMessage());
            }   // End catch
      }   // End if

      try {
          // Commit
          #sql {COMMIT};   // (See Note 9.)
      }
      catch (SQLException ex) {
          System.err.println(ex.getMessage());
      }

   } // End addLineItem

} // End PIManager
```

Notes on `PIManager.sqlj` application:

This application establishes a database connection using the `initContext()` method from the ConnectionManager class and inserts data into the `LINEITEM_ LIST` table.

1. This statement imports a Java utility class that returns a JDBC connection.

2. The constructor connects to the database using the `initContext()` method from the ConnectionManager class.

3. This statement creates an instance of the PIManager class and automatically connects to the database.

4. This statement and the six others that follow it create several Java variables.

5. This statement calls the SQLJ `addLineItem()` method. This method is called with an implicit `DefaultConnection` context created by the

PIManager() constructor. Note that this call and all the host variables (in Step 4) can be removed after the SQLJ application has been tested.

6. This statement declares the SQLJ addLineItem() method. Note that this method has been declared **public static** (see Appendix B for an explanation of Java **public static** methods).

7. This statement selects the next available line number to be inserted into the LINEITEM_LIST table.

8. This statement inserts a row of data into the LINEITEM_LIST table using host variables as input parameters to the INSERT statement.

9. This statement commits the changes to the database.

Step 2   Compile/translate the SQLJ application: PIManager.sqlj.

```
// At the command line, type the following command:
sqlj PIManager.sqlj
```

Step 3   Run the SQLJ application:

```
// At the command line, type the following command:
java PIManager
```

Step 4   Create the Java application: DeploySqljAppInJavaApp.java.

```
/*
** Program Name:        DeploySqljAppInJavaApp.java
**
** Purpose:        Java application that calls a SQLJ method.
**
*/
// Required Java classes for any application
// that needs to access a database
import java.sql.*;

// Import the SQLJ class
import PIManager;        // (See Note 1.)

public class DeploySqljAppInJavaApp {

  public static void main(String[] args) throws SQLException  {

    PIManager sqljProc = new PIManager();    // (See Note 2.)

    // Stop program execution if we cannot connect to the database
    if  (DefaultContext.getDefaultContext() == null ) {
```

```
            System.out.println("I cannot connect to the database "
                            + "-- Stop Execution.");
            System.exit(1);
    }

    // Set Host Variables
    int aRequestno = 501;      // (See Note 3.)
    int aProjectNo = 300;
    int aQuantity = 30;
    String aUnit = "04";
    double anEstimatedcost = 15000;
    double anActualcost = 8500;
    String aDescription = "Datai-Consults";

    try {
        // Call the SQLJ method from
        // the Java application (See Note 4.)
        sqljProc.addLineItem (aRequestno, aQuantity, aProjectNo,
                aUnit, anEstimatedcost, anActualcost, aDescription);
    }  // end try
    catch (SQLException ex) {
            System.err.println("Error calling the SQLJ"
                    + " addLineItem() method : " + ex);
            String sqlMessage = ex.getMessage();
            System.err.println("SQL Message: " + sqlMessage);
    }  // end catch
  }   // End main()

}  // End DeploySqljAppInJavaApp class
```

Notes on `DeploySqljAppInJavaApp.java` application:

This Java application calls a SQLJ method to insert data into the `LINEITEM_ LIST` table.

1. This statement imports a SQLJ class. The SQLJ `PIManager.sqlj` application is used in this example.

2. This statement creates an instance of the `PIManager` SQLJ class and connects to the database using its constructor. This database connection is done using the Oracle JDBC thin driver.

3. These statements set the host variables. Note that you can create a user interface to accept these variables as input parameters.

4. This statement calls the `addLineItem()` SQLJ method contained in the Java application.

Step 5 Compile the Java application: `DeploySqljAppInJavaApp.java.`

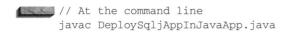

```
// At the command line
javac DeploySqljAppInJavaApp.java
```

Step 6 Run the Java application: `DeploySqljAppInJavaApp.`

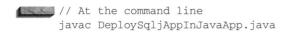

```
// At the command line, run the DeploySqljAppInJavaApp.class
java DeploySqljAppInJavaApp
```

Deploying SQLJ in a Java Applet

A Java applet is a Java program that can start program execution in a Java-compatible browser via an `init()` method. It does not contain a `main()` method (see Appendix B). Every applet is implemented by creating a subclass of the Applet class. The steps to deploy SQLJ in a Java applet are similar to those of deploying SQLJ in a Java application. In addition to the steps in the "Deploying SQLJ in a Java Application" section of this chapter, you must translate the SQLJ `.ser` files (see Chapter 4) into regular Java `.class` files:

1. Create a stand-alone SQLJ application.

2. Compile the SQLJ application using the SQLJ Translator.

3. Run the SQLJ application.

4. Write a Java applet. Include a Java statement to call the SQLJ method.

5. Recompile the SQLJ application with the Java applet.

6. Translate the SQLJ `.ser` files into regular Java `.class` files. Create a root directory and retranslate the SQLJ `.ser` files. Make sure that you set up your path to point to this root directory. You may also need to put a copy of the JDBC driver and the SQLJ Translator into that directory. Failure to do so will generate the runtime error: applet not initialized.

7. Copy the SQLJ `runtime.zip` and `classes111.zip` in the same directory from Step 6.

8. Set your system CLASSPATH to point to this directory.

9. Create an html file for the Java applet.

10. Run the Java applet by calling `AppletViewer`.

Steps 1-3 These steps are identical to Steps 1-3 in the "Deploying SQLJ in a Java Application" section of this chapter. Next you will create the Java applet that will invoke the `addLineItem()` method from the PIManager SQLJ class.

Step 4 Write a Java applet. Include a Java statement to call the SQLJ method. The following is the source code for the Java applet, the `SqljInJavaApplet.java`.

```java
/*
**   Program Name:          SqljInJavaApplet.java
*/
// Import the JDBC classes
import java.sql.*;

// Import the java classes used in applets
import java.awt.*;
import java.io.*;
import java.util.*;

// Import the SQLJ class
import PIManager;

public class SqljInJavaApplet extends java.applet.Applet {

  // The button to call the SQLJ addLineItem() method
  Button execute_button;

  // The place where to dump the applet actions
  TextArea output;

  // Create the User Interface
  public void init ()   {
    this.setLayout (new BorderLayout ());
    Panel p = new Panel ();
    p.setLayout (new FlowLayout (FlowLayout.LEFT));
    execute_button = new Button ("Insert Line_Item");
    p.add (execute_button);
    this.add ("North", p);
    output = new TextArea (10, 60);
    this.add ("Center", output);
  }  // End of init()

  public boolean action (Event ev, Object arg)   {

    if (ev.target == execute_button){
      // Clear the output area
       output.setText (null);

      // Connect to the database
       PIManager sqljProc = new PIManager();
        output.appendText ("Connecting to database" +
```

```
                   " using SQLJ " + "\n");

        // Stop program execution if we cannot connect to the database
        if  (DefaultContext.getDefaultContext() == null ) {
             System.out.println("I cannot connect to the database "
                              + "-- Stop Execution.");
             System.exit(0);
        }

        // Set Host Variables
        int aRequestno = 501;
        int aProjectNo = 300;
        int aQuantity = 30;
        String aUnit = "04";
        double anEstimatedcost = 15000;
        double anActualcost = 8500;
        String aDescription = "Oracle-Support";

        try {
             // Call the SQLJ method from the Java application
             sqljProc.addLineItem (aRequestno, aQuantity, aProjectNo,
                 aUnit, anEstimatedcost, anActualcost, aDescription);
        }  // end try
         catch (SQLException ex) {
                 output.appendText ("Error calling the SQLJ"
                         + " addLineItem() method : " + ex + "\n");
                 String sqlMessage = ex.getMessage();
                 output.appendText ("SQL Message: "
                 + sqlMessage + "\n");
         }  // end catch
    } // End if

   output.appendText ("done.\n");

   return true;

 }  // End action()
}//end SqljInJavaApplet class
```

Notes on the `SqljInJavaApplet.java` applet.

As the foregoing call demonstrates, the call to a SQLJ method from a Java applet is identical to the call from a Java application. This database connection is done via the Oracle JDBC thin driver. This is a required "pure Java" driver for all Oracle Java applets. See Steps 1–4 in "Deploying SQLJ in a Java Application." Next, you will learn the remaining steps needed to run Java applets.

Step 5 Recompile the SQLJ application with the Java applet:

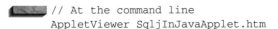

```
// At the command line
sqlj -profile=false PIManager.sqlj SqljInJavaApplet.java
```

Step 6   Translate the SQLJ .ser files into regular Java .class files. Create a root directory and retranslate the SQLJ .ser files. Make sure that you set up your path to point to this root directory. You may also need to put a copy of the JDBC driver and the SQLJ Translator into that directory. Failure to do so will generate the runtime error: applet not initialized:

```
// At the command line
// directory. In NT, you can use the format: -d=c:\dist
sqlj -profile=false -ser2class -d=dist PIManager.sqlj
      SqljInJavaApplet.java
```

Step 7   Copy the SQLJ runtime.zip and classes111.zip in the same directory from Step 6. Use your operating system command to do so.

Step 8   Set your system CLASSPATH to point to this directory.

Step 9   Create an html file for the Java applet.

Step 10   Run the Java applet by calling AppletViewer:

```
// At the command line
AppletViewer SqljInJavaApplet.htm
```

Deploying a SQLJ Applet

Deploying a SQLJ applet is almost identical to deploying SQLJ in a Java applet. You can use SQLJ source code in applets because the SQLJ runtime is pure Java. There are, however, a few considerations to be made. See the *Oracle8*i *SQLJ Developer's Guide and Reference* [63] for more information about the SQLJ packages.

The following SQLJ packages must be packaged with your SQLJ applet:

- sqlj.runtime
- sqlj.runtime.ref
- sqlj.runtime.profile
- sqlj.runtime.profile.ref
- sqlj.runtime.error

Additionally, the packages here must be included if you are using Oracle customization:

- `oracle.sqlj.runtime`
- `oracle.sqlj.runtime.error`

Alternatively, since all these packages are included in the file `runtime.zip`, all you have to do is list the `runtime.zip` as a value for the archive key in your <APPLET> tag. The `runtime.zip` file comes with your Oracle SQLJ installation. You must also specify a pure Java JDBC driver, such as the Oracle JDBC thin driver, for your database connection. Furthermore, Oracle SQLJ requires the runtime environment of JDK 1.1.*x* or higher. You cannot employ browsers using JDK 1.0.*x*, such as Netscape Navigator 3.0 and Microsoft Internet Explorer 3.0, without either using a JRE plug-in or finding some other way of using JRE 1.1.*x* instead of the browser's default JRE.

Deploying SQLJ applets is almost identical to deploying SQLJ in Java applets. You will use the method from the `PIManager` class once more, but this time you will call it a SQLJ applet. The steps are

1. Create a stand-alone SQLJ application.

2. Compile the SQLJ application using the SQLJ Translator.

3. Run the SQLJ application.

4. Write a SQLJ applet. Call the SQLJ method within the program.

5. Recompile the SQLJ application with the SQLJ applet.

6. Translate the SQLJ `.ser` files into regular Java classes.

7. Copy the SQLJ `runtime.zip` and `classes111.zip` in the same directory from Step 6.

8. Set your system CLASSPATH to point to this directory. This step is done only if you wish to use strictly the `AppletViewer` utility program. To view the applet in a browser, make sure that the <APPLET> tag contains the following key/value pair: `archive=classes111.zip,runtime.zip`.

9. Create the html file for the Java applet.

10. Run the SQLJ applet by calling `AppletViewer`.

Note that you can skip Steps 1 to 3 and have all the SQLJ code from the `PIManager` class inside the SQLJ applet. Although it is not advisable, it can be done. The following SQLJ applet performs in a similar manner as the Java applet. In fact,

SqljApplet.sqlj is exactly the same program as the SqljInJavaApplet.java; you only change the class name and of course store the program in a file bearing the same name as required for all Java and SQLJ programs.

```
/*
**   Program Name:          SqljApplet.sqlj
*/
// Import the JDBC classes
import java.sql.*;

// Import the java classes used in applets
import java.awt.*;
import java.io.*;
import java.util.*;

// Import the SQLJ class
import PIManager;

public class SqljInJavaApplet extends java.applet.Applet {

  // The button to call the SQLJ addLineItem() method
  Button execute_button;

  // The place where to dump the applet actions
  TextArea output;

  // Create the User Interface
  public void init ()  {
    this.setLayout (new BorderLayout ());
    Panel p = new Panel ();
    p.setLayout (new FlowLayout (FlowLayout.LEFT));
    execute_button = new Button ("Insert Line_Item");
    p.add (execute_button);
    this.add ("North", p);
    output = new TextArea (10, 60);
    this.add ("Center", output);
  }  // End of init()

  public boolean action (Event ev, Object arg)  {
    if (ev.target == execute_button){
      // Clear the output area
      output.setText (null);

      // Connect to the database
```

```
    PIManager sqljProc = new PIManager();

  // Stop program execution if we cannot connect to the database
  if  (DefaultContext.getDefaultContext() == null ) {
        System.out.println("I cannot connect to the database "
                          + "-- Stop Execution.");
        System.exit(1);
  } // end if

    output.appendText ("Connecting to database" +
          " using SQLJ " + "\n");

  // Set Host Variables
    int aRequestno = 501;
    int aProjectNo = 300;
    int aQuantity = 30;
    String aUnit = "04";
    double anEstimatedcost = 15000;
    double anActualcost = 8500;
    String aDescription = "Oracle-Support";

    try {
        // Call the SQLJ method from the Java application
        sqljProc.addLineItem (aRequestno, aQuantity, aProjectNo,
            aUnit, anEstimatedcost, anActualcost, aDescription);
    }  // end try
    catch (SQLException ex) {
          output.appendText ("Error calling the SQLJ"
                + " addLineItem() method : " + ex + "\n");
                String sqlMessage = ex.getMessage();
                output.appendText ("SQL Message: "
                + sqlMessage + "\n");
    }  // end catch
  }  // End if

  output.appendText ("done.\n");
  return true;
  } // end action()
} // end SqljApplet class
```

In the "Deploying SQLJ in a Java Application" section of this chapter, you created a SQLJ application, the PIManager.sqlj, which you used to deploy SQLJ in a Java application, a Java applet, and a SQLJ applet. Next, you will deploy the SQLJ application, PIManager.sqlj, into the Oracle8*i* JServer (see Chapter 1 to learn more about Oracle JServer).

Deploying SQLJ in an Oracle8*i* Data Server: SQLJ Stored Procedure

SQLJ code can run in the Oracle8*i* Server in the form of stored procedures, stored functions, triggers, Enterprise JavaBeans (EJB), and CORBA objects. See Chapter 4 for a detailed discussion on SQLJ and Java stored procedures, Chapter 8 to learn how to develop enterprise JavaBeans and CORBA objects using SQLJ, and *Oracle8*i *Java Stored Procedures and Developer's Guide, Release 8.1.5* [39].

There is very little difference between coding for server-side use as opposed to client-side use. The main differences involve database connections. Remember that SQLJ clients connect to Oracle database via a JDBC thin or a JDBC OCI driver. SQLJ server-side programs connect through the JDBC KPRB driver (see Chapters 1 and 4). The SQLJ client-side programs must explicitly establish a database connection either via an instance of the `DefaultContext` or a declared connection context class. On the server, the database connection is always implicit.

After you write your SQLJ program, you can translate and compile your code either on a client or in the server. You can load your SQLJ source code directly into the Oracle database, and you can specify that translation and compilation be done automatically. In fact, the Oracle8*i* Server includes a SQLJ translator that can translate the SQLJ source files directly in the server. Alternatively, you can translate and load in one step using the server-side SQLJ Translator. In either case, you use the Oracle `loadjava` utility program to load your SQLJ programs into the server. The recommended way is to have all of your SQLJ `.class` and `.ser` files in a single `.jar` file and then use `loadjava` to upload your SQLJ classes.

The characteristics of the Oracle JDBC KPRB driver include the following:

- You only have one connection.

- The connection must be to the database in which the code is running.

- The connection cannot be closed—any attempt to close it will be ignored.

- The JDBC server-side driver does not support auto-commit. You must commit explicitly.

In this section, you will learn how to transform a SQLJ client-side program into a server-side stored procedure. You will use the SQLJ `PIManager.sqlj` application to do so. To create a SQLJ server-side program from a client-side program, you do the following:

Step 1 Edit the program and remove all explicit database connections and all SQLJ runtime classes.

```
/* Program Name:     PIManager.sqlj
**
*/
// Required Java classes
import java.sql.SQLException;

public class PIManager {

    public static void main (String argv[]) { // Main entry
    } // End Main

    public static void addLineItem
      ( int aRequestno,int aQuantity,int aProjectNo, String aUnit,
          double anEstimatedcost, double anActualcost,
            String aDescription ) throws SQLException {

      int aLineNo = 0;
      #sql {SELECT lineno_seq.NEXTVAL INTO :aLineNo FROM DUAL };

        try {
          #sql { INSERT INTO LINEITEM_LIST
                   ( requestno,lineno,projectno,quantity, unit,
                       estimatedcost, actualcost, description
                   )
                     VALUES
                       ( :IN aRequestno,:IN aLineNo,:IN aProjectNo,
                         :IN aQuantity,:IN aUnit, :IN anEstimatedcost,
                           :IN anActualcost,:IN aDescription
                       )
                 };
        } // End of try
        catch (SQLException er) {
              System.err.println(er.getMessage());
        }   // End of catch

        // Commit
        #sql {COMMIT};    // (See Note 1.)

    } // End addLineItem

} // End PIManager
```

Note on `PIManager.sqlj` as a SQLJ stored procedure:

  1. This statement explicitly commits the changes to the database. Remember that
     the Oracle JDBC-KPRB server-side driver does not support auto-commit. You
     may wish, however, to commit the change to the database in the client-side

program versus the server-side program. In this situation, you can remove the #sql {COMMIT} statement from the PIManager.sqlj and place it into your client-side program.

Step 2   Translate the SQLJ source code. Use the SQLJ ser2class (Chapter 4) translator to do so.

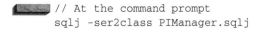

```
// At the command prompt
sqlj -ser2class PIManager.sqlj
```

Step 3   Archive the generated classes and SQL profiles.

```
// At the command line
jar cvf0 PIManager.jar PIManager*.class PIManager*.ser
```

Step 4   Load the PIManager.jar file into the server.

```
// At the command line
call loadjava -thin -resolve -force -user
    scott/tiger@haiti:1521:ORCL PIManager.jar
```

Step 5   Check the load in Step 4 by running the checkload.sql script in SQL*Plus. You wish to find out if your SQLJ classes have been loaded with no error. We provide you with a script that does the work for you. The script uses the user_objects view to determine the status of your classes. Check the listing to find the name and the status of your SQLJ program. Proceed to Step 6 if the status is valid.

```
-- In SQLPLUS
@checkload.sql
```

Step 6   Create PL/SQL wrapper for your SQLJ program using the following syntax:

```
-- Program Name: PI_Actions.sql
CREATE OR REPLACE PACKAGE PI_Actions AS
    PROCEDURE PI_main(p_entry    VARCHAR2);
    PROCEDURE add_Line_Item
        ( p_aRequestno NUMBER,p_aQuantity  NUMBER,
          p_aProjectNo NUMBER,p_aUnit VARCHAR2,
          p_anEstimatedcost NUMBER,p_anActualcost NUMBER,
          p_aDescription VARCHAR2
        );
END PI_Actions;
/
CREATE OR REPLACE PACKAGE BODY PI_Actions AS
```

```
      PROCEDURE PI_main(p_entry     VARCHAR2) AS LANGUAGE JAVA
          NAME 'PIManager.main(java.lang.String[])';
      PROCEDURE add_Line_Item
        ( p_aRequestno NUMBER,p_aQuantity  NUMBER,
          p_aProjectNo NUMBER,p_aUnit VARCHAR2,
          p_anEstimatedcost NUMBER,p_anActualcost NUMBER,
          p_aDescription VARCHAR2 ) AS LANGUAGE JAVA
           NAME 'PIManager.addLineItem(int,int,int,java.lang.String,
                            float,float,java.lang.String)';
END PI_Actions;
/
```

Step 7   Load the PL/SQL wrapper into the server.

```
-- IN SQLPLUS or server manager
@PI_Actions.sql
```

Step 8   Test your SQLJ stored procedure.

```
// In SQLPLUS
BEGIN
PI_Actions.add_Line_Item(501,300,30,'04',15000,8500,'OracleSupport');
END;
/
```

The following SQLJ client applet will call a SQLJ stored procedure.

```
/***   Program Name:          SqljAppletCallsSqljSP.sqlj */

// Import the JDBC classes
import java.sql.*;

// Import the java classes used in applets
import java.awt.*;
import java.io.*;
import java.util.*;

// SQLJ-specific classes
import java.sql.SQLException;
import java.sql.DriverManager;
import sqlj.runtime.ExecutionContext;
import sqlj.runtime.ref.DefaultContext;
import oracle.jdbc.driver.OracleDriver;
import oracle.sqlj.runtime.Oracle;

// Import the Java Utility class
import ConnectionManager;
```

```
public class SqljAppletCallsSqljSP extends java.applet.Applet {

  // The button to call the SQLJ addLineItem() method
  Button execute_button;

  // The place where to dump the applet actions
  TextArea output;

  // Create the User Interface
  public void init ()  {

    this.setLayout (new BorderLayout ());
    Panel p = new Panel ();
    p.setLayout (new FlowLayout (FlowLayout.LEFT));
    execute_button = new Button ("Insert Line_Item");
    p.add (execute_button);
    this.add ("North", p);
    output = new TextArea (10, 60);
    this.add ("Center", output);
  }  // End of init()

  public boolean action (Event ev, Object arg)  {
    if (ev.target == execute_button){

      // Clear the output area
       output.setText (null);

     // Connect to the database    (See Note 1.)
     DefaultContext sqljProcCtx = ConnectionManager.initContext();
      // Stop program execution if we cannot connect to the database
     if  (sqljProcCtx == null ) {
           System.out.println("I cannot connect to the database "
                            + "-- Stop Execution.");
           System.exit(1);
    } // end if
     // Create an execution context instance (See Note 2.)
     ExecutionContext sqljProcExecCtx = new ExecutionContext();

      output.appendText ("Connecting to database using SQLJ " + "\n");

      // Set Host Variables
      int aRequestno = 501;
      int aProjectNo = 300;
      int aQuantity = 30;
      String aUnit = "04";
      double anEstimatedcost = 15000;
      double anActualcost = 8500;
```

```
    String aDescription = "Oracle-Support";

    try {
        // Call the SQLJ method from the SQLJ applet
            #sql [sqljProcCtx,sqljProcExecCtx]     // (See Note 3.)
                { CALL PI_Actions.add_Line_Item
                    ( :IN aRequestno, :IN aQuantity,
                        :IN aProjectNo, :IN aUnit, :IN anEstimatedcost,
                        :IN anActualcost, :IN aDescription
                    )
                };
            output.appendText (" Record has been inserted " +
                                    "- SUCCESS \n");
    }  // end try
    catch (SQLException ex) {
            output.appendText ("Error calling the SQLJ"
                    + " addLineItem() method : " + ex + "\n");
            String sqlMessage = ex.getMessage();
            output.appendText ("SQL Message: " +
                    sqlMessage + "\n");
    }  // end catch

  }  // End of if

  output.appendText ("Work completed \n");
  return true;

  }    // End of action() method

}    // End of SqljAppletCallsSqljSP class
```

Notes on `SqljAppletCallsSqljSP.sqlj` applet:

This SQLJ applet inserts a record in the `LINEITEM_LIST` table via a SQLJ stored procedure in the Oracle8*i* data server.

1. This statement creates an instance of the `DefaultContext` class by calling the `initContext()` method from the Java utility class `ConnectionManager`. Remember that the Oracle JDBC KPRB server-side driver does not support auto-commit. Therefore, you must establish a database connection in your client program prior to calling the SQLJ stored procedure.

2. This statement creates an instance of the `ExecutionContext` class. You should always associate an explicit execution context instance to your SQLJ clause when you create your applet. You wish to be in control of what the

program is executing at the location specified in your connection context instance. More importantly, you may have several applets running and executing concurrently in the browser.

3. This statement calls the SQLJ stored procedure that inserts a record in the `LINEITEM_LIST` table.

In this chapter, you used a "pure" relational database, the financial `PurchaseOrder` schema to implement some of the most advanced SQLJ concepts. You learned the following:

- How to manage single and multiple database connections via instances of the SQLJ `DefaultContext` and of user-defined SQLJ declared `ConnectionContext` class.

- How to design complex SQLJ programs.

- How to deploy SQLJ in several scenarios: SQLJ in applications, SQLJ in Java applications and Java applets, SQLJ in stored procedures, SQLJ in applets, and SQLJ methods and stored procedure embedded in SQLJ applications and SQLJ applets.

In Chapter 6, you will learn how to use SQLJ stream classes to transport information to and from the Oracle8*i* database, the interaction between JDBC and SQLJ, and how to convert JDBC result sets to SQLJ iterators and vice versa.

CHAPTER
6

Advanced SQLJ Features

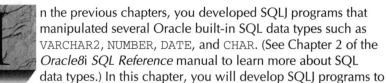

n the previous chapters, you developed SQLJ programs that manipulated several Oracle built-in SQL data types such as VARCHAR2, NUMBER, DATE, and CHAR. (See Chapter 2 of the *Oracle8*i *SQL Reference* manual to learn more about SQL data types.) In this chapter, you will develop SQLJ programs to manipulate additional data types such as LONG, LONG RAW, BLOB, CLOB, and BFILE. SQLJ provides classes that allow you to store and retrieve objects in the database where the data can be ASCII, Unicode, or binary. Additionally, you will create a multi-threaded SQLJ application, that is, a program that executes multiple tasks simultaneously and a SQLJ program that demonstrates the interactions between SQLJ and JDBC constructs. While developing these programs, you will learn the following:

- How to use SQLJ stream classes.

- How to manipulate Large Objects (LOBs) in SQLJ.

- How to create multi-threaded SQLJ programs.

- The interactions between SQLJ and JDBC.

SQLJ Streams

Most programming languages provide the mechanism to bring information from an external source or send information to an external destination. This information can be an object, a sequence of characters, a picture, sound, video, or database objects, and may reside in a file on disk, somewhere on the network, in memory, or in another program. Java provides stream classes as one of its mechanism for moving data. Java programs use input streams for receiving information from external sources and output streams for moving information to external sources. A stream is a sequence of bytes and a byte refers to eight contiguous bits starting on any addressable boundary. A bit or binary digit is the basic unit of computing.

The java.io package provides a collection of stream classes that are divided into two class hierarchies: Character streams and Byte streams. Character streams provide the API to read and write any character in the Unicode character set, whereas Byte streams provide the API to read and write 8-bit bytes of information. The Reader and Writer classes are part of the Character streams used for reading and writing character-based data. The InputStream and OutputStream classes are part of the Byte streams used for reading and writing bytes. They are typically used to read and write binary data such as images and sounds. To learn more about Java streams, see *Java I/O* [22] and the Web site at http://java.sun.com/docs/books/tutorial/essential/io/index.html.

The sqlj.runtime SQLJ package provides stream classes, which are subclasses of the java.io.InputStream class. They can be used to send and receive data from the database:

- The `BinaryStream` class is typically used to process binary files such as graphics, sounds, or documents. You will typically use this class with the `LONG RAW` Oracle data type, but you can also use it with the `RAW` data type.

- The `AsciiStream` class is used to process the ASCII character set, which is represented as ISO-Latin-1 encoding. You will typically use this class for the `LONG` Oracle data type, but you can also use it for the `VARCHAR2` Oracle data type.

- The `UnicodeStream` class is used to process the Unicode character set. Use this class with the `LONG` and the `VARCHAR2` Oracle data types. Note that Unicode is a 2-byte character set capable of having 65,536 possible characters. See http://www.unicode.org for further information on Unicode.

NOTE
Oracle Corporation recommends that you use the Large Object (LOB) data types instead of the `LONG` and `LONG RAW` data types when you wish to store large data in the Oracle8 database. The "LOB— Large Object" section of this chapter introduces the SQLJ-supported LOB classes that include the `BLOB`, `CLOB`, and `BFILE` Oracle data types.

The supported SQLJ stream classes serve as wrappers to provide communication with your application and the database. You can use the classes as iterator columns to receive data from the database or as host variables to send data to the database. The SQLJ stream classes allow you to decompose large pieces of data into small and more manageable chunks, thereby getting better performance when information is transported to and from the database.

Sending Data to the Database with Streams

You can use instances of any of the SQLJ stream classes to transport data to the database, following these steps:

1. Determine the length of the data that you wish to send to the database. For example:

```
// Create an object of type java.io.File
File aFile = new File ("anAsciiFile.txt");
// Get and store the file length into an int variable
int length = (int)aFile.length();
```

2. Create an instance of the `java.io.InputStream` or one of its subclasses:

```
FileInputStream aFileInputStream = new FileInputStream(aFile);
```

3. Create an instance of one of the SQLJ stream classes:

```
AsciiStream anAsciiStream = new AsciiStream(aFileInputStream,
length);
```

4. Use an instance of a SQLJ stream class as a host variable in a SQLJ executable statement:

```
#sql { INSERT INTO LONG_STREAM_TABLE (Filename, StreamData)
        VALUES (:fileName, :anAsciiStream) };
```

5. Close the stream objects of Steps 2 and 3:

```
anAsciiStream.close();
aFileInputStream.close();
```

In the following section, you will develop a SQLJ application to store two ASCII files into the Oracle8 data server.

Storing Files into the Database

You can use SQLJ streams to store ASCII, Unicode, and binary files in a database. The type of file you want to store in the database will determine the type of stream class you should use. Use the LONG data type to store an ASCII or Unicode data file into a table in the database, and use the LONG RAW data type to store a binary file.

The following `AsciiStreamInsert` SQLJ application creates the LONG_STREAM_TABLE table. However, if the table exists, the application deletes the table before re-creating it. The table consists of two columns that are used to store the filename and the contents of the file, respectively. The application reads in ASCII files and stores the data in the database. Here is the listing of the program:

```
/* Program Name: AsciiStreamInsert.sqlj
**
** Purpose: A SQLJ application that will create a table named
** LONG_STREAM_TABLE for storing ASCII files. The program uses
** the SQLJ AsciiStream class to store ASCII files.
 */

// Import class for I/O operations
import java.io.*;

// Import required classes for SQLJ programs and database operations
import java.sql.*;
import oracle.sqlj.runtime.*;
```

```
import sqlj.runtime.*;

public class AsciiStreamInsert {

  public static void  main(String args[])  {
    AsciiStreamInsert streamApp = new AsciiStreamInsert();
    streamApp.connectDB();
    streamApp.createStreamTable();

    // Insert two ASCII files in the database
    // (See Note 1.)
streamApp.insertAsciiStream("AsciiStreamInsert.sqlj");
    streamApp.insertAsciiStream("connect.properties");
  } // End of main

  // Method to connect to database.
  public void connectDB() {  // (See Note 2.)

    // Connect to the database using the connect.properties file.
    try { Oracle.connect(getClass(), "connect.properties"); }

    // Catch SQL exceptions error when connecting to database.
    catch (SQLException ex) {
      System.err.println( "Error connecting to database. " + ex );
      System.exit(1);  // Exit application
    } // End of catch block
  } // End of connectDB

  // Method to create the table for the stream
  public void createStreamTable() {  // (See Note 3.)

    // Delete LONG_STREAM_TABLE table if it already exists.
    try {
      #sql { DROP TABLE LONG_STREAM_TABLE };  // (See Note 4.)
    }
    catch (SQLException ex) {
     // Exception is raised if the table is not in the database.
     // Catch and ignore this exception and move to creating the table
     // to hold the streams.
    }
    // Create a table that will hold the filenames and the content
    try { // (See Note 5.)
      #sql { CREATE TABLE LONG_STREAM_TABLE(Filename  VARCHAR2 (56),
                       streamdata LONG) };
      System.out.println("Table LONG_STREAM_TABLE created.");
    }
```

```
    // Catch SQL exception error when creating the table
    catch (SQLException ex){
      System.err.println( "Could not Create table \n" + ex );
      System.exit(1);   // Exit application
    } // End of catch block
  } // End of createStreamTable method

  void insertAsciiStream(String fileName) {
    try {
      File aFile = new File (fileName);  // (See Note 6.)

    int length = (int)aFile.length();  // (See Note 7.)

      // Create an instance of the FileInputStream class
      // (See Note 8.)
      FileInputStream aFileInputStream = new FileInputStream(aFile);

      // Create stream object to use as host variable
      // (See Note 9.)
      AsciiStream anAsciiStream =
                      new AsciiStream(aFileInputStream, length);

     // (See Note 10.)
     #sql { INSERT INTO LONG_STREAM_TABLE (Filename, StreamData)
                    VALUES (:fileName, :anAsciiStream) };

      // Close stream AsciiStream and objects
      // (See Note 11.)
      anAsciiStream.close();
      aFileInputStream.close();

      #sql { COMMIT };  // Commit insert transaction to the database

      System.out.println("File: " + fileName + " has been inserted.");
    }
    catch (IOException ioe) {
      System.err.println("Error in reading " + fileName + "\n" + ioe);
      System.exit(1); // Exit application
    }
    catch (SQLException SQLe){
      System.err.println("Could not Insert into the table \n" + SQLe);
      System.exit(1);   // Exit application
    }  // End of try block
  }  // End of insertAsciiStream method

}  // End of AsciiStreamInsert application
```

Notes on the `AsciiStreamInsert` application:

1. Pass the names of the two ASCII files that you wish to store in the database as the input parameters of the `insertAsciiStream()` method. This method will insert into the database the `AsciiStreamInsert.sqlj` and `connect.properties` files, respectively.

2. Use the `connectDB()` method to establish a connection with the database. It uses the `Oracle.connect()` method with the `connect.properties` properties file. Remember from Chapters 3 and 5 that the properties file contains the JDBC driver, URL, listener port, Oracle SID, username, and user password parameters. If this method is not able to connect to the database, it will print an error and the application will stop executing.

3. Use the `createStreamTable()` method to create a table that will hold the filenames and the contents of the ASCII files. This method deletes the table if it already exists and creates a new table.

4. This statement deletes the `LONG_STREAM_TABLE` table from the database if it exists.

5. This statement creates the `LONG_STREAM_TABLE` table. The table uses the `VARCHAR2` SQL data type to store the filename and the `LONG` SQL data type to store the contents of the ASCII files. Note that this table is also capable of storing Unicode files.

6. This statement declares and creates a `java.io.File` object file handler that specifies the name of the file that you wish to store in the database.

7. This statement casts (that is, converts a data type to another) the length of the file returned by the `aFile.length()` method from a **long** to an **int** and then assigns the length to the length variable. The `aFile.length()` method returns a **long** value that you need to convert to an integer because the `AsciiStream` constructor that you will use later to create a stream object requires an **int** for the file's length. Note that the Java **long** value may be greater than the value that an **int** variable can hold. If this happens, the integer will contain an erroneous value. To avoid this problem, you may wish to check the length of the file against the largest possible integer value, which is the `java.lang.Integer.MAX_VALUE` (2147483647).

8. This statement creates a `java.io.FileInputStream` object by passing a `java.io.File` object to the constructor of the `FileInputStream` class. This new object holds the contents of the file.

9. This statement creates an `AsciiStream` object that you will use to insert the file into the database. The constructor of the `AsciiStream` requires that you supply a `FileInputStream` object and the length of the file as an integer.

Note that you have to determine the type of file that you wish to store in the database. Choose a corresponding SQLJ stream class that matches the file type, and instantiate an appropriate object of the chosen class. For example, if the file is a Unicode file, you should instantiate a Unicode stream object. You can use one of the following constructors to create a SQLJ stream class object:

```
AsciiStream (InputStream in, int length);
UnicodeStream (InputStream in, int length);
BinaryStream (InputStream in, int length);
```

10. This statement inserts into the `LONG_STREAM_TABLE` table the name of the file and the file's content that you stored in the variables `filename` and `anAsciiStream`, respectively. Note that if the stream object is a `UnicodeStream` or an `AsciiStream` instance, you should insert it into a table whose column is of the `LONG` or `VARCHAR2` SQL data type. However, if the object is a `BinaryStream` instance, you should insert it into a `LONG RAW` or `RAW` column.

11. This statement and the one that follows it close the `AsciiStream` and the Java `FileInputStream` objects, respectively.

Next, you will learn how to retrieve data from the database using SQLJ stream classes.

Retrieving Data from the Database as Streams

SQLJ stream classes can be used to retrieve data from a database and populate a SQLJ named or positional iterators. (See Chapters 2 and 3 to learn more about SQLJ iterators.) Here is an example of a named iterator that uses the SQLJ `BinaryStream` class as an iterator column:

```
#sql iterator BinaryNamedIter (String filename,
                               BinaryStream streamdata);
```

The SQLJ stream classes allow you to retrieve different SQL data types from the database such as `LONG`, `LONG RAW`, `RAW`, and `VARCHAR2`. Remember that you can use the `AsciiStream` and `Unicode` classes to retrieve data for a `LONG` SQL data type column and the `BinaryStream` class for a `LONG RAW` data type column.

NOTE
Oracle8 and the Oracle JDBC drivers do not support the SQLJ clause SELECT INTO *statement with the SQLJ stream classes. Therefore, you must use an iterator.*

Use the following steps to retrieve data from the database using SQLJ stream classes:

1. Declare a SQLJ iterator whose column is a SQLJ stream class. Note that if the iterator is a positional iterator, you can only have one stream column and it must be the last column of the iterator declaration.

2. Create an instance of the SQLJ iterator as defined in Step 1 of this section.

3. Create an instance of a stream class that corresponds to your file type. You can use the object as follows:

   ■ As a host variable in the FETCH INTO clause to retrieve data from a positional iterator. For example:

   ```
   #sql { FETCH :aHostVariable INTO :aBinaryStream };
   ```

   ■ As a host variable that stores query results from a named iterator. In this scenario, however, the type of the holding variable does not need to be of a SQLJ stream class type. It can be the java.io.InputStream class or a subclass of it. For example:

   ```
   InputStream aBinaryStream;
   ```

4. Execute your query with a SQLJ execution statement that will populate the iterator from Step 2.

5. Process the iterator by reading the stream and processing (writing) it to a local stream. After you call the accessor method of the iterator to access the stream column, you must read and process it in the same order that the columns were selected. If you do not, you may lose data.

6. Use the close() method of the input stream instance to close the local instance variable. Close the object immediately after processing the stream. In other words, close the stream object each time you iterate through the loop.

7. Use the close() method of the SQLJ iterator to close the iterator.

In the following section, you will develop a SQLJ application that will retrieve a file from the Oracle data server.

Retrieving Stored Files from a Database

You can use SQLJ stream classes to retrieve ASCII, Unicode, and binary files from a database. Remember that in situations where you wish to transport information that resides in a file to or from a database, you need to determine the file type in order to choose the appropriate stream class in your program.

Next, you will create the `BinarySqljStream` SQLJ application to retrieve files stored as binaries in a database and use the steps from the "Retrieving Data from the Database as Streams" section of this chapter while developing the program.

Before you run the application, create the database table from SQL*Plus that stores the names and the contents of binary files. The following table contains a `VARCHAR2` column for the filename and a `LONG RAW` column for the binary file:

```
CREATE TABLE BIN_STREAM_TABLE(Filename    VARCHAR2 (32),
                              streamdata LONG RAW);
```

Here is the listing of the `BinarySqljStream` SQLJ application:

```
/* Program Name: BinarySqljStream.sqlj
**
** Purpose: An SQLJ application to retrieve data, in the form
** of binary files, from a database to the disk of the local system.
**
** Create a table with SQL*Plus with the following command:
** CREATE TABLE BIN_STREAM_TABLE(Filename VARCHAR2 (32),
**                               streamdata LONG RAW);
**
// Import class for I/O operations
import java.io.*;

// Import required classes for SQLJ programs and database operations
import java.sql.*;
import oracle.sqlj.runtime.*;
import sqlj.runtime.*;

public class BinarySqljStream {

  // Iterator for binary files from the database
  // (See Note 1.)
  #sql iterator BinaryNamedIter (String        filename,
                                 BinaryStream streamdata);

  public static void  main(String args[])  {
    BinarySqljStream aBinaryStreamApp = new BinarySqljStream();
    aBinaryStreamApp.connectDB();
```

```
    // (See Note 2.)
    // Insert binary file into the database.
    aBinaryStreamApp.insertBinaryStream("BinarySqljStream.class");

    // Insert this ASCII file into database as binary stream.
    aBinaryStreamApp.insertBinaryStream("connect.properties");

    // Retrieve all binary files from the database and save
    // them to disk. (See Note 3.)
    aBinaryStreamApp.retrieveBinFiles();
}

// Method to connect to database.
public void connectDB() {  // (See Note 4.)

    // Connect to the database using the connect.properties file.
    try {  Oracle.connect(getClass(), "connect.properties"); }

    // Catch SQL exceptions error when connecting to database.
    catch (SQLException ex) {
      System.err.println( "Error connecting to database. " + ex );
      System.exit(1);  // Exit application
    } // End of try block
} // End of connectDB

void insertBinaryStream(String filename) { // (See Note 5.)
    try {
      File aFile= new File (filename);
      int length = (int)aFile.length();

      // Create an input stream object from the File object
      FileInputStream aFileInputStream = new FileInputStream(aFile);

      // Create a stream object to use as a host variable
      BinaryStream aBinaryStream =
                      new BinaryStream(aFileInputStream, length);

      // Store the filename and the binary stream into the table
      #sql { INSERT INTO BIN_STREAM_TABLE (filename, streamdata)
                  VALUES (:filename, :aBinaryStream) };

      // Close the objects
      aBinaryStream.close();
      aFileInputStream.close();

      #sql { COMMIT };          //Commit insert to the database
    }
    catch (IOException ioe) {
```

```
      System.err.println("Error in reading " + filename + "\n" + ioe);
      System.exit(1);  // Exit application
    }
    catch (SQLException ex){
      System.err.println("Could not Insert into the table \n" + ex);
      System.exit(1);  // Exit application
    }  // End of try block
  } // End of insertBinaryStream

  void retrieveBinFiles() {
    try {
      BinaryNamedIter aBinaryNamedIter = null; // (See Note 6.)
      String fname;

      // Stream variable to hold the retrieved
      BinaryStream aBinaryStream; // (See Note 7.)

      // Populate the iterator with data from the database
      // (See Note 8.)
      #sql aBinaryNamedIter =
                { SELECT filename, StreamData FROM BIN_STREAM_TABLE};

      // Iterate though the named iterator (See Note 9.)
      while (aBinaryNamedIter.next()) {
        fname = aBinaryNamedIter.filename(); // Get the filename

        // Get the stream object from the database (See Note 10.)
        aBinaryStream = aBinaryNamedIter.streamdata();
        // Method to store the retrieved files from the database
        //(See Note 11.)
        saveStreamToFile(aBinaryStream, "binary-directory\\" + fname);

        // With each iteration close the local stream (See Note 12.)
        aBinaryStream.close();
        System.out.println("File " + fname + " has been saved.");
      }

      // Close the named iterator
      aBinaryNamedIter.close();  // (See Note 13.)
    }
    catch (IOException ioe) {
      System.err.println("I/O error: \n" + ioe);
      System.exit(1);  // Exit application
    }
    catch (SQLException ex){
      System.err.println("Could not retrieve \n" + ex);
      System.exit(1);  // Exit application
    } // End of try block
```

```
    } // End of retrieveBinFiles

    // Method to write an input stream to a file on the local system
    // (See Note 14.)
    public void saveStreamToFile(InputStream in, String filename)
                    throws IOException {

        // Create an output file to store the binary files retrieved
        // from the database
        FileOutputStream aFileOutputStream =
                        new FileOutputStream (filename);

        // Loop through stream, read stream and write the data a
        // character at a time to the output file (output stream).
        int ch;
        while ((ch = in.read ()) != -1)
          aFileOutputStream.write (ch);

        // Close the output file
        aFileOutputStream.close ();
    } // End of saveStreamToFile
} // End of BinarySqljStream application
```

Notes on the `BinarySqljStream` application:

   1. This statement declares the `BinaryNamedIter` named iterator whose
   columns contain the filename and contents of the file.

   2. These statements call the method to populate the database with the two
   files. The first file is the Java class file (bytecode) of the application and the
   second one is the `connect.properties` file, which is an ASCII file
   stored as a binary stream in the database. The steps to store a binary file are
   similar to those used to store ASCII and Unicode files. Review the steps
   from the "Storing Files in the Database" section of this chapter.

   3. This method invocation retrieves the files in the database and stores them
   on a local disk.

   4. Use the `connectDB()` method to establish a connection with the database.
   It uses the `Oracle.connect()` method with the `connect.properties`
   properties file.

   5. This method inserts files with the binary stream class into the `BIN_STREAM_`
   `TABLE` table of the database.

   6. This statement declares the `BinaryNamedIter` iterator variable that will
   be used to query the database.

7. This statement declares the stream variable `aBinaryStream` that receives the stream data from the iterator. Note that the declaration data type could have also been the `java.io.InputStream` class or any of its subclasses.

8. This statement queries the database and populates the iterator with the filenames and file's content.

9. Iterate through the iterator and process the stream data from the iterator.

10. This statement uses the `streamdata()` accessor method from the iterator and assigns the instance to the local stream variable specified in Note 7 of this section.

11. This method calls the `saveStreamToFile()` method, which writes the stream to a subdirectory on the local system disk.

12. The statement uses the `close()` method from the stream class to close the local stream instance. Note that it closes the instance after each iteration of the loop.

13. Use the `close()` method of the SQLJ iterator to close the iterator instance.

14. The `saveStreamToFile(...)` method takes a `String` and an `InputStream` object as its input parameters where the first parameter is the name of the file and the second is an input stream object. The method then uses this information to write the data from the stream to a file on the local system.

In the next section, you will learn how to store Large Objects in a database and retrieve them from the database using the Oracle LOB SQL data types.

LOBs—Large Objects

In the previous section, you learned how to use SQLJ stream classes to transport data to and from an Oracle database. Remember that the stream classes provide the mechanism to manipulate the LONG and the LONG RAW SQL data types. Therefore, they can be used with Oracle7 and Oracle8 because they support these data types. However, Oracle Corporation recommends in such cases that you use LOBs (Large Objects) with the Oracle8 data server.

The Oracle8 data server supports three types of LOB data types from the `oracle.sql` package:

■ The BLOB (binary LOB) data type is used to store raw data such as video clips.

- The CLOB (character LOB) data type is used to store single-byte fixed-width character data.

- The BFILE (binary file) data type is an external LOB that is used to store binary files outside of the database.

The CLOB and BLOB data types are called *internal LOBs* because they store their data in the database. The BFILE data type is called an *external LOB* because it stores its data in a file outside of the database.

LOBs provide several improvements over the LONG and LONG RAW data types such as:

- LOBs can store up to 4GB of data, whereas LONG and LONG RAW data types can only store up to 2GB of data.

- A table can have multiple LOB columns, whereas a table can only have one LONG or LONG RAW column.

- LOB data can be accessed incrementally and randomly, whereas LONG and LONG RAW data can only be accessed sequentially.

To manipulate LOBs from SQLJ, you can use either the routines of the DBMS_LOB package or one of the LOB classes from the oracle.sql package. Oracle recommends that you use the LOB classes from Java because they may provide better execution performance than the DBMS_LOB package. The oracle.sql package contains these LOB classes:

- oracle.sql.BLOB

- oracle.sql.CLOB

- oracle.sql.BFILE

See the *Oracle8i Application Developer's Guide—Large Objects (LOBs)* [41] to learn more about LOBs.

Loading Files into BLOB Columns

In this section, you will use the BLOB class from the oracle.sql package to store files into a BLOB column of a database. The steps are as follows:

1. Execute a SQLJ or a SQL statement that creates a table that contains a BLOB column:

```
CREATE TABLE LOBTABLE (blobfilename VARCHAR2 (32), blobdata BLOB);
```

2. Insert a record in the table and make the BLOB column non-null.

Before storing data into a BLOB column, you must first initialize it to make it non-null. If the column is not initialized, you will get an error message when you try to write to it. At initialization time, the database stores a *locator* in the table that points to the storage address of the *LOB's value*—that is, it points to where the actual data is stored. The locator is always stored in the row irrespective of the physical location of where the LOB may be stored. Note that you will need to retrieve the LOB's locator prior to inserting the LOB value.

One way to initialize the BLOB column is to use the EMPTY_BLOB() function, which creates a locator. The BLOB column will not have any data in it after this function is executed.

The following fragment code initializes a BLOB column to give it a location:

```
#sql { INSERT INTO LOBTABLE(blobfilename, blobdata )
            VALUES ('blob-image.jpg', EMPTY_BLOB()) };
```

Note that the physical location of the internal LOB's value depends on its size and is completely transparent to you. Oracle will insert the internal LOB in the row-column of the table if its size is less than or equal to 3964 bytes, or outside the row-column but in the database if it is greater than 3964 bytes.

3. In your SQLJ program, retrieve the LOB's value into a BLOB host variable:

```
BLOB aBLOB;
#sql { SELECT blobdata INTO :aBLOB FROM LOBTABLE
          WHERE blobfilename = 'blob-image.jpg' FOR UPDATE };
```

In order to store data into a BLOB column, you have to get the record locator of the BLOB. To do this, query the database with a SELECT INTO statement to retrieve the locator. This returns the locator to the host variable.

4. Create a File type object, aFile, that holds the contents of the binary file you wish to insert:

```
// Create an object of type File
File aFile = new File(filename);
```

Steps 4 and 5 of this section are similar to Steps 1 and 2 of the "Sending Data to the Database" section of this chapter. You may wish to review the previous section for clarity.

5. Create an instance of the `java.io.InputStream` or one of its subclasses of it:

```
FileInputStream aFileInputStream = new FileInputStream(aFile);
```

6. You will incrementally read chunks of data at a time from the file to store it into the database. So, use the `getChunkSize()` method of the `BLOB` class to determine an ideal chunk size (number of bytes) you should use to incrementally store data to the `BLOB`. You may choose and declare your own chunk size if you wish, but for better performance, Oracle recommends that you use the value returned by the `getChunkSize()` method or a whole-number multiple of that value. The following statement stores the value returned by the method into the `chunkSize` variable:

```
int chunkSize = aBLOB.getChunkSize();
```

7. Create a **byte** array to retrieve the `BLOB` in incremental chunks. The following fragment code creates a **byte** array using the `chunkSize` variable you created in the previous step:

```
byte[] buffer = new byte [chunkSize];
```

Note that you should use a `String` array to store `CLOB` data instead of a **byte** array.

8. Read the contents of the file into the `buffer[]` array and use the `putBytes()` method from the `oracle.sql.BLOB` class to store the file into the database. The following code fragment illustrates the process:

```
// create an int variable to hold the number of bytes read
int lenRead;
// Creates a variable to keep track of how many bytes read
long offset = 1;

// Read data from the file and write the data to the BLOB. A -1 is
// returned when EOF is read from the read() method
while (lenRead = aFileInputStream.read(buffer)) != -1) {
   if ( blobLength < offset)
     buffer = new byte[lenRead];
   aBLOB.putBytes(offset, buffer); // Write to the database
   offset += lenRead;
}
```

9. Close the stream object.

Next, you will learn how to retrieve a BLOB from the database, write its contents into a file, and store the file on a local system disk.

Retrieving Data from BLOB Columns and Writing It to Disk

The following SQLJ application, BlobApplication, uses the oracle.sql.BLOB class and its methods to store and retrieve a BLOB column from a database table. The program will insert three files into the BLOB column, then it retrieves them and writes the contents of the BLOB stored in the database as files on the local system disk. The listing of the program follows:

```
/* Program Name: BlobApplication.sqlj
**
** Purpose: An SQLJ application to store binary files into a BLOB
** column of the database. It will then retrieve and write the
** files from the database back to the disk of the local system.
**
*/

// Import class for I/O operations
import java.io.*;

// Import required classes for SQLJ programs and database operations
import java.sql.*;
import oracle.sql.*;
import oracle.sqlj.runtime.*;
import sqlj.runtime.*;

public class BlobApplication {

  // Named iterator that is used to retrieve BLOB objects (See Note 1.)
  #sql iterator NamedLOBIter (String blobfilename, BLOB blobdata);

  public static void  main(String args[])  {
    BlobApplication lobApp = new BlobApplication();

    lobApp.connectDB(); // Connect to the database

    // Load three files into the database (See Note 2.)
    lobApp.insertIntoLobTable("file1.jpg");
    lobApp.insertIntoLobTable("file2.jpg ");
    lobApp.insertIntoLobTable("file3.jpg ");

    // Now write the files back to your local system disk
```

```
      lobApp.SaveBlobTableToDisk(); // (See Note 3.)
} // End of main

public void connectDB() { // Connect to database (See Note 4.)

    // Connect to the database using the connect.properties file.
    try { Oracle.connect(getClass(), "connect.properties"); }

    // Catch SQL exceptions error when connecting to database.
    catch (SQLException ex) {
      System.out.println( "Error connecting to the database. " + ex );
      System.exit(1);  // Exit application
    } // End of catch block
} // End of connectDB

void insertIntoLobTable( String blobFilename ) {
  try {
      // Insert the filename and initialize the BLOB column to null.
      // During this process, Oracle will store a LOB locator for you.
      #sql { INSERT INTO LOBTABLE(blobfilename, blobdata)
      // (See Note 5.)
                 VALUES (:blobFilename, EMPTY_BLOB()) };

    // Method to insert the file into database
      insertBLOB(blobFilename);  // (See Note 6.)

      // Commit changes to the database (See Note 7.)
      #sql { COMMIT };
  }
  catch (SQLException ex){
      System.err.println( "Could not insert into the table \n" + ex );
      System.exit(1);  // Exit application
  } // End of catch block
} // End of insertIntoLobTable

void insertBLOB(String filename) throws SQLException {
  try {
      BLOB aBLOB;  // (See Note 8.)

      // Select the file to get the locator of the BLOB (See Note 9.)
      #sql { SELECT blobdata INTO :aBLOB FROM LOBTABLE WHERE
                  blobfilename = :filename FOR UPDATE};

      // File from the local disk (See Note 10.)
    File aFile = new File (filename);
    FileInputStream inStreamFile = new FileInputStream(aFile);
```

```
    int chunkSize = aBLOB.getChunkSize(); // (See Note 11.)

    // Buffer to hold chunk of data being read from the input stream
    byte[] buffer = new byte[chunkSize]; // (See Note 12.)

    int lenRead; // For the number of bytes read in (See Note 13.)
    long offset = 1; // To keep track of the # of bytes read (See Note 14.)

    // Read data from the file and write the data to the BLOB
    // (See Note 15.)
    while (lenRead = aFileInputStream.read(buffer)) != -1) {
      if ( blobLength < offset) buffer = new byte[lenRead];
      aBLOB.putBytes(offset, buffer); // Write to the database
      offset += lenRead;
    }

    // Close input file streams (See Note 16.)
    aFileInputStream.close();
  }
  catch (IOException e) {
    System.err.println("Error in reading " + filename + "\n" + e);
    System.exit(1); // Exit application
  } // End of catch block
} // End of insertBLOB

void saveBlobTableToDisk() {
  try {
    NamedLOBIter aNamedLOBIter = null; // Iterator for BLOB

      // Populate the iterator with the filename and BLOB data from
      // the database (See Note 17.)
    #sql  aNamedLOBIter =
        { SELECT blobfilename, blobdata FROM LOBTABLE };

      // Process the iterator by writing the BLOB data to disk
      while ( aNamedLOBIter.next())  // (See Note 18.)
        writeBlobToDisk(aNamedLOBIter.blobfilename(),
                        aNamedLOBIter.blobdata());
  }
  catch (SQLException ex){
    System.err.println( "Could not insert into table \n" + ex );
    System.exit(1); // Exit application
  } // End of catch block
} // End of saveBlobTableToDisk method

void writeBlobToDisk(String filename, BLOB readBlob)
```

```
                throws SQLException {
  try {
    File aFile = new File ("blob_" + filename); // (See Note 19.)
    FileOutputStream aFileOutputStream = new FileOutputStream(aFile);

    long blobLength = readBlob.length();

    int chunkSize = readBlob.getChunkSize();
    // Buffer to hold chunk of data being read from the input stream
    byte[] buffer = new byte [chunkSize];

    // Read data from the BLOB and save data out to a file
    // (See Note 20.)
    for (long pos = 1; pos < blobLength; pos += chunkSize) {
      chunkSize = readBlob.getBytes(pos, chunkSize, buffer);
      aFileOutputStream.write(buffer, 0, chunkSize);
    }

    aFileOutputStream.close(); // Close output file
  }
  catch (IOException e) {
    System.err.println("Error in writing " + filename + "\n" + e);
    System.exit(1);  // Exit application
  } // End of try-catch block
  } // End of writeBlobToDisk method
} // End of BlobApplication
```

Notes on the `BlobApplication` application:

1. This statement declares the `NamedLOBIter` named iterator whose columns are used for the filename and the contents of a binary file, respectively. Note that you can also use the `SELECT INTO` SQLJ clause for single-row queries on a table that contains LOBs columns.

2. This statement and the ones that follow it call the `insertIntoLobTable()` method to store the files into the database.

3. This statement calls the `saveBlobTableToDisk()` method to retrieve all files that are stored in the database and save their contents in files located on the local system disk.

4. This statement declares the `connectDB()` method to establish a connection with the database. It uses the `Oracle.connect()` method with the `connect.properties` properties file to do so. See Chapters 2 and 5 to learn more about SQLJ connections.

5. This statement uses a SQLJ executable statement to insert a filename and call the Oracle EMPTY_BLOB() function which initializes and creates a locator.

6. This statement calls the insertBLOB() method to store the files in the database.

7. This statement commits the changes in the database.

8. This statement declares a BLOB variable that is used to insert data into the database.

9. This statement uses the SELECT INTO clause to query the database to retrieve the BLOB's column locator. The FOR UPDATE clause will implicitly begin a transaction for you. However, you can omit the FOR UPDATE clause if you are already in a transaction. In this statement, you can optionally remove the clause since you are in a transaction. This is because you have not executed the COMMIT statement since your last insert operation.

10. This statement opens the file.

11. This statement gets the optimal chunk size from the database. Remember that the getChunkSize() method returns the chunk data size you should use to incrementally store the data in the database.

12. This statement creates a **byte**[] array that is used to hold the contents of the file and to transport the data to the database.

13. This statement creates an **int** variable that holds the number of bytes that were read from the file.

14. This statement creates a **long** variable that keeps track of the number of bytes that has been read.

15. The statement uses a **while** loop to read the file and to insert the data in the database.

16. This statement uses the close() method to close the input stream object.

17. This statement queries the database and populates the iterator with the filenames and the BLOB data.

18. This statement calls the writeBlobToDisk() method to write the database files into files located on the system disk.

19. Create a file with a blob_ prefix that will be used to store the data retrieved from the database.

20. The **while** loop iterates, reading chunks of data from the BLOB with the putBytes() method. This method reads chunkSize number of bytes into a byte array buffer, and returns the actual number of bytes read from the BLOB instance. The byte array buffer then writes its data to the output stream.

Using the DBMS_LOB Oracle Package with SQLJ

The DBMS_LOB package provides functions and procedures that allow you to manipulate LOBs. SQLJ executable statements can call these routines. In the previous section, you used the oracle.sql.BLOB class to manipulate BLOB columns; in this section, you will use the DBMS_LOB package to manipulate BLOB objects. However, remember that the LOB classes may provide better execution performance than the DBMS_LOB package.

For example, you can use the DBMS_LOB.WRITE procedure instead of the putBytes() method from the BLOB class to store BLOB data in the database. The following fragment code uses the **while** loop listed in the BlobApplication SQLJ application from the "Retrieving Data from BLOB Columns and Writing It to Disk" section of this chapter:

```
// while loop from the BlobApplication.sqlj file
while (lenRead = aFileInputStream.read(buffer)) != -1) {
    if ( blobLength < offset) buffer = new byte[lenRead];
    aBLOB.putBytes(offset, buffer); // Write to the database
    offset += lenRead;
}
```

The equivalent of the preceding code block using DBMS_LOB.WRITE is as follows:

```
// The DBMS_LOB.WRITE() is used in place of the aBLOB.putBytes().
while ( (lenRead = aFileInputStream.read(buffer)) != -1) {
    #sql { call DBMS_LOB.WRITE(:aBLOB, :lenRead, :offset, :buffer) };
    offset += lenRead;
}
```

The parameters of the DBMS_LOB.WRITE routine are as follows:

- aBLOB contains the locator for an internal LOB.

- lenRead is number of bytes to write or that was written.

- offset is the offset position of the BLOB to begin writing.

- buffer is an input **byte** array buffer that holds a chunk of BLOB data.

You can use the Oracle DBMS_LOB.READ routine to read data from the database instead of the getBytes() method of the BLOB class. The following code fragment uses the **for** loop from the `writeBlobToDisk()` method of the BlobApplication SQLJ application:

```
// for loop from the BlobApplication.sqlj using the getBytes method
for (long pos = 1; pos < blobLength; pos += chunkSize) {
        chunkSize = readBlob.getBytes(pos, chunkSize, buffer);
        aFileOutputStream.write(buffer, 0, chunkSize);
}
```

The preceding code block can be rewritten using the `DBMS_LOB.READ` prodecure as follows:

```
// readBlob.getBytes() has been replaced with the DBMS_LOB.READ
for (long pos = 1; pos < blobLength; pos += chunkSize) {
  #sql {  CALL
     DBMS_LOB.READ(:readBlob, :INOUT chunkSize, :pos, :buffer) };
  aFileOutputStream.write(buffer, 0, chunkSize);
}
```

Here is a list of input parameters to the `DBMS_LOB.READ` method:

■ `ReadBlob` is the locator for the LOB to be read.

■ `chunkSize` is the number of bytes to read or that were read.

■ `pos` is the offset in bytes from the begging of the LOB.

■ `buffer` is a **byte** array buffer to read in the data.

Using BFILE in SQLJ

In the previous sections, you learned how to manipulate the `BLOB` internal LOB SQL data type. Remember that the `CLOB` and `BLOB` are called internal LOBs because they store their data in the database. In this section, you will learn how to use the external BFILE LOB, which stores its data outside of the database. BFILE files are read-only files and are located on storage devices such as hard drive, CD-ROM, DVD, and so on. There is one restriction for storing files as BFILE, however: the files have to be a single drive and cannot be striped across multiple disks.

The `BFILE` class provides the mechanism to manipulate the `BFILE` SQL data type. One fundamental difference between internal and external LOBs is that the former can be stored in the database and the latter cannot. In this section, you will learn how to retrieve `BFILE`s on a system disk and store their contents into a `BLOB` column in the database. The steps to do this are as follows:

I. Create a table that contains a `BFILE` column:

```
CREATE TABLE BFILE_LOB_TABLE (catalog VARCHAR2(32), classfile BFILE);
```

Use the `catalog` column name to catalog the bytecode files stored in the `BFILE` column.

2. Use the SQL*Plus or any other tool of your choice to create a directory alias that points to the directory where the binary files are located (Listing 6-1):

Listing 6-1

```
CREATE or REPLACE DIRECTORY "apps" AS 'c:\app\sqlj\files';
```

The `CREATE DIRECTORY` statement specifies the fully qualified directory path. Oracle uses the alias `apps` as its directory name. The `c:\app\sqlj\files` specifies the directory path of where the files are kept. Use the appropriate directory path for the UNIX operating systems, such as `/home/app/sqlj/files`. Modify the path in Listing 6-1 to reflect the location of your file. Note that you must have the `CREATE ANY DIRECTORY` system privilege in order for you to issue a `CREATE DIRECTORY` command.

3. Insert a `BFILE` object (Listing 6-2) in the `BFILE_LOB_TABLE` table that you created in Step 1 of this section:

Listing 6-2

```
INSERT INTO BFILE_LOB_TABLE (catalog, classfile)
  VALUES ('bfile-1', BFILENAME('apps', 'BlobApplication.class'));
COMMIT;
```

As with the internal LOBs, you must initialize the `BFILE`'s column in order to get a LOB locator. To initialize the `BFILE` object, use the `BFILENAME` function (Listing 6-2) whose parameters are the directory alias (Listing 6-1) and the `BlobApplication.class` BFILE file.

Next, you will create the `copyBFILEToBlob()` method that will use the `BFILE` class to read a file on the system and insert it into the `BLOB` column of the `LOBTABLE` table that you created in the `BlobApplication` SQLJ application. You will also modify the application so that it can call the `copyBFILEToBlob()` method. Remember that you created the `BlobApplication` application in the "Retrieving Data from a `BLOB` Column and Writing It to Disk" section of this chapter.

The `copyBFILEToBlob()` method is similar to the `insertBLOB()` method of the `BlobApplication` program where the former uses the `getBytes` method from the `BFILE` class to read the system file and the latter uses the `FileInputStream` stream method from the LOB class. Here is the modified version of the `BlobApplication` SQLJ application that contains the new `copyBFILEToBlob()` method:

```
/* Program Name: BlobApplication.sqlj
**
...
```

```
public class BlobApplication {

  // Named iterator that is used to retrieve BLOB objects
  #sql iterator NamedLOBIter (String blobfilename, BLOB blobdata);

  public static void  main(String args[])  {
    BlobApplication lobApp = new BlobApplication();

    lobApp.connectDB(); // Connect to the database
    lobApp.copyBFILEToBlob("book-1.jpg");

    // Now write the files back to your local system disk
    lobApp.saveBlobTableToDisk();
} // End of main

  ...


void copyBFILEToBlob(String catalogName) {

    BLOB   aBLOB;   // Variable for the BLOB host variable
    BFILE  aBFILE; // BFILE variable for reading a file on the disk
    String filename;  // Variable for storing the retrieved BFILE

    try {
      // Select BFILE column from the database (See Note 1.)
      #sql { SELECT photo INTO :aBFILE FROM BFILE_LOB_TABLE
         WHERE catalog = :catalogName};

      // Test to see if the BFILE is open. If it is not, then open it.
      if (!aBFILE.isFileOpen()) // (See Note 2.)
        aBFILE.openFile();

      // Get the file name of the retrieved file
      filename = aBFILE.getName(); // (See Note 3.)

      // Create a record in the LOBTABLE. The contents of the BFILE
      // will be inserted into this record.
      #sql { INSERT INTO LOBTABLE(blobfilename, blobdata)
              VALUES (:filename, EMPTY_BLOB()) };

      #sql {COMMIT}; // Commit insert transaction

      // Select the file to get the locator of BLOB
      #sql { SELECT blobdata INTO :aBLOB FROM LOBTABLE WHERE
              blobfilename = :filename FOR UPDATE };
```

```
    int chunkSize = aBLOB.getChunkSize();

    // Buffer to hold chunk of data being read from the input stream
    byte[] buffer = new byte[chunkSize];

    int lenRead;

    // Get the length of the binary file
    long blobLength = aBFILE.length();

    // Loop to insert data from the BFILE into the BLOB
    // (See Note 4.)
    for (long offset = 1; offset< blobLength; offset += chunkSize){
      chunkSize = aBFILE.getBytes(offset, chunkSize, buffer);
      if ( blobLength < offset) buffer = new byte[chunkSize];
      aBLOB.putBytes(offset, buffer);
    }
  } // End of try block
  // Catch SQL exception errors.
  catch (SQLException ex){
    System.err.println( "Could not insert into the table \n" + ex );
    System.exit(1);  // Exit application
  } // End of catch block
  } // End of copyBFILEToBlob method
} // End of BlobApplication
```

Notes on the `copyBFILEToBlob` method:

1. This statement gets the locator of the `BFILE` object.

2. This statement uses the Oracle `isFileOpen()` function to check if the file is open.

3. This statement gets the filename of the locator of the `aBFILE` instance.

4. This statement uses a **for** loop to read the `BFILE` object and insert its contents in the `BLOB` column of the database. The first statement in the loop calls the `getbytes()` method to read the file and the `putBytes()` method to write the file in the database.

   In the previous chapters of this book and in the previous sections of this chapter, you created many SQLJ programs that performed several tasks sequentially, that is, one at a time. How can you perform several tasks simultaneously in a single SQLJ program? The following section answers this question.

Multi-threading

Java programs can be designed to perform several tasks simultaneously. For example, a Java program executing in a Web browser can play sounds, communicate with a database, and display images simultaneously. In this scenario, the program is performing multiple tasks, or *threads*, at the same time. The thread concept is a powerful feature of the Java language. A thread is a single sequential flow of execution within a program. The simultaneous processing of multiple threads in a single program is called *multi-threading*.

In situations where you wish to accomplish several tasks simultaneously such as data entry, retrieving data from the database, and so on, performance may be improved with the use of multi-threading. You could develop a multi-thread application where you would create a thread to execute each of the above tasks. The performance gain comes from the fact that the CPU is not idle and is constantly being used.

Multi-threading with SQLJ

You can develop SQLJ multi-threaded applications that perform several tasks simultaneously. You can create SQLJ client-side and server-side multi-threaded programs. SQLJ provides full support for multi-threading. You can use multi-threading in a SQLJ client-side program to gain *throughput* and performance. Throughput is the amount of data that is transferred or processed in a given amount of time. Although you can run multi-threaded applications in the Oracle8*i* JServer, you will not necessarily gain throughput performance as you would with client-side programs because SQLJ threads do not run simultaneously in the Oracle8*i* JServer but rather sequentially.

Multi-threading with Execution Contexts

Recall that a SQLJ operation is always, implicitly or explicitly, associated with an instance of the `sqlj.runtime.ExecutionContext` class. Also remember that an execution context provides a context in which SQL clauses are executed. You learned about execution and connection contexts in Chapter 5's "Relation of the Execution Context to the Connection Context in the SQLJ Executable Statement" section.

When you develop a SQLJ multi-threaded application, if you wish the threads to share the same connection context instance (that is, you connect to the database only once in the program), you must create multiple execution context instances. If you use the same execution context instance for several threads that are retrieving data, you run the risk of overwriting the results from one thread to another. Moreover, the results from one thread may be visible to other threads sharing the same execution context.

You can create different execution context instances in multi-threaded programs in two ways:

■ You can use different connection context instances with each thread where each connection context object implicitly has its own execution context instance. Moreover, the connection context instance allows a SQLJ program to establish a single connection or multiple connections to a single database server.

■ You can declare an execution context instance for each thread. Thus, each thread will have its own execution context instance. You can create an execution context instance with the getExecutionContext() method, which returns an ExecutionContext instance from a connection context instance.

The following code creates an ExecutionContext instance using the default connection context class:

```
String emp;

// Create an execution context instance from the default
// connection context
ExecutionContext anExecutionContext = new ExecutionContext();

// Use the previously declared execution context instance
#sql [anExecutionContext] { SELECT employee INTO :emp
                                FROM EMPLOYEE_LIST };
```

Alternatively, you can create an implicit execution context instance when you use a connection context instance:

```
EmployeeIterator empIter;

// Each thread will have its own default connection context class
dataiConnCtx = Oracle.getConnection
   ("jdbc:oracle:thin:@data-i.com:1521:ORCL","scott","tiger",false);

// Use the previously declared connection context instance
#sql [dataiConnCtx] empIter =
  { SELECT employee, employeeno FROM EMPLOYEE_LIST };
```

Multi-threading with SQLJ Application

It is not difficult to create threads in Java. One way to do this is to declare a subclass of the java.lang.Thread class. The subclass that you declared should override the run() method of Thread class. After overriding the run() method, you can then create and start an instance of the subclass that you created. When the instance is started, it will initially execute the `run()` method. The initial execution of the `run()` method is similar to the `main()` method of a Java or SQLJ application and the `init()` method of a Java or SQLJ applet. Here is an example of a SQLJ class that extends the Java `Thread` class:

```
public class MultithreadApp extends Thread {
  ...
  public void run() {
    // This method is executed when the thread is started.
    // Put the code that you want to multi-thread in this method.
    ...
  }
}
```

The following `MultithreadApp` SQLJ application is a multi-threaded program that queries the database and prints the employee data. It populates a named iterator with all the employee numbers, creates a `Thread` instance for each employee, and starts a thread for each instance. An explicit execution context instance is declared for each `Thread` instance. Here is the listing of the `MultithreadApp` application:

```
Program Name: MultithreadApp.sqlj
**
** Purpose: An SQLJ application that uses threads to print out
** the information of all employees of a schema.
*/

// Import required classes for SQLJ programs and database operations
import java.sql.SQLException;
import sqlj.runtime.ExecutionContext;
import sqlj.runtime.ref.DefaultContext;
import oracle.sqlj.runtime.Oracle;

public class MultithreadApp extends Thread { // (See Note 1.)

  // Iterator for retrieving employee's number to pass to each thread
  #sql iterator Employees (int employeeno);

  // Each thread will have its own employeeNo instance (See Note 2.)
  int employeeNo;

  //Constructor that establishes a connection to the database
  MultithreadApp() { // (See Note 3.)
    try {
      // set the default connection
      Oracle.connect(MultithreadApp.class, "connect.properties");
    }
```

```
  catch (SQLException e) {
     System.err.println("Error connecting to the database: " + e);
  }
}

// Constructor that assigns the employee number to the instance
// variable. (See Note 4.)
MultithreadApp(int employeeNo) {
  this.employeeNo = employeeNo;
}

public static void main (String args[]) { // (See Note 5.)
  MultithreadApp apps = new MultithreadApp();
  apps.processThreads();
} // End of main method

void processThreads()  {
  int numEmp;
  Employees empIter = null;

  try {
    // Get the number of employees in the database (See Note 6.)
    #sql { SELECT COUNT(employeeno) INTO :numEmp
             FROM EMPLOYEE_LIST };

    // Create an array of threads whose size is the # of employees
    Thread[] theThreads = new Thread[numEmp];

    // Get the employee numbers. Each thread will contain
    // an employee number instance. (See Note 7.)
    #sql empIter = { SELECT employeeno FROM EMPLOYEE_LIST };

    // Create a new thread for each employee record. (See Note 8.)
    for (int counter = 0; empIter.next(); counter++) {
     theThreads[counter] = new MultithreadApp(empIter.employeeno());
     theThreads[counter].start();
    }
  }
  catch (Exception e) {
    System.err.println("Error running the example: " + e);
  } // End of try-catch block
} // End of processThreads constructor

public void run() { //(See Note 9.)
  int deptNo;
  String firstName, lastName, pos;

  // This randomly delays each thread (See Note 10.)
  try {
```

```
    Thread.sleep((int)(Math.random() * 2000));
  } catch (InterruptedException e) {}

  try {
    // Create an explicit execution context instance from the
    // default connection context (See Note 11.)
    ExecutionContext anExecutionContext = new ExecutionContext();

    // Use the execution context instance with the thread
    // (See Note 12.)
    #sql [anExecutionContext] {
                  SELECT deptno, firstname, lastname, type
                    INTO :deptNo, :firstName, :lastName, :pos
                      FROM EMPLOYEE_LIST
                        WHERE employeeno = :employeeNo };

    // Print information retrieved from the database.
    System.out.println("Employee Number: " + employeeNo);
    System.out.println("Name: " + firstName + " " + lastName);
    System.out.println("Title: " + pos + "\n");
  }
  catch (SQLException ex) {
    System.err.println("Database Error \n" + ex);
  } // End of try-catch block
} // End of run method
}// End of MultithreadApp application
```

Notes on the `MultithreadApp` application:

1. This statement declares the `MultithreadApp` class as a subclass of the `Thread` class. This declaration allows you to create multiple instances of the `MultithreadApp` class as threads.

2. This statement declares an **int** variable to hold an employee number for each thread. This variable will be initialized when the thread is created.

3. This statement declares the `MultithreadApp()` default constructor to connect to the database. Note that it uses the `connect.properties` file. See Chapters 3 and 5 to learn more about connection context methods and the `connect.properties` file.

4. This statement declares the `MultithreadApp(int employeeNo)` parameterized constructor that is invoked each time a new thread is created. It assigns the value of the parameter `employeeNo` to the instance variable from Note 2.

5. This statement creates the `main()` method that calls the default constructor from Note 3 to establish a connection with the database and the `processThread()` method to create and execute the threads.

6. This statement gets the number of employee records in the database and assigns it to the `numEmp` host variable. The program will create threads based on this number.

7. This statement selects employee numbers from the `EMPLOYEE_LIST` table and stores the results in the `empIter` SQLJ iterator.

8. This statement uses a **for** loop to create a new `Thread` instance for each employee record and start the thread.

9. This statement declares the `run()` method. When a thread begins, it starts execution by invoking this method. This method is the starting point for threads the same way that the `main()` method is the starting point for applications.

10. This statement randomly delays the execution order of the threads. This is to ensure that the threads will not start their execution order sequentially but will execute their code at a random interval between zero and two seconds.

11. This statement creates an execution context instance for each thread.

12. This statement uses an explicit execution context instance. Remember that you must create an execution instance for each thread to avoid possible conflicts during execution.

Next, you will learn about the interoperability of SQLJ and JDBC.

Interoperability SQLJ and JDBC

Recall that SQLJ provides a static embedded SQL interface for Java, whereas JDBC provides a dynamic SQL interface (see Chapter 1). JDBC is the way to use dynamic SQL operations in Java programs when details of database objects are known only at runtime and SQLJ when they are known at compile time. Therefore, you will develop either a JDBC or a SQLJ program depending on the needs of the application. So what happens if the application requires that you construct concurrently dynamic and static SQL statements? This section answers that question.

SQLJ provides interoperability between SQLJ and JDBC—that is, static and dynamic SQL operations can reside in a single SQLJ program. SQLJ and JDBC interact two ways:

- Establishing a single or multiple connections to a database via JDBC and/or SQLJ connection objects.

- Casting JDBC result set objects into SQLJ iterator objects, that is, converting the former to the latter and vice versa.

Note that a good understanding of SQLJ connection contexts is a prerequisite for the subsequent sections of this chapter. See Chapter 5, particularly the "Using SQLJ Connection Context for Database Connections" section, and Appendix D. Next, you will learn how the SQLJ connection context interacts with the JDBC `Connection` class.

Converting a JDBC Connection to a SQLJ Connection

An investigation of the `ConnectionManager` class in the "Using the SQLJ `DefaultContext` Class" in Chapter 5 illustrates the interoperability between SQLJ connections and JDBC connections. The class converts a JDBC `Connection` object to a SQLJ `DefaultContext` object. The following shows a partial listing of the `ConnectionManager` class:

```
/*
** Class Name:     ConnectionManager.java
**
** Purpose:        This is a utility class that uses the
** same concepts, published in the ConnectionManager.class
** provided by Oracle Corporation to create a JDBC
** Connection and a SQLJ DefaultContext object using
** the values of its configuration attributes.
** Applications can use this class to establish a single
** database connection.
...
...
public class ConnectionManager {
  /*
    Set up database connection information. Set these for your
    JDBC driver, database and account. If you leave them set
    to null, any program using this class will not run.
  */
  static public String DRIVER = null ;   //JDBC Driver class
  static public String DBURL  = null ;   //Database URL
  static public String UID    = null ;   //User ID
  static public String PWD    = null ;   //Password
  ...
  ...
  static public Connection aNewConnection() { // (See Note 1.)
    Connection aConnection = null;
    //Verify that the access parameters are defined.
    if (UID== null || PWD==null || DBURL==null || DRIVER==null) {
      System.err.println (
           "Please edit the ConnectionManager.java " +
             "file to assign non-null values " +
```

```
                    "to the static string variables " +
                    "DBURL, DRIVER, UID, and PWD. " +
                     "Then recompile and try again." );
       System.exit(1);
     }
     try {
       Driver d = (Driver)(Class.forName( DRIVER ).newInstance());
       DriverManager.registerDriver(d);
     } // End of try
      catch (Exception e) {
       System.err.println( "Could not load driver: " + DRIVER );
       System.err.println(e);
       System.exit(1);
     } // End of catch
     try { // (See Note 2.)
       aConnection = DriverManager.getConnection (DBURL, UID, PWD);
     } // End of try
      catch (SQLException exception) {
       System.out.println("Error: could not get a connection");
       System.err.println(exception);
       System.exit(1);
     } // End of catch
     return aConnection; // (See Note 3.)
} // End of aNewConnection()
/**
   Returns the currently installed default context. If the current
   default context is null, a new default context instance is
   created and installed using a connection obtained from a call to
   getConnection.
**/

static public DefaultContext initContext() {
   // (See Note 4.)
   DefaultContext aDefaultContext =
          DefaultContext.getDefaultContext();
   if (aDefaultContext == null) {
     try {
          // (See Note 5.)
          aDefaultContext = new DefaultContext(aNewConnection());
     } // End of try
      catch (SQLException e) {
        System.out.println("Error: could not get a default context");
        System.err.println(e);
        System.exit(1);
     } // End of catch

     // (See Note 6.)
     DefaultContext.setDefaultContext(aDefaultContext);
   } // End of if
```

```
    // (See Note 7.)
    return aDefaultContext;
  }
}
```

Notes on the `ConnectionManager` class:

1. This statement creates the `aNewConnection()` method, which in
   turn creates and returns a new JDBC `Connection` object (from the
   `java.sql.Connection` class) using the current values of the `DRIVER`,
   `DBURL`, `UID`, and `PWD` attributes.

2. This statement instantiates the JDBC `Connection` object using the
   `getConnection()` method from the `java.sql.DriverManager` class.

3. This statement returns a JDBC `Connection` object to the method that
   called it.

4. This statement uses the `getDefaultContext()` method of the
   `DefaultContext` SQLJ class to get the default context and assigns
   it to the `aDefaultContext` variable. It will get the current default
   context if it exists.

5. This statement instantiates the `aDefaultContext` object by calling the
   parameterized constructor of the `DefaultContext` SQLJ classes and
   passing to the constructor a JDBC `Connection` object. In other words,
   a JDBC `Connection` object is converted to a SQLJ connection object.

6. This statement sets the connection context as the current default context.

7. This statement returns the SQLJ `DefaultContext` object.

Note that SQLJ programs establish a single connection or multiple connections
through an instance of the `sqlj.runtime.ref.DefaultContext` class, a
declared connection context class, or the `Oracle.connect()` method. You
learned in Chapter 5 that a declared connection context class implements the
`sqlj.runtime.ConnectionContext` class. The `getConnection()` methods
from both the `DefaultContext` and `ConnectionContext` classes return the
underlying JDBC connection object associated with the connection context instance.
That is, in both cases a JDBC `Connection` object is converted to an instance of a
SQLJ `DefaultContext` or `ConnectionContext` class. Remember also that you
can use the `connect()` method of the `oracle.sqlj.runtime.Oracle` class to
connect to a database that instantiates a `DefaultContext` object and implicitly
installs this instance as the default connection. Therefore, the method also returns an
underlying JDBC connection object.

Next, you will learn how to convert a SQLJ connection object to a JDBC object.

Converting a SQLJ Connection to a JDBC Connection

A JDBC `Connection` object is necessary if you wish to use SQL operations dynamically in your program. In this section, you will instantiate JDBC objects from SQLJ connection context objects. You can do so by using the `getConnection()` method of a SQLJ connection context class that gets the underlying SQLJ `Connection` object from the `DefaultContext` or `ConnectionContext` class and returns to your program a JDBC `Connection` object. You can get the JDBC object several ways (Listings 6-3, 6-4, and 6-5):

Listing 6-3

```
// Declare an instance of the DefaultContext class
// to connect to the database.
DefaultContext aDefaultContext = Oracle.getConnection(
        "jdbc:oracle:thin:@data-i.com:1521:ORCL","scott","tiger");

// Use the declared connection context to get the underlying
// Connection instance of the DefaultContext instance
Connection aConnection = aDefaultContext.getConnection();
```

Alternatively, you can get a `DefaultContext` instance with the `getDefaultContext()` method of the `DefaultContext` class and then get its underlying `Connection` instance with the `getConnection()` method:

Listing 6-4

```
Connection aConnection =
        DefaultContext.getDefaultContext().getConnection();
```

Declare a JDBC `Connection` instance while establishing a `DefaultContext` connection by calling the `getConnection()` method of the `Oracle.connect()` method:

Listing 6-5

```
Connection aConnection = Oracle.connect(
    getClass(), "connect.properties").getConnection();
```

Sharing and Closing Connections

When JDBC and SQLJ are interspersed in the same program, the JDBC `Connection` instance and the connection context instance share the same underlying database connection, they inherit properties from each other, and any change to one affects the other. More specifically:

- The JDBC `Connection` instance inherits all the properties of the connection context instance.

- The connection context instances inherit the properties of the JDBC `Connection` instance that was passed as a parameter to its constructor.

- If the state of the `Connection` instance changes, those changes affect the state of the connection context instance because they share the same connection session to the database. For instance, if the `rollback()` method from the `Connection` instance is invoked, any changes made from a previous commit or rollback will be dropped for both the `Connection` and the connection context instances.

- When you close the JDBC `Connection` instance with the `close()` method, you close both the JDBC connection and the SQLJ connection. The resources of the connection context are not freed until the JVM runs the garbage collector. You will get an error if you try to access the data server with the connection context since the underlying connection is closed.

- When you close a SQLJ connection with the `close()` method of the context instance, you close both the SQLJ connection and the JDBC connection.

- By default, connection context closes all shared connections when the `close()` method is invoked.

If you declare JDBC and SQLJ connections in your SQLJ program and they share the same connection, you can close the SQLJ connection without closing the JDBC connection. Recall the options of the `close()` method from the SQLJ connection classes:

```
close(boolean CLOSE_CONNECTION/KEEP_CONNECTION);
```

To keep the JDBC connection open, pass to the parameter of the close method the static **boolean** constant `KEEP_CONNECTION` from the `ConnectionContext` class. The connection context instance will close and release its resources while the JDBC `Connection` instance will not close until it is explicitly closed or the `finalizer()` Java method is used:

```
aDefaultContext.close(ConnectionContext.KEEP_CONNECTION);
```

You can explicitly close the connection object with the static **boolean** constant CLOSE_CONNECTION from the ConnectionContext class:

```
aDefaultContext.close(ConnectionContext.CLOSE_CONNECTION);
```

SQLJ Iterator and JDBC Result Set Interoperability

In this section, you will learn how to convert a JDBC ResultSet object to a SQLJ iterator object.

Converting SQLJ Iterators to JDBC Result Sets

You can develop a SQLJ program that contains static SQL operations (that is, SQLJ statements) that query a database by using iterators. You may wish to iterate the results via a JDBC ResultSet object versus a SQLJ iterator object with JDBC statements. You can use the getResultSet() method from a named or positional SQLJ iterator to get its underlying result set, thereby converting the SQLJ iterator to a JDBC result set. The following fragment code illustrates how to get the underlying result set:

```
// Declare a named SQLJ iterator
#sql iterator VendorIter (int vendorno, String name, String address);
...

VendorIter aVendorIter;
#sql aVendorIter = { SELECT vendorno, name, address FROM VENDOR_LIST };

// Convert the aVendorIter iterator object
// to the aVendorResultSet JDBC ResultSet
ResultSet aVendorResultSet = aVendorIter.getResultSet();

... (process the result set aVendorResultSet)

// close the iterator object and the result set instance
aVendorIter.close();
```

Rules for the result set after converting the iterator:

- Do not access the iterator before or after you get and process the result set. Only access the data through the result set.

- When you close the iterator instance, its underlying result set is also closed. You do not have to close the result set instance.

Casting JDBC Result Sets to SQLJ Iterators

Recall that casting one object to another in effect converts that object type to another. Use the **CAST** operator in a SQLJ executable clause to populate a named or positional iterator from a JDBC ResultSet object. The **CAST** instance must be a ResultSet object:

```
// Declare a SQLJ iterator object
#sql iterator aPositionalIterator (int, String,  String);
...

// A user-defined getMyResultSet() method that returns a ResultSet
// object. See the listing of the JdbcUsingSqljApp for the
// method's contents.
ResultSet aResultSetInstance = getMyResultSet();

// Convert the result set to a positional iterator. The result
// column must match the number and types of the iterator column.
#sql aPositionalIterator = { CAST :aResultSetInstance };
```

Rules for converting iterators to get a result set instance:

- The result set must have the *same* number of columns as the positional iterator columns, and its column types must match the column types of the iterator.

- The result set must have at *least* the same number of columns as the named iterator, and column types must match the column types of the iterator.

- The instance that is being converted must be a java.sql.ResultSet instance.

- When you use the **CAST** operator, the receiving iterator must be declared **public**.

  ```
  #sql public static iterator Employees (int , String , String );
  ```

- Do not access the result set before or after you get and process the iterator. Access the data only through the iterator.

- When you close the iterator instance, the underlying result set is also closed. Therefore, you do not have to close the result set instance. If you do, the iterator will not be closed.

The following `JdbcUsingSqljApp` SQLJ application queries the database with a JDBC `Connection` instance. The results of the query are stored in a `ResultSet` instance. That `ResultSet` instance is converted with the **CAST** operator to a named iterator. Then the iterator's columns are processed and printed:

```
* Program Name: JdbcUsingSqljApp.sqlj
**
** Purpose: An application that gets a Connection instance from the
** DefaultContext connection. The Connection instance is used to
** query and get a JDBC result set. The result set is then cast to
** a named iterator that it printed.
*/

// Import required classes for SQLJ programs and database operations
import java.sql.*; (See Note 1.)
import oracle.sqlj.runtime.Oracle;
import sqlj.runtime.ref.DefaultContext;

public class JdbcUsingSqljApp {

  // Named iterator used to retrieve the department information
  // (See Note 2.)
  #sql public static iterator DepartmentIter
        (int deptno, String shortname, String longname);

  public static void  main(String args[])  {

    JdbcUsingSqljApp JdbcSqljApp= new JdbcUsingSqljApp();
    JdbcSqljApp.runApplication(); // This method begins the program

  } // End of main


  public void runApplication() {
    try {
      // Establish database connection and retrieve a JDBC Connection
      // instance (See Note 3.)
      Connection aConnection = connectDB();

      // (See Note 4.)
      ResultSet aResultset = getResultSetFromDatabase(aConnection);
      // (See Note 5.)
      processResultSetAsIterator(aResultset);
    }
```

```
    catch (SQLException ex) {
      System.err.println( ex );
      System.exit(1);  // Exit application
    }
  } // End of runApplication method

  // Method to connect to database
  Connection connectDB() throws SQLException {

    // Connect to the database using the connect.properties file
    Oracle.connect(getClass(), "connect.properties");

    // Return the Connection instance from the DefaultContext instance
    // (See Note 6.)
    return DefaultContext.getDefaultContext().getConnection();

  } // End of connectDB

  ResultSet getResultSetFromDatabase(Connection aConnection)
                      throws SQLException{

    // Create Statement Object (See Note 7.)
    Statement aStatement = aConnection.createStatement();

    // Query the DEPARTMENT_LIST table (See Note 8.)
    return aStatement.executeQuery("SELECT * FROM DEPARTMENT_LIST");

  } // End of getResultSetFromDatabase method

  void processResultSetAsIterator(ResultSet aResultSet)
                                      throws SQLException {
    DepartmentIter aDepartmentIter;

    // Use the CAST operator to convert the result set to an Iterator
    // (See Note 9.)
    #sql aDepartmentIter = { CAST :aResultSet};

    // Process the iterator by printing out its value
    while(aDepartmentIter.next()){
      System.out.println( aDepartmentIter.deptno() + "   " +
                          aDepartmentIter.shortname() + "   " +
                          aDepartmentIter.longname());
    }

    // Close iterator. It will also close the result set object
    // (See Note 10.)
    aDepartmentIter.close();
```

```
    } // End of processResultSetAsIterator method
} // End of JdbcUsingSqljApp application
```

Notes on the `JdbcUsingSqljApp` application:

1. Import the `java.sql` package (JDBC API). This package provides the classes, libraries, and interfaces for accessing and writing Java applications that connect to databases.

2. Declare a named iterator that will be used to store the converted JDBC `ResultSet` objects. Remember that the iterator must be declared **public**.

3. The method `connectDB()` connects to the database and creates a `java.sql.Connection` instance of the `DefaultContext` class. The instance is returned and is assigned to the `aConnection` variable.

4. This method queries the database and populates a result set using the supplied JDBC `Connection` parameter. The `ResultSet` instance is returned and assigned to the `aResultSet` variable.

5. This method uses the result set from Note 4 to convert the result set to an iterator instance. Then the method prints out the data of the iterator.

6. This statement gets the default connection context using the `DefaultContext.getDefaultContext()` method that gets the underlying `Connection` with the `getConnection()` method that returns a `Connection` instance. This method returns a `ResultSet` instance.

7. The JDBC `Statement` class is responsible for sending dynamic SQL statements to the database. It has methods to update and query the database. Using the `Connection` instance of the parameter of the method, you create a `Statement` object with the `createStatement()` from the `Connection` instance. See Appendix C to learn more about JDBC.

8. This method uses the `Statement` object of Note 7 to execute the dynamic SQL statement with the `executeQuery()` method. The method returns a `ResultSet` object that you will cast into an iterator.

9. This statement uses the **CAST** operator to convert the `aResultSet` JDBC `ResultSet` object to the `aDepartmentIter` SQLJ iterator object. The **CAST** operator binds the result set into the SQLJ executable statement. The `aDepartmentIter` named iterator instance is populated with the contents of the `aResultSet` object.

10. This statement closes the iterator object and the result set object.

In this chapter, you learned the following:

■ How to manipulate some of Oracle's data types such as the LONG, LONG RAW, BLOB, CLOB, and BFILE data types by using the SQLJ streams classes, LOB classes, and the Oracle DBMS_LOB package.

■ How to insert ASCII, Unicode, and binary files into the Oracle database.

■ How to convert SQLJ connection context objects to JDBC Connection objects and vice versa.

■ How to convert JDBC ResultSet objects to SQLJ iterator objects.

This chapter concludes Part II. Chapter 7 marks the beginning of Part III, where you will learn how to use an object-relational database, the scientific Observation schema, to implement SQLJ programs that access objects in the Oracle8*i* data server.

PART
III

SQLJ and Object Deployment

CHAPTER
7

Object-Relational
Processing Using SQLJ

ne of the major accomplishments of modern programming language technology is the emergence of object-oriented programming features. An object-oriented programming language must support:

- **Composite data types**   The nesting of arrays, records, sets, etc.

- **User-defined abstract data types**   Including in the data type definition both data and method members that can have the visibility levels of private or public, so as to separate the implementation of the data type from its use.

- **Inheritance**   The ability to derive a new data type from an old one, appropriately inheriting data and method members.

See *Java with Object-Oriented Programming and World Wide Web Applications* [62] for a discussion.

Advantages of these features include improved data modeling, extensibility, and code reuse. In the mid-1980s, some researchers started investigating the extension of object-oriented programming languages (such as SMALLTALK and C++) so as to support database features, for the purpose of gaining these advantages. Commercial versions of these systems, such as GEMSTONE and OBJECTSTORE, were available in the early 1990s. Notable features of these "pure object-oriented database systems" include the assignment of permanent object identifiers (OIDs) to records, and defining a relationship between two record types by including in one record type a field whose value is a set of OIDs for records in the other record type. The latter sets up a *containment hierarchy* (or a *has-a-set-of relationship*) between the two types of records. Containment hierarchies have the potential for providing a representation of relationships that is more convenient and efficient than the relational foreign key technique, especially where structures with large shared substructures are involved. However, pure object-oriented database systems have been criticized as being too low level, and not comparable in database power to a mature relational DBMS such as Oracle.

The new SQL standard, SQL-1999, which is expected to be approved in late 1999, augments SQL with appropriate object-oriented features. SQL-1999 provides an excellent basis for *object-relational* database systems—that is, systems that combine the power of a relational DBMS with the flexibility and extensibility of the object-oriented approach. These object-relational database systems provide the advantages of pure object-oriented database systems without suffering from their disadvantages. In this chapter, you will examine the object-relational structures of Oracle8*i*, which are based on structures specified in SQL-1999, as well as the techniques for processing these structures in SQLJ. In particular, you will consider

- Oracle8*i* SQL user-defined object types.

- Processing SQL object types in SQLJ.

- Oracle8*i* SQL user-defined collection types.

- Processing SQL collection types in SQLJ.

NOTE
Oracle does not yet support inheritance or visibility levels.

Oracle8*i* User-Defined SQL Object Types

Beginning with the release of Oracle8 in 1997, Oracle provided support for SQL-1999 structures known as *user-defined data types*. A user-defined data type is created by employing the SQL statements CREATE TYPE and CREATE TYPE BODY. With the CREATE TYPE statement, you define an *object type* or a *collection type*. An object type is analogous to a Java class. It contains data fields and methods, and can be used to implement abstract data types. A collection type is either a variable-length array (VARRAY) type or a NESTED TABLE type. The subject of the current section is the object type. In this section, you will learn how to code:

- CREATE TYPE and CREATE TYPE BODY statements for object types and CREATE TABLE statements for object tables.

- INSERT statements for object tables.

- SELECT and UPDATE statements for object tables.

Creating Object Types and Object Tables

In this section, you will learn how to implement object types and object tables. An object type is essentially a record type that can also include methods (that is, subprograms). These methods can be implemented in PL/SQL or Java. An object type can be used as the type of a table column, the type of a table row, or the type of a subprogram parameter or return value. Every instance of an object type in a table is assigned a unique OID. Any table that has an object type as its row type is called an *object table*. OIDs provide a way of referencing rows in an object table that is potentially more efficient and convenient than the foreign key technique.

You will now see examples of some type and object table definitions for an object-relational hurricane database that describes types of platforms where tropical weather observations are made, and that also describes the oceanic observations of those tropical weather sightings. These statements can be submitted to SQL*Plus for execution.

```
/*CREATE TYPE statement for object type declares data fields and
 methods for type.
*/
DREATE TYPE platform_type AS OBJECT
  ( key_id number(8), type varchar2(50), description varchar2(50) );
/

// Create object table.
CREATE TABLE PLATFORM_TYPE_LIST OF platform_type;

CREATE TYPE oceanic_observation AS OBJECT (
    latitude_deg               number(10,4),
    longitude_deg              number(10,4),
    windspeed_mps              number(10,4),
    adj_windspeed_mps          number(10,4),
    wind_direction_deg         number(6),
    pressure_mb                number(6),
    air_temperature_c          number(8,2),
    geohgt_m                   number(8,3),
    wind_gust_mps              number(10,4),
    friction_velocity          number(10,4),
    dew_temperature_c          number(8,2),
    wet_bulb_temperature_c     number(8,2),
    relative_humidity_perc     number(5,2),
    sea_temperature_c          number(8,2),
    sig_wave_hgt_m             number(8,3),
    avg_wave_period_s          number(8,3),
    mean_wave_dir_deg          number(10,4) );
/

// Create type that contains a method.
CREATE TYPE oceanic_observation_type AS OBJECT (
    obs_id        number(8),
    when_t        date,
    at_time       char(8),
    station_id    number(6),
    produced_id   number(8),
    produced_by   REF platform_type,
    obsobj        oceanic_observation,
    member function get_platform_type
      return platform_type,
    pragma restrict_references( get_platform_type, wnds, wnps ) );
/
/* You must restrict the method so that it doesn't suffer side
   effects.  The pragma (compiler directive) disallows the changing
   of database tables (wnds) and package variables (wnps).  The
```

```
     CREATE TYPE BODY statement will not compile without this pragma.
*/

/* CREATE TYPE BODY statement for a type implements methods that are
   declared in the CREATE TYPE statement for that type.
*/
CREATE TYPE BODY oceanic_observation_type AS
  member function get_platform_type is
    pt platform_type;
  begin
    /* Select the PLATFORM_TYPE_LIST record whose OID matches the OID
       in the produced_by field of the oceanic_observation_type instance.
    */
    /* VALUE(pt1) returns the object type record from the
       table.  * wildcard or list of platform_type fields
       would be incompatible with pt variable.
    */
    SELECT VALUE( pt1 ) INTO pt FROM PLATFORM_TYPE_LIST pt1
      WHERE REF( pt1 ) = produced_by;
    return pt;
  end;
end;
/

// Create object table.
CREATE TABLE OCEANIC_OBSERVATION_LIST
  OF oceanic_observation_type;
```

Note that:

- platform_type is an object type for the types of platforms on which the tropical weather observations are recorded. PLATFORM_TYPE_LIST is an object table, the rows of which are of the type platform_type, and which contains a row for each platform type in the database.

- oceanic_observation is an object type that consists of a field for each of the various measurements that could be taken for a tropical weather observation.

- oceanic_observation_type is an object type for the combination of an oceanic_observation and the platform_type for the platform on which the observation was made. oceanic_observation_type contains two fields that merit further discussion: produced_by, which is a reference to a platform_type record, and obsobj, which is a nested oceanic_observation record. In addition, the type contains a member function (method), get_platform_type.

- First, the `produced_by` field is discussed. `produced_by` is of type `REF` `platform_type`. Every object type has a `REF` type with which it is associated. The `REF` type is used to reference instances of the object type with which it is associated. The permissible values of a `REF` type field are OIDs of its associated object type instances. Thus, the value of the `produced_by` field must be an OID for a `platform_type` instance. A `REF` type can be used anyplace in a SQL statement that a SQL type can be used. Using the `produced_by` field, you can get from an `oceanic_observation_type` record to a `platform_type` record without doing a join operation. Depending on the implementation of OIDs, this technique could be more efficient than the join operation.

- The `obsobj` field represents a record of oceanic observations nested within the `oceanic_observation_type` record. An `oceanic_observation_type` record consists of data on where and when an observation was recorded, the OID of the type of platform on which the observation was recorded, and the actual observation itself. Both the platform type and the oceanic observation are represented by distinct records. The difference is that there is a separate table for the platform types, and `produced_by` will reference one of the records in that table, but there is not a separate table for the observations, so that `obsobj` is represented as a nesting of the observation within the `oceanic_observation_type` record. The justification for this difference is that many other `oceanic_observation_type` records share the same platform type, so that you don't want to repeat the `platform_type` within each of those records, but the oceanic observation data is unique to the `oceanic_observation_type` record, so that nesting won't cause any repetitions.

  It can be argued that the nested record representation is more natural than having the oceanic observation fields appear as top-level fields of the table, since in the nested representation those fields are cohesively grouped as a distinct object, just as they are in reality.

- The `CREATE TYPE` statement for the `oceanic_observation_type` declares a member method `get_platform_type` that is implemented in the `CREATE TYPE BODY` statement for `oceanic_observation_type`. `get_platform_type` is a function that returns the `platform_type` record that is referenced by the `oceanic_observation_type` instance on which the method was invoked. Just as in Java, the method for a SQL user-defined type will be invoked on an instance of that type by using the dot operator (`.`). The instance that the method is "dotted with" acts like an implicit parameter for the method, and fields of that instance can be referenced within the method body without using the dot notation. If you wish, you can write `self.produced_by` within the method, instead of just `produced_by`, where `self` refers to the instance on which that method was invoked. The built-in `REF` function, which is invoked within the body of `get_platform_type`, can be applied to any object type instance, and returns the OID of that instance. The `REF` function must be applied to an alias.

■ Finally, `OCEANIC_OBSERVATION_LIST` is an object table, the rows of which are of type `oceanic_observation_type`, and which contains a row for every observation in the database.

The following `SELECT` statement illustrates the invocation of the `get_platform_type` method on records from the `OCEANIC_OBSERVATION_LIST` table.

```
SELECT o.get_platform_type FROM OCEANIC_OBSERVATION_LIST o;
```

The `get_platform_type` method allows you to navigate from an `OCEANIC_OBSERVATION_LIST` record to a `platform_type` record without having to explicitly access the `REF produced_by` field—that is, the method serves to hide that `REF` field. Note that SQL object type methods are invoked using the dot notation, just as they are in Java, and that invocation must be done through an alias (`o` in this example).

INSERT Statements for Object Tables

The fields of the object table `PLATFORM_TYPE_LIST` are all of a simple type, so that you can insert records into `PLATFORM_TYPE_LIST` in a straightforward manner:

```
INSERT INTO PLATFORM_TYPE_LIST VALUES( 1056, 'SURFACE',
                                       'MOORED_BUOY_OCEANIC' );
```

However, the `OCEANIC_OBSERVATION_LIST` object table contains a nested record field and a `REF` field, and both require new techniques, as illustrated by the following `INSERT` statement:

```
INSERT INTO OCEANIC_OBSERVATION_LIST VALUES
   ( 2001, to_date( '11-DEC-1998', 'dd-mon-yyyy' ), 1212, 3000, 4000,
    ( SELECT REF( p ) FROM PLATFORM_TYPE_LIST p WHERE key_id = 1056 ),
       oceanic_observation( 25.928, 270.367, 6.6731, 6.6731, 60, 1070,
                            NULL, NULL, NULL, NULL, NULL, NULL,
                            NULL, NULL, NULL, NULL, NULL ) );
```

The OID of the desired `platform_type` record is obtained by a `SELECT` statement that invokes in its `select_list` the built-in `REF` function described earlier. The `REF` function, when applied to an alias for the `platform_type` table, returns the OID of the record selected by the `WHERE` clause. Recall that the `REF` function must always be invoked through an alias.

The nested `oceanic_observation` record is designated using the *constructor* for the `oceanic_observation` type. Every user-defined type in SQL has a method called a *constructor*, which is analogous to a Java constructor, and is used to construct an instance of that type. The constructor has the same name as the type, and, in the case of an object type, takes as its parameters the field values of the type instance being constructed. The constructor returns the instance that it has constructed.

Note that the date is created by invoking the `to_date` function, where the first parameter indicates a date, and the second parameter indicates the format of that date.

SELECT and UPDATE Statements for Object Tables

The following `SELECT` statement avoids `get_platform_type` method so as to illustrate the explicit dereferencing of `REF` fields using the `DEREF` operator.

```
/* Print the PLATFORM_TYPE_LIST record and obsobj record for
   observation 2001.
*/
SELECT obsobj, DEREF( produced_by ) FROM OCEANIC_OBSERVATION_LIST
  WHERE obs_id = 2001;
```

The built-in `DEREF` function, when applied to an expression of type `REF`, will return the record being referenced by that expression. The `DEREF` function is the inverse of the `REF` function.

The next `SELECT` statement illustrates the implicit dereferencing of `REF` fields, and the accessing of fields in nested records using the cascaded dot notation.

```
/* Print the air temperature in centigrade degrees for oceanic
   observations made with platform_type 1056.
*/
SELECT o.obsobj.air_temperature_c FROM OCEANIC_OBSERVATION_LIST o
  WHERE o.produced_by.key_id = 1056;
```

Note that when you dot a `REF` field with a field in the record being referenced by that `REF` field (here, `o.produced_by.key_id`), you will automatically dereference that `REF` field and get the value of the designated field in the record being referenced (here, `key_id`). However, you must go through an alias (such as

o) in order for this technique to work. Similarly, in order to access the fields in the nested `obsobj` record, you must go through an alias. Thus, the expressions `obsobj.air_temperature_c` and `produced_by.key_id` would be illegal in the `SELECT` statement, generating "Invalid column name" compilation errors. `DEREF(produced_by).key_id` would also be illegal. To retrieve a field in the record being referenced, as opposed to the entire record, you must use implicit dereferencing.

The last examples in this section illustrate the updating of object tables.

```
/* Change the degrees latitude to 105.2 in the
   OCEANIC_OBSERVATION_LIST record with obs_id 2001.
*/
UPDATE OCEANIC_OBSERVATION_LIST o SET o.obsobj.latitude_deg = 105.2
  WHERE o.obs_id = 2001;
```

Note again that the alias is required in order to access particular fields in the nested record.

```
/* Change the type field to balloon in the platform_type record
   referenced by the OCEANIC_OBSERVATION_LIST record with obs_id 2001.
*/
UPDATE PLATFORM_TYPE_LIST p SET type = 'balloon'
  WHERE REF( p ) =
    ( SELECT produced_by FROM OCEANIC_OBSERVATION_LIST
        WHERE obs_id = 2001 );
```

Observe that the following `UPDATE` statement would not work, because you are not allowed to update records through `REF`s to those records.

```
UPDATE OCEANIC_OBSERVATION_LIST o SET o.produced_by.type = 'balloon';
```

Processing SQL Object Types in SQLJ

In order to pass an object or collection between your Java code and your SQLJ statements using a host variable, result variable, or iterator attribute, you must have a Java class, which corresponds to the type of that object or collection, to use in the declaration of the host variable, result variable, or iterator attribute. The preferred way of implementing such a Java class is to have JPublisher generate it for you. These Java classes generated by JPublisher are called *Java custom classes*.

Another option is to use the generic `oracle.sql` classes: `oracle.sql.STRUCT` (for objects), `oracle.sql.REF` (for references), and `oracle.sql.ARRAY` (for collections). However, these classes do not provide the information SQLJ needs to perform strong type checking, and thus provides a less desirable option than the JPublisher-generated Java custom classes.

In this section, you will learn about:

- Creating Java custom classes for user-defined types using JPublisher.

- The Java custom class methods for SQL object types and reference types.

- `ObjectTypes.sqlj`: an example SQLJ program that processes tables containing user-defined SQL object types.

- SQLJ stored subprograms with SQL object type parameters and return values.

Using JPublisher to Create Java Custom Classes for User-Defined Types

You will first examine the JPublisher command line, and then the Java custom classes generated by JPublisher.

You can execute JPublisher on the operating system command line so as to create custom Java classes for the SQL user-defined types that are specified on the command line with the `-sql` option, and which belong to the schema indicated by the `-user` option. For each such specified object type, JPublisher will generate

- A `.java` source file that defines the Java custom class for that object type.

- A `.java` source file that defines the Java custom class for references to that object type.

- For each nested object (record) or collection of the top-level object type, a `.java` source file that defines the Java custom class for the type of that nested object or collection. This makes it unnecessary to explicitly create a custom class for such nested types (by placing the name of the type on the JPublisher command line), but you can do so if you wish.

For example, consider the following JPublisher command line for the object types that were created in the previous section "Creating Object Types and Object Tables."

 `jpub -sql=Platform_Type,Oceanic_Observation_Type -user=scott/tiger`

The execution of this command creates:

- A file named `PlatformType.java` that contains the definition of the Java custom class `PlatformType` for the `platform_type` SQL object type. In order to get a Java custom class that is named according to Java conventions, when you specify the SQL user-defined type on the command line you should capitalize the type name according to how you want the generated Java class name capitalized. That is why the *P* and *T* in Platform_Type were capitalized, even though Oracle SQL is not case sensitive. JPublisher interprets dollar signs ($), underscores (_), and characters that are illegal in Java identifiers as word separators, and they are discarded (that is, they are not inserted into the generated Java class name). However, keep in mind that some versions of JPublisher will not discard $ and _.

Note that if you want to explicitly specify the name for your generated .java file (and, therefore, also the name for your generated Java custom class), you follow the SQL user-defined type name with a colon (:) and the class name you are explicitly assigning:

```
jpub -sql=platform_type:PlatformType -user=scott/tiger
```

This explicit naming option offers a solution to the problem created by the inability of some JPublisher versions to strip the $ and _ from custom class names.

■ A file named PlatformTypeRef.java that contains the definition of the Java custom class PlatformTypeRef for the SQL type REF platform_type.

■ A file named OceanicObservationType.java that contains the definition of the Java custom class OceanicObservationType for the SQL object type oceanic_observation_type.

■ A file named OceanicObservationTypeRef.java that contains the definition of the Java custom class OceanicObservationTypeRef for the SQL type REF oceanic_observation_type.

■ A file named OceanicObservation.java that contains the definition of the Java custom class OceanicObservation for the type of the nested object obsobj of oceanic_observation_type. The default convention used by JPublisher for naming the custom class for a nested object is that specified for the option -case=mixed, as discussed next.

■ A file named OceanicObservationRef.java that contains the definition of the Java custom class OceanicObservationRef for the SQL type REF oceanicobservation.

Of course, each of the generated .java files must be compiled, either using javac or sqlj, in order to generate the corresponding .class files, so that the custom classes can be used in your SQLJ programs.

The -case option for the JPublisher command line allows you to specify how JPublisher uses case in the naming of its generated fields, methods, and classes for nested types.

- ■ -case=mixed (default) indicates that the first character of every word is uppercase except for the first character in a method (underscore (_), dollar sign ($), and characters that are illegal in Java identifiers are treated as word separators, and are discarded). All other characters are lowercase. Note that JPublisher will correctly strip underscores and dollar signs from the names of classes for nested types, fields, and methods, even if it doesn't do so for the class name of the top-level type.

- ■ -case=same indicates that the names should be the same as the SQL user-defined type.

- ■ -case=upper indicates that the names should be all uppercase.

- ■ -case=lower indicates that the names should be all lowercase.

You can use the -methods command-line option (which is a beta feature for release 8.1.5) to have JPublisher generate Java wrappers for the methods in your SQL object type. Such a Java wrapper allows you to invoke the method through an instance of the generated custom class. The default setting for -methods is false (don't generate wrappers). You set -methods=true to enable the generation of Java wrappers for all the methods in your object type. Under the -case=mixed option, the method names start with a lowercase letter, with each subsequent word starting with an uppercase letter.

For example, to generate a Java wrapper for the get_platform_type method in oceanic_observation_type you would enter

```
jpub -sql=oceanic_observation_type:OceanicObservationType
-user=scott/tiger -methods=true
```

This would cause JPublisher to generate the following method for the custom class: OceanicObservationType:

```
PlatformType getPlatformType()
```

When you have JPublisher generate Java method wrappers for your custom class, the custom class definition is placed in a .sqlj file, not a .java file, and you must use sqlj (not javac) to compile that file. If you have a SQLJ program that contains

```
OceanicObservationType oot;
PlatformType pt;
```

```
...
pt = oot.getPlatformType()
```

then `getPlatformType()` will appropriately invoke the `get_platform_type` SQL method so as to obtain the `PlatformType` custom class version of the `platform_type` record that is referenced by `oot`. See Example 6 in the subsequent program `ObjectTypes.sqlj` for sample code that invokes `getPlatformType()`.

By using the `-input` option on the `jpub` command line, you can specify a JPublisher input file that explicitly provides names for custom class fields and Java wrapper methods. For example, the following `jpub` command line specifies the file `newnames` as being the input file for its invocation of JPublisher:

```
jpub -user=scott/tiger -methods=true -input=newnames
```

The file `newnames` consists of a translation statement (in general, a JPublisher input file can contain one or more translation statements) that explicitly provides the custom class names `ObsObj` and `getPT`, respectively, for the `obsobj` field and the `get_platform_type` method:

```
sql oceanic_observation_type
   generate OceanicObservationType
      translate obsobj as ObsObj,
         get_platform_type as getPT
```

This translation statement indicates that for the SQL type `oceanic_observation_type`, a custom class called `OceanicObservationType` should be generated, such that the `obsobj` field will be referred to as `ObsObj` and the `get_platform_type` method will be referred to as `getPT` in the generated custom class.

Java Custom Class Methods for Object Types and Reference Types

The most useful generated methods are described in this section. For more information on generated methods, see Chapter 6 of the *Oracle8i SQLJ Developer's Guide and Reference* [63]. For each field of an object type, there will be an accessor (`get`) method and a mutator (`set`) method generated for the custom class that can be used to, respectively, retrieve and change the value of that field in a custom class instance. The most useful methods in a `REF` type custom class are the `getValue()` method that returns the database object that is being referenced, and the `setValue()` method that can be used to change the field values of the database object that is being referenced. `setValue()` changes the field values of the referenced database object so that they agree with the field values of the argument passed to `setValue()`.

For example, the following methods will be contained in the custom class `PlatformType`:

```
public java.math.BigDecimal getKeyId() throws SQLException,
public void setKeyId( java.math.BigDecimal x ) throws SQLException,
public String getDescription() throws SQLException,
public void setDescription( String x ) throws SQLException
```

Note that JPublisher treats all numeric fields as being of type `java.math.BigDecimal`.

The custom class `PlatformTypeRef` contains the following methods:

```
public PlatformType getValue() throws SQLException,
public void setValue( PlatformType x ) throws SQLException
```

Similar methods are generated for the `OceanicObservation`, `OceanicObservationREF`, `OceanicObservationType`, and the `OceanicObservationTypeRef` classes. The methods generated for the `OceanicObservationType` class include accessor and mutator methods for the nested object:

```
OceanicObservation getObsobj() throws SQLException
```

and

```
void OceanicObservation setObsobj( OceanicObservation x )
    throws SQLException
```

The program, `ObjectTypes.sqlj`, in the following section, illustrates the use of these Java custom class methods as well as situations where the processing of object types can be conveniently accomplished without the use of custom classes.

ObjectTypes.sqlj: An Example SQLJ Program That Processes Tables Containing User-Defined SQL Object Types

The following is an example of a SQLJ program that processes tables containing user-defined SQL object types.

```
/*
** Program Name:  ObjectTypes.sqlj
**
** Purpose:  Illustrate the processing of object tables, REF fields,
**           and nested records in SQLJ.
**
*/
// java.io contains BufferedReader and InputStreamReader classes.
import java.io.*;

// java.util contains StringTokenizer class.
import java.util.*;

// Required SQLException class for SQL errors.
import java.sql.SQLException;

/* oracle.sqlj.runtime.Oracle class contains connect() method for
   connecting to database.
*/
import oracle.sqlj.runtime.Oracle;

/* The PlatObs named iterator will be used to hold a set of records
   consisting of a platform_type record and an oceanic_observation
   record, which have been retrieved using the
   OCEANIC_OBSERVATION_LIST table.
*/
#sql iterator PlatObs( PlatformType plat, OceanicObservation obs );

// Define application class ObjectTypes.
class ObjectTypes {

  // BufferedReader class allows line-at-a-time input.
  private BufferedReader input;
  public static void main( String[] args ) {

    /* Invoke ObjectTypes constructor to connect to database, and to
       direct System.in to a BufferedReader stream.
    */
    ObjectTypes maincode = new ObjectTypes();

    /* The runObjectTypes() method invokes the different methods
       that execute the examples.
    */
    maincode.runObjectTypes();
  }
```

```
/* Initialize database connection, and direct System.in to a
   BufferedReader stream, within application class constructor.
*/
public ObjectTypes() {
  connectDB();
  openInput();
}
// Method to connect to database.
private void connectDB() {
  try {
    Oracle.connect( getClass(), "connect.properties" );
  }
  catch( SQLException e ) {
    System.err.println( "Error connecting to database. \n" + e );
    System.exit(1);
  }
}
/* Method to direct System.in to a character stream, and to direct
   that character stream to a BufferedReader stream.
*/
private void openInput() {
  input = new BufferedReader( new InputStreamReader( System.in ) );
}
// Method to set up a tokenized line of input.
// TokSequence class was presented in Chapter 2.
private TokSequence setupTokSequence() throws IOException {
  String line = input.readLine();
  StringTokenizer st = new StringTokenizer( line );
  TokSequence t = new TokSequence( st );
  return t;
}
// Method that invokes other methods to execute examples.
private void runObjectTypes() {

  /* Example 1 executes an INSERT statement that involves a
     reference field.
  */
  runExample1();

  /* Example 2 executes an UPDATE statement that involves a field
     from a nested record.
  */
  runExample2();

  /* Example 3 uses a SELECT INTO statement to illustrate Java
     custom classes.
  */
  runExample3();
```

```
   /* Example 4 illustrates the getValue() and setValue() methods of
      REF custom classes.
   */
   runExample4();

   /* Example 5 illustrates an iterator class that contains custom
      class attributes.
   */
   runExample5();

   /* Example 6 illustrates the invocation of an object type method
      on a custom class instance.
   */
   runExample6();
}

// SELECT INTO example that doesn't involve custom classes.
void runExample1() {
  try {
    // Get input for insertion.
    System.out.println
      ( "Please enter latitude and longitude separated by blanks " );
    TokSequence t = setupTokSequence();
    double latitude = t.getDouble();
    double longitude = t.getDouble();
    System.out.println( "Please enter observation id, date, time, " );
    System.out.println( "station id, producer id, key id, " );
    System.out.println( "and platform type separated by blanks");
    t = setupTokSequence();
    int obsid = t.getInt();
    String date = t.getString();
    String time = t.getString();
    int stationid = t.getInt();
    int producer = t.getInt();
    int keyid = t.getInt();

    /* Insert input into OCEANIC_OBSERVATION_LIST table.  This
       statement is merely a "stand-alone SQL" statement with
       host variables.
    */
    // Note that REF must be applied to an alias.
    #sql { INSERT INTO OCEANIC_OBSERVATION_LIST VALUES
            ( :obsid, to_date( :date, 'dd-mon-yyyy' ),
               :time, :stationid, :producer,
                ( SELECT REF( p ) FROM PLATFORM_TYPE_LIST p
                    WHERE key_id = :keyid ),
                    oceanic_observation( :latitude, :longitude,
                       NULL, NULL, NULL, NULL, NULL,
```

```
                            NULL, NULL, NULL, NULL, NULL,
                            NULL, NULL, NULL, NULL, NULL ) )
        };
    // Commit insert.
    #sql { COMMIT WORK };
  }
  // Catch exceptions.
  // Invoke error() method to print message and exit.
  catch( SQLException e ) { error( "SQL", 1 ); }
  catch( IOException e )  { error( "IO", 1 );  }
}

// Update example that doesn't involve custom classes.
void runExample2() {
  try {
    /* Input obs_id to identify OCEANIC_OBSERVATION_LIST
       record that is to be updated with a new latitude,
       which is also supplied as input.
    */
    System.out.println
      ( "Please enter observation id and latitude " +
        "separated by blanks " );
    TokSequence t = setupTokSequence();
    int obsid = t.getInt();
    double latitude = t.getDouble();
    /* Update indicated OCEANIC_OBSERVATION_LIST record with
       the supplied latitude.  This statement is merely a
       "stand-alone SQL" statement with host variables.
    */
    #sql { UPDATE OCEANIC_OBSERVATION_LIST o
             SET o.obsobj.latitude_deg = :latitude
               WHERE obs_id = :obsid
        };
    // Commit the update.
    #sql { COMMIT WORK };
  }
  // Catch exceptions.
  // Invoke error() method to print message and exit.
  catch( SQLException e ) { error( "SQL", 2 ); }
  catch( IOException e )  { error( "IO", 2 ); }
}

// The next example illustrates custom classes.
void runExample3() {
  try {
    /* Input obs_id that will identify OCEANIC_OBSERVATION_LIST
       record to be retrieved with a SELECT INTO statement.
    */
```

```
      System.out.println( "Please enter observation id " );
      TokSequence t = setupTokSequence();
      int obsid = t.getInt();
      /* Declare custom class instances for platform_type and
         oceanic_observation object types.
      */
      PlatformType pt;
      OceanicObservation oo;
      /* Select platform_type record that is referenced by, and
         oceanic_observation record that is contained in, the
         desired OCEANIC_OBSERVATION_LIST record.  Select these
         records into the custom class instances pt and oo.  The
         get_platform_type method is not used in this program so
         as to permit the illustration of explicit dereferencing.
      */
      #sql { SELECT DEREF( produced_by ), obsobj  INTO  :pt, :oo
                 FROM OCEANIC_OBSERVATION_LIST
                   WHERE obs_id = :obsid
             };
      /* Use accessor methods generated by JPublisher to get field
         values from custom class instances pt and oo.
      */
      // Print the obtained field values.
      System.out.println( "Key id = " + pt.getKeyId() );
      System.out.println( "Type = " + pt.getType() );
      System.out.println( "Description = " + pt.getDescription() );
      System.out.println
        ( "Latitude degrees = " + oo.getLatitudeDeg() );
      System.out.println
        ( "Longitude degrees = " + oo.getLongitudeDeg() );
    }
    // Catch exceptions.
    // Invoke error() method to print message and exit.
    catch( SQLException e ) { error( "SQL", 3 ); }
    catch( IOException e )  { error( "IO", 3 ); }
}

/* Next, a PLATFORM_TYPE_LIST record is updated by going through
   the produced_by pointer in the OCEANIC_OBSERVATION_LIST table.
   This example will illustrate the getValue() and setValue methods
   of REF custom classes.
*/
void runExample4() {
  try {
    /* Input obs_id to identify OCEANIC_OBSERVATION_LIST record
       whose platform_type record will have its description changed
       to the input description.
    */
```

```
    System.out.println
      ( "Please enter observation id and description " +
        "separated by blanks ");
    TokSequence t = setupTokSequence();
    int obsid = t.getInt();
    String desc = t.getString();

    /* Declare ptr to be instance of REF custom class for
       platform_type.
    */
    PlatformTypeRef ptr;

    /* Select desired produced_by value into REF custom class
       instance ptr.
    */
    #sql { SELECT produced_by INTO :ptr
             FROM OCEANIC_OBSERVATION_LIST
               WHERE obs_id = :obsid
         };
    /* Use the getValue() method to get platform_type record that
       is referenced by selected produced_by field that is in ptr.
       Place this record in platform_type custom class instance pt.
    */
    PlatformType pt = ptr.getValue();

    /* Use mutator method in platform_type custom class instance pt
       to change the description value in that instance.
    */
    pt.setDescription( desc );

    /* Use the setValue() method in REF custom class instance to
       update the referenced record in the PLATFORM_TYPE_LIST table.
    */
    ptr.setValue( pt );

    // Commit the update.
    #sql { COMMIT WORK };
  }
  // Catch exceptions.
  // Invoke error() method to print message and exit.
  catch( SQLException e ) { error( "SQL", 4 ); }
  catch( IOException e )  { error( "IO", 4 ); }
}

/* Example 5 illustrates the use of an iterator that has custom
   class fields.
*/
void runExample5() {
```

```
try {
  /* For each OCEANIC_OBSERVATION_LIST record matching the input
     station_id, its platform_type record and oceanicobservation
     record will be retrieved and printed.
  */
  System.out.println( "Please enter station id " );
  TokSequence t = setupTokSequence();
  int stationid = t.getInt();

  // Declare iterator instance aPlatObs.
  PlatObs aPlatObs;

  /* Populate iterator instance aPlatObs using desired
     platform_type and oceanicobservation records.
     Note that field aliases are required to provide
     conformity with iterator attribute names.
  */
  #sql aPlatObs =
    { SELECT DEREF( produced_by ) AS plat, obsobj AS obs
        FROM OCEANIC_OBSERVATION_LIST
          WHERE station_id = :stationid
    };
  PlatformType pt;
  OceanicObservation oo;

  /* In each iteration of this loop, the iterator accessor methods
     will be used to place a platform_type custom class record and
     an oceanicobservation custom class record in the custom class
     instances pt and oo, respectively.  Then the custom class
     accessor methods will be used to retrieve and print the
     desired fields.
  */
  while ( aPlatObs.next() ) {
    pt = aPlatObs.plat();
    oo = aPlatObs.obs();
    System.out.println( "Key id = " + pt.getKeyId() );
    System.out.println( "Type = " + pt.getType() );
    System.out.println( "Description = " + pt.getDescription() );
  }
  // Close iterator instance.
  aPlatObs.close();
}
// Catch exceptions.
// Invoke error() method to print message and exit.
catch( SQLException e ) { error( "SQL", 5 ); }
catch( IOException e )  { error( "IO", 5 ); }
}
```

```
/* This example illustrates the invocation of an object type method
   on a custom class instance.
*/
void runExample6() {
  try {
    /* Input obs_id that will identify OCEANIC_OBSERVATION_LIST
       record to retrieve.
    */
    System.out.println( "Please enter observation id" );
    TokSequence t = setupTokSequence();
    int obsid = t.getInt();

    // Declare custom class instances pt and oot.
    PlatformType pt;
    OceanicObservationType oot;

    // Select desired OCEANIC_OBSERVATION_LIST record into oot.
    #sql { SELECT VALUE(o) INTO :oot
             FROM OCEANIC_OBSERVATION_LIST o
               WHERE obs_id = :obsid
         };
    /* Invoke Java custom class method wrapper (for SQL
       oceanic_observation_type method get_platform_type)
       on oot, to retrieve platform_type record that is
       referenced by oot.
    */
    pt = oot.getPlatformType();

    // Use custom class accessor method to print the key_id in pt.
    System.out.println( "key id = " + pt.getKeyId() );
  }
  // Catch exceptions.
  // Invoke error() method to print message and exit.
  catch( SQLException e ) { error( "SQL", 6 ); }
  catch( IOException e )  { error( "IO", 6 ); }
}

// Method to print error message and exit.
void error( String what, int where ) {
  System.out.println(what + " error in example " + where );
  System.exit(1);
}
}
```

SQLJ Stored Subprograms with SQL Object Type Parameters and Return Values

The Java custom classes for user-defined SQL types provide a means for
implementing stored subprograms in SQLJ that have user-defined SQL types as

parameter and return types. For example, suppose you wanted to implement a SQLJ version of the `get_platform_type` method for the `oceanic_observation_type` class. You will implement it first as a top-level stored function, and then as a member method of `oceanic_observation_type`, replacing the PL/SQL version of the method. You start by coding a Java class `OceanicProjections` that contains a Java method, `getPlatformType`, that will be used to implement the desired stored function.

```
/*
** Program Name:  OceanicProjections.sqlj
**
** Purpose:  Provide the java method getPlatformType() to be used
**           for implementing the get_platform_type top-level stored
**           function.
**
*/
import java.sql.SQLException;
class OceanicProjections {
  public static PlatformType getPlatformType
    ( OceanicObservationType oot ) {
    PlatformTypeRef
      ptr = oot.getProducedBy();
      return ptr.getValue();
  }
}
```

Then you

- Translate and compile `OceanicProjections.sqlj`:

  ```
  sqlj -ser2class OceanicProjections.sqlj
  ```

- Place all generated .`class` files and relevant custom classes in a .`jar` file:

  ```
  jar -cvf0 OceanicProjections.jar OceanicProjections*.class
  OceanicObservationType.class PlatformTypeRef.class
  PlatformType.class OceanicObservation.class
  ```

- Load your .`jar` file classes into the Oracle8*i* server:

  ```
  loadjava -resolve -verbose -thin
  -user scott/tiger@data-i.com:1521:ORCL OceanicProjections.jar
  ```

- Create in SQL*Plus a top-level SQL wrapper for your stored function:

  ```
  /*
  ** Program Name: getplatformtype.sql
  **
  ```

```
    */
    CREATE FUNCTION get_platform_type
      ( oceanicobs oceanic_observation_type )
      return platform_type AS
      LANGUAGE java
      NAME 'OceanicProjections.getPlatformType
        ( OceanicObservationType )
      return PlatformType';
    /
```

Your stored function `get_platform_type` now exists. The following `SELECT` statement provides an example invocation of that function:

```
SELECT get_platform_type( value(o) ) FROM OCEANIC_OBSERVATION_LIST o;
```

Now suppose that instead of (or in addition to) implementing `get_platform_type` as a top-level stored function, you wished to implement it as a SQLJ coded member method of `oceanic_observation_type`, replacing the PL/SQL version. In order to accomplish this, you have to modify the `OceanicProjections` class in two ways. First, since `get_platform_type` is an object type method, the `oceanic_observation_type` parameter is an implicit parameter, and thus you must declare the method `getPlatformType()` so that it doesn't take any parameters. Second, you must declare the `OceanicProjections` class as an extension of the `OceanicObservationType` class, so that the method `getPlatformType()` has access to the fields of its implicit parameter through the `OceanicObservationType` accessor methods (specifically, `getProducedBy()`, in this example). This modified `OceanicProjections` class is called `OceanicProjections2`.

```
/*
** Program Name:  OceanicProjections2.sqlj
**
** Purpose:  Provide the java method getPlatformType() to be used
**           for implementing the get_platform_type method in the
**           oceanic_observation_type SQL object type.
**
*/
import java.sql.SQLException;
class OceanicProjections2 extends OceanicObservationType {
  public static PlatformType getPlatformType() {
    PlatformTypeRef
      ptr = getProducedBy();
      return ptr.getValue();
  }
}
```

After you have compiled this class, and loaded it and related classes into the server as described previously, you only have to drop the type body for `oceanic_observation_type`, and then appropriately re-create it in SQL*Plus:

```
DROP TYPE BODY oceanic_observation_type;
CREATE TYPE BODY oceanic_observation_type AS
  member function get_platform_type
    RETURN platform_type IS
    LANGUAGE java
    NAME 'OceanicProjections2.getPlatformType()
    return PlatformType';
end;
/
```

You can now invoke the member method with the dot notation, just as you did when it was implemented in PL/SQL:

```
SELECT o.getplatformtype() FROM OCEANIC_OBSERVATION_LIST o;
```

Note that if you were implementing the `get_platform_type` method as a SQLJ method from the outset, you would

1. Create the `oceanic_observation_type` type, but not the type body.

2. Use `jpub` to create a custom class for `oceanic_observation_type`.

3. Compile `OceanicProjections2` and load it into the server (along with the related classes).

4. Create the `oceanic_observation_type` body.

Oracle8*i* User-Defined SQL Collection Types

There are two kinds of collection types in Oracle, NESTED TABLEs and VARRAYs (variable-length arrays). In order for a table to contain a field that is of either of these collection types, a CREATE TYPE statement first has to be executed for the type. For example, suppose you wish to have a table of observations that passed quality control, which is to contain a field that itself is to be a table. Each record in the NESTED TABLE is to consist of an observation id and a one-character code indicating how well the observation passed. You first create in SQL*Plus a type for the records in the NESTED TABLE, and then a type for the NESTED TABLE. Only then can you create the table that contains the NESTED TABLE:

```
CREATE TYPE passedobs AS
   object( obsid number, passed char(1) ) ;
/

CREATE TYPE passedobsarray AS TABLE OF passedobs;
/

CREATE TABLE PASSED_OBSERVATION_LIST
   ( passed_id number(5),
     qcid       number(5),
     when_t     date,
     at_time    char(8),
     idobj      passedobsarray )
     NESTED TABLE idobj STORE AS POBSID_LIST;
```

Note that the table PASSED_OBSERVATION_LIST is not defined to be an object table (that is, there is no explicitly defined row type for it), since there will be no REF fields in the database that will reference its records, nor any other tables in the database having its record type as a field or a record type. Thus, there is no need to give the record type of PASSED_OBSERVATION_LIST a special name.

However, the question remains as to the advantages of nesting the idobj table in the PASSED_OBSERVATION_LIST table as compared to implementing it as a separate table (which is how it will be physically implemented, anyway). It could be argued that the idobj information inherently belongs grouped with the other PASSED_OBSERVATION_LIST data, and that the naturalness of this representation is reflected in the relative simplicity of the "join-free" queries on this table given later in this section. The judgment concerning the validity of this argument is left up to you.

Another argument to justify the NESTED TABLE construct concerns the traffic between client programs and the Oracle server. NESTED TABLE types allow you to transfer a NESTED TABLE between the client and server as a single unit. Without such a construct, you would have to map complex structures into simple SQL types. The many separate components in the mapping would each require a separate trip to the server, appreciably degrading performance. In fact, this reduction of network traffic can be considered a general advantage of the object-relational approach, including not only collection types, but nested records and REFs as well. The Java custom classes can be viewed as an efficient, type-secure mechanism for providing a convenient unit of transfer between the SQLJ client program and the Oracle server.

The CREATE TABLE statement for a table that contains a NESTED TABLE must have a nested_table_clause that indicates which table will actually hold the records of the NESTED TABLE. In this case, POBSID_LIST will hold the records for the idobj field.

An alternative way of representing the passed observation information is as a variable-length array (VARRAY) within the PASSED_OBSERVATION_LIST record. The following statements are executed to create a table, PASSED_OBSERVATION_ LIST2, that is analogous to PASSED_OBSERVATION_LIST, except that it contains a VARRAY instead of a NESTED TABLE. Note that the maximum size of the VARRAY (here, 100) must be supplied in the CREATE TYPE statement for the VARRAY.

```
CREATE TYPE passedobsarray2 AS VARRAY( 100 ) OF passedobs;
/

CREATE TABLE PASSED_OBSERVATION_LIST2
  ( passed_id number(5),
    qcid      number(8),
    when_t    date,
    at_time   char(8),
    idobj     passedobsarray2 );
```

How do you determine whether you should use a NESTED TABLE or a VARRAY? You do that by considering the two fundamental differences between a NESTED TABLE and a VARRAY:

- The NESTED TABLE is dynamic, whereas the VARRAY is static. This has several important implications. Records can be inserted, deleted, and updated in a NESTED TABLE after that table has been inserted into the outer record.

   In order to change a VARRAY in an outer record, the entire VARRAY has to be replaced. On the other hand, because of its static nature, a VARRAY can occupy less space than a NESTED TABLE. Also, if the VARRAY is small enough, its static nature allows it to be stored close to the rest of its outer record. This closeness can lead to a faster access time, as compared to the NESTED TABLE that is stored separately from its outer record.

- Ordering has meaning for VARRAYs, but not for NESTED TABLEs. If ordering is important for your collection, you may prefer to implement it as a VARRAY. (Of course, the exploitation of ordering position at the logical level violates the relational philosophy.)

The following statements will insert records into the PASSED_OBSERVATION_ LIST and PASSED_OBSERVATION_LIST2 tables:

```
/* Use the NESTED TABLE type constructor to create and initially
   load the NESTED TABLE instance in record.
*/
```

```
INSERT INTO PASSED_OBSERVATION_LIST VALUES
  ( 1032, 10999, '23-Aug-1978', '14000',
    passedobsarray( passedobs( 99999, '1' ),
    passedobs( 6777, '1' ) ) );

/* To insert into NESTED TABLE after it has been created, use the
   table operator, which is an unnesting operator that extracts the
   desired NESTED TABLE for the desired operation (insertion in this
   case).
*/
INSERT INTO TABLE( SELECT idobj FROM PASSED_OBSERVATION_LIST
  WHERE passed_id = 1032 ) VALUES( 33333, '1' );

// Insert into the VARRAY version of PASSED_OBSERVATION_LIST.
/* Use VARRAY type constructor to create and initialize VARRAY
   instance.
*/
INSERT INTO PASSED_OBSERVATION_LIST2 VALUES
  ( 1032, 10999, '23-Aug-1978', '14000',
    passedobsarray2( passedobs( 99999, '1' ), passedobs( 6777, '1' ) )
  );

/* You can't change an already existing VARRAY.  In order to insert
   a new record, you have to replace the VARRAY with an entirely new
   VARRAY.
*/
UPDATE PASSED_OBSERVATION_LIST2
  SET idobj = passedobsarray2( passedobs( 99999, '1' ),
    passedobs( 6777, '1' ), passedobs( 33333, '1' ) )
      WHERE passed_id = 1032;
```

You will now consider some queries on the PASSED_OBSERVATION_LIST and PASSED_OBSERVATION_LIST2 tables.

```
// Print the idobj sets that contain an observation with obsid 99999.
// p alias is required in table expression.
// Table operator extracts NESTED TABLE.
SELECT idobj FROM PASSED_OBSERVATION_LIST p WHERE 99999 IN
  ( SELECT i.obsid FROM TABLE( p.idobj ) i );

/* Solution to preceding query when idobj is implemented as a VARRAY
   (note that there is no difference in the solutions).
*/
SELECT idobj FROM PASSED_OBSERVATION_LIST2 p WHERE 99999 IN
  ( SELECT i.obsid FROM TABLE( p.idobj ) i );

/* Print the passed_id of each record that contains obsid 99999 as
   its first observation.  This can only be done for the VARRAY case
```

```
        (since ordering is meaningless for the NESTED TABLE case, although
        you can subscript NESTED TABLEs in PL/SQL), and the VARRAY case
        requires a technique such as a PL/SQL block since VARRAY
        subscripts can't be used in stand-alone SQL.
*/
begin
    for i in ( SELECT * FROM PASSED_OBSERVATION_LIST2 )
        loop
            if i.idobj( 1 ).obsid = 99999
                then dbms_output.put_line( i.passed_id );
            end if;
        end loop;
end;
/

/* For each PASSED_OBSERVATION_LIST record, print the passed_id
    from that record, and the obsids from the idobj collection
    nested in that record.
*/
SELECT passed_id, CURSOR
    ( SELECT i.obsid FROM TABLE( p.idobj ) i )
        FROM PASSED_OBSERVATION_LIST p;

/* Solution to preceding query when idobj is implemented as a
    VARRAY (again, it is the same).
*/
SELECT passed_id, CURSOR
    ( SELECT i.obsid FROM TABLE( p.idobj ) i )
        FROM PASSED_OBSERVATION_LIST2 p;
```

There is still a third alternative structure for implementing the `idobj` field, namely, as a NESTED TABLE of references to `passedobs` records. These `passedobs` records must then be stored in a separate table. The following statements implement and illustrate this third alternative structure.

```
CREATE TYPE passedobsarray3 AS
    TABLE OF REF passedobs;
/

CREATE TABLE PASSED_OBSERVATION_LIST3 (
    passed_id   number(5),
    qcid        number(5),
    when_t      date,
    at_time     char(8),
    idobj       passedobsarray3 )
    NESTED TABLE idobj STORE AS POBSID_LIST3;
```

```
/* PASSEDOBS_LIST is the separate table to contain
   passedobs records.
*/
CREATE TABLE PASSEDOBS_LIST
  of passedobs;

INSERT INTO PASSEDOBS_LIST VALUES( 99999, '1' );
INSERT INTO PASSEDOBS_LIST VALUES( 6777, '1' );

/* The set of passedobs references selected must be cast
   to the passedobsarray3 type before it is inserted into
   the PASSED_OBSERVATION_LIST3 record.  Note that in order
   for a subquery to be an operand of the CAST function, the
   MULTISET function must first be applied to the subquery
   causing the output of the subquery to be treated as a set
   (possibly containing duplicates).
*/
INSERT INTO PASSED_OBSERVATION_LIST3
  VALUES( 1032, 10999,'23-AUG-78', '14000',
    CAST( MULTISET( SELECT REF(p) FROM PASSEDOBS_LIST p
      WHERE OBSID = 99999
        OR OBSID = 6777 ) AS passedobsarray3 ) );

/* For each PASSED_OBSERVATION_LIST3 record, print the
   passed_id from that record, and the obsids from the
   passedobs records that are referenced by the idobj
   collection nested in that PASSED_OBSERVATION_LIST3
   record.  column_value is the system generated field
   for a NESTED TABLE of scalars.
*/
SELECT passed_id,
  cursor( SELECT i.column_value.obsid FROM TABLE( p.idobj ) i )
    FROM PASSED_OBSERVATION_LIST3 p;
```

The three structures – NESTED TABLE of passedobs records, nested array of passedobs records, and NESTED TABLE of passedobs references—provide three alternative implementations of the (two-level) containment hierarchy between PASSED_OBSERVATION_LIST records and passedobs records.

Processing SQL Collection Types in SQLJ

Your first step is to create Java custom classes for your SQL collection types using JPublisher. You execute JPublisher exactly as in the object type case. For example,

here is what you would run in order to generate custom classes for the
`passedobsarray` and `passedobsarray2` types:

```
jpub -sql=PassedObsArray,PassedObsArray2 -user=scott/tiger
```

Capitalize just as you did in the object type case in the earlier section "Processing
SQL Object Types in SQLJ." When you generate a custom class for a collection
type, JPublisher automatically generates custom classes for your element types.
Thus, in this example, JPublisher will automatically generate a custom class
`Passedobs` for the SQL object type `passedobs` (and therefore also a `REF` custom
class `PassedobsRef`). Each `.java` file generated for these classes—namely,
`PassedObsArray.java`, `PassedObsArray2.java`, `PassedObs.java`,
`PassedObsRef.java`—must then be compiled using `javac` or `sqlj`. If you
don't like the name JPublisher generated for the `passedobs` custom class
(`Passedobs`), you can explicitly list `PassedObs` on the `jpub` command line
to get the o capitalized:

```
jpub -sql=PassedObs,PassedObsArray,PassedObsArray2 -user=scott/tiger
```

For each collection custom class, the methods that JPublisher generates include:

- A **constructor method** (of course, having the same name as the custom
  class) that initializes the new custom class instance with an array that is
  passed in as an argument.

- A **getArray() method** that returns as an array the collection that is
  represented by the custom class instance.

- A **setArray() method** that replaces the collection that is represented by
  the custom class instance with the collection that is represented by an array
  that is passed as the argument to `setArray()`.

- A **length() method** that returns the number of elements in the collection
  that is represented by the custom class instance.

- A **getElement() method** that returns an individual element in the
  collection that is represented by the custom class instance.

- A **setElement() method** that updates an individual element in the
  collection that is represented by the custom class instance.

In the current example, JPublisher will generate (among others) the following
methods for the `NESTED TABLE` class `PassedObsArray`:

```
public PassedObsArray( Passedobs[] p );
public PassedObs[] getArray()throws SQLException;
public void setArray( PassedObs[] p ) throws SQLException;
public int length() throws SQLException;
public PassedObs getElement( long index ) throws SQLException;
public void setElement( PassedObs p, long index );
```

The index argument in getElement() and setElement() indicates which element in the collection is being retrieved or updated.

Methods with corresponding signatures are generated for the VARRAY class PassedObservationList2. In the next section, you will see a program CollectionTypes.sqlj that illustrates the use of these methods.

CollectionTypes.sqlj: An Example SQLJ Program That Processes Tables Containing NESTED TABLEs and VARRAYs

Following is an example of a SQLJ program that processes tables containing NESTED TABLEs and VARRAYs.

```
/* The following two iterators must be declared public, since they
   will be nested in other iterators, and therefore must be defined
   in their own files.
*/

/*
** Program Name:  PassedArray.sqlj
**
** Purpose:   PassedArray is a named iterator used for the SELECT
**            statement in Example 4.  PassedArray will hold a set
**            of records from the PASSED_OBSERVATION_LIST.idobj
**            NESTED TABLE.
**
*/
#sql public iterator PassedArray( int obsid, String passed );

/*
** Program Name:  ObsId.sqlj
**
** Purpose:   ObsId is a named iterator used for the SELECT statement
**            in Example 6.  ObsId will hold a set of obsids from the
**            PASSED_OBSERVATION_LIST.idobj NESTED TABLE.
**
*/
#sql public iterator ObsId( int obsid );
```

```
/*
** Program Name:  CollectionTypes.sqlj:
**
** Purpose:   Provide a series of examples that illustrate the use of
**            iterators and collection custom classes in retrieving
**            collections.
*/
/* java.math contains the BigDecimal class that is used by
   JPublisher generated code.
*/
import java.math.*;

// java.io contains BufferedReader and InputStreamReader classes.
import java.io.*;

// java.util contains StringTokenizer class.
import java.util.*;

// Required SQLException class for SQL errors.
import java.sql.SQLException;

/* oracle.sqlj.runtime.Oracle class contains connect() method for
   connecting to database.
*/
import oracle.sqlj.runtime.Oracle;

/* IdObsIdSet is a named iterator class for the SELECT statement in
   Example 7.  ObsIdSet is a Java custom class for a table of numbers
   (obsids).  IdObsIdSet will be used to hold a set of records each
   consisting of a passed_id and a set of obsids.
*/
#sql iterator IdObsIdSet( int passed_id, ObsIdSet obsidset );

/* IdObsId is a named iterator class for the SELECT statement in
   Example 6.  ObsId is an iterator class for a set of obsids.
   IdObsIdSet and IdObsId provide two alternative ways of
   retrieving the same output: a set of records each consisting
   of a passed_id and a set of obsids.
*/
#sql iterator IdObsId( int passed_id, ObsId obsid );

/* IdPassedObsArray is a named iterator class for the SELECT statement
   in Example 5.  PassedObsArray is the custom class for the nested
   table type passedobsarray, which is a set of records consisting of
   an obsid field (int) and a passed field (String) - that is, the
   type of PASSED_OBSERVATION_LIST.idobj.  IdPassedObsArray will hold
   a set of records each consisting of a passed_id and a set of
   PASSED_OBSERVATION_LIST.idobj records.
```

```
*/
#sql iterator IdPassedObsArray( int passed_id, PassedObsArray idobj );

/* IdPassedArray is a named iterator class for SELECT statement in
   Example 4.  PassedArray is a named iterator class designed to hold
   the records of the NESTED TABLE PASSED_OBSERVATION_LIST.idobj.
   IdPassedObjArray and IdPassedArray provide two alternative ways
   of retrieving the same output: a set of records each consisting of
   a passed_id and a set of PASSED_OBSERVATION_LIST.idobj records.
*/
#sql iterator IdPassedArray( int passed_id, PassedArray idobj );

// Define application class CollectionTypes.
class CollectionTypes {

  // BufferedReader class allows line-at-a-time input.
  private BufferedReader input;
  public static void main( String[] args ) {

    /* Invoke CollectionTypes constructor to connect to database,
       and direct System.in to a BufferedReader stream.
    */
    CollectionTypes maincode = new CollectionTypes();

    /* The runCollectionTypes() method invokes methods to execute
       examples.
    */
    maincode.runCollectionTypes();
  }
  /* Initialize database connection, and direct System.in to a
     BufferedReader.
  */
  public CollectionTypes() {
    connectDB();
    openInput();
  }
  // Method to connect to database.
  private void connectDB() {
    try {
      Oracle.connect( getClass(), "connect.properties" );
    }
    catch( SQLException e ) {
      System.err.println( "Error connecting to database. \n" + e );
      System.exit(1);
    }
  }
  /* Method to direct System.in to a character stream, and to direct
     that character stream to a BufferedReader stream.
```

```
*/
private void openInput() {
  input = new BufferedReader( new InputStreamReader( System.in ) );
}
/* Method to set up a tokenized line of input.  See Chapter 2 for
   the definition of the TokSequence class.
*/
private TokSequence setupTokSequence() throws IOException {
  String line = input.readLine();
  StringTokenizer st = new StringTokenizer( line );
  TokSequence t = new TokSequence( st );
  return t;
}
// Method that invokes other methods to run the examples.
private void runCollectionTypes() {
 try {
  /* Example 1 illustrates selecting into a Java custom class
     instance for a NESTED TABLE, and using the getArray()
     method to load the NESTED TABLE records from the custom
     class instance into an array.
  */
  runExample1();

  /* Example 2 produces the same output as Example 1, without
     loading the NESTED TABLE records into an array.
  */
  runExample2();

  /* Example 3 is equivalent to Example 2, except it works with
     the PASSED_OBSERVATION_LIST2 table that implements idobj as
     a VARRAY.  The code of Example 3 is essentially identical to
     the code of Example 2.
  */
  runExample3();

  /* Example 4 illustrates the use of a nested iterator in
     retrieving a set of records, where one of the fields
     being retrieved is a NESTED TABLE.
  */
  runExample4();

  /* Example 5 is equivalent to Example 4, except instead of a
     nested iterator being used, an iterator with a collection
     custom class attribute is used.
  */
  runExample5();

  /* Example 6 illustrates the extraction of a portion of a nested
```

```
        table for loading into an iterator attribute.
    */
    runExample6();

    /* Example 7 is equivalent to Example 6, except the portion of
       the NESTED TABLE is loaded into a collection custom class
       instance instead of into an iterator.
    */
    runExample7();

    /* Example 8 illustrates the construction of a VARRAY whose exact
       size is not known at compile time, and the insertion of that
       VARRAY into a PASSED_OBSERVATION_LIST2 record.  Without the
       collection custom class for the VARRAY, you would have to
       insert extra elements to compensate for the fact that you did
       not know the exact size of the array at compile time.
    */
    runExample8();

    System.out.println( "Examples complete. " );
  }

  catch( SQLException e ) {
    System.out.println( "SQL error in example: " + e );
    System.exit(1);
  }
  catch ( IOException e ) {
    System.out.println( "IO error in example: " + e );
    System.exit(1);
  }
}

  void runExample1() throws SQLException, IOException {
    PassedObsArray poa;
    TokSequence t;
    int obsid;
    PassedObs[] po;
    int passedid;

    /* Input an observation id so as to print the passed_id and idobj
       fields of the PASSED_OBSERVATION_LIST record whose idobj nested
       table contains that observation id.
    */
    System.out.println( "Please enter observation id. ");
    t = setupTokSequence();
    obsid = t.getInt();

    /* Select the passed_id and nested idobj table of the
```

```
       OCEANIC_OBSERVATION_LIST record that contains the
       input observation id in its nested idobj table.
       (Assume that there is only one such record.)  idobj
       is selected into poa, an instance of the Java custom
       class instance that was generated for the NESTED TABLE
       type of idobj.
    */
    #sql { SELECT passed_id, idobj INTO :passedid, :poa
             FROM PASSED_OBSERVATION_LIST p
               WHERE :obsid IN
                 ( SELECT i.obsid FROM TABLE( p.idobj ) i )
         };
    System.out.println( "passedid = " + passedid );

    /* Invoke the getArray() method on poa to move the nested
       table elements into the po array.
    */
    po = poa.getArray();

    /* In the for loop, the accessor methods for the NESTED TABLE
       elements are used to obtain and print the fields of the
       elements that were loaded into the po array.  Note that the
       array length attribute for po is used to terminate the loop.
    */
    for ( int i = 0; i < po.length; i++ ) {
      System.out.println( " obsid = " + po[i].getObsid()
        + " passed code = " + po[i].getPassed() );
    }
}

void runExample2() throws SQLException, IOException {

  // Input an observation id.
  System.out.println( "Please enter observation id. " );
  TokSequence t = setupTokSequence();
  int obsid = t.getInt();

  /* Same SELECT INTO statement as in Example 1 to select
     passed_id field and idobj NESTED TABLE of desired record.
     As in Example 1, the NESTED TABLE is selected into the Java
     custom class instance poa.
  */
  int passedid;
  PassedObsArray poa;
  #sql { SELECT passed_id, idobj INTO :passedid, :poa
           FROM PASSED_OBSERVATION_LIST p
             WHERE :obsid IN
               ( SELECT i.obsid FROM TABLE( p.idobj ) i )
```

```
    };
  System.out.println( "passed id = " + passedid );

  /* In the for loop, the getElement() method for poa is
     invoked to access the i-th record of the NESTED TABLE.
     getElement() enables you to access the records in a
     collection custom class directly, without first loading
     them into an array (as was done in Example 1). The generated
     custom class method is used to terminate the loop.
  */
  for ( long i = 0; i < poa.length(); i++ ) {
    System.out.println
      ( " obs id = " + poa.getElement(i).getObsid() +
          " passed code = " +
              poa.getElement(i).getPassed() );
  }
}

void runExample3() throws SQLException, IOException {
  System.out.println( "Please enter observation id. " );
  TokSequence t = setupTokSequence();
  int obsid = t.getInt();
  int passedid;

  /* PassedObsArray2 is the Java custom class for a
     VARRAY of passedobs records (designed to hold
     PASSED_OBSERVATION_LIST2.idobj records).
  */
  PassedObsArray2 poa2;
  #sql { SELECT passed_id, idobj INTO :passedid, :poa2
           FROM PASSED_OBSERVATION_LIST2 p
             WHERE :obsid IN
                ( SELECT i.obsid FROM TABLE( p.idobj ) i )
       };
  PassedObs[] po = poa2.getArray();
  System.out.println( "passed id = " + passedid );
  for ( int i = 0; i < po.length; i++ ) {
    System.out.println
      ( "obs id = " + po[i].getObsid() +
          " passed code = " + po[i].getPassed() );
  }
}


void runExample4() throws SQLException, IOException {

  /* Input a quality control id so as to print the passed_id
     and idobj fields of all PASSED_OBSERVATION_LIST table
     records that match that quality control id.
```

```
*/
System.out.println( "Please enter quality control ID. " );
TokSequence t = setupTokSequence();
int qcid = t.getInt();

/* Declare anIdPassedArray as an instance of IdPassedArray.
   IdPassedArray is an iterator that contains an int
   attribute for the passed_id field and a nested iterator
   attribute for the idobj NESTED TABLE of the
   PASSED_OBSERVATION_LIST table.
*/
IdPassedArray anIdPassedArray;

/* Populate anIdPassedArray (outer iterator) with the passed_id
   and idobj field values from the PASSED_OBSERVATION_LIST table
   records that match the input quality control id.
*/
/* The nested cursor must be used to extract the fields of idobj.
   If you merely place i.idobj in the select_list, there will be
   a type mismatch between that field and the iterator idobj
   attribute.
*/
#sql anIdPassedArray =
  { SELECT passed_id,
      cursor( SELECT i.obsid, i.passed
        FROM TABLE( p.idobj ) i )
          AS idobj
            FROM PASSED_OBSERVATION_LIST p
              WHERE qcid = :qcid
  };
/* while loop uses iterator next() method to retrieve records
   from outer iterator.
*/
while ( anIdPassedArray.next() ) {

  // Extract passed_id and print it.
  System.out.println
    ( "passed id = " + anIdPassedArray.passed_id() );

  /* Extract idobj and place it in iterator for the idobj
     field (inner iterator).
  */
  PassedArray aPassedArray = anIdPassedArray.idobj();

  /* while loop uses the next() method to retrieve records
     with obsid and passed fields from inner iterator.
  */
  while ( aPassedArray.next() ) {
```

```
        // Print the obsid and passed fields.
        System.out.println
          ( "obs id = " + aPassedArray.obsid() +
             " passed code = " + aPassedArray.passed() );
      };
      // Close the inner iterator.
      aPassedArray.close();
    }
    // Close the outer iterator.
    anIdPassedArray.close();
}

void runExample5() throws SQLException, IOException {
  System.out.println
    ( "Please input the desired quality control id. " );
  TokSequence t = setupTokSequence();
  int qcid = t.getInt();

  /* Declare anIdPassedObsArray as an instance of
     IdPassedObsArray.  IdPassedObsArray is an iterator that
     contains an int attribute for the passed_id field, and
     a Java collection custom class attribute for the idobj
     field of the PASSED_OBSERVATION_LIST table.
  */
  IdPassedObsArray anIdPassedObsArray;

  /* Populate anIdPassedObsArray with a SELECT statement
     similar to, but simpler than, the SELECT statement in
     Example 4.
     (See Note 1.)
  */
  #sql anIdPassedObsArray =
    { SELECT passed_id, idobj
        FROM  PASSED_OBSERVATION_LIST
          WHERE qcid = :qcid
    };
  /* while loop uses iterator next() method to retrieve
     records from iterator.
  */
  while ( anIdPassedObsArray.next() ) {
    System.out.println
      ( "passed id = " + anIdPassedObsArray.passed_id() );

    /* Move the idobj NESTED TABLE from the iterator instance
       into a collection custom class instance poa.
    */
    PassedObsArray poa = anIdPassedObsArray.idobj();
```

```
      // Load the collection from poa into an array po.
      PassedObsArray[] po = poa.getArray();

      /* The for loop retrieves the fields from the records in the
         array, and prints them.
      */
      for ( int i = 0; i < po.length; i++ ) {
        System.out.println
          ( "obs id = " + po[i].getObsid() +
              " passed code = " + po[i].getPassed() );
      }
    }
  // Close iterator.
  anIdPassedObsArray.close();
}

void runExample6() throws SQLException, IOException {

  /* Input a quality control id so as to retrieve from each
     PASSED_OBSERVATION_LIST record that matches the quality
     control id, the passed_id and the set of obsids from the
     nested idobj table.
  */
  System.out.println( "Please enter quality control id. " );
  TokSequence t = setupTokSequence();
  int qcid = t.getInt();

  /* Declare anIdObsId to be an instance of the iterator
     IdObsId.  IdObsId contains an int passed_id attribute
     and an ObsId nested iterator attribute obsid to hold
     a set of obsids.
  */
  IdObsId anIdObsId;

  /* Declare anObsId to be an instance of the ObsId iterator.
     ObsId contains a single int attribute.
  */
  ObsId anObsId;

  /* Populate anIdObsId (outer iterator) with the passed_id and
     set of idobj obsids from the PASSED_OBSERVATION_LIST records
     that match the input quality control id.  The obsid set goes
     into the ObsId nested iterator attribute.  Note that the nested
     cursor expression must be given the obsid alias so as to be
     consistent with the named iterator.
  */
  #sql anIdObsId =
    { SELECT passed_id,
```

```
           cursor( SELECT i.obsid FROM TABLE( p.idobj ) i ) AS obsid
             FROM PASSED_OBSERVATION_LIST p
               WHERE qcid = :qcid
      };
    /* while loop used the next() method to retrieve outer iterator
       records.
    */
    while ( anIdObsId.next() ) {

      // Extract passed_id from outer iterator record and print it.
      System.out.println( "passed id = " + anIdObsId.passed_id() );
      System.out.println( "obs ids " );

      /* Populate anObsId (inner iterator) with obsid set from outer
         iterator record.
      */
      anObsId = anIdObsId.obsid();

      /* while loop uses next() method to retrieve inner iterator
         records.
      */
      while ( anObsId.next() ) {
        System.out.println( anObsId.obsid() );
      }
      // Close inner iterator.
      anObsId.close();
    }
    // Close outer iterator.
    anIdObsId.close();
  }

  void runExample7() throws SQLException, IOException {

    /* Declare anIdObsIdSet to be an instance of the IdObsIdSet
       iterator.  IdObsIdSet contains two attributes: an int
       attribute to hold a passed_id and an ObsIdSet custom class
       attribute to hold a set of obsids.
       (See Note 2.)
    */
    IdObsIdSet anIdObsIdSet;
    System.out.println( "Please enter quality control id. " );
    TokSequence t = setupTokSequence();
    int qcid = t.getInt();

    // (See Note 3.)
#sql anIdObsIdSet =
    { SELECT passed_id,
        CAST( MULTISET( SELECT i.obsid FROM TABLE( p.idobj ) i )
```

```
            AS obs_id_set )AS obsidset
              FROM PASSED_OBSERVATION_LIST p
                WHERE qcid = :qcid
    };
  // while loop uses next() method to retrieve iterator records.
  while ( anIdObsIdSet.next() ) {
    System.out.println( "passed id = " + anIdObsIdSet.passed_id() );
    System.out.println( "obs ids " );

    /* Declare ois to be an instance of the ObsIdSet collection
       custom class.
    */
    ObsIdSet ois;

    // Extract the set of obsids from iterator record into ois.
    ois = anIdObsIdSet.obsidset();

    // Load collection from ois into an array of BigDecimals.
    // JPublisher treats all numeric fields as BigDecimal.
    BigDecimal[] oia = ois.getArray();

    // for loop extracts elements from array and prints them.
    for ( int i = 0; i < oia.length; i++ ) {
      System.out.println( oia[i] );
    }
  }
  // Close iterator.
  anIdObsIdSet.close();
}

void runExample8()throws SQLException, IOException {

  /* Input a passed_id that identifies the PASSED_OBSERVATION_LIST2
     record into which the VARRAY will be inserted.
  */
  System.out.println( "Please enter a passed id. " );
  TokSequence t = setupTokSequence();
  int passedid = t.getInt();
  int n;

  // Input size of VARRAY to be inserted.
  System.out.println
    ( "Please enter number of passed observations. " );
  t = setupTokSequence();
  n = t.getInt();
  System.out.println
    ( "Please enter one obsid and passed code per line. " );
```

```
/* Create array of custom class PassedObs records (slots for
   references to PassedObs records are created).
*/
PassedObs[] po = new PassedObs[n];

/* Create PassedObs records, have array slots reference them,
   and input into them.
*/
for ( int i = 0; i < n; i++ ) {
  t = setupTokSequence();
  po[i] = new PassedObs();

  /* JPublisher treats all numeric fields as BigDecimal.  You
     input obsid field as String, pass it to the appropriate
     BigDecimal constructor, and then insert the constructed
     BigDecimal into the custom class record in the array.
  */
  BigDecimal b = new BigDecimal( t.getString() );
  po[i].setObsid(b);

  // Input passed code and place it in the custom class record.
  po[i].setPassed( t.getString() );
}
/* Create a VARRAY custom class instance and initialize it to
   the array of custom class PassedObs records, using a VARRAY
   custom class constructor.
*/
PassedObsArray2 poa2 = new PassedObsArray2( po );
/* Update the desired PASSED_OBSERVATION_LIST2 record with the
   VARRAY in the VARRAY custom class instance.
*/
#sql { UPDATE PASSED_OBSERVATION_LIST2
         SET idobj = :poa2
           WHERE passed_id = :passedid
     };
// Commit the update.
#sql { COMMIT WORK };
 }
}
```

Notes on `CollectionTypes.sqlj`:

I. The SELECT statement here simply contains the `idobj` field, instead of a cursor expression involving the `idobj` field, as was used in Example 4. The reason for this is that the iterator here contains a Java custom collection type attribute (whose type corresponds to the type of the `idobj` field in the record) instead of a nested iterator attribute that itself contains two attributes, as in Example 4 (which forced you to extract two fields from the `idobj` field using the cursor expression in order to have type compatibility).

2. In SQL*Plus, a special type for a set of `numbers` was created:

```
CREATE TYPE obs_id_set AS TABLE OF number;
/
```

A java custom class `ObsIdSet` was then created for `obs_id_set`.

3. This `SELECT` statement is similar to the `SELECT` statement in Example 6, except it doesn't use a `cursor` expression to generate the set of `obsids`. Instead, the set of `obsids` selected is cast to the `obs_id_set` type, so that it can be loaded into the `ObsIdSet` attribute of the iterator (`ObsIdSet` is the Java custom class for the SQL type `obs_id_set`). Note that in order for a subquery to be an operand of the `CAST` function, the `MULTISET` function must first be applied to the subquery causing the output of the subquery to be treated as a set (possibly containing duplicates).

In this chapter, you learned about Oracle user-defined types and the JPublisher-generated Java custom classes that represent them. These Java custom classes provide a convenient, secure, and efficient way for the Java program and its embedded SQLJ statements to communicate through host expressions, result expressions, and iterator attributes. In Chapter 8, you will see that these custom classes provide an excellent unit of transfer between your SQLJ program and CORBA, EJB, and RMI.

CHAPTER

8

SQLJ Business and Scientific Object Deployment

n the previous chapters, you developed several SQLJ applications, applets, stored procedures, and database triggers. Moreover, you deployed SQLJ applications that encapsulate business logic into the Oracle8*i* data server. When you were building these programs, you had the responsibility to design, create, and verify every piece. Your design structures had to capture enough detail to support the development of each line of code. In fact, you had complete control over every piece of the development process. In this chapter, you will learn how to relinquish this control as you acquire the skills to design and develop software components. A component is a functional and operational piece of software consisting of several classes logically grouped together within a specific business task. More importantly here, you will learn how to decompose SQLJ applications into object components and distribute them to different computers over a network or different network systems.

During object deployment, you will ship a SQLJ component-based object—that is, a SQLJ component—across a network from one process to another using Java Remote Method Invocation (RMI), Enterprise JavaBeans (EJB), and Common Object Request Broker Architecture (CORBA). Remember that RMI is used to call Java remote objects, EJB allows you to create server-side Java remote objects, and CORBA gives you access to remote objects written in any language including Java. As you go deeper into this chapter, you will learn more about these distributed paradigms.

While developing and deploying a SQLJ component-based object, you will learn the following:

- The basic concepts of distributed computing systems

- How to design and develop a SQLJ component-based object

- How to deploy a SQLJ component using the Java Remote Method Invocation

- How to deploy an Enterprise JavaBeans component object using a SQLJ implementation

- How to deploy a CORBA component object using a SQLJ implementation

Basic Concepts of Distributed Computing Systems

Large computer networks such as corporate and government intranets, the Internet, and the World Wide Web (WWW) have one common characteristic: heterogeneity.

Heterogeneous systems consist of a combination of hardware—heterogeneous networks, that is, numerous operating systems (OS) running on several different hardware configurations such as mainframes, UNIX workstations, PCs, Apple Macintosh, and so on—and software components where each of these components represents a valuable and indispensable portion of an enterprise as a whole. Presently, the challenge is to develop the software infrastructure to integrate or unify these components and enable communication between the objects that reside within them, in spite of their different designs and physical locations.

In response to this challenge, the concept of distributed object computing systems was born. Distributed object models extend an object-oriented programming system by allowing the object components to be distributed on different computers throughout a heterogeneous network. In this scenario, each component remains within its own environment, occupies its own address space, and yet interoperates with other components as if each one were part of a unified whole.

The term *distributed computing* (Figure 8-1) refers to programs or applications that make calls—that is, remote object invocation calls—to other programs located at different address spaces, possibly on different computers. In this situation, although these objects may reside within their own address space—possibly on another computer, on a different network, or both—they appear as though they are local to the application that makes the calls. An address space is the range of memory locations to which a CPU can refer. Underlying all distributed computing architectures is the notion of communication between computers. In a distributed object model, server-side objects provide services, and client-side applications (which may reside on the same computer that provides the services) issue requests for those services to be performed on their behalf. More importantly, clients gain access to information transparently, without having to know on which software or hardware platform the information resides or where it is located on an enterprise's network.

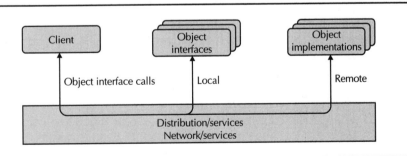

FIGURE 8-1. *Distributed object architecture*

Distributed computing systems have many advantages. You can:

- Wrap legacy systems and enable communication with them. For example, CORBA provides mappings to specific languages such as C and C++ that allow you to wrap a FORTRAN application (that is, create C or C++ classes that publicly define the behavior of the FORTRAN application) so that a CORBA client application written in these languages can access the FORTRAN code. The code that is combined with another piece of code to determine how that code is executed is called a *wrapper.* This implies that the wrapped code (the FORTRAN code) can only be accessed via the wrapper (the C or C++ code).

- Perform systems integration at many levels so that these systems may become less complex, and thereby more efficient and flexible.

- Decompose complex software applications into object components and distribute the objects to computers that best fit the task of each object.

- Isolate software development as specific tasks that can be delegated to several developers concurrently and assembled together later during the development life cycle.

- Allow components easily to be reused by multiple projects.

Standards to create and develop component-based applications in a distributed heterogeneous environment came about in late 1989 with the formation of the Object Management Group (OMG). The OMG introduced an abstract object model for distributed systems, the Object Management Architecture (OMA). There now exists several distributed object paradigms, but the most popular ones are CORBA, the Distributed Component Object Model (DCOM), RMI, JavaBeans, and EJB:

- CORBA, developed by the OMG in the early 1990s, employs an Object Request Broker (ORB) to create and manage client and server communications between objects. ORBs allow objects on the client side to make requests of objects on the server side without any prior knowledge of where those objects reside, in which language they are written, or on which hardware platform they are running. CORBA objects are packaged as binary components that remote clients can access via method invocations. CORBA uses the Internet Inter-ORB Protocol (IIOP) to access its remote objects. IIOP defines the way the bits are sent over a wire between CORBA clients and servers.

■ DCOM is a component technology from Microsoft for distributing applications on the Windows (DNA) architecture. It uses a protocol called the Object Remote Procedure Call (ORPC) for "remoting" objects.

■ The RMI system, from Sun JavaSoft, allows an object running in one Java Virtual Machine (JVM) to invoke methods on an object running in another JVM. RMI uses a protocol called the Java Remote Method Protocol (JRMP) for remote method invocation calls. The Java remote method invocation system described in the JDK 1.2 specification (October 1998) was designed to operate in the Java environment and thus lacked interoperability with other languages. To address this problem, a solution known as RMI-IIOP was presented in the JavaOne Conference (June 1999). Presently, RMI objects can use the IIOP protocol to communicate with non-Java CORBA objects. The RMI-IIOP specification was developed jointly by Sun and IBM and runs on both JDK 1.1 (from release 1.1.6 onwards) and Java 2. See http://java.sun.com/products/rmi-iiop/ [43] for more information regarding RMI-IIOP.

■ JavaBeans (Sun JavaSoft) equips Java with a client/server remote method invocation capability with more robust distribution services. It is used to build client-side applications by assembling visual (GUI) and non-visual widgets and is not a server-side component model. With the JavaBeans API you can create reusable, platform-independent components and combine them into Java applets, Java applications, or both.

■ Enterprise JavaBeans, developed by numerous groups at Sun and its partner companies, extends the JavaBeans architecture to a higher level by providing an API optimized for building scientific and business applications as reusable server components. It is a server-side component model and is designed to address issues involved with managing distributed business objects in a three-tier architecture. Based conceptually on the RMI model, EJB is a cross-platform component architecture for the development and deployment of multi-tier, distributed, and object-oriented Java applications. EJB server components are application components that usually run in an application server. With the release of Oracle8*i*, EJB components can now run in a database server. In EJB applications, object "remoting" follows the RMI specification, but vendors are not limited to the RMI transport protocol. For example, the Oracle8*i* EJB server uses RMI over IIOP for its transport protocol. In the "Deploying an Enterprise JavaBeans Object Using a SQLJ Implementation" section of this chapter, you will develop an EJB application component that runs in the Oracle8*i* data server (see *Enterprise JavaBeans* [33] and *Enterprise JavaBeans, Developing Component-Based Distributed Applications* [61] to learn more about EJB).

See the bibliography at the end of the book for more information regarding distributed computing systems.

In the following sections, you will use the Unified Modeling Language (UML) to design a SQLJ component, the Java programming language and SQLJ to develop the source code, and finally you will deploy the SQLJ component using RMI, EJB, and CORBA. UML is a language for constructing (modeling) and documenting software systems.

Designing and Developing a SQLJ Component-Based Object

In this section, you will create a SQLJ component-based object to manipulate an Oracle table, the `PLATFORM_TYPE_LIST`, of a user-defined datatype, `PLATFORM_TYPE`. Remember how you defined the `PLATFORM_TYPE` type and the `PLATFORM_TYPE_LIST` table (see the Introduction and Chapter 7 of this book). Listing 8-1 shows the SQL statements that created both the `TYPE` and the `TABLE` in the Oracle8*i* data server.

Listing 8-1

```
-- In SQLPLUS or svrmgr
-- Create an Oracle type
CREATE TYPE PLATFORM_TYPE AS OBJECT(
    key_id      NUMBER(5),
    type        VARCHAR2(20),
    description VARCHAR2(50))
/
-- Create a table of PLATFORM_TYPE objects
CREATE TABLE PLATFORM_TYPE_LIST OF PLATFORM_TYPE
/
```

What Is a Component?

"A software component is a unit of composition with contractually specified interfaces and explicit context dependencies only. A software component can be deployed independently and is subject to composition by third parties" (Workshop on Component-Oriented Programming, ECOOP, 1996). An object is not necessarily a component. Nor is a component necessarily an object. An example of an object is an atmospheric observation object in the HRD Wind Analysis system (HWIND), developed at the Hurricane Research Division in Miami, where the attributes and operations associated with that observation object are designed solely with the HWIND application in mind. An example of a component is a SQLJ application that has been wrapped with an object interface and is being used to check business or scientific rules in an application or database server.

Component Composites

A component is the unit of work and distribution that packs together small, tightly coupled objects in larger units of independent deployment (see Figure 8-2). It is a set of modules and consists, at a minimum, of the following:

- An object `interface` defines the behavior of the component. The behavior is the contract that the object `interface` offers publicly. The contract guarantees that the invocation of one of its `interface` methods produces either the result or one of the exceptions specified. A client that wishes to use a component will do so via the component interface that defines its access points. For example, a Java `interface` consists of a class name and a set of method signatures. A method signature consists of a method name and its parameter types along with its return values and exceptions. This `interface` must be declared public in order to be visible to a client; otherwise a client gets an error when it invokes the object.

- An object *implementation* provides the method (behavior) definitions that precisely defined the circumstances in which the object will react. The method implementation assures that, under the specified circumstances, the object will always produce a precisely defined result. Additionally, the component may be extended to include other classes that extend the implementation class.

What Is a Component Model?

Before software complexity becomes overwhelming, you should use modeling to stay in control. A component model defines a set of interfaces and classes that must be used in a particular way to isolate and encapsulate a set of functionality. In response to complexity, use component modeling to raise the level of abstraction in order to get a higher-level view of the software. You can use object modeling CASE tools that offer abstraction from the source code to create a model for your component. There are many modeling tools such as Oracle Designer (database modeling, Oracle Corporation), Rational Rose (software systems modeling, Rational Software), Visio (general-purpose modeling, Visio Corporation), and so on. Most popular modeling tools use the UML methodology to create a component model. In Figure 8-3, you use UML to design the SQLJ component.

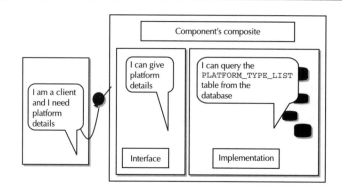

FIGURE 8-2. *Component composite*

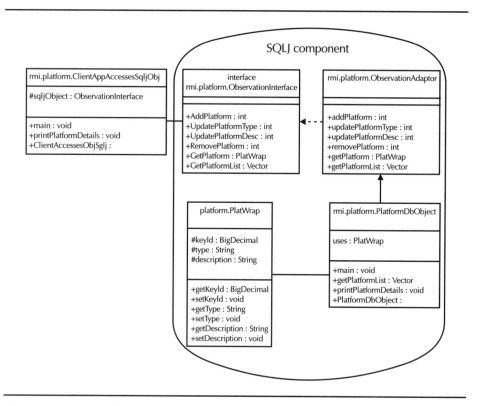

FIGURE 8-3. *High-level view of a client and a SQLJ component-based object*

Notes on Figure 8-3:

The SQLJ component-based object consists of the `ObservationInterface` **interface**, the `ObservationAdaptor` *implementation* class, the `PlatformDbObject` *child* class, and the `PlatWrap` class. See Appendix B to learn more about **interface**, **implements**, and child classes.

■ The `ObservationInterface` **interface** consists of a class name and a set of method signatures. The object's interface provides a public contract that describes the operations that are allowed on the `PLATFORM_TYPE_LIST` table. It defines the behavior of the SQLJ component.

■ The `ObservationAdaptor` *implementation* class provides, in this scenario, only the method definitions of the SQLJ component. You may create additional classes that extend the implementation class to provide the method bodies. The design offers a lot of flexibility as you may decide to create several child classes where each provides a method body for a specific method definition.

■ The `PlatWrap` class is a Java class that wraps or maps the `PLATFORM_TYPE` Oracle type. It provides a set of "getter" and "setter" methods that allow you to treat and manipulate the `PLATFORM_TYPE` SQL data type as a regular Java object. The getter and setter methods allow you to get

■ and to set the value of data members, respectively.

■ The `PlatformDbObject` class is a subclass of the `ObservationAdaptor` class. The class provides a method body for the `getPlatformList()` method. Note that users can examine and manipulate the SQLJ component only via the public methods defined in the object interface and are therefore unaware of how it is implemented.

■ The `ClientAppAccessesSqljObj` class is a client-side SQLJ application that uses the SQLJ component.

Developing a SQLJ Component

Next, you will create a SQLJ component and a SQLJ client-side application to access the component. Note that a software component is also called a *business object*. In this scenario, the term business object, like the term *component,* refers to an object that performs a set of tasks associated with a particular business process. Throughout the remainder of this chapter, the term SQLJ object, SQLJ business object, SQLJ component-based object, or SQLJ component will be used interchangeably and all of them will refer to a software component written in SQLJ.

Use the steps listed here to create a SQLJ business object and a client-side SQLJ application that uses the business object:

1. Create the directories that you wish to use to build and deploy your SQLJ component.

2. Create an object **interface**: `ObservationInterface`.

3. Create an implementation class: `ObservationAdaptor`. Note that both the interface and the implementation class could have been defined in files with the `.sqlj` extension.

4. Create the `PlatWrap` Java class that maps the `PLATFORM_TYPE` Oracle type. This class provides all the getter and setter methods to manipulate the `PLATFORM_TYPE` SQL data type. Remember that you defined the `PLATFORM_TYPE` in Listing 8-1.

5. Create the `PlatformDbObject` SQLJ class, defined in a file with the `.sqlj` extension, that extends the implementation class. This SQLJ application provides the method body for the `getPlatformList()` method defined in the `ObservationInterface` **interface**.

6. Compile the classes from Steps 2 to 5. Use the `javac` compiler and the SQLJ translator to do so.

7. Run the `PlatformDbObject` class to make sure it delivers the expected result. You do so either at the command line by invoking the JVM (for example, `java PlatformDbObject`) or by using the facility of the tool that you use to develop the source code.

8. Create the `ClientAppAccessesSqljObj` SQLJ client-side application that uses the SQLJ business object.

9. Recompile all the programs as you did in Step 6.

10. Run the client-side application, the `ClientAppAccessesSqljObj`.

Step 1   Create the directories that you wish to use to build and deploy your SQLJ component.

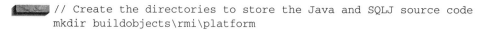
```
// Create the directories to store the Java and SQLJ source code
mkdir buildobjects\rmi\platform
```

```
// Create the directories to store
// the Java classes and the SQLJ .ser classes
mkdir deployobjects\rmi\platform
```

Step 2   Create an object **interface**: ObservationInterface. As you create a program, you may wish to compile it immediately so that you may correct any syntax errors. If you decide to do so, remember to set your CLASSPATH as specified in Step 6 of this section.

```
/*      Program Name: ObservationInterface.java   (See Note 1.)
**      Purpose:      A java interface to query the
**      obsschema schema stored in Oracle8i data server.
*/

package rmi.platform;           // (See Note 2.)

import java.sql.SQLException;
import java.util.*;

public interface ObservationInterface {    // (See Note 3.)

    int addPlatform (PlatWrap p)
            throws SQLException; // (See Note 4.)

    int updatePlatformType (int platformId, String type)
            throws SQLException; // (See Note 5.)

    int updatePlatformDesc (int platformId, String desc)
            throws SQLException;

    int removePlatform (int platformId)
            throws SQLException;   // (See Note 6.)

    PlatWrap getAPlatform(int platformId)
            throws SQLException; // (See Note 7.)

    Vector getPlatformList()
            throws SQLException;   // (See Note 8.)
}   // End of ObservationInterface interface
```

Notes on the ObservationInterface **interface**:

   1. Program documentation. This section is optional but is highly recommended.

   2. This statement defines the package name, rmi.platform. The Java programming language requires a mapping between the fully qualified package name of a class and the directory path to that class. This mapping lets the Java compiler know the directory in which to find the class files mentioned in a program. Before you begin writing any code in Java, you should decide on package and directory names. Do not be surprised, however, if you need to change your design in the future.

3. This statement declares the `ObservationInterface` **interface**. Remember that the behavior of an object is defined and possibly described in its **interface**, and also that client-side programs can only access the object via the entry points defined in the object's **interface**.

4. This statement defines a method signature to add a row of data of type `PlatWrap` to the `PLATFORM_TYPE_LIST` table stored in the Oracle8*i* data server. Note the clause **throws** `SQLException`, which defines the exception mechanism for database applications. Remember that a method signature consists of a method name and its parameter names and types along with its return values and exceptions.

5. This statement and the one that follows it define two method signatures that can change the values of the column attributes `type` and `description`, respectively.

6. This statement defines a method signature that removes a row of data from the `PLATFORM_TYPE_LIST` table.

7. This statement defines a method that returns an object of type `PlatWrap`.

8. This statement defines a method that returns a Java `Vector` of `PlatWrap` objects.

Step 3   Create an implementation class: `ObservationAdaptor`. Remember that both the interface and the implementation class could have been defined in files with the `.sqlj` extension.

```
/*    Program Name: ObservationAdaptor.java
**    Purpose:     A java Class that implements
** the ObservationInterface class to
** query the obsschema stored in Oracle8i. This
** implementation class provides ONLY the method
** definitions for all the methods specified
** in the ObservationInterface interface
*/

package rmi.platform;
```

```
import java.sql.SQLException;
import java.util.*;

public class ObservationAdaptor
     implements ObservationInterface  {    // (See Note 1.)
//  Method definition to add a new PlatWrap object in the database.
    public int addPlatform (PlatWrap p)
            throws SQLException {

        return 0;
    }    // End of addPlatform
//  Method definition to change the type attribute in the database.
    public int updatePlatformType (int platformId, String type)
            throws SQLException {

        return 0;
    }    // End of updatePlatformType
//  Method definition to change the description attribute.
    public int updatePlatformDesc (int platformId, String desc)
            throws SQLException {

        return 0;
    }    // End of updatePlatformDesc
//  Method definition to remove a PlatWrap object.
    public int removePlatform (int platformId)
            throws SQLException {

        return 0;
    }    // End of removePlatform
//  Method definition to get a specific PlatWrap object
//  whose key_id = platformId.
    public PlatWrap getAPlatform(int platformId)
            throws SQLException {

        return null;
    }  // End of getAPlatform

//  Method definition to get a list of all the PlatWrap objects.
    public Vector getPlatformList()
            throws SQLException {

        return null;
    }  // End of getPlatformList
}    // End of ObservationAdaptor class
```

Note on the `ObservationAdaptor` class:

1. This statement declares an implementation class for the SQLJ object. Note that the implements clause is part of the class definition. For more flexibility, the `ObservationAdaptor` class provides only the method definitions for the `ObservationInterface` **interface**. Remember that in Java, when a class declares that it implements an interface, a contract is formed between the class and the compiler. By entering into this contract, the class agrees that it will provide method bodies or definitions for each of the method signatures declared in that interface.

Step 4   Create the `PlatWrap` Java class that maps the `PLATFORM_TYPE` Oracle type. This class provides all the getter and setter methods to manipulate the `PLATFORM_TYPE` SQL data type.

```
/*      Program Name:      PlatWrap.java
**
**      Purpose:           Serialize the PlatformType class
**                         from Oracle jpub utility program
*/

package rmi.platform;

import java.math.BigDecimal;

public class PlatWrap
      implements java.io.Serializable {     // (See Note 1.)

  // Declare data members
  protected BigDecimal keyId;
  protected String type;
  protected String description;

  // Default constructor
  public PlatWrap() {
  }   // End of constructor

  // Parameterized constructor that initializes
  // the data members with the input parameters.
  public PlatWrap(BigDecimal keyId,
                  String type, String description ) {
    this.keyId = keyId;
    this.type = type;
    this.description = description;
```

```
}    // End of constructor

// getter method returns the value of the keyId
// data member that has been previously set
// by the setKeyId() method
public java.math.BigDecimal getKeyId() {
  return keyId;
}

// setter method that assigns the input parameter
// to the keyId data member.
public void setKeyId(BigDecimal keyId) {
  this.keyId = keyId;
}
// getter method returns the value of the type
// data member that has been previously set
// by the setType() method
public String getType() {
  return type;
}
// setter method that assigns the input parameter
// to the type data member.
public void setType(String type) {
  this.type = type;
}
// getter method returns the value of the description
// data member that has been previously set
// by the setDescription () method
public String getDescription() {
  return description;
}
  // setter method that assigns the input parameter
// to the description data member.
public void setDescription(String description) {
  this.description = description;
}
} // End of PlatWrap class
```

Note on the `PlatWrap` class:

This class provides a getter and a setter method for each column attribute of the `PLATFORM_TYPE_LIST` table. Note the use of the **this** Java keyword in the parameterized constructor as well as in the getter methods. Remember that the keyword **this** refers to the immediate object and removes the ambiguity between the member variables of the class and the arguments of the constructor and the methods. (See Appendix B to learn more about the **this** keyword and other Java constructs.)

1. This statement defines the `PlatWrap` class as a Java serializable object. A Java class becomes a serializable object when it implements the `java.io.Serializable` **interface**. When you create a serialized object, Java stores the state of the object in a stream. A stream is a sequence of bytes. It does so with sufficient information so that the object can be reconstructed at the receiving end of the stream. The concept of serialization is very important when you wish to ship Java objects across a network. For example, Java requires processes called *marshaling* and *unmarshaling* in order to send data across different address spaces. Marshaling packs a method call's parameters (at a client's space) or return values (at a server's space) into a standard format for transmission. Unmarshaling, the reverse operation, unpacks the standard format to an appropriate data presentation in the address space of a receiving process. Marshaling and unmarshaling can only be used on serialized objects. The SQLJ application that you are developing does not require that the `PlatWrap` be a serialized object, but the RMI and the EJB applications that you will develop in the subsequent sections do require a serialized object.

Step 5   Create the `PlatformDbObject` SQLJ class, defined in a file with the `.sqlj` extension, that extends the implementation class. This SQLJ application provides the method body for the `getPlatformList()` method defined in the `ObservationInterface` **interface**. Note that the class also provides the `printPlatformDetails()` method for displaying the column attributes of the table. This method is only visible within the scope of the `PlatformDbObject` class. No other program can access it. This method was created only to enable you to test the SQLJ application before creating the client application. After testing the output from the class, you may remove it from the `PlatformDbObject` class if you wish.

```
/*     Program Name: PlatformDbObject.sqlj
**     Purpose:     A SQLJ Class that extends the
**  ObservationAdaptor and fully implements the
**  getPlatformList(): Vector from the ObservationInterface
**  to query the obsschema schema stored in Oracle8i
*/

package rmi.platform;

// Required SQLJ classes for any SQLJ program
import sqlj.runtime.*;
import sqlj.runtime.ref.*;

// Required Oracle classes for Oracle database
```

```java
import oracle.sql.*;
import oracle.sqlj.runtime.Oracle;
import oracle.jdbc.driver.*;

import java.sql.*;
import java.math.BigDecimal;
import java.util.Vector;

// (See Note 1.)
public class PlatformDbObject extends ObservationAdaptor {

    // Declare a named iterator
    #sql iterator PlatformColumnIter (int  aPlatformId,
      String aType, String aDesc); // (See Note 2.)

    public PlatformDbObject () {
      try {
          // Instantiate Default Context for the database server
          Oracle.connect(PlatformDbObject.class,
            "connect.properties");  // (See Note 3.)
      } // end try
      catch (Exception ex) {
        System.err.println(" Contructor Error from "
          + "PlatformDbObject: " + ex);
      } // end catch
   }   // end constructor

  public static void main(String [] args)
    throws SQLException {

    PlatformDbObject app = new PlatformDbObject();

    // Stop program execution because I cannot connect to DB.
    // (See Note 4.)
    if  ( DefaultContext.getDefaultContext() == null ) {
        System.out.println("I cannot connect to the database"
            + " -- Stop executing PlatformDbObject.sqlj");
        System.exit(1);
    }  // End if

    // Retrieve platform data from the database (See Note 5.)
    Vector platformVector = app.getPlatformList();
    if  (platformVector == null) {
        System.out.println("No records found ");
        System.exit(1);
    }  // End if

    // Create an array of PlatFormType
```

```
    PlatWrap[] platformTypes =
      new PlatWrap[platformVector.size ()];   // (See Note 6.)

    // Copy the vector content into the PlatFormType[]
    platformVector.copyInto(platformTypes);    // (See Note 7.)

    // Print the details
    printPlatformDetails(platformTypes);      // (See Note 8.)
  }  // End main()

public Vector getPlatformList()throws SQLException {

    // Use platformVector to store PlatFormType objects
    Vector platformVector = new Vector();

    // Use PlatformColumnIter to retrieve
    // rows of data from PLATFORM_TYPE_LIST table
    PlatformColumnIter aPlatformColumnIter = null;

    try {
        #sql aPlatformColumnIter =          // (See Note 9.)
           { SELECT P.key_id AS aPlatformId,
                    P.type AS aType,
                    P.description AS aDesc
             FROM PLATFORM_TYPE_LIST P
           };

        while (aPlatformColumnIter.next()) {  // (See Note 10.)
          int keyId = aPlatformColumnIter.aPlatformId();
          String type = aPlatformColumnIter.aType();
          String description = aPlatformColumnIter.aDesc();

          // Instantiate aPlatformType   (See Note 11.)
          PlatWrap aPlatformType = new PlatWrap();

          // Set the data members of the aPlatformType object
          // (See Note 12.)
          aPlatformType.setKeyId(new BigDecimal(keyId));
          aPlatformType.setType(type);
          aPlatformType.setDescription(description);

          // add a PlatformType object to the platformVector
          // (See Note 13.)
          platformVector.addElement(aPlatformType);
        }  // End while

        // Close the SQLJ iterator
```

```
      aPlatformColumnIter.close();
  }  // End of try
  catch (SQLException e) {
        e.printStackTrace();
  }  // End of catch

  System.out.println("Number of records found: "
          + platformVector.size());
  return platformVector;  // (See Note 14.)

}   // End getPlatformList()

public static void printPlatformDetails(PlatWrap[] p)
   throws SQLException {
   if ( p[0].getKeyId()== null )  {
      System.out.println("Platforms do not exist ");
      return;
   }  // End if

   int i;
   for (i = 0; i < p.length; i++) {   // (See Note 15.)
       System.out.println(
          ((p[i].getKeyId()==null) ?
             "NULL keyId" : p[i].getKeyId().toString())
             + " " + ((p[i].getType()==null) ?
             "NULL type" : p[i].getType())
             + " " + ((p[i].getDescription()==null) ?
              "NULL description" : p[i].getDescription()) );
   } // End of for loop

}   // End printPlatformDetails ()

}  // End of PlatformDbObject class
```

Notes on the `PlatformDbObject` SQLJ application:

1. This statement declares the `PlatformDbObject` class as a subclass of the `ObservationAdaptor` class (see Appendix B for a definition and examples of Java subclasses).

2. This iterator declaration clause declares a named iterator, the `PlatformColumnIter`, which is used to select rows from the `PLATFORM_TYPE_LIST` table. Remember that when you specify an iterator in a SQLJ application, SQLJ generates a class named `PlatformColumnIter`. (See Chapters 2 and 3 to learn more about SQLJ iterators.)

3. This statement uses the `Oracle.connect()` method to create an instance of the `DefaultContext` class. The method installs the new connection as the static default context. The database connection uses the JDBC driver, URL, listener port, Oracle SID, username, and user password parameters listed in the properties file. (See Chapters 2 and 5 to learn more about the `Oracle.connect()` method.)

4. This statement uses the `getDefaultContext()` method from the `DefaultContext` class to determine if a connection instance exists. You will want to stop program execution if the program did not establish a database connection.

5. This statement calls the `getPlatformList()` method and stores the results into a `Vector` variable. The method returns a `Vector` (set) of `PlatWrap` objects.

6. This statement creates an array of `PlatWrap` objects. Note that the array length is equal to the size of the vector that is returned by a call to the `platformVector.size()`. (See Appendix B to learn about Java arrays.)

7. This statement uses the `copyInto()` method from the Java `Vector` class to copy all the vector's elements into the `platformTypes[]` array.

8. This statement calls the `printPlatformDetails()` method to print the objects' values from the `platformTypes[]` array. Note that a class can define methods that are not specified in the **interface**. These methods, however, can only be invoked within the JVM that is running these services. If you later decide to use the SQLJ object as a remote object, the methods that you declare in this class that are not specified in the **interface** cannot be invoked remotely.

9. This assignment clause executes a `SELECT` statement, constructs an iterator object that contains the result table for the `SELECT` statement, and assigns the iterator object to the variable `aPlatformColumnIter`. Note that an execution context instance is associated implicitly with this SQL operation. Also, because the application is using a default connection, it is not necessary to specify a connection context instance. (See Chapters 3 and 5 to learn more about SQLJ iterator, connection, and execution context statements.)

10. The `next()` method, which belongs to the generated class, `PlatformColumnIter`, advances the iterator to successive rows in the SQLJ result set. This method is similar to the `next()` method for the JDBC `ResultSet`. The `next()` method returns a value of true when the next

row is available or a value of false when all table rows have been fetched from the iterator. (See Appendix C to learn more about JDBC `ResultSet`.)

11. This statement creates an instance of `PlatWrap` class. You wish to store a set of these objects in the `platformVector` variable.

12. This statement and the two that follow it use the `setKeyID()`, `setType()`, and `setDescription()` methods from the `PlatWrap` class to set the values for the `keyId`, `type`, and `description`, respectively. Remember that those methods are called "setters."

13. This statement adds a `PlatWrap` object into the `platformVector` `Vector` variable.

14. This statement returns a vector of `PlatWrap` objects.

15. This statement prints all the objects' values from the `PlatWrap` object array. Note the use of the Java tertiary operator, the "`expression ? op 1: op 2`," to test for null values. After evaluating the expression "`p[i].getKeyId()==null`," the tertiary operator returns "op 1" if the expression evaluates to be true or "op 2" if it evaluates to false. Remember also that SQL nulls from the database are converted to Java null values. Also note that if the receiving Java type is primitive and an attempt is made to retrieve a SQL null, then a `sqlj.runtime.SQLNullException` is thrown and no assignment is made.

Step 6 Compile the classes from Steps 2 to 5. Use the `javac` compiler and the SQLJ translator to do so. Your `connect.properties` file must reside in the same directory as the `.class` files that the programs generated. The .class files are located in the `device:\deployobjects\rmi\platform` directory, where `device` is a driver letter (see Listing 8-2).

Listing 8-2

```
// At the command line
// First:   Set your CLASSPATH.
set CLASSPATH=%CLASSPATH%;device:\buildobjects

// Go to the directory that you created in Step 1
cd device:\buildobjects\rmi\platform

// Compile all programs using the SQLJ Translator.
// The *.java allows you to compile all Java source code.
// The "-d" option sends the classes to the deployobjects directory
sqlj -profile=false -d=device:\deployobjects
  PlatformDbObject.sqlj *.java
```

Step 7   Run the `PlatformDbObject` class to make sure it delivers the expected result. You do so either at the command line by invoking the JVM (for example, `java PlatformDbObject`) or by using the facility of the tool that you use to develop the source code (see Listing 8-3).

Listing 8-3

```
// At the command line
// First:    Set your CLASSPATH.
set CLASSPATH=%CLASSPATH%device:\deployobjects;

// Go to the deployobjects directory
cd device:\deployobjects\rmi\platform

// Execute the following command to run the SQLJ application
java rmi.platform.PlatformDbObject
```

Note that you must qualify the name of the program with its package name. This maps the fully qualified package name of a class and the directory path to that class. The mapping lets the Java compiler know the directory in which to find the class files mentioned in a program. In Listing 8-3, you run the program using the package name, `rmi.platform`.

Step 8   Create the `ClientAppAccessesSqljObj` SQLJ client-side application that uses the SQLJ business object.

```
/*      Program Name:      ClientAppAccessesSqljObj.sqlj
**
**      Purpose:           This SQLJ application will access
**   the SQLJ object via the interface ObservationInterface.
*/

package rmi.platform;

// Required SQLJ classes for any SQLJ program
import sqlj.runtime.*;
import sqlj.runtime.ref.*;

// Required Oracle classes for Oracle database
import oracle.sql.*;
import oracle.sqlj.runtime.Oracle;
import oracle.jdbc.driver.*;

import java.sql.*;
import java.math.BigDecimal;
import java.util.*;
```

```java
import java.util.Vector;

public class ClientAppAccessesSqljObj {

  // (See Note 1.)
  protected static ObservationInterface sqljObject;
  public ClientAppAccessesSqljObj()
    throws SQLException {

    // Connect to the database
    sqljObject = new PlatformDbObject();   // (See Note 2.)
  } // End of constructor

  public static void main(String[] args)
    throws SQLException  {

    ClientAppAccessesSqljObj app =
              new ClientAppAccessesSqljObj();

    if  (DefaultContext.getDefaultContext() == null ) {
        System.out.println("I cannot connect to "
                    + "the database "
                    + "-- Stop Execution.");
        System.exit(1);
    }   // End if

    // Declare a platform vector
    Vector platformVector = null;

    try {
        platformVector =
          sqljObject.getPlatformList();  // (See Note 3.)
    }   // End of try
    catch (SQLException ex) {
        System.out.println("Error calling the SQLJ"
              + " object " + ex + "\n");
        String sqlMessage = ex.getMessage();
        System.out.println("SQL Message: "
              + sqlMessage + "\n");
        System.exit(1);
    }  // end of catch

    try {
        // Print the details
        printPlatformDetails(platformVector); // (See Note 4.)
    }  // End of try
    catch (SQLException ex) {
        System.out.println("Error printing platform"
```

```
                        + " details " + ex + "\n");
              String sqlMessage = ex.getMessage();
              System.out.println("SQL Message: "
                        + sqlMessage + "\n");
        }  // end of catch
    }  // End of main()

    public static void printPlatformDetails(Vector platformVector)
        throws SQLException {
      if  (platformVector == null) {
          System.out.println("No Data FOUND");
          return;
      }  // End if

      PlatWrap p = null;
      Enumeration enum = platformVector.elements();

      // Iterate to get the column
      // attributes from the table
      while (enum.hasMoreElements()) {    // (See Note 5.)
          // Get PlatformType from the platformVector
          p = (PlatWrap)enum.nextElement();

          // Get the column values
          System.out.println(
            ((p.getKeyId()==null) ? " " : p.getKeyId().toString())
              + " " + ((p.getType()==null) ? " " : p.getType()) + " "
              +((p.getDescription()==null) ? " " : p.getDescription()
                  ) );
      }     // End of while

    }  // End of printPlatformDetails()

}  // End of ClientAppAccessesSqljObj class
```

Notes on the `ClientAppAccessesSqljObj` application:

This client application uses the `getPlatformList()` method defined in the SQLJ object's **interface**, `ObservationInterface`, to query the `PLATFORM_TYPE_LIST` table. It calls the `getPlatformList()` method whose body is in the `PlatformDbObject` SQLJ program. The `ClientAppAccessesSqljObj` application uses its own method, `printPlatformDetails()`, to print the values from a `Vector` variable.

    1. This statement declares an instance of the `ObservationInterface` **interface**, the `sqljObject`.

2. This statement instantiates `sqljObject` to an object of type `PlatformDbObject`. You need to do this because you wish to access the `getPlatformList()` method specified in the **interface**, `ObservationInterface`, whose method body resides in the `PlatformDbObject` class.

3. This statement calls the `getPlatformList()` method in the `PlatformDbObject` program.

4. This statement calls the local function `printPlatformDetails()` from the `ClientAppAccessesSqljObj` application to print the values of the objects from the `platformVector` variable. It does *not* call `printPlatformDetails()` method from the `PlatformDbObject` class. Remember that the latter method is visible only within the scope of the `PlatformDbObject` class. See Note 8 from the "Notes on the `PlatformDbObject` SQLJ application" section of this chapter.

5. This statement uses an object of the Java `Enumeration` type to print the values from the platformVector variable.

Step 9 Recompile all the programs as you did in Step 6.

```
// Review Step 6 to set your classpath
sqlj -profile=false -d=path\deployobjects PlatformDbObject.sqlj *.java
```

Step 10 Run the client-side application, `ClientAppAccessesSqljObj`.

```
// Set your classpath. Review Step 7 to do so.
java rmi.platform.ClientAppAccessesSqljObj
```

In the following section, you will develop an RMI application that uses the SQLJ business object that you created in the "Designing and Developing a SQLJ Component-Based Object" section of this chapter.

Deploying a SQLJ Component Using the Java Remote Method Invocation

In the previous section, you created a SQLJ component-based object and a client program that uses the object. In this scenario, both the client and SQLJ object resided on the same machine, the `datai` server. In this section, you will develop an application where a client located on any machine on a network will use a business object that resides on a different machine, possibly on the same network or on different networks. In the situation where the two objects reside on different machines, you need a mechanism by which these objects can communicate. The Java Remote Method Invocation provides that mechanism.

What Is RMI?

Java RMI provides distributed facilities for software components written in Java. Developing and deploying a distributed application using RMI is fairly quick and easy. RMI uses a network-based registry to keep track of the distributed objects. It depends on a naming mechanism called the *rmiregistry*. The rmiregistry runs on a server machine and holds information about the available server objects. A server object makes a method available for remote invocation by binding it to a name in its registry. A Java/RMI client (see Figure 8-4) accesses the remote server object by acquiring an object reference to a Java/RMI server object. It uses a stub class to invoke remote objects. A client first does a lookup for a server object reference and then invokes methods on the server object as if the server object resided in the client's address space. Alternatively, another Java class can do the lookup. In this section, you will develop an RMI-based application where a Java class other than the client, the `RmiPlatformDbObject` class (Figure 8-5), will do the object lookup for you. Note that a Java class acquires a server object via a URL address. You will use a URL to name your server objects the same way you would name an HTML page. For example, the "`rmi://datai/PlatformServer`" specified in the listing of the `RmiPlatformDbObject` class is the URL address of the server object that you will create. For more information concerning the RMI distributed

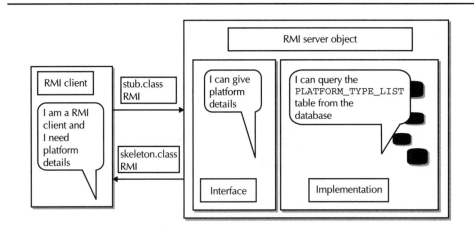

FIGURE 8-4. *RMI client invokes RMI server object*

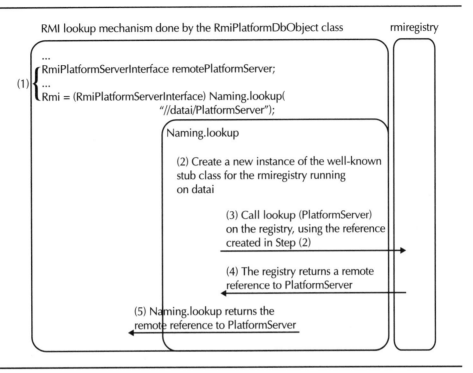

RMI lookup mechanism done by the RmiPlatformDbObject class

rmiregistry

```
...
RmiPlatformServerInterface remotePlatformServer;
(1) ...
Rmi = (RmiPlatformServerInterface) Naming.lookup(
                    "//datai/PlatformServer");
```

Naming.lookup

(2) Create a new instance of the well-known stub class for the rmiregistry running on datai

(3) Call lookup (PlatformServer) on the registry, using the reference created in Step (2)

(4) The registry returns a remote reference to PlatformServer

(5) Naming.lookup returns the remote reference to PlatformServer

FIGURE 8-5.   *RMI lookup mechanism*

model, see the Java Remote Method Invocation Specification, http://java.sun.com/products/jdk/1.2/docs/guide/rmi/spec/rmiTOC.doc.html [26].

RMI Object Composites

An RMI-based application consists of:

- An object **interface** which, as in the SQLJ component, specifies the behavior of the RMI object.

- An implementation class that specifies the behavior definitions specified by the object interface class.

- A client object that makes requests by invoking methods on the remote objects.

Developing an RMI Object

The steps to create a distributed version of your SQLJ component using RMI are as follows:

1. Create a high-level view of the RMI-based application.

2. Create a Java **interface** server object, RmiPlatformServerInterface.

3. Create a Java implementation server object, RmiPlatformServerImplementation.

4. Create a Java class, RmiPlatformDbObject, to do the object lookup in the rmiregistry located on the datai server, get a reference to the SQLJ object, and load its class.

5. Create the ClientAppAccessesRmiObj client-side application that uses the remote service.

6. Compile all the classes from Steps 2 to 6 including the classes for the SQLJ object.

7. Run the implementation class through the rmic compiler to create the stub and skeleton classes for the client and the server.

8. Start the RMI registry.

9. Start the rmi.platform.RmiPlatformServerImplementation implementation server class.

10. Start the client.

Step 1 Create a high-level view of the application (see Figure 8-6).

Step 2 Create the RmiPlatformServerInterface Java **interface**. The primary function of the **interface**, like the ObservationInterface of the SQLJ business object, is to inform the clients of available methods on the server. In your RMI application, the only available method from the class is the getPlatformList() method. You may specify more methods if you wish. If you do so, do not forget to provide the method bodies. Remember that you created the getPlatformList() method body in the PlatformDbObject SQLJ application in the "Designing and Developing a SQLJ Component-Based Object" section of this chapter.

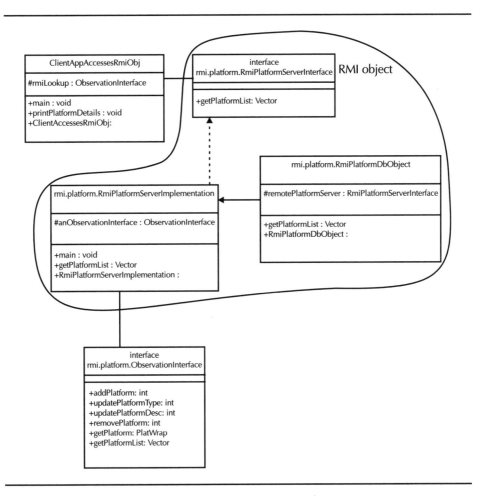

FIGURE 8-6. *RMI object that uses a SQLJ business object*

```
/*      Program Name: RmiPlatformServerInterface.java   */

package rmi.platform;      // (See Note 1.)

import java.rmi.*;       // (See Note 2.)
import java.sql.SQLException;
import java.util.*;

public interface RmiPlatformServerInterface
    extends java.rmi.Remote { // (See Note 3.)
  // This interface advertises only the getPlatformList() method.
```

```
// When you design a RMI remote interface, you must include
// in this class all the methods that you want to be accessed by
// your RMI client.
Vector getPlatformList()
  throws RemoteException, SQLException;  // (See Note 4.)
}  // End of RmiPlatformServerInterface interface
```

Notes on the `RmiPlatformServerInterface` **interface**:

1. This statement specifies that the class resides in the same package as the SQLJ business object interface, the `rmi.platform` package.

2. This statement and the one that follows it make the `java.rmi.*` package and the `java.sql.SQLException` class available to the `RmiPlatformServerInterface` **interface**.

3. This statement declares a **public interface**. Remember that you must declare this **interface public**, otherwise an error will be generated when a client calls the `getPlatformList()` method. More importantly, an RMI **interface** must extend the `java.rmi.Remote` **interface**.

4. This statement declares the remote method that can be invoked by a client. Each method specified in the **interface** class must declare `java.rmi.RemoteException` or a superclass of `RemoteException` in its **throws** clause. With RMI-based applications, the Java language reports network-related communication and server problems by throwing `java.rmi.RemoteException` exceptions. In addition to the `RemoteException` in the **throws** clause, you also need to specify any application-specific exceptions. For example, you have to add the `SQLException` in the **throws** clause because the `getPlatformList()` method accesses a database. Also remember that you need to declare the data type of the remote object as the remote interface type. In this program, the Java `Vector` is the return data type.

Step 3 Create the `RmiPlatformServerImplementation` server class. The functions of an RMI remote implementation class are as follows:

■ Implement a remote **interface**.

■ Get the object ready so that it can accept incoming remote calls. To do so, the object needs to be "exported" when the client instantiates the object. Object exportation is done by the constructor of the `java.rmi.server.UnicastRemoteObject` class. For more information regarding object's exportation, see Note 4 in the "Notes on the RmiPlatformServerImplementation class" section of this chapter.

■ Declare a constructor that throws a java.rmi.RemoteException and any application-specific exceptions.

Here is the listing of the RmiPlatformServerImplementation class:

```
/*      Program Name:     RmiPlatformServerImplementation.java
**
**      Purpose:          This is the RMI implements class.
*/

package rmi.platform;

import java.rmi.server.*;          // (See Note 1.)
import java.rmi.*;
import java.sql.SQLException;
import java.util.*;

public class RmiPlatformServerImplementation
    extends java.rmi.server.UnicastRemoteObject
    implements RmiPlatformServerInterface {  // (See Note 2.)
  // (See Note 3.)
  protected ObservationInterface anObservationInterface;

  public RmiPlatformServerImplementation ()
    throws RemoteException, SQLException {  // (See Note 4.)
    // (See Note 5.)
    anObservationInterface = new PlatformDbObject();
  }  // End of constructor

  public Vector getPlatformList()
    throws RemoteException, SQLException {  // (See Note 6.)

    Vector platformVector = null;
    // (See Note 7.)
    platformVector = anObservationInterface.getPlatformList();
    return platformVector;
  }  // End of getPlatformList()

  public static void main(String[] args) {

    // Create and install a security manager
    if (System.getSecurityManager() == null) {  // (See Note 8.)
      System.setSecurityManager(new RMISecurityManager());
    }  // End if
```

```
try {    // (See Note 9.)
    RmiPlatformServerImplementation myServer =
            new RmiPlatformServerImplementation();
    System.out.println("Binding the object");

    // Bind this object instance to the name PlatformServer
    // (See Note 10.)
    Naming.rebind("//datai/PlatformServer", myServer);
    System.out.println("Platform Server ready!");
} // End of try
catch (Exception e) {
    System.out.println(e.getMessage());
    e.printStackTrace();
} // End of catch

} // End of main()

} // End of RmiPlatformServerImplementation class
```

Notes on the `RmiPlatformServerImplementation` class:

1. This statement makes the `java.rmi.server.*` and the `java.rmi.*` packages available to the class.

2. This statement extends the `java.rmi.server.UnicastRemoteObject` interface class. In the Java language, a remote object implementation must implement, at a minimum, one remote **interface**. The `java.rmi.server.UnicastRemoteObject` class provides the capability to create a remote object that can use RMI's default socket-based transport for communication between a client and a server and also enables the `RmiPlatformServerImplementation` class to run all the time.

3. This statement creates a variable of type `ObservationInterface`. Remember that you want to use the SQLJ object you created in the "Designing and Developing a SQLJ Component-Based Object" section of this chapter. Note that you can only access the object via its access points as specified in the object's interface.

4. This statement declares the constructor for the remote object. This constructor, like any other Java constructor, calls the constructor of its superclass, "`java.rmi.server.UnicastRemoteObject`," which allows an instance of the class to be exported. Exporting a remote object makes the object available to accept incoming remote requests by listening for incoming calls to the remote object on an anonymous or designated port number. When you instantiate the `RmiPlatformServer`

Implementation class via a call to its constructor, the class will automatically be exported. Remember that Java requires that you include the RemoteException in the **throws** clause even if the constructor does nothing else. If you forgot the constructor, the javac compiler will generate an error.

5. This statement creates an instance of the PlatformDbObject class and stores the result in a variable of type ObservationInterface. You can use the instance to call the getPlatformType() method, whose method body resides in the PlatformDbObject class.

6. This method declaration includes the RemoteException and the application-specific exception, the SQLException. This class provides the method body as required.

7. This statement calls the getPlatformList() method of the PlatformDbObject using RMI.

8. First, the main() method of the class must create and install a security manager. This is done by invoking the System.getSecurity Manager() method from the RmiSecurityManager class. The security manager guarantees that the loaded class performs only the allowed operations. RMI clients or servers cannot load a class when there is no security manager. Second, the main() creates an instance of the remote object implementation and binds that instance to a name in the rmiregistry.

9. The first statement in the try block creates an instance of the remote object. Upon instantiation, the remote object is exported and is therefore ready to receive incoming requests from clients.

10. This statement registers the remote object in the rmiregistry on the datai server with the name PlatformServer. Remember that a rmiregistry is a server name service that allows remote clients to get a reference to a remote object. Also, the rmiregistry binds an URL-formatted name of the form "//localhost/YourObjectBindingName," where localhost is your host, like datai, and the YourObjectBindingName is a user-defined string like the PlatformServer string. Once you register a remote object in the rmiregistry, clients can do object lookups using the URL-formatted name that you defined in the program. In this example, clients will use the //datai/PlatformServer URL to get a reference to the remote object associated with this name. Note that the rmiregistry runs on a default port number, 1099. You may use a port number other than the default, but in this case, you will need to provide your own. For example, you could use port number 1620. If you do, you must specify the 1620 port

in your program, "//datai:1620/PlatformServer". The `myServer` is a reference to the object implementation on which remote methods will be invoked. Remote implementation objects never leave the JVM where they are created. Clients that do remote requests always get a serialized instance of the implementation stub class and never get an actual copy of the object. For example, clients will get an instance of the `RmiPlatformServerImplementation_Stub` class. The stub and the skeleton classes will be generated in Step 7 of this section where you will invoke the *rmic* compiler. Since clients get a reference to the remote object instead of an actual copy, they would need to reconstruct the object in their address space. This is one of the reasons why Java requires that the object be serialized. Remember that Java stores a serializable object in a stream with sufficient information to reconstruct the object. Note that for security reasons for the Java language, an application can only bind or unbind an object on the rmiregistry running on the same host. Object lookups, however, can be done from any host.

Step 4   Create a Java class, the `RmiPlatformDbObject` class, to get a reference to the SQLJ object and load its class.

```
/*      Program Name:    RmiPlatformDbObject.java
**
**      Purpose:         This class does a lookup to
** get the server object reference.
*/

package rmi.platform;

import java.rmi.*;       // (See Note 1.)
import java.sql.SQLException;
import java.util.*;

public class RmiPlatformDbObject
     extends ObservationAdaptor {    // (See Note 2.)

  protected RmiPlatformServerInterface remotePlatformServer;

  public RmiPlatformDbObject ()
     throws RemoteException, SQLException {   // (See Note 3.)

   try {
       if (System.getSecurityManager() == null) { // (See Note 4.)
          System.setSecurityManager(new RMISecurityManager());
       }    // End if

       // (See Note 5.)
       remotePlatformServer =
          (RmiPlatformServerInterface)
```

```
              Naming.lookup("rmi://datai/PlatformServer");

          System.out.println ("Naming lookup WORKED");
      }    // End of try
    catch (Exception e) {
        System.out.println ("Naming lookup did not work");
        e.printStackTrace();
      }   // End of catch()

  }   // End of constructor

  public Vector getPlatformList()
      throws SQLException {

    Vector platformVector = null;
    try {      // (See Note 6.)
        platformVector =
          remotePlatformServer.getPlatformList();
      }   // End of try
    catch (RemoteException e) {    // (See Note 7.)
        e.printStackTrace();
      }   // End of catch

    return platformVector;

  }   // End of getPlatformList()

}   // End of RmiPlatformDbObject class
```

Notes on the `RmiPlatformDbObject` class:

1. This statement makes the `java.rmi` package available to the program.
   RMI clients need some classes from this package such as the `Naming` and
   `RemoteException` classes.

2. This statement extends the `ObservationInterface` **interface** of the
   SQLJ object.

3. This statement creates a Java variable, the `remotePlatformServer`, of
   type `RmiPlatformServerInterface`.

4. This statement will create and install a security manager if none is present.

5. This statement does an object lookup by calling the `Naming.lookup()`
   method. This method will return a reference to the remote object
   implementation from the rmiregistry on the `datai` server. The
   `Naming.lookup()` method uses a format similar to the
   `Naming.rebind()` method from Note 10 in the "Notes on the
   `RmiPlatformServerImplementation` class" part of this section.

The string, the "rmi://datai/PlatformServer", specifies that you wish to get a reference of the remote object called PlatformServer from the rmiregistry located on the datai server. The Naming.lookup() method, with the arguments that you provide, will construct an instance of the RmiPlatformServerImplementation_Stub class and will return this instance to the program. Then the program will use the stub instance to load the stub class from the CLASSPATH. The RmiPlatformServerImplementation_Stub class will be generated in Step 7 when you run the RmiPlatformServerImplementation class through the rmic compiler.

6. This statement calls the getPlatformList() method specified in the RmiPlatformServerInterface interface class whose body resides in the PlatformDbObject class.

7. The method does not use the RemoteException in its **throws** clause but instead it does so in a **catch** block.

Step 5   Create the ClientAppAccessesRmiObj client-side application that uses the remote service.

The ClientAppAccessesSqljObj SQLJ client that you created in the "Designing and Developing a SQLJ Component-Based Object" section of this chapter is similar to the RMI client, but they differ from each other in the way each accesses the business object. In the previous section, you created an application where both client and business objects resided in the same address space, in the same computer. If you wanted to move the client code to another computer, you would have to move the business object code to the same computer because you did not provide the mechanism for the client to remotely access the SQLJ component.

In this application, you use RMI, which provides the mechanism to remotely access the SQLJ component, where both client and server objects reside in different address spaces. In this scenario, the RMI client code can reside anywhere on a network (possibly in another computer) independently of the location of the SQLJ component code. RMI allows the client to invoke a remote method by making a call to a client stub class (referred to as a *proxy*). The client proxy packs the call parameters into a request message and invokes the JRMP wire protocol to ship the message to the server. The server-side stub, called a *skeleton,* unpacks the message and calls the actual method on the object.

```
/*     Program Name:      ClientAppAccessesRmiObj.java
**
**     Purpose:           This Java application will access
```

```
**   a remote object using JAVA RMI.
*/
package rmi.platform;

import java.awt.*;
import java.io.*;
import java.sql.*;
import java.util.*;

// Mandatory Java classes for RMI calls
import java.rmi.Naming;
import java.rmi.RemoteException;

public class ClientAppAccessesRmiObj {

  protected static ObservationInterface rmiLookup;  // (See Note 1.)

  public ClientAppAccessesRmiObj()
      throws RemoteException, SQLException {

    // Connect to the database
    rmiLookup = new RmiPlatformDbObject();  // (See Note 2.)

  }  // End of constructor

  public static void main(String[] args)
      throws RemoteException, SQLException  {

    try {
        ClientAppAccessesRmiObj app =
             new ClientAppAccessesRmiObj();
    }  // End of try
    catch (Exception ex) {
        System.out.println("Cannot Instantiate  "
            + "the RmiPlatformDbObject class ");
        System.exit(1);
    }  // End of catch

    // Declare a platform vector
    Vector platformVector = null;

    try {
        platformVector =
            rmiLookup.getPlatformList();  // (See Note 3.)
    }    // End of try
    catch (SQLException ex) {
        System.out.println("Error calling the SQLJ"
                + " object " + ex + "\n");
```

```
            String sqlMessage = ex.getMessage();
            System.out.println("SQL Message: "
                    + sqlMessage + "\n");
            System.exit(1);
        }   // End of catch

        try {
            // Print the details
            printPlatformDetails(platformVector);
        }   // End of try
        catch (SQLException ex) {
            System.out.println("Error printing platform"
                    + " details " + ex + "\n");
            String sqlMessage = ex.getMessage();
            System.out.println("SQL Message: "
                    + sqlMessage + "\n");
        }   // End of catch

    }   // End of main()

    public static void printPlatformDetails(Vector platformVector)
        throws SQLException {
        if  (platformVector == null) {
            System.out.println("No Data FOUND");
            return;
        }   // End if

        PlatWrap p = null;
        Enumeration enum = platformVector.elements();

        // Iterate to get the column
        // attributes from the table
        while (enum.hasMoreElements()) {
            // Get PlatformType from the platformVector
            p = (PlatWrap)enum.nextElement();
            // Get the column values
            System.out.println(
              ((p.getKeyId()==null) ? " " : p.getKeyId().toString())
                + " " + ((p.getType()==null) ? " " : p.getType()) + " "
                + ((p.getDescription()==null) ? " " : p.getDescription()
                ) );
        }     // End of while

    }   // End of printPlatformDetails()

}   // End of ClientAppAccessesRmiObj class
```

Notes on the `ClientAppAccessesRmiObj` client:

1. This statement creates a Java variable of type `ObservationInterface` named `rmilookup`. Remember that you wish to access the SQLJ object from this client.

2. This statement creates an instance of the `RmiPlatformDbObject` class and stores it in the `rmilookup` variable.

3. This statement calls the `getPlatformList()` method, whose body resides in the `PlatformDbObject` class. When a client invokes the remote `getPlatformList()` method, the client's JVM looks at the `RmiPlatformServerImplementation_Stub` class. The class defined within the stub is an image of the server class. The client's request is then routed to the skeleton class located on the server, the `RmiPlatformServerImplementation_Skel` class, which in turn calls the appropriate method on the server. In this scenario, the stub acts as a proxy to the skeleton and the skeleton is a proxy to the actual object's method. Finally, RMI serializes the `PlatWrap` objects and returns them to the client.

Step 6 Compile (Listing 8-4) all the classes from Steps 2 to 6 including the classes for the SQLJ object. Set your CLASSPATH and recompile all the programs in the `rmi.platform` package. To do so, review Step 6 from the "Designing and Developing a SQLJ Component-Based Object" section of this chapter.

Listing 8-4

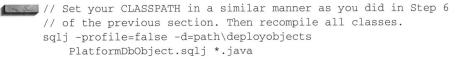

```
// Set your CLASSPATH in a similar manner as you did in Step 6
// of the previous section. Then recompile all classes.
sqlj -profile=false -d=path\deployobjects
    PlatformDbObject.sqlj *.java
```

Step 7 Run the implementation class through the rmic compiler to create the stub and skeleton classes for the client-side and server-side object, respectively. Run the compiler on the fully qualified class file name, `rmi.platform.RmiPlatformServerImplementation`, that contains the remote object implementation. When you invoke the rmic compiler (Listing 8-5), the compiler generates the class files `RmiPlatformServerImplementation_Stub.class` and `RmiPlatformServerImplementation_Skel.class`. The generated stub classes implement exactly the same set of remote interfaces as the remote object itself. Remember that a RMI client uses a reference to the stub class to load the remote object class. In fact, the stub acts as a proxy for the remote object.

Listing 8-5

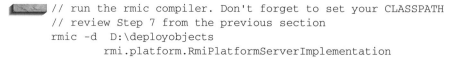

```
// run the rmic compiler. Don't forget to set your CLASSPATH
// review Step 7 from the previous section
rmic -d  D:\deployobjects
          rmi.platform.RmiPlatformServerImplementation

// The rmic compiler generates the stub and the skeleton classes
RmiPlatformServerImplementation_Stub.class
RmiPlatformServerImplementation_Skel.class
```

Step 8 Start the RMI registry (see Listing 8-6) on the datai server. At the command line, set your path and start the registry. Note that if you use a port number other than the default one, you need to specify it when you start the registry. For example, if you use port number 1620, enter rmiregistry 1620 at the command line.

Listing 8-6

```
// Get a new window and Set your CLASSPATH.
set CLASSPATH=%CLASSPATH%device:\deployobjects;

// Go to the directory where your classes are located
cd device:\deployobjects\rmi\platform

// start the rmiregistry (UNIX)
rmiregistry &

// Windows NT
rmiregistry
```

Step 9 Start the rmi.platform.RmiPlatformServerImplementation server class (see Listing 8-7).

Listing 8-7

```
// Set your CLASSPATH.  Use a new window
set CLASSPATH=%CLASSPATH%device:\deployobjects;

// Go to the directory where your classes are located
cd device:\deployobjects\rmi\platform
```

```
// Start the client
java rmi.platform.RmiPlatformServerImplementation
```

When you start the server in Listing 8-7, you will get the following output:

```
// Output when you start the server
Binding the object
Platform Server ready!
```

Step 10 Start the client (see Listing 8-8). Once the registry and the server are up and running, then you can start the client.

Listing 8-8

```
// Set your CLASSPATH
set CLASSPATH=%CLASSPATH%device:\deployobjects;

// Go to the directory where your classes are located
cd device:\deployobjects\rmi\platform

// Start the client
java rmi.platform.ClientAppAccessesRmiObj
```

In the remaining sections of this chapter, you will develop distributed applications where the business objects reside in the Oracle database. You will use EJB and CORBA to do so. In Chapters 4 and 5, you stored Java and SQLJ logic into the Oracle8*i* data server. With Java and SQLJ stored procedures and call specifications, you were limited to the set of Java classes that represent some SQL data types. With CORBA and EJB, methods take objects as arguments and return objects. Moreover, these objects maintain object identity during the entire database session.

Next, you will develop an EJB application and you will deploy the EJB object in the Oracle8*i* data server. For more information on EJB technology, consult the *Enterprise JavaBeans and CORBA Developer's Guide* [52], the bibliography at the end the book, and the Enterprise JavaBeans Specification Version 1.0 (http://java.sun.com/products/ejb/docs10.html [56]).

Deploying an Enterprise JavaBeans Object Using a SQLJ Implementation

In the previous section, you developed a RMI-based application that allowed a RMI client to use the SQLJ object you created in the "Designing and Developing a SQLJ Component-Based Object" section of this chapter. The ClientAppAccessesRmiObj client used the Java Remote Method Invocation to remotely invoke the `getPlatformList()` method of the SQLJ object. In this section, you will develop an Enterprise JavaBeans object that resides in the Oracle8*i* database and an EJB client application program (that can reside anywhere on the network) that uses the EJB object.

What Is Enterprise JavaBeans?

Enterprise JavaBeans (EJB) is a component architecture for developing and deploying distributed transaction-oriented applications written in Java. EJB is based on the RMI specification model. Remoting EJB objects is supported through the standard Java API for remote method invocation. Remember that remote invocation method is done via the Java Remote Method Invocation. You learned about RMI in the "Deploying a SQLJ Component Using the Java Remote Method Invocation" section of this chapter. The Java API, as in the RMI-based applications, allows a client to invoke an EJB object using any distributed object protocol, including the IIOP protocol (TCP/IP with some CORBA-defined message exchanges). The EJB specification 1.0 defines a standard mapping of EJB to CORBA that enables a non-Java CORBA client to access EJB objects and any other client that uses an ORB to access EJB objects that reside on CORBA-based EJB servers (see Figure 8-7). Also, Web browser clients can use the HTTP protocol (set of rules for exchanging files over the World Wide Web) to invoke servlets that invoke EJB objects. Servlets are Java modules that extend request/response-oriented servers such as Java-enabled Web servers. They provide a way to generate dynamic documents. The `javax.servlet` package provides interfaces and classes for writing servlets. Servlets can be embedded in many different servers but are mostly embedded within HTTP servers.

Enterprise JavaBeans Roles

The EJB architecture defines six roles in the development and deployment of enterprise Beans. Each role can be performed by a different party, but also a single party may perform several roles. The roles are as follows:

1. An *enterprise Bean provider* develops a component called *enterprise Bean* that implements a business task. In this section you will assume the role of an enterprise Bean provider and as such you will develop an enterprise Bean that produces a listing of the platforms from the Observation schema.

2. An *application assembler* composes applications (for example, GUI, servlets, applets, or scripts) that use the enterprise Bean.

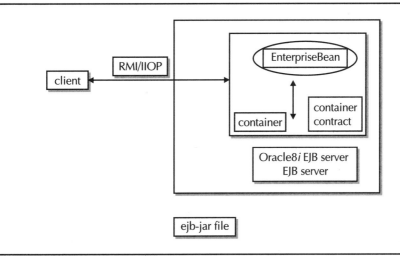

FIGURE 8-7.   *Enterprise JavaBeans container contract (specification 1.0)*

3. A *deployer* is responsible for the deployment of enterprise Beans and their containers. An enterprise Bean lives in a container and a container lives in an application or database server.

4. An *EJB server* provider is usually an operating system, a middleware, or a database vendor. An EJB server is a collection of services for supporting EJB installations. An EJB server manages the resources needed to support EJB components.

5. An *EJB container provider* provides an API that insulates the enterprise Bean from the specifics of an underlying EJB server. EJB components reside in an EJB container. An EJB container is a system that manages the life of an enterprise Bean. It provides the environment in which the Beans can operate, handles the object life cycle, including creating and destroying an object, and also the state management of the Beans. In the next section, you will learn about the state management of an enterprise Bean.

6. A *system administrator* is responsible for monitoring the system where the enterprise Beans are running.

Types of Enterprise JavaBeans

The EJB architecture defines two types of enterprise Beans, the session object type and the entity type Bean, where the former lives in an EJB session container and the latter in an EJB entity container:

■ A *session object type* is a logical extension of a single-client program and executes on behalf of the client that creates it. It is relatively short-lived—that is, its life is that of its client, and it is removed when the client quits or the EJB server crashes. EJB server providers—like Oracle, provide session containers where an EJB session is just a database session. A fundamental characteristic of a database session is that the session dies when the user disconnects with the database or when the data server crashes.

In order to manage the session Bean container (Figure 8-7), one must know its *state management mode.* At deployment time, a session Bean is specified as having either a STATELESS or a STATEFUL state management mode. A session Bean is said to be STATELESS when the Bean can be used by any client (moreover, its state is not retained across methods and transactions), or STATEFUL when the session Bean does retain its state. A STATELESS session Bean is referred to as a Bean that contains no conversational state, whereas a STATEFUL session Bean contains a conversational state. Note that the Oracle8*i* EJB server implements only the EJB session container contract as specified by the EJB specification and does not differentiate between a STATELESS and a STATEFUL session Bean. In other words, the Oracle8*i* EJB server identifies both STATELESS and STATEFUL session Beans as STATELESS.

■ An *entity enterprise Bean* is a persistent object that represents an object view of an entity stored in a persistent storage (for example, a database) or an entity that is implemented by an application. Unlike an enterprise session Bean, an entity Bean can be accessed concurrently by multiple clients, its client object view is location independent, and its lifetime is not limited by the lifetime of the JVM process in which it executes, that is, an entity Bean does not die when the EJB server crashes.

Enterprise JavaBeans Object Composites

An EJB object consists of four major components (see Figure 8-8):

■ *The Bean home* **interface.** An EJB container implements the home interface for the EJB objects that it provides. A client accesses an enterprise

Bean, irrespective of its implementation and its container, via the enterprise Bean home **interface**. The home interface allows the client to create, look up, and remove EJB objects. A client uses the Java Naming and Directory Interface (JNDI) to locate the home interface. The JNDI architecture (developed by Sun and the other partners such as IBM, Hewlett Packard, Netscape, Novell, and so on) provides naming and directory functionality to Java applications and consists of an Application Programming Interface (API) and a Service Provider Interface (SPI). Remember that the EJB container is a system that manages the life of an enterprise Bean. The EJB container also provides the Bean instances with a SessionContext interface class that consists of several methods that allow a client to manipulate Context instances maintained by the container. The notion of a context, defined by the Context package, is the core interface for clients to look up, bind, unbind, and rename EJB objects, and create and destroy sub-contexts. For example, a client uses an instance of the InitialContext class to look up an EJB home interface. One context might require a specification of security credentials in order to access a service, whereas another might require a specification of the server configuration. The required specifications are referred to as the environment of a Context. The Context **interface** also provides methods for retrieving and updating the environment of a Context. For example, the ClientJavajForEjbPlatform client, which you will develop in this section, uses the following segment code to locate the container for the PlatformDb EJB object:

```
serviceURL = "sess_iiop://haiti:2481:orcl";
objectName = "/test/PlatformDb";
// where "/test" is the directory where you
// published the PlatformDb EJB object.

// Create an instance of the Context class
Context ic = new InitialContext (env);
// Use the lookup method of the Context class
// to get a reference of the PlatformHome interface object.
PlatformHome home =
      (PlatformHome)ic.lookup (serviceURL + objectName);
```

For more information regarding JNDI, see http://java.sun.com/products/jndi/ [25] and the bibliography at the end of the book.

■ *The EJB container.* This provides the enterprise Bean remote **interface**. A client uses an instance of an enterprise Bean remote **interface** to create an instance of an EJB object.

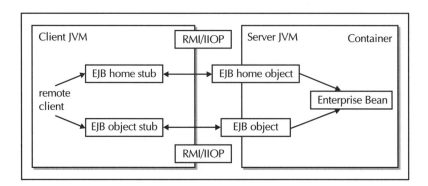

FIGURE 8-8. *EJB client-side and server-side objects*

■   *The enterprise Bean implementation class.*   This is the actual class that implements the Bean remote **interface**. The business logic methods reside in the implementation class.

■   *The Bean deployment descriptor.*   An enterprise Bean provider must include a deployment descriptor for each enterprise Bean. Deployment descriptors are serialized classes that serve a function similar to property files. They allow you to describe and customize runtime attributes, that is, runtime behaviors of server-side components (for example, security, transactional context, and so on) without having to change the Bean class or its interfaces. Deployment descriptors are created after you create the interfaces and the Bean class for your enterprise Bean. A deployment descriptor is a serialized instance of a `javax.ejb.deployment.EntityDescriptor` or `javax.ejb.deployment.SessionDescriptor` object.

Developing an Enterprise Session Bean Application

The steps to develop an EJB session Bean are as follows:

1. Create a high-level view of the EJB-based application.

2. Create the directories that you wish to use for your package name.

3. Create a Bean remote **interface** server object, the `Platform` **interface**.

4. Create a Bean home **interface** server object, the `PlatformHome` **interface**.

5. Create a Java class to map the Oracle PLATFORM_TYPE type. You will use the PlatWrap class that you created for your SQLJ component-based object.

6. Create the Bean itself, PlatformDb class. This class, like the PlatformDbObject, implements the business logic. Remember that PlatformDbObject implements the getPlatformList() method in the "Designing and Developing a SQLJ Component-Based Object" section of this chapter. The PlatformDb class implements the identical business logic and will use the PlatWrap class to ship the EJB object to the client.

7. Set your CLASSPATH and compile all the classes from Steps 3 to 6.

8. Create the deployment descriptor file, the Platform.ejb file.

9. Create a JAR file of the classes that you created from Steps 3 to 6. See Chapters 4 and 5 for more information on JAR files.

10. Load and deploy the EJB object into the Oracle8*i* EJB server.

11. Create the EJB client, the ClientJavaForEjbPlatform, to use the EJB object.

12. Set your CLASSPATH and compile the client class.

13. Run the EJB client.

CAUTION
The length of an object name that resides in the Oracle8i database is limited to 30 characters. Oracle stores the fully qualified name of the object, that is, the path and the object name. For example, the Platform ***interface*** *is stored in the database under the* platform\Platform *name. Also note that the* PIter *SQLJ iterator declared in the* PlatformDb *class is stored under the* platServer\Piter *name. Remember this limitation when you name your server-side programs.*

Step 1   Create a high-level view of the EJB-based application (see Figure 8-9).

Step 2   Create the directories you wish to use for your package name.

```
// Create the directories to store the Java and SQLJ source code
mkdir deployobjects\platform\platServer
```

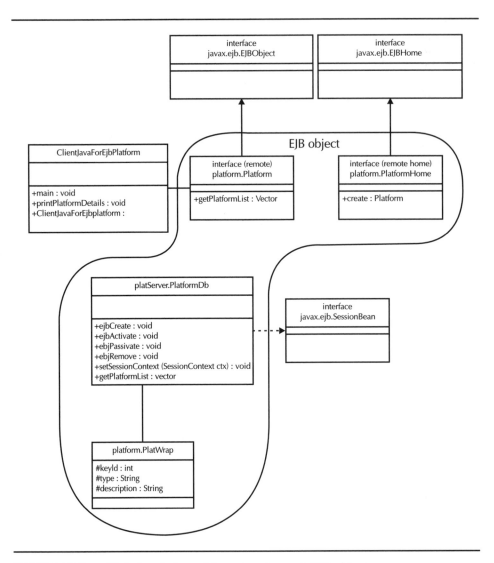

FIGURE 8-9. *High-level view of the* `PlatformDb` *EJB object*

Step 3   Create a Bean remote **interface** server object, the `Platform` **interface**:

```
/*      Program Name:    Platform.java
**
**      Purpose:    EJB remote interface
*/
```

```
package platform;
import javax.ejb.*;
import java.rmi.RemoteException;
import java.util.Vector;

public interface Platform extends EJBObject  {  // (See Note 1.)

  // Note that the Platform EJB remote interface is
  // advertising the getPlatformList() in a similar manner
  // to the RmiPlatformServerInterface in the
  // "Deploying a SQLJ Component Using the Java
  // Remote Method Invocation" section of this chapter.
  public Vector getPlatformList()
   throws java.sql.SQLException,
       RemoteException;  // (See Note 2.)

} // End of Platform interface
```

Notes on the remote Platform **interface**:

1. The Bean remote interface must be a subclass of the java.ejb. EJBObject class. The EJBObject interface must be extended by all EJB remote interface classes. The EJB remote interface, like the RMI interface, defines the methods that are callable by an EJB client. The EJBObject is an object that exposes only the remote interface that you specified. It acts like a proxy, intercepting the remote object invocations and calling the appropriate methods on the enterprise Bean instance.

2. This statement defines the methods—those that implement the business logic—that the Bean contains. As in the RMI-based applications, you must declare all the methods you wish EJB clients to have access to, and the methods must include in their **throws** clause the Java RemoteException and any application-specific exceptions. In this example, the java.sql. SQLException exception for database applications is included in the **throws** clause of the method.

Step 4: Create a Bean home **interface** server class, the PlatformHome class:

```
/*     Program Name:     PlatformHome.java
**
**     Purpose:          EJB home interface
*/

package platform;
```

```
import javax.ejb.*;
import java.rmi.RemoteException;

public interface PlatformHome extends EJBHome {  // (See Note 1.)

  public Platform create()
    throws CreateException, RemoteException;   // (See Note 2.)

}  // End of PlatformHome EJB home interface
```

Notes on the `PlatformHome` **interface**:

1. This class must be declared as a subclass of the `EJBHome` interface and must define the enterprise Bean type-specific `create()` method. An EJB container implements the `EJBHome` interface of each enterprise Bean installed in the container. It makes the `EJBHome` interfaces available to the client through JNDI, allowing the client to create and delete Beans, and query information or "metadata" about the Beans. You will need to publish the enterprise Bean home interface in order for a client to access the class. You do so with the `deployejb` tool provided by Oracle. The `deployejb` tool publishes in the database a reference to the home object as well as the EJB object, and the EJB client looks up at the home reference object to create instances of the Bean. (See Appendix D to learn more about this tool.)

2. This statement declares the `create()` method that returns a type of the EJB `PlatForm` **interface** object. EJB clients use the Bean home interface to create a Bean instance. For each create method in the home interface, there must be a corresponding method called `ejbCreate()` specified in the implements class, with the same signature (see the listing of the `PlatformDb` class following Step 6). The `create()` method is specified to return the Bean type whereas the `ejbCreate()` is a void method (see Appendix B to learn more about Java void methods). When a client invokes the `create()` method on the home, the container invokes the corresponding `ejbCreate()` method in the Bean itself. Note that the method declaration must include the `CreateException` and the `RemoteException` exceptions in its **throws** clause.

Step 5   Create a Java class to map the Oracle `PLATFORM_TYPE` type. You will use the `PlatWrap` class that you created for your SQLJ component-based object. See the listing for the `PlatWrap` class in Step 4 of the "Designing and Developing a SQLJ Component-Based Object" section of this chapter.

Step 6   Create the Bean itself, `PlatformDb` class. This class, like the
`PlatformDbObject`, implements the business logic. Remember that
`PlatformDbObject` implements the getPlatformList() method in the "Designing
and Developing a SQLJ Component-Based Object" section of this chapter. The
`PlatformDb` class implements the identical business logic and will use the
`PlatWrap` class to ship the EJB object to the client:

```
/*     Program Name: PlatformDb.sqlj
**     Purpose:       A SQLJ Class that implements the
**   SessionBean interface and fully implements the
**   getPlatformList(): Vector from the EJB remote
**   interface, the platform.java class
**   The class implements the logic to query
**   the PLATFORM_TYPE_LIST table.
**
*/
package platServer;

// import the serializable object
import platform.PlatWrap;

import java.rmi.RemoteException;
import java.sql.*;

import java.math.BigDecimal;
import java.util.Vector;
import javax.ejb.*;

public class PlatformDb implements SessionBean {    // (See Note 1.)
  SessionContext sessionCtx;

  public void ejbCreate()
    throws CreateException, RemoteException {   // (See Note 2.)
  }
  public void ejbActivate() { // (See Note 3.)
  }
  public void ejbPassivate() {
  }
  public void ejbRemove() {
  }
  public void setSessionContext(SessionContext ctx) {
      this.sessionCtx = ctx;
  }

  // Declare a named iterator
  #sql iterator PIter (int  aPlatformId,
          String aType, String aDesc);
```

```
// This is the method body for the method
// specified in the EJB remote interface: platform.java
public Vector getPlatformList()
    throws SQLException, RemoteException {

  // Use platformVector to store PlatFormType objects
  Vector platformVector = new Vector();

  // Use PIter to retrieve
  // rows of data from PLATFORM_TYPE_LIST table
  PIter anPIter = null;

  try {
      #sql anPIter =
          { SELECT P.key_id AS aPlatformId,
                   P.type AS aType,
                   P.description AS aDesc
            FROM PLATFORM_TYPE_LIST P
          };

    while (anPIter.next()) {

        int keyId = anPIter.aPlatformId();
        String type = anPIter.aType();
        String description = anPIter.aDesc();

        // Instantiate aPlatformType
        PlatWrap aPlatformType = new PlatWrap();

        // Set the data members of the aPlatformType object
        aPlatformType.setKeyId(new BigDecimal(keyId));
        aPlatformType.setType(type);
        aPlatformType.setDescription(description);

        // add a PlatformType object to the platformVector
        platformVector.addElement(aPlatformType);

    }  // End of while

    // Close the iterator
    anPIter.close();

  }  // End of try
  catch (SQLException e) {
        e.printStackTrace();
  }  // End of catch
```

```
    return platformVector;

  }   // End of getPlatformList()
} // End of PlatformDb class
```

Notes on the `PlatformDb` class:

This Bean implementation class shows the minimum methods required for an EJB implementation method. Note that the enterprise Bean class does not implement the Bean's remote interface, the `EJBObject` class does so when you install the EJB object. At invocation time, the `EJBObject` acts as a proxy, passing method invocations through to the Bean instance installed in the server.

1. The `SessionBean` **interface** must be implemented by every enterprise session Bean implementation class. The container uses the `SessionBean` methods to notify the EJB instances of the instance's life cycle events.

2. This statement implements the method that will be invoked on the server when the EJB client invokes the `create()` method from the Bean home interface.

3. This statement and the ones that follow it implement the four required methods specified by the `javax.ejb.SessionBean` interface class:

   ■ *The `ejbActivate()`*. This method is called when the instance is activated from its "passive" state. Note that the temporary transfer of the state of an idle session Bean to some form of secondary storage is called *passivation,* and the transfer back is called *activation.* At activation time, the EJB instance will acquire any resource that it had released earlier with the `ejbPassivate()` method. Oracle8*i* EJB server does not use the `ejbActivate()` method nor the `ejbPassivate()`.

   ■ *The `ejbPassivate()`*. This method is called before the instance enters the "passive" state. It will release any resource that it can reacquire later in the `ejbPassivate()` method.

   ■ *The `ejbRemove()`*. A container invokes this method before it ends the life of a session object to release system resources and destroy a Bean instance at the client's request.

   ■ *The `setSessionContext(SessionContext ctx)`*. The container can use this method to store a reference to the context object into a variable. This method is called at Bean's creation.

Step 7   Set your CLASSPATH and compile all the classes from Steps 3 to 6. Note that the Oracle `deployejb` tool cannot use any JDK version that ends with a letter (for example, JDK 1.1.7A or 1.1.7B). Use JDK 1.1.6 or JDK 1.1.8 to compile and deploy the EJB application.

```
// At the command line
set ORACLE_HOME=C:\Oracle\Ora81
// Use your database server name, your iiop port listener number.
// This is a default port number that you find in the
// listener.ora file. If you do not have access to this
//  file, ask your DBA.
set ORACLE_SERVICE=sess_iiop://datai:2481:orcl

// Use the JDK 1.1.6 or 1.1.8
set JDK_CLASSPATH=D:\jdk1.1.8\lib\classes.zip

// get to the directory that you created in step 2
cd deployobjects\platform

// Set the CLASSPATH
set CLASSPATH=.;D:\deployobjects;% \
   ORACLE_HOME%\lib\aurora_client.jar; \
 %ORACLE_HOME%\jdbc\lib\classes111.zip; \
 %ORACLE_HOME%\sqlj\lib\translator.zip; \
 %ORACLE_HOME%\lib\vbjorb.jar;  \
 %ORACLE_HOME%\lib\vbjapp.jar;%JDK_CLASSPATH%

// Compile the classes in the platform directory
javac -g *.java

// Compile the sqlj class
cd platServer
sqlj -ser2class PlatformDb.sqlj
```

Step 8   Create the deployment descriptor file, `Platform.ejb`. This is an ASCII file. By convention, you use the `.ejb` extension. The EJB container provider will provide a deployment tool that can read the descriptor file, parse it, signal parse errors, and then verify that the descriptor file, the interface declaration, and the Bean implementation declaration meet the EJB standard. Oracle provides the `deployejb` tool to do the task for you.

```
// File Name:   Platform.ejb
// platform EJB deployment descriptor.

SessionBean platServer.PlatformDb {  // (See Note 1.)
```

```
BeanHomeName = "test/PlatformDb";   // (See Note 2.)
// (See Note 3.)
RemoteInterfaceClassName = platform.Platform;
HomeInterfaceClassName = platform.PlatformHome;

AllowedIdentities = {OBSSCHEMA};  // (See Note 4.)

//  SessionTimeout = 20; (See Note 5.)
StateManagementType = STATEFUL_SESSION; // (See Note 6.)

RunAsMode = CLIENT_IDENTITY; // (See Note 7.)

TransactionAttribute = TX_REQUIRED; // (See Note 8.)
} // End of platServer.PlatformDb
```

Notes on the `Platform.ejb` deployment descriptor file:

The deployment descriptor file uses the transaction and security attributes defined by the `javax.ejb.deployment.ControlDescriptor` and the `javax.ejb.deployment.DeploymentDescriptor` classes.

1. This statement declares the `platServer.PlatformDb` EJB object as a `SessionBean`. Note that the name of the object is fully qualified with the directory where the class resides.

2. This statement declares the name of the EJB published object and the directory associated with the object. When you install Oracle8*i*, the software creates for you a directory called `test` that you can use to store the published EJB home class of the EJB object. Use the `sess_sh` tool provided by Oracle to create directories of your choice. (See Chapter 6 of the *Enterprise JavaBeans and CORBA Developer's Guide* [52] to learn more about EJB and CORBA tools.) The `sess_sh` (session shell) tool is an interactive interface to a database instance's session namespace. You specify database connection arguments when you start `sess_sh`. It then presents you with a prompt to indicate that it is ready for commands. Each database instance running the Oracle8*i* JServer software has a session namespace, which the Oracle8*i* ORB uses to activate CORBA and EJB objects. A session namespace is a hierarchical collection of objects known as `PublishedObjects` and `PublishingContexts` and is analogous to UNIX file system files and directories. A namespace incorporates the idea of a session directly in the URL, allowing the client to easily manipulate multiple sessions. In the string `"test/PlatformDb"`, the test directory is the namespace and the `PlatformDb` is the name of the `PublishedObject`. Each `PublishedObject` is associated with a class

schema object that represents a CORBA or EJB implementation in the database. From the `PublishedObject`, the Oracle8*i* ORB obtains the information necessary to find and launch the corresponding class schema object. Use the following syntax to invoke the session shell:

```
// At the command line
sess_sh [options] -user <user> -password <password>
   -service <serviceURL>
   [-d | -describe]  [-h | -help]
   [-iiop]  [-role <rolename>]  [-ssl]  [-version]
```

3. This statement and the one that follows it store the name of the remote **interface** and the remote home **interface** in the `RemoteInterfaceClassName` and the `HomeInterfaceClassName`, respectively.

4. This statement specifies which user is allowed to access the enterprise Bean. In this example, only the `obsschema` user can use the Bean.

5. This commented statement indicates that you can set the session timeout value. You set the value in seconds. In this scenario, the session will use the EJB container-specific default value.

6. This statement declares an enterprise Bean State Management Mode. The argument to the method is `STATEFUL_SESSION` or `STATELESS_SESSION`. Remember that the Oracle8*i* EJB server does not distinguish a `STATEFUL` from a `STATELESS` session Bean.

7. The `CLIENT_IDENTITY` attribute instructs the container to run the EJB method with the client's security identity.

8. The `TX_REQUIRED` attribute specifies that the enterprise Bean requires that the method be executed in a global transaction. In other words, if the caller is associated with a transaction, the EJB method will be associated with the caller's transaction; otherwise start a new global transaction.

Step 9 Create the `platform.jar` JAR file (Listing 8-9) of the classes that you created from Steps 3 to 6:

Listing 8-9

```
// At the command line, do the following:
// Set your CLASSPATH if you have not done so yet.
// Review Step 7 of this section.
```

```
jar cvf0 platform.jar platform\Platform.class \
   platform\PlatWrap.class  \
   platform\PlatformHome.class  \
   platServer\PlatformDb$PIter.class  \
   platServer\PlatformDb.class \
   platServer\PlatformDb_SJProfile0.class \
   platServer\PlatformDb_SJProfileKeys.class
```

Step 10   Load and deploy the EJB object into the Oracle8*i* EJB server (see Listing 8-10). Use the Oracle tool, `deployejb`, to load and publish the EJB object in the Oracle8*i* EJB server. (See Appendix D for a list of the Oracle tools and their associated options.) The `deployejb` tool "publishes" the EJB object into a namespace using the `platformDb` name that you declared in the `platform.ejb` file (see Note 2 in the "Notes on the `Platform.ejb` deployment descriptor file" part of this section). Remember that you used the `PlatformServer` name to "publish" the RMI object into the server's rmiregistry whereas you use the `platformDb` name to publish your EJB object into a namespace. When you install Oracle8*i*, the software creates the test directory as a default namespace, which you can use to publish your EJB and CORBA objects. At deployment time, the `deployejb` tool reads the deployment descriptor file (`Platform.ejb`) that you created in Step 8 and the JAR file (`platform.jar`) in Step 9 of this section to create the `platform_generated` JAR file. The EJB client that you will develop later in this section uses the `platform_generated` JAR file to access your Platform Bean. At the command line:

Listing 8-10

```
// First set your CLASSPATH - review Step 7 of this section
// Go to the directory where the files are
// located and invoke the EJB tool
cd device:\deployobjects\platform
deployejb -republish -temp temp \
   -u obsschema -p obsschema -s %ORACLE_SERVICE% \
   -descriptor platform.ejb platform.jar

// Output file from deployejb
platform_generated.jar
```

Note that if the deployment is not successful, you may use the `dropjava` tool to remove all the Java classes that you loaded via the `deployejb` tool and the `sess_sh` tool to remove the Bean home interface name from the published object namespace (see Listing 8-11). You can also create new directories under the root directory to hold objects for separate projects, but you must have access as database user `SYS` to do so:

Listing 8-11

```
// Remove all the classes using the JAR file that deployejb
// tool created for you. For example, the platform_generated.jar.
// You can use the Oracle oci8 driver or the Oracle JDBC-THIN driver
// The following example uses the THIN driver. At the command line:
dropjava -thin -u obsschema/obsschema@datai:1521:orcl  \
    platform_generated.jar

// Open a shell session:
sess_sh -user obsschema -password obsschema \
  -service sess_iiop://datai:2481:orcl
// go to the test directory
cd test
// Remove the PublishedObject name
rm -r /test/PlatformDb
```

Step 11   Create the `ClientJavaForEjbPlatform` EJB client that will use the `Platform` EJB object:

```
/*      Program Name: ClientJavajForEjbPlatform.java
**      Purpose:      A Java client to access Platform EJB
**   object stored in Oracle8i data server.
**      Client tasks:
**      1. Locates the remote home Bean interface.
**      2. Authenticates the client to the server.
**      3. Activates an instance of the Platform bean.
**      4. Invokes the getPlatformList() method on the bean
*/

// import the EJB platform remote interface  (See Note 1.)
import platform.Platform;
// import the EJB  platform home interface
import platform.PlatformHome;
// import the serializable object
import platform.PlatWrap;

// import the ServiceCtx class from the Oracle package
// (See Note 2.)
import oracle.aurora.jndi.sess_iiop.ServiceCtx;

// import the Java mandatory classes to use JNDI  (See Note 3.)
import javax.naming.Context;
import javax.naming.InitialContext;
```

```java
// import application-specific Java classes
import java.util.Hashtable;
import java.sql.*;
import java.math.BigDecimal;
import java.util.*;
import java.util.Vector;

public class ClientJavaForEjbPlatform {

  public static void main(String[] args)
      throws Exception  {
    if (args.length != 4) {
      System.out.println("usage: Client "
          +"serviceURL objectName user password");
      System.exit(1);
    }  // End if

    String serviceURL = args [0];
    String objectName = args [1];
    String user = args [2];
    String password = args [3];

    Hashtable env = new Hashtable();

    // Set the JNDI environment for the client
    // to locate the EJB object (See Note 4.)
    env.put(Context.URL_PKG_PREFIXES, "oracle.aurora.jndi");
    env.put(Context.SECURITY_PRINCIPAL, user);
    env.put(Context.SECURITY_CREDENTIALS, password);
    env.put(Context.SECURITY_AUTHENTICATION,
        ServiceCtx.NON_SSL_LOGIN);

    // Create an instance of the Context class
    Context ic = new InitialContext (env);

    // Create an instance of the EJB object home interface.
    PlatformHome home = null;
    // Create an instance of the EJB Bean class.
    Platform myPlatformBean = null;

    try {
        // Use the home interface to
        // locate the EJB object (See Note 5.)
        home =
            (PlatformHome)ic.lookup (serviceURL + objectName);

        // Create a Bean instance  (See Note 6.)
```

```
            myPlatformBean = home.create();

    }   // End of try
    catch ( Exception ex ) {
        System.out.println("Cannot locate"
            +" or create Platform home");
        System.exit(1);
    }   // End of catch

    Vector platformVector = null;
    try {
        // Invoke the EJB object's method   (See Note 7.)
        platformVector =
            platformVector = myPlatformBean.getPlatformList();
    }   // End of try
    catch ( Exception ex ) {
        System.out.println("Cannot locate or "
            + "getPlatformList()");
        System.exit(1);
    }   // End of catch

    // Print the details. Code REUSE! (See Note 8.)
    printPlatformDetails(platformVector);
}   // End of main()

public static void printPlatformDetails(Vector platformVector)
        throws SQLException {

    if  (platformVector == null) {
        System.out.println("No Data FOUND");
        return;
    }   // End if

    PlatWrap p = null;
    Enumeration enum = platformVector.elements();
    // Iterate to get the column attributes from the table
    while (enum.hasMoreElements()) {
        // Get PlatformType from the platformVector
        p = (PlatWrap)enum.nextElement();
        // Get the column values
        System.out.println(
          ((p.getKeyId()==null) ? " " : p.getKeyId().toString())
            + " " + ((p.getType()==null) ? " " : p.getType()) + " "
            + ((p.getDescription()==null) ? " " : p.getDescription()
                ) );
    }       // End of while

  }   // End of printPlatformDetails()
}   // End of ClientJavaForEjbPlatform class
```

Notes on the `ClientJavajForEjbPlatform` client application:

1. This statement and the ones that follow it import in the program the EJB remote, remote home, and the serialized classes of the EJB object.

2. You must import this class from the `oracle.aurora.jndi.sess.sess_iiop` package.

3. This statement and the one that follows it import the Java classes specified in the `javax` package. You must import these classes if you wish to use the JNDI API.

4. The following four statements store the environment parameters in a Java HashTable. The JNDI `Context` object needs these parameters. Use the `put()` method provided by the HashTable class to store the parameters in a hash table. For more information regarding JNDI, see the first bullet of the "Enterprise JavaBeans Object Composites" section of this chapter.

5. To get the root of the JNDI naming hierarchy, create an instance of the `Context` class using the JNDI `InitialContext()` method.

6. The first thing a client does is to locate the enterprise Bean home interface. Remember that the client uses the home interface to look up, create, and remove EJB objects. Once you acquire an initial context, you can invoke its methods to get a reference to the EJB home interface. To look up the Bean, you need an URL address and the published full path name of the EJB object. Use the following syntax to construct a URL for the `Platform` enterprise Bean:

```
<service_name>://<hostname>:<iiop_listener_port>:<SID>
   /<published_obj_name>
```

```
// Use the following for your Platform EJB object
// 2481 is a default listener port for IIOP and is configured
// in the listener.ora file.
sess_iiop://yourHost:2481:ORCL/test/PlatformDb
```

Note that, because the actual location of the EJB container is transparent to the client, a client that uses JNDI might be written to include EJB containers that are located on multiple machines.

7. Once you get the Bean, create a new session Bean by invoking the `create()` method of the `PlatformHome` home remote interface class. The `create()` method returns a reference to the program. Use the reference to invoke the `getPlatformList()` method of the EJB object.

8. This statement calls your client method to print the platform details.

Step 12   Set your CLASSPATH and compile the client class:

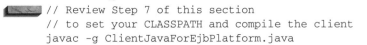

```
// Review Step 7 of this section
// to set your CLASSPATH and compile the client
javac -g ClientJavaForEjbPlatform.java
```

Step 13   Run the EJB client. When you set the CLASSPATH to run the client, you must include the file that the `deployejb` tool had generated for you in Step 10 of this section. The client needs the file to locate your EJB object. Use the following syntax to set your CLASSPATH and run the client program (see Listing 8-12).

Listing 8-12

```
// Set your variables as you did in Step 7 of this section.

// Then set your CLASSPATH. Please note that the JAR file
// generated at deployment time,
// the platform_generated.jar, has been added.

set CLASSPATH=.;D:\deployobjects; \
%ORACLE_HOME%\lib\aurora_client.jar; \
%ORACLE_HOME%\jdbc\lib\classes111.zip; \
%ORACLE_HOME%\sqlj\lib\translator.zip; \
%ORACLE_HOME%\lib\vbjorb.jar; \
%ORACLE_HOME%\lib\vbjapp.jar;%JDK_CLASSPATH%; \
platform_generated.jar

// Run the client program using the following arguments:
// 1.  Oracle service name
// 2.  The EJB object and its full path
// 3.  Username (owner or authorized user)
// 4.  password
java ClientJavaForEjbPlatform
  %ORACLE_SERVICE% /test/PlatformDb obsschema obsschema
```

Note that we provide a `makeit.bat` file to compile and load all the programs and publish the EJB object, and also a `runit.bat` file to run the client.

In the following section, you will learn how to deploy a CORBA object in the Oracle8*i* data server. To learn more about CORBA, see the "CORBA/IIOP 2.2 Specification" at http://www.omg.org/corba/cichpter.html#idls&s [13] and the *Enterprise JavaBeans and CORBA Developer's Guide* [52].

Deploying a **CORBA** Object Using a **SQLJ** Implementation

In the previous sections of this chapter, you developed a SQLJ business object and a SQLJ client that uses the object where both the client and object resided in the same address space. Next, you created an RMI object and an RMI client that uses the SQLJ object by making a remote invocation call on its `getPlaformList()` method. Finally, you developed an EJB object that resides in the Oracle8*i* data server and an EJB client that also remotely invoked the EJB object's method, `getPlaformList()`. In both cases, the RMI and EJB applications, you use SQLJ to implement the business logic. More importantly, you use distributed object technologies, RMI and RMI/IIOP, respectively, to establish communication between client and components that reside in different address spaces.

In this section, you will develop a CORBA distributed application consisting of a CORBA object that encapsulates the business logic that you implemented in the previous sections and a CORBA client, like the SQLJ client, the RMI client, and the EJB client, that will use the object.

What Is CORBA?

Underlying distributed object paradigms is the notion of establishing the relationships between objects that live in different address spaces. It is hard to develop distributed objects that communicate transparently, efficiently, and reliably. CORBA specification addresses this challenge.

As previously stated in the "Basic Concepts of Distributing Systems" section of this chapter, CORBA is a distributed object architecture that allows business objects to interoperate (communicate) across network systems regardless of the programming language in which they are written or the platform on which they are running. CORBA supports remote, local, and client/server object collaboration. CORBA clients and servers use IIOP to communicate. The separations of interface and implementation objects and location and access transparency are the fundamental design principles behind CORBA. Interfaces to remote objects are described in a platform-neutral interface definition language (IDL). Mappings from IDL to specific programming languages are implemented, binding the language to CORBA/IIOP. Today, over 800 companies such as hardware, software, and database vendors support CORBA.

CORBA specifies a set of bus-related services for creating and deleting objects, accessing them by name, and storing them in persistent storage. The CORBA specification contains several components (Figure 8-10):

- *The Object Request Broker (ORB)* core is responsible for client and server object communication. ORB is the object bus that lets objects make requests to and receive responses from other objects located in the same address space or remotely.

- *The Interoperability Specification*, whose elements are the General and Internet Inter-ORB (GIOP and IIOP), defines the elements of interoperability between independently produced ORBs.

- *Interface Definition Language (IDL)* defines the interfaces and the types of objects that the interfaces use. IDL provides operating system and programming language independent interfaces to all the services and components that reside on a CORBA bus, allowing client and server objects written in different programming languages to interoperate.

- *The Programming language mappings for IDL* (for example, C, C++, Java, and so on) include definition of the language-specific data types and interfaces to access CORBA objects through the ORB.

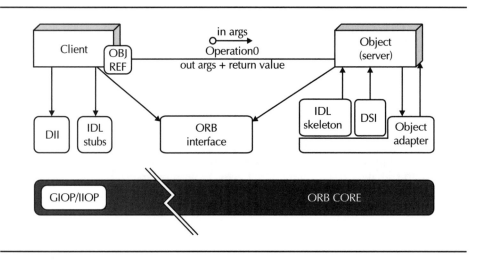

FIGURE 8-10. *CORBA component architecture*

- *The Static Invocation Interface (SII)* is a programming interface to the stub class that provides communication between client and server objects written in non-object-oriented languages.

- *Dynamic Invocation Interface (DII)* allows the dynamic construction of object invocations rather than calling a stub class that is specific to a particular operation. DII lets you discover methods to be invoked at runtime. Dynamic invocations are difficult to program, but they provide maximum flexibility and are very useful tools to discover services at runtime.

- *Static Skeleton Interface (SSI) and Dynamic Skeleton Interface (DSI)* allow static and dynamic handling of objects.

- *Portable Object Adapter (POA)* provides an object adapter that can be used with multiple ORBs. An ORB provides services through an object adapter (generation and interpretation of object references, method invocations, and so on). Object implementations use object adapters to access the ORB. Note that the current release of Oracle8*i* does not support POA.

- *ORB Interface and Implementation Repositories (IR)*, respectively, are the interface that goes directly above the ORB and the repository of information for the ORB to locate and activate implementation objects. The Interface Repository APIs allow you to obtain and modify the descriptions of the registered component interfaces, the methods they support, and the parameters they require.

This section provides a short introduction on the ORB component. Detailed discussion of all CORBA components is beyond the scope of this book. For more information on CORBA components, see the bibliography at the end of the book and particularly the CORBA 2.2 Specification [13], *Client/Server Programming with Java and CORBA* [35], and *Instant CORBA* [36].

Object Request Broker

CORBA uses an ORB (Figure 8-11) middleware that handles the communication details between client and server objects. The ORB is structured to provide a high degree of interoperability of a wide variety of object systems. It is responsible for the mechanisms to locate the object's implementation, activate the object, and communicate the requested data to the client. The CORBA client communicates via the object interface, which is completely independent of where the object is located. Like the RMI and the EJB clients, the CORBA client uses a stub class to invoke remote objects. Additionally, it can use the Dynamic Invocation Interface (DII) or can directly interact with the ORB for some functions. In CORBA, the term

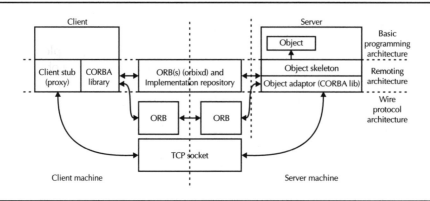

FIGURE 8-11. *CORBA ORB architecture*

Dynamic Invocation refers to client's request being constructed at runtime instead of being known at compiled time.

CORBA Object Composites

The CORBA object components are similar to the RMI and EJB object components and consist of:

■ An application **interface** source file defined in the OMG Interface Definition Language (OMG IDL) that must have an .idl extension. The IDL file describes the interfaces that client objects call and object implementations provide. When you write the IDL **interface** file, you need to specify the interfaces, the interfaces' operations (that is, the method definitions or the behavior of the object), and the data types used in these interfaces. The OMG IDL grammar is a subset of the proposed ANSI C++ standard and supports C++ syntax for constant type and operation declarations. Client programs are not written in OMG IDL but in languages for which IDL mappings have been defined. For example, IDL mappings exist for programming languages such as C, C++, Smalltalk, COBOL, ADA, and Java. After you create the IDL file, the next step is to run the file through the IDL compiler. The IDL compiler generates the "type" information for each interface's method and stores it in a repository called the Interface Repository (IR). The interface's information is generated in the programming language of your choice depending on the IDL mapping that you have in your system. For example, Inprise provides a mapping of IDL for Java, the VisiBroker for Java. To map IDL files to Java, you can use the idl2java, java2idl, and java2iiop tools (Inprise's VisiBroker for Java) that are distributed with Oracle8*i*.

■ An **interface** *implementation*, like an RMI or an EJB implementation class, provides the actual state and behavior of an object. The object implementation interacts with the ORB to establish its identity, create new objects, and obtain ORB services.

■ A client object sends a request during which it obtains an Object Reference for the CORBA object. A client initiates the request when it calls either the stub class that is specific to the object or by using the Dynamic Invocation Interface (DII). Note that the new release of Oracle8*i* supports requests only via a stub class. When a client makes a request, it first gets an Object Reference, which it then uses to activate the object. Object activation (that is, preparing an object to execute an operation) is done when the client invokes an object's method. The client knows how to find or create the CORBA objects and, like the RMI and the EJB clients, can access the object's functionality only via the object's public interface. Note that CORBA server objects are located by name through the CORBA Naming Service. Also, note that CORBA clients, like EJB clients, use the JNDI to locate CORBA objects stored in the Oracle8*i* database (Figure 8-12). Remember that the CORBA ORB is an object bus. The CORBA Naming Service allows components on the bus to locate other components by name.

Next, you will develop a CORBA object and deploy it into the Oracle8*i* data server.

Developing a CORBA Object

The steps to develop and deploy a CORBA object using a SQLJ implementation are as follows:

1. Create the directories that you wish to use to store and deploy your object.

2. Create a high-level view of your object.

3. Create the OMG IDL file, platform.idl.

4. Generate the stub and the skeleton classes. The IDL compiler will generate the stub and the skeleton classes for you when you run the platform.idl file through the compiler (Listing 8-14). The client IDL stubs provide the static interfaces to object services. These precompiled stubs define how clients invoke corresponding services on the servers and act like local proxy for a remote server object. Static invocations are easier to program, faster,

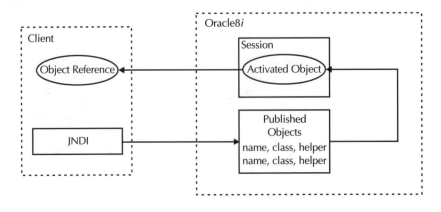

FIGURE 8-12. *Client using JNDI for EJB and CORBA object lookup (Oracle8*i*)*

and self-documenting. The server IDL stubs (skeletons) provide static
interfaces to each service exported by the server.

5. Create the server object implementation class, the `PlatformImpl` class.

6. Create the `ClientJavaForCorbaPlatform` CORBA client that will use
the CORBA object.

7. Set your CLASSPATH and compile all the programs.

8. Create the `platform.jar` JAR file.

9. Load the programs into the Oracle8*i* data server.

10. Publish the CORBA object.

11. Run the CORBA client.

Step 1 Create the directories that you wish to use to store your source code:

```
// Create the directories to store the Java and SQLJ source code
mkdir deployobjects\corba\platform\platServer
```

Step 2 Create a high-level view of your object (see Figure 8-13).

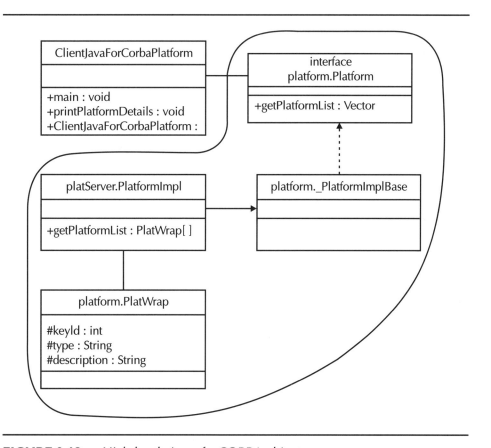

FIGURE 8-13. *High-level view of a CORBA object*

Step 3 Create the IDL file, `platform.idl`. An OMG IDL specification consists of type, constant, exception, and/or module definitions. The `platform.idl` file is a very basic IDL file:

```
//      File Name:     platform.idl                          */
//      Purpose:    OMG IDL file for the
//                  Platform CORBA Object
//

module platform { // (See Note 1.)
  struct PlatWrap {  // (See Note 2.)
    long keyId;
    wstring aType;
    wstring aDescription;
  };  // End of PlatWrap struct

  typedef sequence <PlatWrap> PlatWrapArr; // (See Note 3.)

  exception SQLError {  // (See Note 4.)
    wstring message;
  };  // End of SQLError exception

  interface Platform {  // (See Note 5.)
    // (See Note 6.)
    PlatWrapArr getPlatformList () raises (SQLError);
  };  // End of Platform interface

}; // End of CORBA module
```

Notes on the `platform.idl` file:

1. This statement declares a CORBA module. A module consists of a group of usually related object interfaces. CORBA module is used to prevent name clashing between CORBA and other programming languages. Note that an IDL module is mapped to a Java package with the same name. Also, note that all IDL type declarations within the module generate corresponding Java class or interface declarations within the generated package.

2. This statement declares a CORBA *struct*. A struct is mapped to a **final** Java class with the same name. The `keyId`, `aType`, and `aDescription` fields are called *attributes* and correspond to Java instance variables. An attribute is made visible to clients as a pair of operations, `get_XXXX` and `set_XXXX`, and consequently are mapped to a pair of Java accessor and modifier methods. When you compile the IDL file, the compiler also generates a *holder* and a *helper* class for the struct. For example, the IDL compiler will generate the `PlatWrapHolder` and the

PlatWrapHelper classes for the PlatWrap struct. See Note 5 below for more information regarding generated helper and holder classes. See Listing 8-13 for a listing of the Java classes generated by the IDL compiler.

3. This statement declares a CORBA *sequence* that maps to a Java array with the same name. Consequently, the PlatWrapArr sequence defines a Java array of PlatWrap objects.

4. This statement declares the SQLError user-defined exception. IDL exceptions are mapped very similarly to CORBA struct. User-defined exceptions are mapped to final Java classes that extend the org.omg.CORBA.UserException class. A holder and a helper class, as for the struct, are also generated. They are the SQLErrorHolder and the SQLErrorHelper classes, respectively.

5. This statement declares an IDL **interface** header that consists of an interface name and an optional inheritance specification (that is, an interface can be derived from another interface; this is called a *single inheritance*). Also, CORBA allows an interface to inherit from multiple interfaces; this is called *multiple inheritance.* The **interface** declaration may include constant, type, exception, and operation declarations. An IDL **interface** is mapped to a public Java **interface** with the same name that contains the mapped operation signatures. Clients use the object interface to look up an object. The lookup method returns a reference to the interface and clients use the reference to invoke methods on the object. In addition to the Java **interface**, the IDL compiler generates two other Java classes, the PlatformHelper helper and the PlatformHolder holder classes. A helper class contains methods that read and write the object to a stream and cast the object to and from the type of the base class, whereas a holder class is used by the application when parameters in the interface operation are of type out or inout.

6. This statement declares an operation in the **interface** body. Operation declarations in OMG IDL are similar to C function declarations. You normally declare the published operations on the object in the **interface** body.

Step 4   Generate the _st_Platform stub and the _PlatformImplBase skeleton classes (Listing 8-13). The _<interfaceName>ImplBase skeleton class, like the EJB Object's implementation class, is installed on the server and communicates with the stub file on the client side. The server skeleton also returns parameters and return values to the client. The CORBA ORB handles the communication between the client's stub and the server's skeleton. The IDL compiler will generate the Java classes corresponding to the declarations specified in the `platform.idl` file including the stub and the skeleton classes. Refer to the "Notes on the `platform.idl` file" part of this section for more information regarding the generated Java classes. Note that the _example_Platform ("_st_" is a VisiBroker-specific prefix) class is also included. This class gives you an example of how you should implement the interface on the server. See the listing of the _example_Platform in Listing 8-14. Use the `idl2java` tool to compile the OMG IDL file.

Listing 8-13

```
// First, set the following variables. At the command prompt:
set ORACLE_HOME=Device:\Oracle\Ora81
// Please edit the host name to correspond to your host name:
set ORACLE_SERVICE=sess_iiop://datai:2481:orcl
// Set a variable to hold your JDK path
set JDK_CLASSPATH=Device:\jdk1_1_8\jdk1.1.8\lib\classes.zip

// Get to the directory where you stored your platform.dl file
// Review Step 1 of this section.
cd Device:\deployobjects\corba

// Set your CLASSPATH.
set CLASSPATH=.;Device:\deployobjects; \
%ORACLE_HOME%\lib\aurora_client.jar; \
%ORACLE_HOME%\jdbc\lib\classes111.zip; \
%ORACLE_HOME%\sqlj\lib\translator.zip;  \
%ORACLE_HOME%\lib\vbjorb.jar; \
%ORACLE_HOME%\lib\vbjapp.jar;%JDK_CLASSPATH%

// Compile the OMG IDL file
idl2java -no_comments platform.idl

// Expected Java output files from compiled IDL file:
Traversing platform.idl
Creating: platform\PlatWrap.java
Creating: platform\PlatWrapHolder.java
Creating: platform\PlatWrapHelper.java
Creating: platform\PlatWrapArrHolder.java
Creating: platform\PlatWrapArrHelper.java
Creating: platform\SQLError.java
Creating: platform\SQLErrorHolder.java
Creating: platform\SQLErrorHelper.java
Creating: platform\Platform.java
Creating: platform\PlatformHolder.java
Creating: platform\PlatformHelper.java
Creating: platform\_st_Platform.java
```

```
Creating: platform\_PlatformImplBase.java
Creating: platform\PlatformOperations.java
Creating: platform\_tie_Platform.java
Creating: platform\_example_Platform.java
```

Listing 8-14

```
//    File Name:    _example_Platform.java
package platform;
public class _example_Platform
    extends platform._PlatformImplBase {  // (See Note 1.)
  public _example_Platform(java.lang.String name) {
    super(name);
  }
  public _example_Platform() {
    super();
  }
  public platform.PlatWrap[] getPlatformList()
        throws platform.SQLError {
    // IMPLEMENT: Operation
    return null;
  }
}
```

Note on Listing 8-14:

I. The implementation class must be a subclass of the `_PlatformImplBase` skeleton class. Remember that the client uses the `_st_Platform` stub class on the client side to communicate with the `_PlatformImplBase` server skeleton class.

Step 5   Create the `PlatformImpl` server object implementation class.

The `PlatformImpl`, like the `PlatformDbObject` from the SQLJ component and the `Platform` from the EJB object, implements the application-specific business logic. It provides the information needed to create an object and the services to invoke its methods. The following is a listing of the `PlatformImpl` class:

```
/*    Program Name: PlatformImpl.sqlj
**    Purpose: A SQLJ Class that extends the
**    _PlatformImplBase interface generated by
**    IDL compiler and fully implements the
**    getPlatformList(): Array from the IDL
**    interface Platform declaration
**    The class implements the logic to query
```

```
**   the PLATFORM_TYPE_LIST table.
*/
package platServer;

import platform.*;
import platform.PlatWrap;

// (See Note 1.)
import oracle.aurora.AuroraServices.ActivatableObject;

import java.sql.*;
import java.util.Vector;

// Declare a named iterator
#sql iterator PIter (int  aPlatformId,
         String aType, String aDesc);

public class PlatformImpl
   extends platform._PlatformImplBase
     implements ActivatableObject {  // (See Note 2.)

  public platform.PlatWrap[] getPlatformList ()
     throws platform.SQLError {  // (See Note 3.)
    try {
       Vector platformVector = new Vector ();

       // Use the PIter SQLJ iterator to retrieve
       // rows of data from the PLATFORM_TYPE_LIST table
       PIter anPIter = null;

       #sql anPIter =
          { SELECT P.key_id AS aPlatformId,
                  P.type AS aType, P.description AS aDesc
            FROM PLATFORM_TYPE_LIST P
          };

       // Store the contents of the SQLJ iterator in
       // the platformVector object
       while (anPIter.next()) {  // (See Note 4.)
          platformVector.addElement
            ( new PlatWrap
              ( anPIter.aPlatformId(),anPIter.aType(),
                anPIter.aDesc()
              )
            );
       }  // End of while
```

```
      // Close the SQLJ iterator
      anPIter.close();

      // Create an array of PlatWrap objects whose
      // length is equal to the vector length
      PlatWrap[] queryResult =
            new PlatWrap[platformVector.size()];
      // Copy the contents of the platformVector object
      platformVector.copyInto(queryResult);
      // Return an array of PlatWrap objects to the caller
      return queryResult;

  }   // End of try
  catch (SQLException e) {
     throw new SQLError (e.getMessage ());   // (See Note 5.)
  }   // End of catch

 }  // End of getPlatformList ()

 public org.omg.CORBA.Object
   _initializeAuroraObject () {  // (See Note 6.)
   return this;
 } // End of _initializeAuroraObject ()

} // End of PlatformImpl class
```

Notes on the `PlatformImpl` class:

1. This statement imports the `oracle.aurora.AuroraServices.ActivatableObject` **interface** that provides the mechanism to activate CORBA objects stored in the database. Remember that the Oracle8*i* JVM is called Aurora and that the Aurora/JVM is part of JServer, which provides the `oracle.aurora.*` protected package. The `oracle.aurora.*` includes Java classes that allow you to store and manipulate Java in the database. See Chapter 1 of this book and the *Oracle8i Java Developer's Guide and Reference* [23] to learn more about Aurora.

2. This statement declares a subclass of the `platform._PlatformImplBase` class generated by the IDL compiler in Step 4 and implements the `oracle.aurora.AuroraServices.ActivatableObject` class. Remember that the generated class mapped the operation signatures for the CORBA object. The `PlatformImpl` class provides the operation body for the object.

3. This statement declares the `getPlatformList()` method. Note that the user-defined error is included in the method's **throws** clause.

4. This statement declares a `while` loop to retrieve the column values of the database table, the `PLATFORM_TYPE_LIST` table, stored in the `anPIter` iterator variable. The statement that follows it first constructs a `PlatWrap` object by calling the parameterized constructor of the `PlatWrap` class using the accessor methods from the SQLJ iterator and then inserts the object into the `platformVector` variable. The remaining code of the program is identical to the `PlatformDbObject` class from the "Designing and Developing a SQLJ Component-Based Object" section of this chapter.

5. This statement raises the `SQLerror` user-defined error in its **throws** clause.

6. This statement declares the `_initializeAuroraObject()` method that returns an object of `type org.omg.CORBA.Object`. The `_initializeAuroraObject()` method returns a class delegate rather than the object itself. If you define a class, such as the `PlatformImpl` class, that implements the `ActivatableObject` class, then you must include the `_initializeAuroraObject()` method in your class file.

Step 6   Create the `ClientJavaForCorbaPlatform` CORBA client that will use the CORBA object.

```
/*      Program Name: ClientJavaForCorbaPlatform.java
**      Purpose:      A Java client to access CORBA
**   object stored in Oracle8i data server.
*/

// Import the CORBA platform interface
import platform.*;
import platServer.*;

import oracle.aurora.jndi.sess_iiop.ServiceCtx;
import javax.naming.Context;
import javax.naming.InitialContext;

import java.util.Hashtable;
import java.sql.*;
import java.math.BigDecimal;
import java.util.*;
import java.util.Vector;

public class ClientJavaForCorbaPlatform {

  public static void main(String[] args) throws Exception {

    if (args.length != 4) {
        System.out.println("usage: Client "
```

```
            + "serviceURL objectName user password");
        System.exit(1);
    }  // End if

    String serviceURL = args [0];
    String objectName = args [1];
    String user = args [2];
    String password = args [3];

    // Setup environment for JNDI  (See Note 1.)
    Hashtable env = new Hashtable();
    env.put(Context.URL_PKG_PREFIXES, "oracle.aurora.jndi");
    env.put(Context.SECURITY_PRINCIPAL, user);
    env.put(Context.SECURITY_CREDENTIALS, password);
    env.put(Context.SECURITY_AUTHENTICATION,
        ServiceCtx.NON_SSL_LOGIN);

    // Get an initial context instance
    Context ic = new InitialContext (env);

    try {
        // Create a Platform object and invoke
        // the lookup() method to get a reference
        // of the Platform interface.
        // (See Note 2.)
        Platform aPlatform =
            (Platform)ic.lookup (serviceURL + objectName);

        // Use the instance to invoke
        // the remote object's method  (See Note 3.)
        PlatWrap[] platformArray = aPlatform.getPlatformList();

        // Print the details. Code REUSE!
        printPlatformDetails(platformArray);

    }   // End of try
    catch ( Exception ex ) {
        System.out.println("Cannot locate"
            +" or create Platform");
        System.exit(1);
    }  // End of catch

}  // End of main()

public static void printPlatformDetails(PlatWrap[] p)
    throws SQLException {
    int i;
    for (i = 0; i < p.length; i++) {
```

```
            System.out.println(p[i].keyId + " "
                + p[i].type + " "  +p[i].description );
      } // End of for loop

   }    // End printPlatformDetails()

}   // End of ClientJavaForCorbaPlatform class
```

Notes on the `ClientJavaForCorbaPlatform` application:

The CORBA client is almost identical to the EJB client that you created in the "Deploying an Enterprise JavaBeans Object Using a SQLJ Implementation" section of this chapter.

1. This statement and the ones that follow it are identical to the statement in the EJB client in the "Deploying an Enterprise JavaBeans Object Using a SQLJ Implementation" section of this chapter. You use JNDI to look up a CORBA object that resides in the Oracle8*i* data server the same way that you look up an EJB object. Note that a CORBA application requires that an ORB be active on both the client system and the system running the server. The client-side ORB is normally initialized as part of the processing that goes on when the client invokes the `lookup()` method on the JNDI `InitialContext` object that it instantiates. The ORB on the server is started by the presentation that handles IIOP requests. Oracle8*i* JServer provides a JNDI interface to CosNaming (CORBA naming service) so that you use URL-based naming to refer to and activate CORBA objects in a session. For information regarding JNDI environment settings, see the *Enterprise JavaBeans and CORBA Developer's Guide* [52], the "Notes on the `ClientJavajForEjbPlatform` client application" part of the "Deploying an Enterprise JavaBeans Object Using a SQLJ Implementation" section of this chapter, and the bibliography at the end of the book.

2. This statement creates an instance of the `Platform` **interface** that the IDL compiler generated for you in Step 4 of this section. When you call the lookup method, it returns an object reference to the **interface**.

3. This statement invokes the `getPlatformList()` method of the CORBA object using the object reference from the previous statement. Note that CORBA objects are activated on demand, that is, the client activates the object when it invokes the method; at invocation time, the ORB loads the object into memory and caches it. A cache is a buffer of high-speed memory filled often with instructions from main memory. In CORBA, to invoke a remote function, the client makes a call to the client stub. The stub packs the call parameters into a request message, and invokes a wire protocol to ship the message to the server. At the server side, the wire protocol delivers the message to the server stub, which then unpacks the request message and calls the actual function on the object.

Step 7 Set your CLASSPATH and compile all the programs generated by the IDL compiler from Step 4 including your CORBA client and your SQLJ class:

```
// Review Step 4 of this section to set your CLASSPATH
// and then compile all Java source code. At the command line:
javac -g  platform\PlatWrap.java
javac -g  platform\PlatWrapHolder.java
javac -g  platform\PlatWrapHelper.java
javac -g  platform\PlatWrapArrHolder.java
javac -g  platform\PlatWrapArrHelper.java
javac -g  platform\SQLError.java
javac -g  platform\SQLErrorHolder.java
javac -g  platform\SQLErrorHelper.java
javac -g  platform\Platform.java
javac -g  platform\PlatformHolder.java
javac -g  platform\PlatformHelper.java
javac -g  platform\_st_Platform.java
javac -g  platform\_PlatformImplBase.java
javac -g  platform\PlatformOperations.java
javac -g  platform\_tie_Platform.java

// Compile the platServer\PlatformImpl.sqlj program
sqlj -ser2class platServer\PlatformImpl.sqlj

// Compile the  CORBA client
javac -g ClientJavaForCorbaPlatform.java
```

Step 8 Create a JAR file of all your `.class` files from `platform` and `platServer` directories. Oracle recommends using a JAR file consisting of `.class` files to load SQLJ and Java into the Oracle8*i* data server. See Appendix D to learn more about the `jar` tool.

```
// Set your CLASSPATH if you have not done so.
// Create the platform.jar JAR file
jar cvf0 platform.jar platform\PlatWrap.class \
 platform\PlatWrapHolder.class \
 platform\PlatWrapHelper.class \
 platform\PlatWrapArrHolder.class \
 platform\PlatWrapArrHelper.class \
 platform\SQLError.class \
 platform\SQLErrorHolder.class \
 platform\SQLErrorHelper.class \
```

```
platform\Platform.class \
platform\PlatformHolder.class \
platform\PlatformHelper.class \
platform\_st_Platform.class \
platform\_PlatformImplBase.class \
platform\PlatformOperations.class \
platform\_tie_Platform.class \
platServer\PIter.class \
platServer\PlatformImpl.class \
platServer\PlatformImpl_SJProfile0.class \
platServer\PlatformImpl_SJProfileKeys.class
```

Step 9 Load the programs into the Oracle8*i* data server using the `platform` JAR file that you created in Step 8. At the command line, use the `loadjava` tool to do this (see Appendix D):

```
// At the command line:
loadjava -verbose -oracleresolver -resolve -thin -u \
 obsschema/obsschema@datai:1521:orcl platform.jar
```

Step 10 Publish the CORBA object into the Oracle8*i*. This is the final step in preparing a CORBA object. When you publish a CORBA object, that is, you are putting a CORBA object into the namespace. Objects are published in the Oracle database using the OMG CosNaming service and can be accessed using Oracle's JNDI interface to CosNaming. Remember that the namespace in the database looks just like a typical file system and also, you can examine and manipulate objects in the publishing namespace using the session shell tool (`sess_sh`). See Step 10 of the "Deploying an Enterprise JavaBeans Object Using a SQLJ Implementation" section of this chapter for more information regarding Oracle namespace. Use the `publish` tool specifying the `corbaPlatform` user-defined name for the CORBA object that you wish to publish or any name of your choice, the `platServer.PlatformImpl` implementation class, and the `platform.PlatformHelper` class. See Appendix D for more information on the Oracle8*i* tools and their options.

```
// Set your CLASSPATH and publish the object into the database
publish -republish -u obsschema \
  -p obsschema -schema OBSSCHEMA -s %ORACLE_SERVICE% \
 /test/corbaPlatform platServer.PlatformImpl platform.PlatformHelper
```

Step 11 Run the `ClientJavaForCorbaPlatform` CORBA client. If you have no error from the preceding steps, then run the client:

```
// Please, set your CLASSPATH. Review Step 4 to do so.
Java ClientJavaForCorbaPlatform sess_iiop://datai:2481:orcl \
/test/PlatformCorbaObject obsschema obsschema
```

Note that a `makeit.bat` file is provided to compile and load all the programs and publish the CORBA object, and also a `runit.bat` file to run the CORBA client.

In this chapter, you used an object-relational database, the scientific Observation schema, to develop components implemented in SQLJ. While developing a software component, you learned the following:

- Some basic concepts of distributed objects.

- How to design and develop a SQLJ component and a client that uses the component. In this scenario, both component and client resided in the same address space.

- How to design and develop distributed objects and clients that use these objects by making remote invocation calls on the components' methods. And while the object and the client were located on different address spaces, it appears as though they were local to the clients that make the call. You created the RMI, EJB, and CORBA objects to demonstrate this concept and also, in all three cases, you used SQLJ to implement the business logic encapsulated in the object. In addition, you learned that EJB and CORBA clients use database sessions just like any other Oracle client, but unlike a session in which the client communicates through SQL*Net, you access CORBA and EJB sessions through IIOP.

This chapter concludes Part III. Chapter 9 marks the beginning of Part IV, where you will learn performance-tuning techniques that will help you use SQLJ effectively.

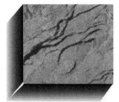

PART
IV

Effective Use of SQLJ

CHAPTER
9

SQLJ Applications:
Performance Tuning

n the previous chapters, you learned how to design, implement, and deploy SQLJ programs. In this chapter, you will learn how to tune your SQLJ source code and thereby improve performance. Oracle JDBC drivers support the standard JDBC (version 1.*x*) of the Sun Microsystems JDK and further enhance it with the Oracle-defined extensions for Oracle-specific data types, object types, and their mappings to Java. The Oracle-defined extensions (`oracle.jdbc.driver` package) includes the `oracle.jdbc.driver.OracleConnection` class that implements the `java.sql.Connection` interface and provides methods to set values to the Oracle performance extensions for SQL statements executing in a current connection.

In this chapter, you will revisit the `ConnectionManager` class that you created in Chapter 5 and extend its capability to connect to the Oracle8*i* data server using the `OracleConnection` class. You will also develop a SQLJ program that uses the mechanisms provided by the `OracleConnection` class to improve performance.

Specifically, in this chapter you will

- Extend the `ConnectionManager` class created in Chapters 5 and 6 so that it can be used as a utility class that includes methods that convert an instance of the `sqlj.runtime.ref.DefaultContext`, `sqlj.runtime.ConnectContext`, and `java.sql.Connection` classes to instances of the `oracle.jdbc.driver.OracleConnection` class. See Chapter 5 to learn more about SQLJ connection classes.

- Develop efficient SQLJ programs that improve performance.

- Tune SQL statements from SQLJ with the Oracle Optimizer.

- Consider other ways to improve performance by reducing network traffic.

Extending the ConnectionManager Class

In this section, you will create additional methods in the `Connection-Manager` class that convert an instance of the SQLJ `DefaultContext`, `ConnectionContext`, or the JDBC `java.sql.Connection` classes to an instance of the `OracleConnection` class. The `OracleConnection` class supports the following:

■ *Row prefetch* is the retrieval of multiple rows from the database with a single round-trip versus retrieving each row with a single round-trip.

■ *Batch updates* or *batch inserts* is the process of sending a group of SQL DML statements to the database in one round trip versus making one round trip to the database for each SQL execution statement. In this scenario, the DML statements are saved in the client's memory until a batch value is created, that is, a threshold value has been reached. Once this value is reached, groups of updates or inserts are sent to the database as a batch in one trip.

A partial listing of the ConnectionManager class is presented in Chapter 6; you may wish to review it before proceeding. Here is the listing of the modified version of the class that uses the OracleConnection class:

```
/*  Class Name: ConnectionManager.java
**
**  Purpose:    Java utility program to establish
**    connections to Oracle databases
*/

import oracle.jdbc.driver.OracleConnection;
import sqlj.runtime.ref.DefaultContext;
import sqlj.runtime.ConnectionContext;
import oracle.sqlj.runtime.Oracle;
import java.sql.Connection;
import java.sql.SQLException;

public class ConnectionManager {

  // An instance variable used to hold an OracleConnection instance
  private OracleConnection anOracleConnection = null;

  /*
    Set up database connection information. Set these variables for
    your JDBC driver, database and account. If you leave them set
    to null, any program using this class will not run
  */

  static private String DBURL   = null ;   //Database URL
  static private String UID     = null ;   //User ID
  static private String PWD     = null ;   //Password
```

```
static {
  /* Start of Oracle configuration
     Modify the DBURL, UID, and PWD variables to reflect the
     user, driver, and database that you wish to connect to
  */

  //  Required for programs using OCI 7 driver
  //  DBURL  = "jdbc:oracle:oci7:@" ;

  //  Required for programs using OCI 8 driver
  //  DBURL  = "jdbc:oracle:oci8:@" ;

  //  Required for programs using oracle thin driver
  //  DBURL  = "jdbc:oracle:thin:@localhost:port#:SID" ;

  // (See Note 1.)
  DBURL  = "jdbc:oracle:thin:@data-i.com:1521:ORCL";
  UID    = "scott";
  PWD    = "tiger";
  // End of Oracle configuration
} // End of static initializer

public ConnectionManager() {
  try {
    // Get a Connection instance from the underlying JDBC
    // connection. Cast the returned Connection to an
    // OracleConnection instance (See Note 2.)
    anOracleConnection = (OracleConnection)
      DefaultContext.getDefaultContext().getConnection();
  } // End of try block
  // (See Note 3.)
  catch (java.lang.NullPointerException e) {
    // An exception is raised if there is no previous connection
    // to the database. The following method establishes a
    // connection and test to see if the DBURL, UID, and PWD
    // variables are defined. It then establishes a connection with
    // the database
    connectDB();
  } // End of catch block
} // End of ConnectionManager() constructor

public ConnectionManager(Connection aConnection) {
  try {
    // Cast the Connection parameter to an OracleConnection
    // instance (See Note 4.)
    anOracleConnection = (OracleConnection)aConnection;
  } // End of try block
  catch (java.lang.NullPointerException e) {
    // Establish a connection if there is no associated connection
```

```
      // with the Connection parameter object
      connectDB();
   } // End of catch block
} // End of ConnectionManager() constructor

public ConnectionManager(DefaultContext aDefaultContext) {
   try {
      // Cast the underlying JDBC connection of the DefaultContext
      // object to the OracleConnection instance variable
      anOracleConnection =
         (OracleConnection)aDefaultContext.getConnection();
   } // End of try block
   catch (java.lang.NullPointerException e) {
      // Establish a connection if there is no associated connection
      // with the DefaultContext parameter object.
      connectDB();
   } // End of catch block
} // End of ConnectionManager() constructor

public ConnectionManager(ConnectionContext aConnectionContext) {
   try {
      // Cast the underlying JDBC connection of a declared
      // ConnectionContext object to the OracleConnection
      // instance variable.
      anOracleConnection =
         (OracleConnection)aConnectionContext.getConnection();
   } // End of try block
   catch (java.lang.NullPointerException e) {
      // Establish connection if there is no associated connection
      // with the ConnectionContext parameter object
      connectDB();
   } // End of catch block
} // End of ConnectionManager() constructor

/*
   Creates a new OracleConnection object using the current values
   of the DBURL, UID, and PWD variables, or the installed
   default context. If any of the needed attributes is null, or a
   connection is not able to be established, an appropriate error
   message is printed to System.out and the programs exits.
*/
private void connectDB() {
   // Verify that the access parameters are set. (See Note 5.)
   if (UID==null || PWD==null || DBURL==null) {
      System.err.println (
         "Please edit the ConnectionManager.java file to assign " +
         "non-null values to the static string variables " +
         "DBURL, UID, and PWD. Then recompile and try again." ) ;
      System.exit(1) ;
```

```
    } // End of if

    try {
      // If there is no connection to the database, establish one
      // while converting and casting the underlying JDBC connection
      // to an OracleConnection instance
      //  (See Note 6.)
      anOracleConnection = (OracleConnection)
        Oracle.connect(DBURL, UID, PWD, false)
          .getDefaultContext().getConnection();
    } // End of try block
    catch (SQLException e) {
      System.err.println("Error connecting to the database");
      System.err.println(e);
      System.exit(1) ;
    } // End of catch block
  } // End of connectDB() method

  public void resetOracleConnection(Connection aConnection) {
    // Using the Connection or an OracleConnection object from the
    // parameter, reset the anOracleConnection instance variable
    anOracleConnection = (OracleConnection)aConnection;
  } // End of resetOracleConnection() method

  public void resetOracleConnection(DefaultContext aDefaultContext) {
    // Using the DefaultContext object parameter, reset the
    // anOracleConnection instance variable
    anOracleConnection =
      (OracleConnection)aDefaultContext.getConnection();
  } // End of resetOracleConnection() method

  public void resetOracleConnection(ConnectionContext
                                    aConnectionContext) {
    // Using the ConnectionContext object parameter, which
    // represents a declared connection context object, reset
    // the anOracleConnection instance variable
    anOracleConnection =
      (OracleConnection)aConnectionContext.getConnection();
  } // End of resetOracleConnection() method

  public Connection getConnection() {
    // Return a java.sql.Connection object by casting it from the
    // OracleConnection instance variable
    return (Connection)anOracleConnection;
  } // End of getConnection() method

  public OracleConnection getOracleConnection() {
    // Return the OracleConnection instance variable
```

```
        return anOracleConnection;
    } // End of getOracleConnection() method

    public DefaultContext getDefaultContext() {
        // Return the current installed DefaultContext instance
        return DefaultContext.getDefaultContext();
    } // End of getDefaultContext() method
}
```

Notes on the `ConnectionManager` class:

1. Set the database access information by assigning values to the DBURL (database URL), UID (user id), and PWD (password) instance variables of this `ConnectionManager` class. These variables are used to establish connections to the database.

2. This statement gets a `Connection` object from the installed `DefaultContext` and then casts the returned instance to an `OracleConnection` object.

3. This catch block catches a `java.lang.NullPointerException` exception error that is thrown if there were no previous connections made to the database. In this case, the program will call the `connectDB()` method to establish a connection to the database.

4. This statement converts a `java.sql.Connection` object to an `OracleConnection` object and assigns the `Connection` to the `OracleConnection` instance variable.

5. This statement checks if the DBURL, UID, and PWD variables have been set. The method will print an error message and exit the program if any of the variables are not defined.

6. Using the DBURL, UID, and PWD class variables, establish a connection to the database with the `Oracle.connect()` method. Use the `getConnection()` method of the `DefaultContext` connection to get the underlying JDBC connection. Cast the returned `Connection` instance to an `OracleConnection` instance and assign it to the `anOracleConnection` variable.

Developing Efficient SQLJ Programs

In this section, you will learn the features provided by the Oracle JDBC drivers to improve the program's performance by reducing the number of round trips made to the database. To learn the ways for reducing traffic to the database, you will develop a SQLJ application that uses these features. Note that the Oracle JDBC-OCI and JDBC-THIN drivers provide these performance features for client-side SQLJ programs, whereas the Oracle JDBC-KPRB driver of the Oracle8*i* data server supports the same features for SQLJ server-side programs.

Performance Enhancements

Use the following features to improve the performance of your SQLJ program:

- **Disabling the auto-commit mode**   When auto-commit mode is enabled (that is, the auto-commit flag is set to true), it indicates to the database to commit the transaction after every SQL statement is executed. In situations where the auto-commit mode is enabled, program execution can be quite expensive in terms of time and processing efforts. When auto-commit mode is disabled, the JDBC driver groups the connection's SQL statement without committing the statements. By disabling auto-commit, you combine the set of SQL statements into a single transaction. You can commit or discard the transaction by either specifying an explicit `COMMIT` or `ROLLBACK` statement in the program. See Chapter 3 to learn more about the auto-commit flag in SQLJ connections.

    In SQLJ programs, you can enable or disable auto-commit mode as follows:

    - Auto-commit mode is disabled by default when you use the `Oracle.connect()` method to establish a database connection.

    - Use the auto-commit flag parameter in the `getConnection()` method of the `sqlj.runtime.ref.DefaultContext` class or the `sqlj.runtime.ConnectContext` class to enable or disable the auto-commit mode. Remember the syntax for this method (see Chapter 5):

        ```
        getConnection(String   URL,
                      String   username,
                      String   password,
                      boolean  auto-commit-flag)
        ```

    - Use the `setAutoCommit(false/true)` method of the `java.sql.Connection` or the `oracle.jdbc.driver.OracleConnection` classes to disable or enable auto-commit mode.

- **Row prefetch**   Use the row prefetch to retrieve a group of rows. Both the Oracle JDBC and the Oracle SQLJ support this feature.

■ **Batch updates and/or batch inserts** Batching allows you to send groups of SQL insert and update statements to the database in batches. This feature is not currently supported by Oracle SQLJ but is supported by Oracle JDBC. The `insertWithJdbcBatch()` method of the `PerformanceApp` SQLJ program demonstrates how to use the JDBC batch mechanism.

Row Prefetching with SQLJ

When you have to retrieve a large number of records from the database or perform many updates and inserts in the database, one way to improve performance is to reduce the number of round trips to the data server. For performance improvements, the Oracle JDBC drivers provide the row prefetching and batching mechanisms. See the *Oracle8i JDBC Developer's Guide and Reference* [38] for more information on Oracle JDBC batch updates and inserts.

The Oracle JDBC drivers allow you to set a *prefetch* value, that is, specify a value indicating the number of rows of data that you wish to retrieve in one round trip. When you query the database with no prefetch value, SQLJ retrieves rows one row at a time.

Specifically, the `OracleConnection` class provides methods that allow you to set the number of rows to prefetch in the client. In order for you to use the methods of the `OracleConnection` class, you must create an instance of it. You can get an instance of this class from the underlying JDBC `Connection` instance. Recall that in Chapter 6 you created SQLJ connection objects by converting a JDBC `Connection` object from the underlying connection. Listing 9-1 illustrates how to convert a `DefaultContext` object to a JDBC `Connection` object, and then convert the latter to an `OracleConnection` object. Use the `setDefaultRowPrefetch()` method of the `OracleConnection` object to set the default prefetch value to 10:

Listing 9-1

```
// Get an OracleConnection object by first converting the installed
// DefaultContext object to a java.sql.Connection object with the
// DefaultContext.getDefaultContext().getConnection() method, then
// cast the returned java.sql.Connection object to an
// OracleConnection object. Finally, use the setDefaultRowPrefetch()
// method to set the prefetch value to 10.
(OracleConnection)
  DefaultContext.getDefaultContext().getConnection()
    .setDefaultRowPrefetch(10);
```

Note that, in addition to the SQLJ DefaultContext class, you can convert an instance of the SQLJ ConnectionContext class to an instance of the OracleConnection class. For example, set the prefetch value to 100 by converting an instance of a declared connection context class to a JDBC Connection object, cast the Connection object to an OracleConnection object, and then use the setDefaultRowPrefetch() method to specify the prefetch values (Listing 9-2):

Listing 9-2

```
// Assume that you have created an instance
// of a declared ConnectionContext class named declaredCtx.
// Use the declaredCtx.getConnection() method to convert the
// declaredCtx object to a JDBC Connection object, cast
// the latter to an OracleConnection object, and use the
// setDefaultRowPrefetch() method to specify a
// prefetch value of 100.

(OracleConnection)
  declaredCtx.getConnection().setDefaultRowPrefetch(100);
```

When you wish to know the current setting of the row prefetch value, use the getDefaultRowPrefetch() method of an OracleConnection instance to do so:

```
int current_value;
current_value = anOracleConnection.getDefaultRowPrefetch();
```

The steps for using the row prefetching mechanism in SQLJ programs are as follows:

I. Convert an instance of the DefaultContext class or a declared connection context class (Listing 9-3) to a java.sql.Connection object and cast the latter to an OracleConnection object. See the "Interoperability of SQLJ and JDBC" section of Chapter 6 to learn more about converting SQLJ connection objects to JDBC Connection objects.

Listing 9-3

```
// Cast a DefaultContext object to a java.sql.Connection object
OracleConnection anOracleConnection = (OracleConnection)
  DefaultContext.getDefaultContext().getConnection();

// Cast the declared ConnectionContext object named declaredCtx
// to a java.sql.Connection object.
```

```
OracleConnection anOracleConnection = (OracleConnection)
    declaredCtx.getConnection();
```

2. Specify the row prefetch value with the `setDefaultRowPrefetch()` method of the `OracleConnection` instance:

```
// This statement sets the default row prefetch value to 20 by
// calling the method and passing it the value 20.
anOracleConnection.setDefaultRowPrefetch(20);
```

NOTE
The default prefetch value will automatically be set to one (1) when you retrieve data from an iterator that contains the LONG or the LONG RAW data types regardless of the prefetch value you pass to the setDefaultRowPrefetch() method.

The `PerformanceApp` SQLJ application illustrates how to use Oracle JDBC classes to perform row prefetch and batch updates in SQLJ. More specifically, it performs the following tasks:

- Insert records using SQLJ statements.

- Insert records with different Oracle JDBC batch values using JDBC statements.

- Retrieve rows of data by setting different prefetch values using SQLJ statements.

```
/* Program Name: PerformanceApp.sqlj
** Purpose:     A SQLJ application that demonstrates how to
** insert records as a batch and query the database by setting
** prefetch values.
**
*/

import oracle.jdbc.driver.OracleConnection;
import oracle.jdbc.driver.OraclePreparedStatement;
import java.sql.PreparedStatement;
import java.sql.SQLException;

public class PerformanceApp {

  #sql public static iterator PrefetchIter (int anumber);

  public static void main(String[] args){
    PerformanceApp Prefetchapp = new PerformanceApp();
```

```
        ConnectionManager aConnectionManager = new ConnectionManager();

        // Establish connection with the database and return an
        // OracleConnection instance. This instance is used to set values
        // of the JDBC row prefetch and the batch. (See Note 1.)

        OracleConnection anOracleConnection =
          aConnectionManager.getOracleConnection();
        Prefetchapp.runApplication(anOracleConnection);
      } // End of main() method

void runApplication(OracleConnection anOracleConnection) {
        // The number of rows to insert into the database (See Note 2.)
        int rowsToInsert = 1000;
        try {
          #sql { DROP TABLE PERF_TABLE}; // (See Note 3.)
        }
        catch (SQLException ex){ }

        try { // (See Note 4.)
          #sql { CREATE TABLE PERF_TABLE(anumber NUMBER)};

          System.out.println("*** Inserting rows in the database ***\n");
          System.out.println("********* Please Wait *********\n");

          System.out.println("******** Inserting with SQLJ ********\n");
          // Insert 1000 records into database with SQLJ (See Note 5.)
          insertWithSqlj(rowsToInsert);

          System.out.println("\n**** Inserting with JDBC BATCH ****\n");
          // (See Note 6.)
          // Insert an additional 1000 records with a batch value of 10
          insertWithJdbcBatch(rowsToInsert, anOracleConnection, 10);
          // Insert an additional 1000 records with a batch value of 100
          insertWithJdbcBatch(rowsToInsert, anOracleConnection, 100);
          // Insert an additional 1000 records with a batch value of 1000
          insertWithJdbcBatch(rowsToInsert, anOracleConnection, 1000);

          System.out.println("\n********* Query the table *********\n");

          System.out.println("*** Querying the database by" +
                            " row prefetching *\n");
          // Query database using the default prefetch value of 10
          // (See Note 7.)
          prefetchWithSqlj(anOracleConnection,
                        anOracleConnection.getDefaultRowPrefetch());
          // Query database with SQLJ by setting the prefetch value to 100
          prefetchWithSqlj(anOracleConnection, 100);
          // Query and set database row prefetch value to 1000
          prefetchWithSqlj(anOracleConnection, 1000);
        } // End of try block
```

```
    catch (SQLException e){
      System.out.println(e);
      System.exit(1);
    } // End of catch block
} // End of runApplication() method

static void insertWithSqlj(int insertMax) throws SQLException {
  // Get the time when record insertions begin (See Note 8.)
  long start = System.currentTimeMillis();

  // Add 'insertMax' number of rows into the database (See Note 9.)
  for(int i= 1; i <= insertMax; i++)
    #sql{ INSERT INTO PERF_TABLE VALUES(:i) };

  // Get the time it took to insert the rows (See Note 10.)
  long finish = System.currentTimeMillis() - start;

  // Print the number of records inserted in the database and the
  // time it took to insert those records.
  System.out.print("** With SQLJ, " + insertMax
          + " records inserted ");
  System.out.println("in " +(finish / 1000.0)+ " seconds.\n");
} // End of insertWithSqlj() method

static void insertWithJdbcBatch(
              int insertMax,
              OracleConnection anOracleConnection,
              int batchNumber)  throws SQLException {

  // Set the batch value with the value of the parameter
  // (See Note 11.)
  anOracleConnection.setDefaultExecuteBatch(batchNumber);

  long start = System.currentTimeMillis(); // Get the start time

  // Get a PreparedStatement object for sending the insertions
  // to the database (See Note 12.)
  PreparedStatement aPreparedStatement =
    anOracleConnection.prepareStatement(
      "INSERT INTO PERF_TABLE VALUES (?)");

  // Insert new records into the database (See Note 13.)
  for (int i=1; i <= insertMax; i++) {
    aPreparedStatement.setInt(1,i);
    aPreparedStatement.execute();
  }
  // Send the inserted records to the database in batches
  // (See Note 14.)
  ((OraclePreparedStatement)aPreparedStatement).sendBatch();

  // Get the time that it took for the record insertions
```

```
    long finish = System.currentTimeMillis() - start;

    aPreparedStatement.close(); // Close statement object

    System.out.print("** With JDBC BATCH set to " +
            anOracleConnection.getDefaultExecuteBatch() + " rows. ");
    System.out.println(insertMax + " rows inserted in " +
            (finish / 1000.0)+ " seconds.\n");
} // End of insertWithJdbcBatch() method

static void prefetchWithSqlj(OracleConnection anOracleConnection,
                             int prefetchValue)
                                 throws SQLException {
  int rows = 0;
  // Set the row prefetch value (See Note 15.)
  anOracleConnection.setDefaultRowPrefetch(prefetchValue);

  PrefetchIter aPrefetchIter = null;

  long start = System.currentTimeMillis(); // Get the start time

  #sql aPrefetchIter = { SELECT anumber FROM  PERF_TABLE };

  // Iterate through the iterator (See Note 16.)
  while (aPrefetchIter.next()){
    rows++;      // Count the number of rows read
  }

  // The time it took to accomplish the retrieve and process the
  // iterator
  long finish = System.currentTimeMillis() - start;

  aPrefetchIter.close();

  System.out.print("** PREFETCH value set to " +
          anOracleConnection.getDefaultRowPrefetch() + " rows. ");
  System.out.println(rows + " rows retrieved in " +
                      (finish / 1000.0)+ " seconds.\n");
} // End of prefetchWithSqlj() method
} // End of PerformanceApp class
```

Notes on the `PerformanceApp` SQLJ application:

1. Call the `connectDB()` method to connect to the database. This method
   returns an `OracleConnection` instance. Later in the program, you will
   use methods provided by this instance to specify values to the row prefetch
   and the batch update values.

2. The `rowsToInsert` variable holds the number of insertions to be made in the database. You can change this value to insert more or less rows in the database.

3. This statement drops the table if it exists. If the table does not exist, a `SQLException` error is raised and caught by the catch block.

4. Create a table that will be used for inserting data into the database.

5. Use the `insertWithSqlj()` method to insert 1,000 records in the database. Remember that the `rowsToInsert` parameter holds the value of the number of rows to insert. This method is used to show the amount of time it takes to insert records with SQLJ versus inserting records with JDBC batch update.

6. Insert rows in the database with the `insertWithJdbcBatch()` method. The last parameter of this method is the value for the JDBC batch. The method is called three times with update batch values of 10, 100, and 1,000 passed as its parameter.

7. This method will query the database using an `OracleConnection` object and a prefetch value as its parameters. In the first method call, the `prefetchWithSqlj()` method uses the default row prefetch value of 10. The method does so by calling the `getDefaultRowPrefetch()` method. In the second and third call, the prefetch value is set to 100 and 1,000, respectively.

8. This statement gets the current time in milliseconds. This time is used with the stop time in Note 10 to calculate the time it takes the insert operations to complete.

9. This statement inserts records into the database with a SQLJ executable statement.

10. This statement gets the stop time and calculates the time it took, in milliseconds, to complete the insert operations with SQLJ.

11. Set the batch value to the number supplied by the parameter of the `insertWithJdbcBatch()` method.

12. The `PreparedStatement` class extends the JDBC `Statement` class (see Appendix C). It is responsible for sending information to the database. The question mark (?) refers to the placeholder for the data that will be inserted into the database with the `setInt()` method in Note 13.

13. This loop inserts data into the database. When the execute() method is called and when the batch value is reached, it will automatically send and insert the data as a batch to the database. The setInt() method refers to the question mark of Note 12. The value that is sent to the database is passed as a parameter to this method.

14. The sendBatch() method will flush and send any remaining statements waiting to be sent to the database.

15. Using the prefetchValue variable of the prefetchWithSqlj() method, set the row prefetch value with the setDefaultRowPrefetch() method by passing to it the prefetchValue variable parameter.

16. This loop statement iterates through the result set. The data from the database is retrieved a batch at a time. When the default row prefetch value is reached, it will go to the database and retrieve the default prefetch number of rows.

Tuning SQLJ Statements with the Oracle Optimizer

The Oracle SQL *optimizer* provides an efficient way to execute SQL statements in the Oracle database. The optimizer selects the best access path for your SQL statements by using either the rule-based or the cost-based approach. See the *Oracle8i Tuning* [7] and the *Oracle8i SQL Reference* [28] for further information on the Oracle optimizer:

■ The *rule-based* approach is based on the access paths available and the ranks of these access paths.

■ Using the *cost-based* approach, the optimizer determines which execution plan is most efficient by considering available access paths and factoring in information based on statistics for the schema objects (tables or indexes) accessed by the SQL statement. The cost-based approach also considers *hints*, which are optimization suggestions to the optimizer placed in a comment in the statement.

Since you, the Oracle database designer or implementer, may have more information on the data than the Oracle optimizer and know how you wish the database to handle the data, you can pass hints to the optimizer to tune your SQL statements. For instance, you may know that a certain index is more selective for certain queries. Based on this information, you may be able to choose a more efficient execution plan than the optimizer. In such a case, use hints to force the optimizer to use your optimal execution plan.

Oracle SQLJ allows you to pass hints to the Oracle optimizer to tune your SQL statements. You pass the hints with a comment (/* or --) notation followed by a plus sign (/*+ or --+). The comments containing hints must follow the Oracle keyword DELETE, SELECT, or UPDATE statement block. At runtime, the SQLJ translator will recognize the hints, combine them with your SQL statement, and send them to the database. For example, you can use a /*+ ORDERED */ or a --+ ORDERED hint in your SQLJ executable statement to tell the Oracle optimizer to join tables in the order in which they appeared in the FROM clause. Listing 9-4 illustrates this concept:

Listing 9-4

```
#sql static iterator EmployeeIter (String lastname, String longname);
…


EmployeeIter anEmployeeIter;

// Pass a hint to the Oracle optimizer to first join the EMPLOYEE_LIST
// table and then join the department_list table.
#sql anEmployeeIter = { SELECT /*+ ORDERED */ lastname, longname
                            FROM EMPLOYEE_LIST emp, DEPARTMENT_LIST dept
                            WHERE emp.deptno = dept.deptno };
… (process iterator)
```

Consider Other Ways to Reduce Network Traffic

When you use two-tier client/server applications, where the application's processing is performed on the client's machine, you may experience network bottleneck. You can reduce or possibly eliminate this problem by using a three-tier approach. Remember that in the three-tier architecture, the processing of the data from the database is done on an application server versus a client's machine. In this scenario, the client (first tier) connects to an application server (middle tier). See Chapters 1 and 5 to learn more about application servers. The middle tier processes clients' requests by handling and processing data from and to a database server (third tier). In a three-tier approach, only the processed results of the middle tier are sent over the network to the client, thus eliminating the need for the client to retrieve and process data from the database. The three-tier architecture can also eliminate some of the restrictions of the network connections and security imposed by Java applets and Web browsers.

SQLJ can be deployed in various scenarios including in a three-tier architecture. Instead of processing the database business logic from a SQLJ client, you can reduce the client's processing by removing the business logic that processes database data and moving that logic from the client to an application server. Note that the application server can be located on a stand-alone server or on a database server.

As Chapter 8 showed, you can develop Java RMI, Enterprise JavaBeans (EJB), and CORBA objects using SQLJ. Moreover, with the Oracle8*i* data server, your SQLJ applications can reside inside the Oracle8*i* JServer in the form of Java stored procedures, EJB and CORBA objects. More importantly, the performance techniques that you learned in the previous sections of this chapter such as row prefetching and JDBC batching can be implemented in SQLJ applications residing either internally or externally to the Oracle8*i* database. (See Chapter 8 to learn how to develop RMI, EJB, and CORBA objects.)

In this chapter, you extended the functionality of the `ConnectionManager` class that you developed in Chapter 5 to include methods that convert any SQLJ connection object and the JDBC `Connection` object to an object of the `OracleConnection` class. You learned how to design SQLJ programs that use the features provided by the Oracle extension package to reduce network traffic, thereby improving performance.

In Chapter 10, you will learn about the Oracle Internet development tools. In particular, you will be acquainted with the Oracle *JDeveloper* tool, a user-friendly development tool that allows you to build, debug, and deploy database applications written in Java and SQLJ.

CHAPTER
10

Survey of Oracle8*i* Development Tools

racle provides several Internet development tools such as Designer, WebDB, JDeveloper, Developer (formerly Developer/2000), and so on. This chapter provides a brief overview of these tools, particularly Oracle Designer, WebDB, and JDeveloper. Additionally, it provides a walkthrough that teaches you step-by-step how to create, compile, and run a SQLJ application using Oracle JDeveloper.

In this chapter, you will find the following:

■ A brief overview of Oracle Internet development tools.

■ A description of some features of the JDeveloper tool.

■ A step-by-step walkthrough that demonstrates how to create, compile, and run a SQLJ application using the JDeveloper Integrated Development Environment (IDE).

Brief Overview of Oracle Internet Development Tools

Oracle provides several tools that you can use to develop and deploy database applications over the Web. The following section introduces some of them. Note that you can get a free evaluation copy of most Oracle products. You can either download them from http://technet.oracle.com or order the CDs from the Oracle store, whose link is found at the same address.

Oracle Designer Tool

Designer is a visual development modeling tool that provides an environment to model database applications. It allows you to generate server-side Database Definition Language (DDL) statements that can be used to create new schemas or update old ones. You can use Designer to develop database applications for many databases such as Oracle7, Oracle8, Oracle8*i*, Oracle Lite, Oracle Rdb, IBM DB/2, Sybase Adaptive Server, Microsoft SQL Server, or any ODBC-compliant database. Applications designed with Designer for an Oracle database are stored in a repository in the Oracle database. Additionally, you can create architectures for client/server or Web-based application deployment, Dynamic HTML, Visual Basic, or C++.

You can use Designer to model "pure" relational databases using Entity Relationship (ER) modeling techniques and object-relational databases using features of the Unified Modeling Language (UML) object analysis and design methodology. The UML features are part of the *Designer Object Extension* tool formerly called *Object Database Designer*. Remember that UML features notation for analyzing and designing software components. (See Chapter 8 for more information regarding UML.)

Designer Generators

You can use Designer to automatically generate the following:

- *Oracle Developer Forms Generator* creates screen layouts, client-side application logic, and database access definitions.

- *Oracle WebServer Generator* produces applications to run over the Web.

- *C++ Generator* generates C++ classes that map the Oracle types that you wish to access from a C++ client-side application. (See Chapters 7 and 8 to learn how to develop and access Oracle types for Oracle8 and Oracle8*i* databases.)

- *Visual Basic Generator* generates Visual Basic applications based on module and database design specifications recorded in the repository.

- *Oracle Report Generator* defines report modules and their usage.

- *Oracle Server Generator* creates server-side components such as SQL DDL that include the table, column, Foreign Key constraint, Check constraint, and Primary Key constraint definitions.

See http://technet.oracle.com for technical information on Oracle Internet tools.

Oracle WebDB

WebDB is an HTML-based development tool for building Web database applications (for example, HTML forms, reports, charts, menus, and so on) and Web sites. It provides many wizards that guide the user during the entire development process. Additionally, WebDB contains the tools that DBAs can use to manage a Web site such as:

- The capability to create database users and assign roles and development privileges to them.

- The capability to configure the WebDB Listener and PL/SQL gateway.

- The capability to organize the structure of WebDB sites.

Both types of users, Oracle application developers and database administrators (DBAs), can use WebDB to build applications over the Web. WebDB applications are stored in the Oracle database and can be used with Oracle7.3.4 or later. When you build a Web site with WebDB, all the maintenance tools are included in the site itself—that is, you can change the site wherever you are (for example, in your office or on the road). WebDB also includes an HTTP listener that you can install to act as a Web server and a PL/SQL interface to the database. Use WebDB to browse databases over the Web, build components (for example, reports, menus, and so on), and monitor users and database activity.

Oracle JDeveloper

JDeveloper is a user-friendly development tool that allows you to build, debug, and deploy database applications written in Java and SQLJ. When you wish to develop Java or SQLJ client-side and server-side programs, you may use your favorite editor or the Oracle JDeveloper tool. In this chapter, you will use JDeveloper to develop the `MySqljAppUsingJDev` SQLJ application.

JDeveloper Features

Use the Oracle JDeveloper to:

- Create Java and SQLJ client-side applications and applets.

- Create and deploy Java and SQLJ server-side applications to Oracle8*i*.

- Create, debug, and deploy Java servlets. Remember that servlets are Java programs that extend request/response-oriented servers such as Java-enabled Web servers.

- Create, debug, and deploy Enterprise JavaBeans (EJB) applications to Oracle8*i*. (See Chapter 8 to learn more about EJB applications.)

- Create, debug, and deploy CORBA applications to Oracle8*i*. (See Chapter 8 to learn more about CORBA objects.)

- Generate *InfoBus* Data Forms using *JFC/Swing* components.

- Switch JDK versions between 1.1 and 1.2.

This section provides you with a brief overview of the JDeveloper IDE. While reading this section, you will learn how to use the Navigator component to create, organize, and access workspaces, projects, packages, and Java and SQLJ classes. See the "Developing a SQLJ Application Using JDeveloper" section of this chapter to learn more about these components.

Primary Components of the JDeveloper IDE

When you open JDeveloper, you see its command, development, and message areas (see Figure 10-1).

Command Area

The *command area* (see Figure 10-1) contains the following components:

- The menu bar displays a list of the available commands within the tool such as File, Edit, Search, View, Project, Run, Wizards, Tools, Windows, and Help.

- The toolbar displays the shortcut keys to open and save a file, save all files, undo an operation, search, search again, debug a program, redo an operation, replace, browse a symbol, make and rebuild a program.

- The component palette displays the Java Beans that reside in the tool library. It allows you to add components to your user interface, install custom or third-party components, and customize the palette.

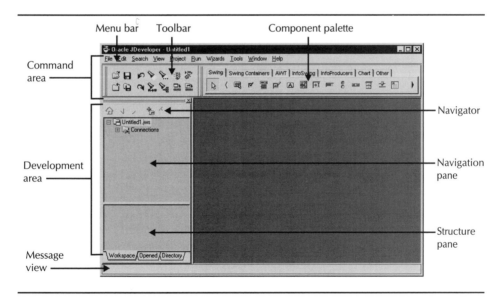

FIGURE 10-1. *Oracle JDeveloper tool*

Development Area

You use the *development area* (refer to Figure 10-1) to access your Java and SQLJ source files. In other words, you can create, edit, and view your source code in that area.

Message Area

The *message view* area at the bottom of the JDeveloper window displays errors and messages during a debugging session.

Developing a SQLJ Application Using JDeveloper

The steps to develop a SQLJ application are as follows:

1. Create a workspace.

2. Create a project.

3. Add a SQLJ file to your project to create the source code file.

4. Set project properties so that JDeveloper can check SQLJ syntax at compile time. This step is optional but highly recommended.

5. Compile the program.

6. Run the program.

1. Creating a New Workspace

In JDeveloper IDE, a *workspace* keeps track of the projects that you use and environment settings while developing your Java or SQLJ program. When you start JDeveloper, the tool navigator automatically displays the last project that you created—that is, the last workspace is opened by default, enabling you to pick up where you left off. If you wish to create a new workspace and a new project, you need to close the current workspace. You do so by clicking File | Close Workspace. After you close the workspace, the screen looks like the one in Figure 10-1. Workspaces are stored in files with the extension .jws.

The steps to create a workspace are as follows:

1. Choose File | New Workspace.

2. If prompted, select the files in the current workspace that you wish to save and click OK.

Alternatively, you can rename the default workspace. See the "Renaming a Workspace" section of this chapter.

2. Creating a New Project

To create a project, use the Project Wizard that creates a project file with the file extension .jpr. This project file contains the project properties and a list of all the files in the project. The tool uses the list of files and the project settings when you load, save, or build a project. You can see the project file at the top node of the project tree in the Navigation pane. The Project Wizard creates a project file, which stores the project properties and an optional HTML file that contains default project information. You can edit the HTML page to record pertinent information about the project. Here are the steps to create a new project:

1. Click File | New Project. You'll see the Project Wizard screen shown here:

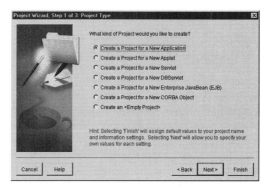

2. Select "Create an <Empty Project>" and click the Next button. The second wizard screen appears with a default project and package names, as shown next:

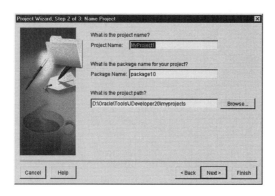

3. Enter new project and package names if you wish to override the defaults. For example, enter `MySqljAppUsingJDev` and `sqljproject` for the project name and the package name, respectively, and click Next to continue. Alternatively, you may click Next without entering additional information to accept the default project and package names. By default, JDeveloper stores the source code files that you created in the `myprojects` directory and the class files in the `myclass` directory. If you wish to store your projects in a different directory path, click Browse, select your directory path, and then click OK.

4. JDeveloper allows you to document your application. If you want to accept the default, click Next. Otherwise, edit the necessary fields such as Title, Author, Description (as shown here), and click Next.

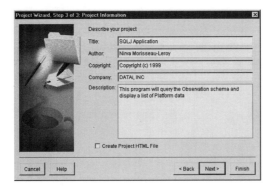

5. The tool displays the Finish screen, shown next. Click Finish to create the project.

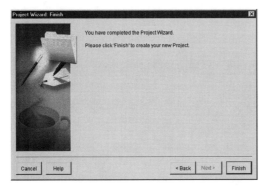

Note that a project is created using the name that you entered in Step 3. The navigator reflects these changes, as shown in Figure 10-2.

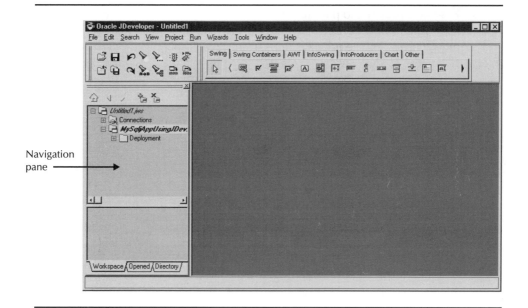

Navigation
pane

FIGURE 10-2. *Navigator shows the new project*

Renaming a Workspace

In Figure 10-2, the navigator displays the `Untitled1.jws` filename of the default
workspace. Follow these steps to rename the workspace:

1. Click `Untitled1.jws`.

2. Click File | Rename. You'll see a Save As dialog box like the one
   shown here:

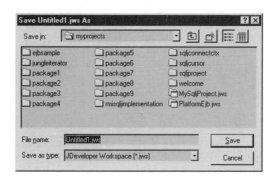

3. Change `Untitled1.jws` to `MySqljAppUsingJDev`, select the `sqljproject` package, and click Save to save the workspace file in the `sqljproject` package.

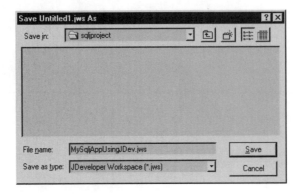

Note that the navigator reflects the changes that you make (see Figure 10-3).

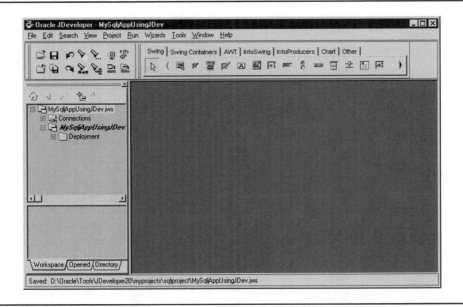

FIGURE 10-3. *Navigator shows the new name of the workspace*

3. Adding a SQLJ Source File to the Project

In this section, you will create your SQLJ source file. The steps are as follows:

1. Click File | New.

2. JDeveloper displays the New panel and its icons.

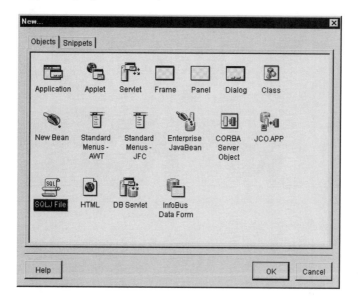

3. You can select the icon that corresponds to your need, in this case the SQLJ File icon, and then click OK. The tool creates the Untitled1.sqlj file, as shown in Figure 10-4.

4. Double-click to display the Untitled1.sqlj source file (see Figure 10-4). By default, JDeveloper inserts two import statements to make the sqlj.runtime.* and the sqlj.runtime.ref.* available to your SQLJ program.

5. Rename the file by entering MySqljAppUsingJDev, and save the new file in the sqljproject package. Note that the navigator reflects your changes (as shown in Figure 10-5).

Congratulations. You have just created an empty SQLJ program. The next step is to enter your SQLJ source code, as shown in Figure 10-6 (see the listing of the MySqljAppUsingJDev SQLJ application at the end of this chapter).

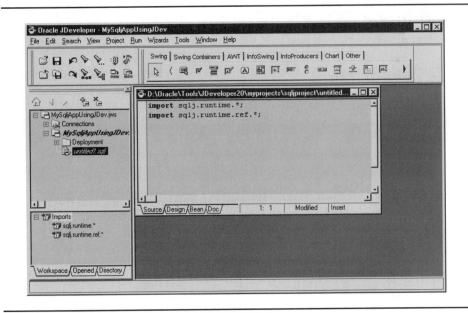

FIGURE 10-4. *SQLJ source file*

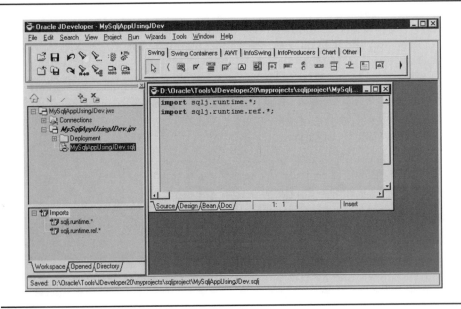

FIGURE 10-5. *Navigator shows the new name for the SQLJ source file*

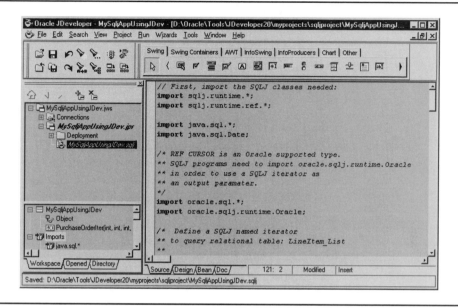

FIGURE 10-6. *SQLJ source code*

4. Setting the Project Properties

JDeveloper allows you to set the project properties so that the SQLJ translator can connect to the database and check SQLJ semantics at compile time. To enable this functionality, you need to create a connection object in the tool. To do so, follow these steps:

  1. Click Project | Project Properties to open the Properties dialog box shown here:

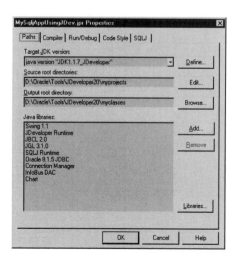

2. Click SQLJ, and then click "Check SQL semantics against database schema," as shown next:

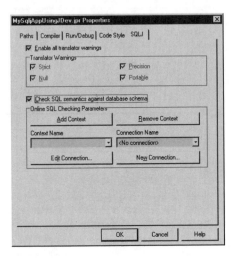

3. Click New Connection.

4. Enter username and password. The default is your local host. If the database is not on your local host, then replace the "localhost" string with the URL address of your database—for example, data-i.com. Note that the name of the connection object is Connection2; you may change it to a more meaningful name if you wish.

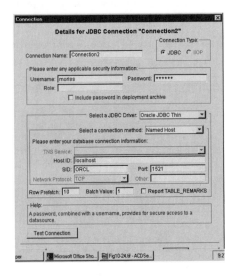

5. Click the Test Connection button to connect to the database and test your connection. If the test is successful, the connection object named `Connection2` appears as shown next:

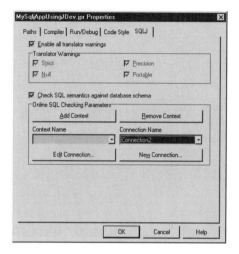

6. Click OK.

Next, you will learn how to compile a SQLJ program using JDeveloper.

5. Compiling a SQLJ Program

Compiling a program in JDeveloper is very easy. To do so:

1. Click the name of the SQLJ program you wish to compile.

2. Click `Project | Rebuild`.

JDeveloper invokes the SQLJ translator that compiles your program. If compilation errors are generated (warning or fatal), JDeveloper will list them in the message area at the bottom of the screen. Note that in Figure 10-7 the program was compiled successfully, and a list of warning messages is presented in the message area.

Remember that when you compile a SQLJ program, the SQLJ translator generates a Java source file and a class file. By default, JDeveloper stores the Java source file in the package directory that you created in Step 2 in the "Creating a New Project" section of this chapter. If you wish to run the SQLJ program from the Navigator tree, you need to include the Java source file in your project. To do so, click the green plus sign (+) in the Navigator tree, select the `MySqljAppUsingJDev.java` file, and click Open (see Figure 10-8). You are now ready to run the SQLJ program.

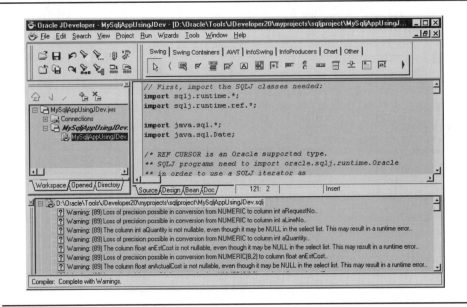

FIGURE 10-7. *List of warning messages generated at compilation time*

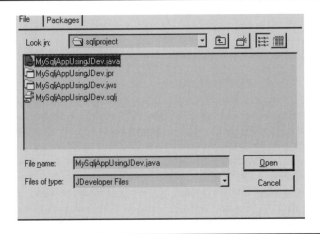

FIGURE 10-8. *Add a Java source file to your project*

6. Running a SQLJ Program

In the previous section, you learned how to compile a SQLJ program using JDeveloper. Fortunately, you had no syntax errors while compiling the program. In situations where the translator generates fatal errors, you need to edit the source code, correct the errors, and recompile the program using the steps listed in the "Compiling a SQLJ Program" section of this chapter. Next, you will run the program.

Before you do so, however, JDeveloper's documentation suggests that you rebuild the entire project, particularly in a situation where you have compiled each program individually as in the scenario described in the "Compiling a SQLJ Program" section of this chapter. When you rebuild the project, the tool creates the appropriate file dependencies and ties any loose ends that may exist. To rebuild the project:

1. Click the `MySqljAppUsing.jpr` file.

2. Click Project | Rebuild "`MySqljAppUsing.jpr`" or click the Rebuild icon on the toolbar. JDeveloper will recompile all programs within the project, as shown in Figure 10-9.

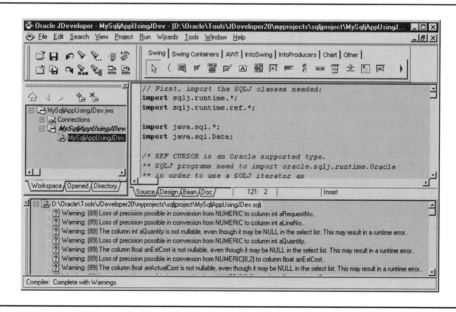

FIGURE 10-9. *JDeveloper recompiles all programs in the project*

Hopefully, you have no errors. You can therefore run the program. To do so, follow these steps:

1. Click the `MySqljAppUsing.java` file.

2. Click Run | Run using the options from the command area or alternatively click the Run button on the toolbar. Note that when you use the run option to execute the program, JDeveloper recompiles the program before running it. So, at subsequent times when you wish to recompile a program, you only need to click the program name and then click the Run button.

Figure 10-10 shows that the output of the program is listed in the window named Compiler associated with the `MySqljAppUsing` program located at the bottom of the tool main window. Use the Compiler window's scroll bar to view the results generated by the SQLJ application.

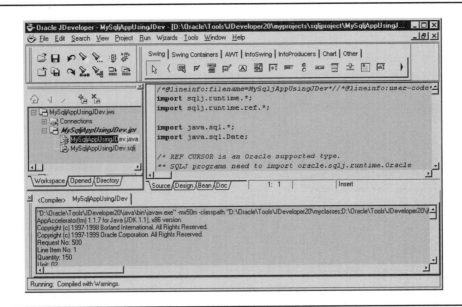

FIGURE 10-10. *Program output is listed in the window named Compiler*

Here is the listing of the MySqljAppUsingJDev SQLJ application:

```
/*   Program Name: MySqljAppUsingJDev.sqlj
**
**   Purpose:       Use a SQLJ named iterator to
** retrieve purchase orders and their associated
** line items.
*/

// Import the SQLJ runtime classes
import sqlj.runtime.*;
import sqlj.runtime.ref.*;

// Import the Java classes
import java.sql.*;
import java.sql.Date;

import oracle.sql.*;
import oracle.sqlj.runtime.Oracle;

public class MySqljAppUsingJDev {

    /*  Declare a public SQLJ named iterator
    ** to query the LineItem_List relational table.
    **
    ** Columns listed in the SQLJ named iterator
    ** must match directly the database name columns.
    ** Database data type must also match iterator
    ** data type.  */
    #sql public iterator PurchaseOrderIter
            ( int aRequestNo, int aLineNo,
              int aQuantity, String aUnit,
              float anEstCost, float anActualCost,
              String aDesc
            );
  // Default constructor
  public MySqljAppUsingJDev() {  // (See Note 1.)
      try {
          /* Register the driver and set the default context
          ** The constructor is the best place to do this.
          ** Edit the setDefaultContext call for a URL
          ** appropriate to your system. */
          DriverManager.registerDriver
              (new oracle.jdbc.driver.OracleDriver());
```

```
            DefaultContext.setDefaultContext
                (new DefaultContext
                   ("jdbc:oracle:thin:@data-i.com:1521:ORCL",
                     "scott","tiger",false)
                );
        } // End try
        catch (Exception ex) {
           System.err.println("Database Connection failed: " + ex);
           } // end catch
        }   // End constructor

   public static void main (String [] args) throws SQLException {
       // Instantiate MySqljAppUsingJDev()    (See Note 2.)
       MySqljAppUsingJDev app = new MySqljAppUsingJDev();

       // Stop program execution if we cannot connect to the database
       // (See Note 3.)
       if  (DefaultContext.getDefaultContext() == null ) {
             System.out.println("I cannot connect to the database "
                                       + "-- Stop Execution.");
             System.exit(1);
        } // End if
        try {
            app.runMySqljAppUsingJDev ();   // (See Note 4.)
        } // End try
        catch (SQLException ex) { // (See Note 5.)
          System.err.println("Error running the " +
                  "MySqljAppUsingJDev application: " + ex);
          String sqlState = ex.getSQLState();
          System.err.println("SQL State: " + sqlState);
          String sqlMessage = ex.getMessage();
          System.err.println("SQL Message: " + sqlMessage);
          int errorCode = ex.getErrorCode();
          System.err.println("SQL Error Code: " + errorCode);
        }   // End catch
   } // End main()

 void runMySqljAppUsingJDev () throws SQLException {
   // Instantiate PurchaseOrderIter iterator
   // and initialize it: purchaseOrder
   PurchaseOrderIter aPurchaseOrderIter = null;

  // Query Purchase_List database table using
  // aPurchaseOrderIter. (See Note 6.)
  #sql aPurchaseOrderIter =
      { SELECT L.requestno AS aRequestNo,
            L.lineno AS aLineNo,
            L.quantity AS aQuantity,
```

```
          L.unit AS aUnit,
          L.estimatedcost AS anEstCost,
          L.actualcost AS anActualCost,
          L.description AS aDesc
        FROM lineitem_list L
        ORDER BY L.requestno
      };  // end of SQLJ statement

      // Iterate and print purchase order info. (See Note 7.)
      while (aPurchaseOrderIter.next() ) {
         System.out.println("Request No: " +
            aPurchaseOrderIter.aRequestNo() );
         System.out.println("Line Item No: " +
            aPurchaseOrderIter.aLineNo() );
         System.out.println("Quantity: " +
            aPurchaseOrderIter.aQuantity() );
         System.out.println("Unit: " +
            aPurchaseOrderIter.aUnit() );
         System.out.println("Estimated Cost: " +
            aPurchaseOrderIter.anEstCost() );
         System.out.println("Actual Cost: " +
            aPurchaseOrderIter.anActualCost() );
         System.out.println("Quantity: " +
            aPurchaseOrderIter.aDesc() );
      }  // End while

      /* Close the iterator
      **
      ** Iterators should be closed when you no longer need them
      */
      aPurchaseOrderIter.close();
   } // End runMySqljAppUsingJDev()

} // End MySqljAppUsingJDev.class
```

Notes on the `MySqljAppUsingJDev` SQLJ application:

1. This statement creates a default constructor that, when invoked, will automatically connect to the Oracle database. See Chapters 2, 5, and 6 to learn more about SQLJ connection objects and Appendix B for Java default constructors. Remember that a SQLJ constructor is identical to a Java constructor.

2. This statement instantiates the `MySqljAppUsingJDev` SQLJ class.

3. This statement ensures that the program stops execution if it fails to connect to the database.

4. This statement calls the `runMySqljAppUsingJDev` method.

5. The catch block includes several statements:

   - The first statement prints a user-defined error message.

   - The following statements use the methods from the `java.sql.SQLException` class and its subclasses to provide more information on the SQL errors generated by the program (see Chapter 4 to learn more about generated SQL errors):

     - The next statement calls the `getSQLState()` method that returns a five-digit string containing the SQL state.

     - The next statement prints the SQL state retrieved from the previous statement.

     - The next statement calls the `getMessage()` method that returns an error message.

     - The next statement prints the error message.

     - The next statement calls the `getErrorCode()` method that returns 0. This information is really meaningless.

     - The next statement prints the error code.

6. This statement selects all purchase orders and their associated line items and stores the results in a SQLJ iterator object. Remember that multi-row queries are stored in SQLJ iterator objects. See Chapters 2, 3, and 5, and Appendix D to learn more about SQLJ iterators.

7. This statement uses a while loop to iterate the results stored in the iterator object.

This chapter concludes Part IV. It introduced some of the Oracle Internet development tools such as Oracle Designer, Oracle WebDB, and JDeveloper. Additionally, it presented a step-by-step walkthrough that taught you how to create, compile, and run a SQLJ program.

Appendix A, "Basic Oracle SQL," marks the beginning of Part V, where you will learn basic SQL and PL/SQL concepts that will help you understand SQLJ constructs.

PART

V

Appendices

APPENDIX

A

Basic Oracle SQL

n this appendix, you will find:

- Some basic material on the relational database model.
- A tutorial for the SQL relational database language.
- A discussion of embedded SQL, the approach which allows SQL statements to be executed from general-purpose programming languages such as C and C++.
- A discussion of PL/SQL, Oracle's procedural extension of SQL.

The Relational Model for Databases

Clearly, the seminal advance in database technology was the creation of the relational model for databases by E. F. Codd as presented in *A Relational Model of Data for Large Shared Data Banks* [12]. The basic advantage of the relational model is that it provides power through simplicity. In particular, the model is based on a simple data structure, the table, and simple very high-level database languages such as SQL, in which the user indicates what is to be done instead of how to do it. You are referred to Chapter 3 of *An Introduction to Database Systems, Sixth Edition* [15] for a description of the advantages provided by such simplicity.

Some fundamental definitions for the relational model are now presented. A *file* is a set of records, where a *record* is a set of fields, and a *field* is the smallest unit of named data in the file. Figure A-1 illustrates a file called EMPLOYEE_LIST that contains a record for each employee in a company, containing the fields employeeno, lastname, firstname, phone, and departmentno.

employeeno	lastname	firstname	phone	departmentno

FIGURE A-I. *EMPLOYEE_LIST*

This `EMPLOYEE_LIST` file enjoys a special property that is very important in the relational model; it is an example of a *table*. A *table* is a file in which every record has the same structure, that is, the same number, and the corresponding semantic type, of fields. The *semantic type* of a field is the meaning of the field. `EMPLOYEE_LIST` is a table since each record in it contains exactly the same semantic type (although not necessarily the same values) of fields. Specifically, each `EMPLOYEE_LIST` record consists of an employee number, a last name, a first name, a phone number, and a department number.

In the relational model, each table should be equipped with a *primary key*, that is, a field (or collection of fields) that satisfies the following two properties:

- **Uniqueness**   No two records in the table will have the same primary key values.

- **Fully defined**   Every record in the table must have a value for each field in its primary key. This means that when a record is inserted into a table, a value must be given to each field in the primary key.

The primary key is the principal means of identifying a record in a table.

The primary key for the `EMPLOYEE_LIST` table consists of one field, the `employeeno` field. This is designated in Figure A-1 (and generally in this appendix) by circling the primary key field.

The `MARRIAGE` table in Figure A-2 represents the marriages, both past and present, between a set of men and a set of women. Since it is possible for a person to have ex-spouses, both the `husband_ssn` and the `wife_ssn` are required fields in the primary key. Such a primary key that contains more than one field is called a *composite primary key*.

A *relational database* is a logically related collection of tables. In general, a database describes *entities* (that is, distinguishable objects) and relationships between entities (see *The Entity-Relationship Model—Toward a Unified View of Data* [10]).

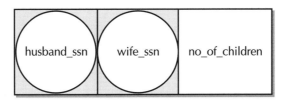

FIGURE A-2.   *MARRIAGE*

For example, the database in Figure A-3 describes the entities employee, department, and project, as well as the relationship between employees and departments, and the account relationship between projects and departments.

As is typical in relational databases, each entity is represented by its own table. The relationship between departments and employees is represented by placing departmentno, the primary key of the DEPARTMENT_LIST table, in the EMPLOYEE_LIST table. The account relationship between departments and

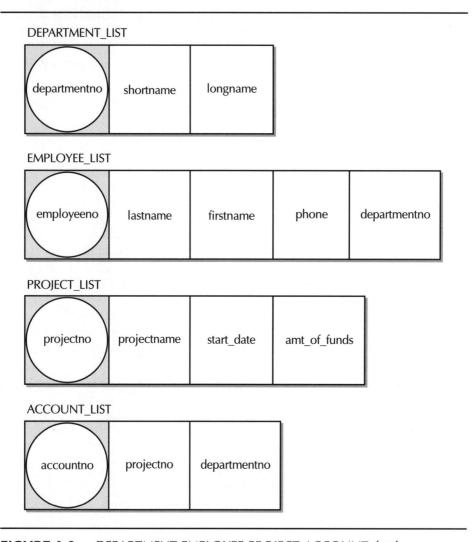

FIGURE A-3. *DEPARTMENT-EMPLOYEE-PROJECT-ACCOUNT database*

projects is represented by its own table, ACCOUNT_LIST, containing the primary keys of the DEPARTMENT_LIST table (departmentno) and the PROJECT_LIST table (projectno). Thus, in both of these relationships, the primary keys of the entities being related are used to define the relationships.

However, the account relationship gets its own table while the department-employee relationship does not. The reason for this difference is that the account relationship is a many-many relationship (each department can have an account with many projects, and each project can have an account with many departments), whereas the department-employee relationship is a one-many relationship (each department can have many employees, but each employee works in only one department). Since placing the departmentno in the PROJECT_LIST table, or placing the projectno in the DEPARTMENT_LIST table, would generate too much redundancy, it is indeed desirable to represent the account relationship as a separate table.

As you have seen in the preceding discussion, relationships are represented in the relational model by using the primary keys of the entities being related (actually, *alternate keys*; keys that could have been chosen to be the primary key, but were not so chosen, can also be used). The primary key of one table (the referenced table) that appears in another table (the referencing table) is called a *foreign key* for the referencing table. The *referential integrity rule* states that no foreign key can reference a nonexistent record in the referenced table. Hence, if departmentno 100 appears in an EMPLOYEE_LIST record, there must be a departmentno 100 in a DEPARTMENT_LIST record. Most relational database systems support the referential integrity rule. You will see later how this rule is enforced in SQL.

A *relational database language* is a language for setting up the structure of, and manipulating, relational databases. The commands in a relational database language that are used to set up the structure of a database (for example, creating a new table) are called DDL (Data Definition Language) commands. The commands for manipulating a database (for example, inserting, deleting, updating, and retrieving records) are called DML (Data Manipulation Language) commands. SQL is by far the most widely used relational database language.

A *relational database management system* (RDBMS) is an implementation of one or more relational database languages. Most RDBMSs implement SQL, but some implement other relational database languages as well. The first two significant RDBMSs were the research systems INGRES (see *The Design and Implementation of INGRES* [55]), developed at the University of California at Berkeley, and System R (see *System R: Relational Approach to Database Management* [5]), developed at IBM Research, San Jose. System R was based on SQL, while INGRES was based on the relational database language QUEL. However, the commercial version of INGRES, available in the early 1980s, supported both SQL and QUEL, with SQL being the principal language for the system.

The first commercially available RDBMS, and the first commercial implementation of SQL, was the Oracle RDBMS, which was available by 1979.

SQL

In the next two sections, you will consider the DDL and DML commands of SQL, respectively. You are referred to *An Introduction to Database Systems, Sixth Edition* [15] and *Oracle8i SQL Reference Manual* [28] for more information on these commands.

In Oracle, you can submit SQL commands interactively to the SQL*Plus and SQL*DBA utilities.

SQL DDL Commands

The most important SQL DDL command is the CREATE TABLE command, which creates a new database table. A simplified syntax of the CREATE TABLE command is presented:

```
CREATE TABLE tablename ( list_of_field_definitions_and_constraints )
```

where a `list_of_field_definitions_and_constraints` is a *field definition* or a sequence of field definitions and constraints separated by commas. Each field definition consists of a *field name* followed by a *field data type*. A *constraint* is a condition that the database must satisfy in order to be consistent, such as a primary key constraint or a foreign key constraint. For example, the following CREATE TABLE command creates the database table described in Figure A-1.

```
CREATE TABLE
   EMPLOYEE_LIST
      ( employeeno   number(5),
        lastname     varchar2(30),
        firstname    varchar2(30),
        phone        varchar2(13),
        departmentno number(5),
        PRIMARY KEY  ( employeeno ),
        FOREIGN KEY  ( departmentno ) REFERENCES DEPARTMENT_LIST )
```

`number` is the SQL numeric data type, which includes integers and floats, with `number(5)` indicating an integer with a maximum of five digits, and `varchar2` is the SQL data type for variable length strings. The primary key constraint ensures that:

- No two records in EMPLOYEE_LIST can have the same employeeno value.

- Every record inserted into EMPLOYEE_LIST must have a non-NULL employeeno value. Note that when a field has not been given a value in a record, SQL by default will assign a special NULL value to the field in that record.

The foreign key constraint insures the enforcement of the referential integrity rule, by constraining operations on both the referencing table (EMPLOYEE_LIST) and the referenced table (DEPARTMENT_LIST). Specifically, the RDBMS will not allow an EMPLOYEE_LIST record to be inserted if it contains a departmentno that is not in the DEPARTMENT_LIST table. Similarly, the departmentno field of an already existing record cannot be changed to a departmentno that is not in the DEPARTMENT_LIST table. Also, the RDBMS will not allow a DEPARTMENT_LIST record to be deleted if the departmentno of that record is still in the EMPLOYEE_ LIST table (that is, if there is still an employee in that department). Similarly, an update of a departmentno field in the DEPARTMENT_LIST table is not allowed if that update would cause a departmentno to "disappear" from the DEPARTMENT_ LIST table, and if that departmentno is still in the EMPLOYEE_LIST table. However, SQL allows foreign keys to be NULL, and therefore reference no record at all.

The inverse of the CREATE TABLE command is the DROP TABLE command, which purges a table from the database. For example,

DROP TABLE EMPLOYEE_LIST

will purge the EMPLOYEE_LIST table from the database.

Other SQL DDL commands include the ALTER TABLE command, which changes the logical structure of an already existing table; the CREATE VIEW command which creates a virtual table (one that exists as a stored definition instead of a stored set of records in the database); and the CREATE INDEX command which creates a B-tree index on a table to speed up retrievals. You are referred to *An Introduction to Database Systems, Sixth Edition* [15] and *Oracle8i SQL Reference Manual* [28] for information on these commands.

SQL DML Commands

SQL contains four DML commands:

- The INSERT statement (to insert records into a table)
- The DELETE statement (to delete records from a table)
- The UPDATE statement (to change the field values of already existing records in a table)
- The SELECT statement (to retrieve data from the database)

The syntax of the DELETE and UPDATE statements, as well as the syntax of one of the two types of INSERT statements, the INSERT SELECT statement, is based on the syntax of the SELECT statement. Therefore, these statements will be discussed after the SELECT statement.

First, the INSERT VALUES statement, the type of INSERT statement that is not based on the SELECT statement, is discussed. A CREATE TABLE statement creates an empty table. The INSERT VALUES statement can be used to load a record into a table. The syntax of the INSERT VALUES statement is

```
INSERT INTO tablename ( field_list ) VALUES ( values_list )
```

The field_list indicates the order in which field values will be inserted, and values_list contains those field values. For example,

```
INSERT INTO EMPLOYEE_LIST
    ( employeeno, lastname, firstname, phone, departmentno )
        VALUES ( 1056, 'Jones', 'Rachel', '(305)555-0359', 15 )
```

will insert the indicated record into the EMPLOYEE_LIST table. Note that string literals are delimited by single quotes (') in SQL.

SELECT Statements

First, the simplest kind of SELECT statement—namely, a SELECT statement that involves only one table—is considered.

One-Table SELECT Statements

The simplified syntax of a one-table SELECT statement is

```
SELECT expression_list FROM tablename [ where_clause ]
```

where the square brackets indicate that the where_clause is optional. The expression_list is a list of expressions, with each expression built up using operators, constants, and the fields from tablename. A where_clause is the keyword WHERE, followed by a Boolean combination of comparison_clauses using the Boolean operators AND, OR, NOT, where a comparison_clause has the form:

```
expression1 comparison_operator expression2
```

expression1 and expression2 are as in the expression_list, and the comparison_ operators are <, <=, >, >=, =, <> (inequality operator). For example,

```
SELECT employeeno, phone
    FROM EMPLOYEE_LIST
        WHERE departmentno = 15
            AND firstname = 'Michelle'
```

will print the employeeno and phone number for each employee with the first name Michelle who works in department number 15. The comparison clauses in the preceding example can be called `compare-against-constant` clauses, as they each compare the value of a specific field to a specific constant. Such `compare-against-constant` clauses are very common in `SELECT` statements.

In general, the one-table `SELECT` statement will print the indicated expressions from the indicated table for records that satisfy the `WHERE` clause condition. The * wildcard may appear in place of the `expression_list` in the `SELECT` statement, indicating that all the fields in the table should be printed, and a missing `where_clause` indicates that each record in the table will contribute output. For example,

```
SELECT * FROM EMPLOYEE_LIST
```

will print the entire `EMPLOYEE_LIST` table.

Multiple-Table SELECT Statements

Next, `SELECT` statements that involve more than one table are considered. These are true database commands in that they act across tables at the database level. Consider the following query:

```
Print the project names of projects that have an account
with department number 15.
```

This query involves both the `ACCOUNT_LIST` table, to find the project numbers of projects that have an account with department number 15, and the `PROJECT_LIST` table, to "translate" the project numbers found in `ACCOUNT_LIST` into the project names that are to be printed. This query can be coded as the following `SELECT` statement:

```
SELECT PROJECT_LIST.projectname
    FROM PROJECT_LIST, ACCOUNT_LIST
        WHERE ACCOUNT_LIST.departmentno = 15
            AND ACCOUNT_LIST.projectno = PROJECT_LIST.projectno
```

Note that field names are modified with table names, using the dot (`.`) operator, to protect against the ambiguity that would arise when the same field name appears in different tables in the query.

The `compare-against-constant` clause `ACCOUNT_LIST.departmentno = 15` can be thought of as identifying the desired `ACCOUNT_LIST` records. The join clause `ACCOUNT_LIST.projectno = PROJECT_LIST.projectno` can be thought of as obtaining the `PROJECT_LIST` record that "matches" such an `ACCOUNT_LIST` record in that it contains the same `projectno`. In general, a join clause has the form:

```
fieldreference1 comparison_operator fieldreference2
```

where a `fieldreference` has the form `[ tablename. ]fieldname` and the referenced fields come from different records.

A special type of join clause involves fields from different records in the same table. This type of join clause requires the *alias* construct. For example, consider the query:

Print the pairs of first names of employees who have the same last names, but different first names.

This query can be expressed in SQL as:

```
SELECT EX.firstname, EY.firstname
  FROM EMPLOYEE_LIST EX, EMPLOYEE_LIST EY,
    WHERE EX.lastname = EY.lastname
      AND EX.firstname <> EY.firstname
```

In the FROM clause, EX and EY are assigned as two aliases for EMPLOYEE_LIST records that can be used in the WHERE clause, allowing you to compare different records from the EMPLOYEE_LIST table. Specifically, the two join clauses obtain EMPLOYEE_LIST records EX and EY for different employees (their first names are different) who have the same last names.

Nested SELECT Statements

A *nested SELECT statement* is a SELECT statement that contains another SELECT statement in its WHERE clause. A subquery is a SELECT statement that is contained in the WHERE clause of a nested SELECT statement. A common reason for including a subquery in the WHERE clause of a SELECT statement is that the WHERE clause contains the IN operator. You can use the IN operator to test if a value belongs to a set of values that is designated by a subquery. For example, consider the problem, which was solved previously without subqueries, of printing the project names of projects that have an account with department number 15. A nested solution to this problem is

```
SELECT projectname FROM PROJECT_LIST
  WHERE projectno IN
    ( SELECT projectno FROM ACCOUNT_LIST
        WHERE departmentno = 15 )
```

Here we print the names of projects whose project number belongs to the set of numbers of projects that have an account with department number 15. In general, the form of such a *membership test* is

```
expression IN ( subquery )
```

where the IN operator returns true if the value of the indicated expression belongs to the set designated by the indicated subquery.

Some prefer a nested solution of a query to a flat (that is, nonnested) solution because the nested solution can be a simple connection of simple (often one-table) selects. When the nesting structure does provide a sequence of one-table SELECT statements, as in the preceding example, it is not necessary to qualify field names with table names. Also, there are some queries that do not have flat solutions. These are queries that involve the NOT IN operator in a negative membership test. The *negative membership test* has the form:

```
expression NOT IN ( subquery )
```

which returns true if the value of the expression does not belong to the set designated by the subquery, and returns false otherwise. For example, the query:

```
Print the project names of projects that do not have an account
with department number 15.
```

does not have a flat solution. However, this query has the following nested solution:

```
SELECT projectname FROM PROJECT_LIST
    WHERE projectno NOT IN
      ( SELECT projectno FROM ACCOUNT_LIST
          WHERE departmentno = 15 )
```

Observe that the following query prints the project names of projects that have an account with at least one department number other than 15, instead of the desired output:

```
SELECT PROJECT_LIST.projectname
    FROM PROJECT_LIST, ACCOUNT_LIST
      WHERE ACCOUNT_LIST.departmentno <> 15
          AND PROJECT_LIST.projectno = ACCOUNT_LIST.projectno
```

In general, the inequality operator cannot be used to simulate the NOT IN operator.

Aggregate Functions

Roughly speaking, an *aggregate function* is a function that assigns a number to a set of field values or a set of records. In the SELECT statement, aggregate functions can appear in the expression_list after the keyword SELECT, or in a HAVING clause (which will soon be introduced). The aggregate functions supported by SQL include AVG, SUM, MAX, MIN, and COUNT. Oracle SQL supports additional aggregate functions, namely, VARIANCE and STDDEV (standard deviation).

For example, you can code the query:

Print how many accounts involve department number 15.

as:

```
SELECT COUNT(*) FROM ACCOUNT_LIST
   WHERE departmentno = 15
```

where COUNT(*) indicates that you are counting records. The other form of the COUNT aggregate function is

```
COUNT( DISTINCT expression )
```

where you are counting distinct expression values.

Each of the other aggregate functions takes an expression, optionally prefixed with the keyword DISTINCT or the keyword ALL, as its argument. For example, AVG(DISTINCT qty) indicates that duplicate qty values should be removed before computing the average qty. AVG(ALL qty) indicates that the average should be computed for all the qty values, including duplicates. ALL is the default for the SUM, AVG, MAX, MIN, VARIANCE, and STDDEV aggregate functions.

Suppose you are required to print, for each department, the department number and the number of accounts that involve that department. You can do this using the GROUP BY clause:

```
SELECT departmentno, COUNT(*) FROM ACCOUNT_LIST
   GROUP BY departmentno
```

Here, the GROUP BY clause partitions the ACCOUNT_LIST table into groups, with one group for each departmentno, and generates one line of output— namely the departmentno and number of accounts—for each group. You can modify this query so that only groups that satisfy a specified condition generate output. You accomplish this with the HAVING clause. For instance, the following SELECT statement prints the department number and number of accounts for each department that has more than ten accounts:

```
SELECT departmentno, COUNT(*) FROM ACCOUNT_LIST
   GROUP BY departmentno HAVING COUNT(*) > 10
```

In closing, please note that Oracle SQL aggregate functions are referred to as group functions.

UNION, INTERSECT, and MINUS Operators
Please observe that all the SELECT statements that you have seen so far take each field from a designated table. However, suppose you want to print the department

numbers that appear either in the `ACCOUNT_LIST` table or the `EMPLOYEE_LIST` table. You cannot do this using the constructs discussed thus far. However, SQL supports a `UNION` operator, the output of which is the set-theoretic union of the outputs of the `SELECT` statements that are its operands, and which you can use to solve this problem.

```
SELECT departmentno FROM EMPLOYEE_LIST
   UNION
SELECT departmentno FROM ACCOUNT_LIST
```

This query will print the department numbers that are in the `ACCOUNT_LIST` table or in the `EMPLOYEE_LIST` table, with duplicate records removed.

SQL also provides the `INTERSECT` and `MINUS` operators. The department numbers common to the `ACCOUNT_LIST` and the `EMPLOYEE_LIST` table are given by:

```
SELECT departmentno FROM ACCOUNT_LIST
   INTERSECT
SELECT departmentno FROM EMPLOYEE_LIST
```

Similarly, the department numbers that are in the `ACCOUNT_LIST` table but are not in the `EMPLOYEE_LIST` table will be printed by:

```
SELECT departmentno FROM ACCOUNT_LIST
   MINUS
SELECT departmentno FROM EMPLOYEE_LIST
```

Observe that the `MINUS` and `NOT IN` operators provide alternate solutions to the same type of problem. For example, the preceding query can also be expressed as:

```
SELECT departmentno FROM ACCOUNT_LIST
   WHERE departmentno NOT IN
     ( SELECT departmentno FROM EMPLOYEE_LIST )
```

The query that was previously solved with the `NOT IN` operator, namely:

```
Print the project names of projects that do not have an account with
department number 15.
```

has the following solution with the `MINUS` operator:

```
SELECT projectname FROM PROJECT_LIST
   WHERE projectno IN
     ( SELECT projectno FROM PROJECT_LIST
         MINUS
       SELECT projectno FROM ACCOUNT_LIST
         WHERE departmentno = 15 )
```

DISTINCT and ORDER BY

Finally, the keyword DISTINCT and the ORDER BY clause are discussed. In order to suppress duplicate records in the output from a SELECT statement, follow the keyword SELECT with the keyword DISTINCT. For example:

```
SELECT DISTINCT departmentno FROM ACCOUNT_LIST
```

will print the department numbers in the ACCOUNT_LIST table, without duplication.

In order to guarantee that the output from a SELECT statement is sorted on one or more fields, you use an ORDER BY clause following the WHERE clause in the SELECT statement. For example, the following query prints the ACCOUNT_LIST records involving department number 15, sorted on the accountno and projectno fields:

```
SELECT * FROM ACCOUNT_LIST WHERE departmentno = 15
   ORDER BY accountno, projectno
```

INSERT SELECT, DELETE, and UPDATE Statements

The SELECT statement syntax is used in the INSERT SELECT statement, the DELETE statement, and the UPDATE statement. The syntax of the INSERT SELECT statement is

```
INSERT INTO tablename ( field_list ) select_statement
```

where the expression_list in the SELECT statement must be type compatible with the field_list after the tablename. When you execute the INSERT SELECT statement, the records delivered by the SELECT statement are inserted into the indicated table. For example:

```
INSERT INTO ACCOUNT_LIST( accountno, projectno, departmentno )
   SELECT * FROM NEW_ACCOUNTS
```

will insert the NEW_ACCOUNTS records into the ACCOUNT_LIST table, where NEW_ ACCOUNTS is a table that has the same structure as the ACCOUNT_LIST table.

The syntax of the DELETE statement is

```
DELETE FROM tablename [ where_clause ]
```

The optional where_clause has the same syntax as the WHERE clause in a one-table SELECT statement on tablename (however, it can contain subqueries). When executed, the records in tablename that satisfy the where_clause are deleted from tablename. For example, the following statement will delete the ACCOUNT_LIST records for department number 15:

```
DELETE FROM ACCOUNT_LIST WHERE departmentno = 15
```

Similarly, the UPDATE statement can contain a WHERE clause that indicates which records should be updated. For example, the following UPDATE statement changes the last name of employee 1056 to Smith and changes the phone number to (305)555-0873:

```
UPDATE EMPLOYEE_LIST
   SET lastname = 'Smith', phone = '(305)555-0873'
     WHERE employeeno = 1056
```

The general form of the UPDATE statement is

```
UPDATE tablename SET set_list [ where_clause ]
```

where set_list is a list of elements of the form:

```
field  =  expression
```

When you execute the UPDATE statement, the values of the indicated fields will be changed to the indicated expressions on the records in tablename that satisfy the WHERE clause.

Transaction Control Commands

In addition to DDL and DML commands, SQL supports *transaction control commands*. A *transaction* is a unit of database work (that is, a section of an embedded SQL program or online session that is guaranteed, among other things, to be completely done or completely undone). Examples of transaction control commands are the COMMIT WORK statement:

```
COMMIT [ WORK ]
```

which makes all database changes in the transaction permanent, and the ROLLBACK statement:

```
ROLLBACK [ WORK ]
```

which undoes all database changes in the transaction. Typically, the COMMIT WORK and ROLLBACK statements divide the program or session into transactions.

Embedded SQL

An *embedded SQL program* is a program in a general-purpose programming language, such as C or C++, which directly contains SQL statements within it. An embedded SQL program in a general-purpose programming language is processed by a precompiler that translates it into a program in the general-purpose programming language without

SQL statements. In particular, the SQL statements are translated into function calls to a SQL runtime library for the programming language. The Oracle precompiler for C is called Pro*C. SQL statements are specially marked in the embedded SQL program by prefixing them with the keywords exec sql. Most SQL statements can be directly placed in such an exec sql statement. A notable exception, as you will see, is the SELECT statement.

Embedded SQL Example Program

The following is a Pro*C acceptable embedded SQL program that inserts records into the ACCOUNT_LIST table from a data file called ACCT_DATA (Pro*C source files have the extension .pc).

```
/*
** Program Name:  load_acctlist.pc
**
** Purpose:  Load the ACCOUNT_LIST table from the text file ACCT_DATA.
**
*/
#include<stdio.h>
#include<string.h>
#include<stdlib.h>

/* (See Note 1.) */
exec sql include sqlca;

main()
{ /* Declare host variables (C variables that will appear
     in exec sql statements) in the declare section.
  */
  /* (See Note 2.) */
  exec sql begin declare section;
    int accountno, projectno, departmentno;
    varchar2 user[21], pass[20];
  exec sql end declare section;

  /* Declare C variables that won't appear in exec sql statements.
  */
  /* fp is a standard I/O file pointer that will be used to read
     the ACCT_DATA file.
  */
  FILE * fp;
  int i;

  /* Connect to the database with username = scott and
     password = tiger.
  */
  strcpy( user.arr, "scott" );
```

```
        user.len = strlen( user.arr );
        strcpy( pass.arr, "tiger" );
        pass.len = strlen( pass.arr );
        exec sql CONNECT :user IDENTIFIED BY :pass;

        /* Test sqlcode to see if connected.  If not connected,
           terminate program.
        */
        if ( sqlca.sqlcode != 0 )
          { fprintf( stderr, "Sorry, cannot connect to database,
                              program terminated. \n" );
            return;
          }

        /* Open data file. */
        if ( ( fp = fopen( "ACCT_DATA", "r" ) == NULL ) );
          { fprintf
             ( stderr, "Cannot open data file, program terminated. \n" );
            return;
          }

        /* Read data file records, and insert them into the
           ACCOUNT_LIST table.
        */
        /* Fields in the data file are separated by blanks, and records
           are terminated with newlines.
        */
        while( fscanf
          ( fp, "%d%d%d", &accountno, &projectno, &departmentno) != EOF )
          { exec sql INSERT INTO ACCOUNT_LIST
              VALUES ( :accountno, :projectno, :departmentno );

            /* Test sqlcode to see if insert worked.
               If it worked, commit the insert.
            */
            if ( sqlca.sqlcode != 0 )
              { fprintf( stderr, "%d%d%d could not be inserted\n",
                         accountno, projectno, departmentno );
              } else COMMIT WORK;
          }
          printf ( "Program complete. \n" );
          fclose(fp);
}
```

Notes on `load_acctlist.pc`:

  1. The SQL communications area `sqlca` (a struct) is included into the program
   by the `exec sql include sqlca` statement. One of the fields in `sqlca` is

the `sqlcode` field which is set to zero by the system whenever a SQL statement successfully executes, and is set to a nonzero value whenever the execution of a SQL statement generates a warning or an error. `sqlca.sqlcode` should be checked after the execution of each SQL statement.

2. C variables that appear in `exec sql` statements are called *host variables* and must be declared in the `declare` section of the program. When host variables appear in `exec sql` statements, they must be prefixed by a colon (for example, `:accountno`). You can use host variables any place in an *exec sql* statement that an expression can appear.

The SQL `varchar2` variable-length data type is implemented as a struct with a data field (`arr`) that contains a pointer to a string, and a length field (`len`) that contains the logical length of the string referenced by `arr`.

Cursors

A `SELECT` statement cannot be directly executed as an `exec sql` statement. The reason for this is that the designers of embedded SQL decided that they wanted the output from the `SELECT` statement to be automatically buffered, and then read by the program from the buffer one record at a time. Such a transparent buffer is called a *cursor*, and is manipulated by several types of statements. The DECLARE CURSOR statement attaches a `SELECT` statement to a cursor identifier. The OPEN statement activates a cursor and binds the values of any host variables that appear in the DECLARE CURSOR SELECT statement. The FETCH statement reads the next record from the cursor into host variables (the `SELECT` statement output records are fetched from the cursor sequentially, one record at a time). The CLOSE statement deactivates the cursor.

The following embedded SQL program repeatedly reads a project number, and prints the department numbers and account numbers for accounts involving that project. When the program reads a -1 instead of a valid project number, it terminates.

```
/*
** Program Name:  accts_for_projs.pc
**
** Purpose:   Prints department numbers and account numbers for
**            accounts involving the input project.
*/
#include<stdio.h>
#include<string.h>
#include<stdlib.h>
exec sql include sqlca;
main()

{ /* Declare host variables. */
```

```
exec sql begin declare section;
int accountno, projectno, departmentno;
varchar2 user[21], pass[20];
exec sql end declare section;

/* Declare cursor. */
/* (See Note 1.) */
exec sql DECLARE xa CURSOR FOR
    SELECT departmentno, accountno FROM ACCOUNT_LIST
       WHERE projectno = :projectno;

/* Connect to the database with username = scott and
   password = tiger.
*/
strcpy( user.arr,"scott" );
strcpy( pass.arr,"tiger" );
user.len=strlen( user.arr );
pass.len=strlen( pass.arr );
exec sql CONNECT :user IDENTIFIED BY :pass;

/* Check sqlcode to see if connected. */
if( sqlca.sqlcode !=0 )
  { fprintf ( stderr, "Sorry, cannot connect to database,
                       program terminated. \n" );
    return;
  }

/* Main loop. */
for( ; ; )
  { printf( "Please enter a project number
           (enter -1 to terminate)>>\n " );
    scanf( "%d", &projectno );
    if( projectno == -1 ) { printf( "BYE\n" );
                            return;
                          }

    /* Open cursor, which binds projectno value to cursor
       SELECT statement, and fetch records for that projectno.
    */
    exec sql OPEN xa;

    /* Fetch loop. */
    for( ; ; )
      { exec sql FETCH xa INTO :departmentno, :accountno;

        /* sqlcode is nonzero when there are no more records
           to be fetched.
        */
```

```
        if( sqlca.sqlcode !=0 ) break;
        printf( "Department number = %d Account number = %d /n",
                departmentno, accountno );
    }

    /* Close cursor, so it can be reopened at the beginning
       of the main loop.
    */
    /* (See Note 2.) */
    exec sql CLOSE xa;
    }
}
```

Notes for `accts_for_projs.pc`:

1. The SELECT statement that is attached to the cursor xa contains a host variable :projectno. The values of host variables are bound to cursors at OPEN time, not at DECLARE CURSOR time, and not at FETCH time. Therefore, it is irrelevant that projectno has not been given a value at the point where the DECLARE CURSOR appears, and if you changed the value of the projectno variable in the FETCH loop, that will not affect the records that are fetched in the FETCH loop.

2. You cannot open a cursor if it is already open. This is the reason for closing the cursor at the end of the main loop.

This discussion of embedded SQL is closed by considering why a facility for invoking SQL from a host programming language is even needed. Why is a stand-alone interactive interface like SQL*Plus not sufficient? First, a program, such as a process control system (instead of a human end-user) may need direct access to a database. Second, SQL was not initially intended to be computationally complete. SQL is considered a data sublanguage that specializes in data retrieval facilities, at the expense of omitting computational structures such as looping statements. Thus, the computational facilities of a language such as C complement the very high-level data access facilities of SQL.

For more information on embedded SQL, you are referred to *Oracle Developer's Guide* [29] and *Oracle8i Pro*C Manual* [17].

PL/SQL

PL/SQL is Oracle's procedural extension to SQL, which was strongly influenced by the Ada programming language. SQL and PL/SQL are the basic languages used throughout the Oracle RDBMS. However, starting with the Oracle8*i* release, SQLJ has begun to offer PL/SQL some competition for its central position in the Oracle RDBMS.

In some cases, PL/SQL provides an easier to use alternative to embedded SQL, which is more tightly integrated to SQL than the latter approach. In other cases it can be used in conjunction with embedded SQL.

PL/SQL Block

The basic unit of PL/SQL is the *PL/SQL block*. You can submit a PL/SQL block interactively to SQL*Plus and SQL*DBA, as well as invoking it from embedded SQL. A PL/SQL block has the form:

```
[ declare section ]
begin
  list_of_statements
  [ exception section ]
end;
```

The optional `declare section` contains declarations that are local to the block. The `list_of_statements` is a sequence of one or more PL/SQL statements, each of which is terminated by a semicolon (;). The optional `exception section` starts with the keyword `exception`, and contains exception handlers for the block that handle user-defined or predefined exceptions (*exceptions* are identifiers that correspond to error conditions).

A PL/SQL statement can be any transaction control command, any SQL DML command except a `SELECT` statement (SQL DDL commands are not allowed), a `SELECT INTO` statement, a control statement (`loop`, `if`, `exit`, `return`), an assignment statement, a procedure call, a cursor manipulation statement (`OPEN`, `FETCH`, `CLOSE`), a raise statement (to raise an exception), or a (nested) PL/SQL block. You are referred to *Oracle8 PL/SQL Programming* [60] and *Oracle8i PL/SQL Manual* [40] for extensive treatments of PL/SQL statements, and to *Oracle8i Application Developer's Guide Fundamentals* [42] for helpful information on the effective use of PL/SQL. In this appendix, you will find a few key examples.

The following PL/SQL block, which prints the department numbers of departments that have an account with every project, illustrates the `SELECT INTO`, `if`, and `for loop` statements.

```
declare
nprojs number(5); nprojsd number(5);
begin

  /* Count the total number of projects. */
  SELECT COUNT(*) INTO nprojs FROM PROJECT_LIST;

  /* For each department, check if the number of projects supplied
     by the department equals the total number of projects, that is,
```

```
          if the department has an account with each project.  If so,
          print the department number.
      */
      for i in ( SELECT departmentno FROM DEPARTMENT_LIST )
        loop

          /* Count the number of projects with which the current
             department has an account.
          */
          /* Note that expressions involving PL/SQL variables, such as
             i.departmentno, can appear any place in a SQL statement that
             an expression is expected.
          */
          SELECT COUNT( DISTINCT projectno ) INTO nprojsd
            FROM ACCOUNT_LIST
              WHERE departmentno = i.departmentno;

          /* If the department has an account with each project,
             use the put_line procedure of the dbms_output package
             to print the department number.
          */
          if nprojs = nprojsd
            then dbms_output.put_line( i.departmentno );
          end if;
        end loop;
    end;
```

The constructs used in this PL/SQL block are now discussed. In the `declare section` of this PL/SQL block, `number` PL/SQL variables are declared that will hold the total number of projects (`nprojs`) and the number of projects that have an account with a particular department (`nprojsd`). Note that most of the SQL data types, in addition to other data types, are supported in PL/SQL.

A `SELECT INTO` statement, which can be directly used in embedded SQL as well as in PL/SQL, is a `SELECT` statement whose `WHERE` clause returns a single record, and such a statement stores the field values of that record in the variables listed in the `INTO` clause. Here, the first `SELECT INTO` statement in the PL/SQL block computes the total number of projects, and stores that value in `nprojs`.

Next, there is a `for loop` that iterates over the department numbers in the `ACCOUNT_LIST` table. Before discussing the exact type of loop used in the preceding PL/SQL block, a few statements about PL/SQL loops in general are made. PL/SQL supports a `loop` statement with the syntax:

```
loop
    list_of_statements
end loop
```

This construct sets up an infinite loop (a do forever), that must be terminated by the execution of an exit statement (exit), which, like the break statement in C, will cause control to be transferred out of the loop to the first statement following the loop. Optionally, the keyword loop can be prefixed with a while clause or a for clause. A while clause has the syntax:

```
while Boolean_condition
```

which converts the loop into a while loop as in C, that is, a pretest loop where the loop is terminated when the Boolean condition evaluates to false.

There are several types of for clauses. One type has the form:

```
for var in initial_expression ... final_expression
```

which sets up a counter-driven for loop, with integer counter in var, in which the list_of_statements is repeatedly executed, with var taking on, in successive iterations, initial_expression, initial_expression+1, ..., final_expression. The form of the for clause used in the preceding PL/SQL block has the syntax:

```
for var in ( subquery )
```

where the list_of_statements is repeatedly executed for each record generated by the subquery, with the var taking on, in successive iterations, each of the records generated by the subquery. In either form, the for var is implicitly declared, and should not be explicitly declared in a declaration section.

The syntax of the PL/SQL if statement is

```
if condition then list_of_statements
zero-or-more [ elsif condition then list_of_statements ]
    [ else list_of_statements ]
end if
```

An if statement can contain zero or more elsif clauses. When an if statement is executed, if the Boolean condition before the first then evaluates to true, the list_of_statements following the first then is executed. Otherwise, the list_of_statements following the then of the first elsif whose condition evaluates to true is executed. If all the conditions evaluate to false, the list_of_statements following the else is executed.

In the if statement in the preceding PL/SQL block, the put_line procedure of the dbms_output package is used to print the department number. put_line takes one argument, which it prints followed by a newline, and is overloaded to take as an argument various built-in SQL types. The dbms_output package is a collection of procedures that are useful for accomplishing "quick and dirty" output. You will see more about procedures and packages in the next two subsections.

PL/SQL Subprograms

A *PL/SQL subprogram* is a named, parameterized PL/SQL block that can be called (invoked) from various places, including other PL/SQL blocks. When a subprogram is called, *actual parameters* are passed that are matched up with the corresponding formal parameters in the subprogram declaration, in a manner indicated by the *mode* of the formal parameters.

The PL/SQL blocks that you have seen so far have not been named, and are therefore referred to as *autonomous PL/SQL blocks*.

There are two kinds of subprograms in PL/SQL: procedures and functions. A *procedure* does not return a value, and a *procedure call* must be used as a statement (not as an expression). On the other hand, a *function* returns a value, and a *function call* must be used as an expression, and cannot stand by itself as a statement. Thus, a function call must be used as part of a statement, for example, as the right hand side of an assignment statement. A subprogram can be declared local to a PL/SQL block in the declare section of that block, or it can be directly stored globally in the database; or, as you will see, it can be stored globally in the database by including it in a package that is stored globally in the database.

The Oracle SQL CREATE FUNCTION (CREATE PROCEDURE) statement is used to store a function (procedure) in a database. You can submit such a statement, as you can any Oracle SQL statement, to SQL*Plus. A stored subprogram can be called from any PL/SQL block that has access to the database in which the subprogram is stored. In addition, stored functions can be used any place in a SQL statement that an expression is expected. You are now given a slightly simplified syntax of the CREATE FUNCTION statement (the CREATE PROCEDURE syntax is similar):

```
CREATE FUNCTION functionname ( formal_parameter_list )
   return returntype is declaration_list
     begin
       statement_list
[ exception_section ]
     end [ functionname ] ;
```

A `formal_parameter_list` element has the form:

```
formal_parameter_name [ mode ] type
```

The mode can be `in` (the value of the formal parameter is initialized to the value of the corresponding actual parameter, that is, the parameter in the function call, at call time, but trying to change the formal parameter value results in a

PL/SQL syntax error); out (the actual parameter is set to the value that the formal parameter has at return time); or in out (the combination of the in mode and out mode). If the mode is missing for a formal parameter, the in mode is assumed.

The following CREATE FUNCTION statement stores a function named insertemp in the database. This function inserts a new employee record into the EMPLOYEE_LIST table and returns true, if EMPLOYEE_LIST does not already contain an employee record with the same employeeno, and returns false, otherwise.

```
CREATE FUNCTION insertemp
   ( empno         EMPLOYEE_LIST.employeeno%type,
     lastname      EMPLOYEE_LIST.lastname%type,
     firstname     EMPLOYEE_LIST.firstname%type,
     phone         EMPLOYEE_LIST.phone%type,
     departmentno  EMPLOYEE_LIST.departmentno%type ) return Boolean is
x integer
begin

   /* Check for duplicate employee number. */
   /* Return false, if a duplicate exists. */
   SELECT COUNT(*) INTO x FROM EMPLOYEE_LIST
     WHERE employeeno = empno;
   if x > 0 then return false;
   end if;

   /* Otherwise, insert employee record, commit insert and return
      true.
   */
   /* PL/SQL variables can be used any place in a SQL statement that
      an expression is expected.
   */
   INSERT INTO EMPLOYEE_LIST
     VALUES ( empno, lastname, firstname, phone, departmentno );
   COMMIT WORK;
   return true;
end insertemp;
```

Note that in the preceding example, the data types of the formal parameters are inherited from the corresponding ACCOUNT_LIST field data types, by using the type attributes of the ACCOUNT_LIST fields (field name followed by %type). The data type number could have been directly used here, but it is safer (in lieu of the possibility of table field type change) to use the %type attributes. A type attribute expression can be used anywhere in PL/SQL that a data type is expected. Observe also that the keyword declare is omitted in the declare section of subprograms.

An example of a PL/SQL block that calls the preceding `insertemp` function is

```
begin
  if not insertemp ( 1111, 'Smith', 'Michelle', '(305)555-0359', 15 )
  then dbms_output.put_line ( 'Employee 1111 already exists.' );
end;
```

In this example, each actual parameter of the `insertemp` function call is matched up with its corresponding formal parameter in the `insertemp` function definition by these parameters having the same position in their respective parameter lists. There is also a facility in PL/SQL for matching up actual and formal parameters by name. You are referred to *Oracle8i PL/SQL Manual* [40] for a description of this facility.

Advantages of using subprograms in PL/SQL, as in any other programming language, include modularity, extensibility, reliability, maintainability, and abstraction (see *Oracle Developer's Guide* [29, p. 385] for details). The specific advantages of using stored subprograms in Oracle include higher productivity (applications can exploit a central repository of common code), better performance (to execute ten individual SQL statements involves ten database calls, but to execute a stored subprogram containing ten SQL statements causes one database call), and conservation of memory (the shared memory capability of Oracle allows for only one copy of a stored subprogram to be loaded into memory for all applications that access it). See *Oracle Developer's Guide* [29, p. 399] for more details.

PL/SQL Packages and Exceptions

In this section, an example illustrating packages and exceptions is presented. A PL/SQL *package* is a construct that groups together logically related resources such as variables, subprograms, cursors, and exceptions. If the `package` is stored in a database, all these resources are available to any SQL or PL/SQL construct that has access to the database. A `package` consists of two units: a required package specification and an optional `package body`. The package specification is the interface to the `package` in that it declares the variables, exceptions, cursors, subprograms, and so on that are available for use by clients of the `package`. The `package body` fully defines subprograms that are specified in the package specification, and so implements the specification (only subprogram specifications, and not the complete subprogram, can appear in a package specification). A package specification is stored in a database by the SQL `CREATE PACKAGE` statement. A `package body` is stored in a database by the `CREATE PACKAGE BODY` SQL statement.

Consider a `package emppak` that provides resources for the manipulation of the `EMPLOYEE_LIST` table.

```
CREATE PACKAGE emppak is
exception norec;
procedure deleteemp ( empno EMPLOYEE_LIST.employeeno%type );
function insertemp
  ( empno          EMPLOYEE_LIST.employeeno%type,
    lastname       EMPLOYEE_LIST.lastname%type,
    firstname      EMPLOYEE_LIST.firstname%type,
    phone          EMPLOYEE_LIST.phone%type,
    departmentno EMPLOYEE_LIST.departmentno%type )
    return number;
end emppak;

CREATE PACKAGE BODY emppak is
  procedure deleteemp ( empno EMPLOYEE_LIST.employeeno%type ) is
  x integer;
  begin

    /* Check if employee record exists. */
    SELECT COUNT(*) INTO x FROM EMPLOYEE_LIST
      WHERE employeeno = empno;

    /* If it doesn't exist, raise an exception, terminating
       the procedure.
    */
    /* If it does exist, delete employee, and commit the delete.
    */
    if x = 0 then raise norec;
    end if;
    DELETE FROM EMPLOYEE_LIST WHERE employeeno = empno;
    COMMIT WORK;
  end deleteemp;
  function insertemp
    ( empno          EMPLOYEE_LIST.employeeno%type,
      lastname       EMPLOYEE_LIST.lastname%type,
      firstname      EMPLOYEE_LIST.firstname%type,
      phone          EMPLOYEE_LIST.phone%type
      departmentno EMPLOYEE_LIST.departmentno%type ) return boolean is
  x integer;
  begin

    /* Check for duplicate employee number. */
    /* Return false, if a duplicate exists. */
    SELECT COUNT(*) INTO x FROM EMPLOYEE_LIST
      WHERE employeeno = empno;
    if x > 0 then return false;
    end if;
```

```
      /* Otherwise, insert employee record, commit insert, and
         return true.
      */
      /* Recall that PL/SQL variables can be used any place in a
         SQL statement that an expression is expected.
      */
      INSERT INTO EMPLOYEE_LIST
        VALUES ( empno, lastname, firstname, phone, departmentno );
      COMMIT WORK;
      return true;
   end insertemp;
   /* Local block in package body. */
   begin
     CREATE TABLE EMPLOYEE_LIST
        ( employeeno    number(5),
          lastname      varchar2(30),
          firstname     varchar2(30),
          phone         varchar2(13),
          departmentno number(5),
          PRIMARY KEY   ( employeeno ),
          FOREIGN KEY   ( departmentno ) REFERENCES DEPARTMENT_LIST );
   end;
end emppak;
```

This package specification for `emppak` exports three resources: the `norec` exception, the `deleteemp` procedure, and the `insertemp` function.

An exception is a PL/SQL identifier that corresponds to an error. There are only two operations that can be applied to an exception: an exception can be raised (that is, activated) and an exception can be handled. When an exception is raised in a PL/SQL block, that block is terminated and a handler is sought in the exception section of that block. If a handler is found, the exception is deactivated and control is passed to the statement following the one that invoked the block (the statement following the block, if the block is not the outer block of a subprogram, or the statement following the subprogram call, if the block is the outer block of a subprogram).

If a handler is not found in the exception section of the block, the exception remains active, and a handler is searched for (and executed, if found) in the block containing the statement that invoked the block (that is, the invoking block), followed by the termination of the invoking block. This method is repeated until a handler is found, or there are no more blocks left. In our case, the `norec` exception is raised in the `deleteemp` procedure and is intended to be handled by the block that invoked the `deleteemp` procedure, since a handler is not provided in the `deleteemp` procedure. `norec` is an example of a user-defined exception, that is, declared by the programmer in an exception declaration, and is explicitly raised by a raise statement.

The other type of exception is a predefined exception that corresponds to an Oracle internal error, and is automatically raised by the system (or also can be explicitly raised). An example of a predefined exception is `no_data_found`, which is automatically raised by the system when a SELECT INTO statement does not retrieve any data. Predefined exceptions are handled just like user-defined exceptions.

The procedure deleteemp and the function insertemp illustrate two different ways of reporting errors. The function insertemp returns an error code, while the procedure deleteemp raises an exception. It is probably best to use the return code technique, unless the error is a serious one, because the user-defined exception method suffers a performance overhead. On the other hand, the repeated explicit checking of error codes can make the PL/SQL code harder to read.

Note that the package body can contain its own local block that is executed when the package is created. You can use such a local block to accomplish initializations. This local block is analogous to a Java constructor. In our case, the EMPLOYEE_LIST table is created when the package is created. The reason for this is to try and use the emppak package to encapsulate the EMPLOYEE_LIST table as much as possible, encouraging the users of the package to go through the exported subprograms as much as possible.

The following PL/SQL block illustrates how the resources of the package emppak can be used.

```
begin
   /* Insert a new employee record with emppak.insertemp. */
   if not emppak.insertemp
     ( 3000, 'Smith', 'Damon', '(954)555-0172', 15 )
     then dbms_output.put_line
       ( 'Employee 3000 already exists in table.' );
       else dbms_output ( 'Employee 3000 inserted' );

   /* Now delete the 3000 record. */
   emppak.deleteemp( '3000' );

   /* Exception handler for norec exception. */
   when emppak.norec then dbms_output.put_line
     ('Employee 3000 cannot be fired since employee does not exist.' );
end;
```

Notes:

1. An emppak resource is referenced by "dotting" the package name with the resource name (for example, emppak.norec). In particular, this is exactly what is done when put_line is referenced (dbms_output.put_line).

2. An exception handler has the syntax:

   ```
   when exceptionname then list_of_statements
   ```

3. The statements in the list are executed, and then control is passed out of the block, as previously described.

Finally, it should be remarked that PL/SQL blocks can be invoked from Oracle-embedded SQL programs. The syntax for invoking a PL/SQL block from a Pro*C program is

```
exec sql execute

   PL/SQL_block

end-exec;
```

For example,

```
exec sql execute
   begin

      /* Select number of accounts into the C host variable naccts. */
      SELECT COUNT(*) INTO :naccts FROM ACCOUNT_LIST;

      /* Select number of employees into C host variable nemps. */
      SELECT COUNT(*) INTO nemps FROM EMPLOYEE_LIST;
   end;
end-exec;
```

A performance advantage of including a PL/SQL block in an `exec sql` statement is that the entire block is passed to the Oracle server in one call, as opposed to requiring multiple calls which would be the case if each SQL statement in the block were coded in its own `exec sql` statement.

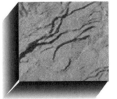

APPENDIX

B

Java Basics

n this appendix, you will to learn about the following:

- The Java constructs to develop an application: Java Application

- The concepts of classes and objects in the Java language

- The Java constructs to develop an applet: Java applet

The Java Application

This section examines and explains the application, `JavaApplication`, which is a simple Java program consisting of one method called `main()`. Through a line-by-line investigation of this program, you will learn some features of Java such as variables, operators, expressions, control flow statements, and so on. In the subsequent sections that follow the `JavaApplication`, you will learn more about the syntax and semantics of the Java language.

A Java program that contains a `main()` is called a *Java application*. It is a stand-alone program that runs independently of any Java-compatible browser. At runtime, the Java Virtual Machine (JVM) invokes the `main()` method and generates an error if this method is not found. See Chapter 1 to learn more about the JVM.

The source code for a Java class resides in a file with the same name as the class and with the `.java` extension. For example, the source code of the `JavaApplication` class resides in a file named `JavaApplication.java`. In this section, you will use the `JavaApplication` application to print the values of an array of strings that you supply at the command line when you run this program.

```
//Program name: JavaApplication.java
public class JavaApplication {
  public static void main(String[] args){
    //Loop control variable. 0 is the first index of an array.
     int loopVar = 0;

    // Loop to print each word from the command line argument iterate
    // until there are no elements left in the array
    while( loopVar < args.length ){ System.out.println(args[loopVar++]);
    }
  }
}
```

Variables and Data Types

Java allows you to declare variables in your programs. All variables in Java have a data type, a name, and scope. When you declare a variable, you must associate it with a data type.

Java supports a complete set of *primitive* data types and *reference* (non-primitive) data types. The primitive data types are handled by value, that is, the actual values are stored in the variable. The non-primitive data types, such as objects and arrays, are handled by references, that is, the address of an object or an array is stored in the variable. Table B-1 lists Java's primitive data types and the range of their values.

The following code fragment demonstrates how to declare Java variables and their associated data types:

```
// Create the loopVar int primitive data type and
// assign to it the value of 0
int loopVar = 0;

// Create the args reference variable
// to store the address of an array of strings
String[] args
```

Type	Size	Minimum Value	Maximum Value
boolean	1 bit	N.A.	N.A.
char	16 bits	\u0000 (0)	\uFFFF (65535)
byte	8 bits	-128	127
short	16 bits	-32768	32767
int	32 bits	-2147483648	2147483647
long	64 bits	-9223372036854775808	9223372036854775807
float	32 bits	±1.402E-45	±3.40282347E+38
double	64 bits	±4.9E-324	±1.7976931348E+308

TABLE B-1.   *Primitive Data Types*

Arrays and Strings

Two important data types in any programming language are *arrays* and *strings*. Like most programming languages, Java provides a mechanism for collecting and managing a set of values through an array. In Java, both arrays and strings are objects. In the subsequent sections of this appendix, you will learn more about the concept of objects. The `main()` method of the `JavaApplication` uses an array that holds a set of strings as its argument.

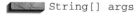 `String[] args`

Operators

Java provides a set of operators that you use to perform a function on the variables. The following code fragment lists some examples of Java operators:

```
// Assignment operator: '='
// Assign the value of 0 to the integer variable loopVar
int loopVar = 0;

// Use args.length to determine the size of the array and
// the arithmetic operator '<' (less than) to compare the
// value stored in the loopVar against the size of the array
loopVar < args.length
```

Expressions

Java expressions combine into a sequence of operators, variables, and method calls. They are used to help with the execution control within the program, compute, and assign values to variables. The following example uses the arithmetic operator "++", a pre/post increment operator, to increment the value by 1 of the `loopVar` variable:

 `loopVar++`

Control Flow Statements

There are two types of control flow statements: *branching* and *looping*. These statements control the flow of the program, that is, the sequence in which the program's statements are executed. The branching control flow statements include the **if-then-else** and the **switch** statements. The looping control flow statements include the **for**, the **while**, and the **do-while** loops.

The `JavaApplication` application uses a `while` *statement* to iterate through the `args` array and print its value. A **while** loop iterates and repeatedly executes statements until a Boolean expression is evaluated to false (condition not met). The following iterates through statements until `loopVar` is evaluated to be less than `args.length`:

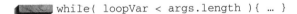
```
while( loopVar < args.length ){ … }
```

Compilation and Execution

Now that you have written a Java application, the next step is to compile the program. You can do so with the `javac` compiler by invoking it at the command line:

```
javac JavaApplication.java
```

If the compilation is successful, the `javac` compiler will generate a `.class` file (bytecode) for the `JavaApplication` application named `JavaApplication.class`. Next, you can run the application by issuing the following command at the command line:

```
java JavaApplication position department company
```

After executing the application, the output of the application displays on your console the following:

```
position
department
company
```

Java Classes and Objects

The Java programming language is an object-oriented programming language that is based on classes and objects. A *class* is a collection of attributes and methods that serves as a blueprint for creating objects and an object is an instance of the class. Since Java is based on objects and classes, you will need to understand some basic object-oriented programming concepts in order for you to successfully write Java programs.

The topics covered in this section will help you learn how to build and construct Java classes and objects:

- Creating and using objects
- Creating and using constructors
- Using **this**
- Class members

- Access modifiers

- Method return types

- Creating subclasses

- Creating packages

- Importing classes and packages

- Abstract classes

- Interfaces

You will use the following `Employee` class to learn how to create and use Java classes and objects throughout this section by adding some additional functionality to the class. As in the section "The Java Application" earlier in this appendix, you will learn more about Java through a line-by-line investigation of the `Employee` class as you build it.

```
//Class name: Employee.java
public class Employee {
  public String name;
  public double salary;
  public double hours;
}
```

Creating and Using Objects

An *object* is an instance of a class where each object has its own copy of the attributes and methods of the class. In Java, you have to instantiate an object, which dynamically allocates memory for the object, thereby, creates an instance of a class. The exception to the rule, since it is used heavily in Java, is the Java `String` class that does not need to be instantiated.

Creating Objects

Now that you have the data type `Employee`, you need to create an instance of the class by declaring a variable and instantiating an `Employee` object:

- **Declaration**   Before creating an object, however, you must *declare* a variable that will refer to an `Employee` object.

  ```
  Employee emp;
  ```

  The `emp` variable refers to the data type `Employee`. It is important to understand that `emp` is not an object. You need an instance of the class to have an object.

■ **Instantiation**   After you have declared a variable, you have to use a class constructor to instantiate or allocate memory for an object. This is accomplished by using the operator **new** followed by a constructor of the class:

```
emp = new Employee();
```

Alternatively, the declaration and instantiation could be accomplished all in one line:

```
Employee emp = new Employee();
```

Note that in Java, since strings are so commonly used, you do not have to use the **new** operator to instantiate them. You can create an instance of the `String` class simply by enclosing the characters between double quotes. For example:

```
String name = "John";
```

Deleting Objects

Java will automatically delete any object that is no longer being referenced by a variable. This memory cleanup is called *garbage collection*. The garbage collector runs in a low-priority thread usually when the system is idle. However, when the JVM runs out of memory, the garbage collector will run in high-priority mode to reclaim resources. Setting a variable to **null** will eliminate the reference to the object. Since the object is no longer referenced, the garbage collector will delete it from memory.

Accessing Member Variables of Objects

After you have created an object, use the dot (.) member separator to access the members of the class. The following example uses the member separator to assign values to the member attributes of the object:

```
emp.name = "John";     // Set value of name
emp.salary = 11.50;    // Assign the hourly salary
emp.hours = 40.0;      // Set value to 40 hours
```

The following `ObjectClassProgram` instantiates the `Employee` class, assigns values to the data members, and prints these values:

```
// Program name: ObjectClassProgram.java
public class ObjectClassProgram {
  public static void main(String[] args){
    // Create a new Instance of the Employee class
```

```
        Employee emp = new Employee();
        emp.name = "John";   // Set the value of name
        emp.salary = 11.50; // Assign the hourly salary
        emp.hours = 40.0;    // Set value to 40 hours
        System.out.println( "Name: " + emp.name + " | Hourly salary: $" +
                            emp.salary + " | Hours worked " + emp.hours);
    }
}
```

Creating and Using Constructors

By default, all Java classes have at least one implicit constructor to initialize a new
instance of the class. You can also create a constructor explicitly.

Default Constructor

If you look at the declaration and the instantiation of the emp object in the
ObjectClassProgram application, you will notice that a call is made to the
Employee() constructor. The Employee() constructor is the *default constructor*
for the Employee class and has no arguments. The following example illustrates
the way to call the default constructor:

```
Employee emp = new Employee();
```

Constructor Overloading

Constructor overloading is when you overload a method, that is, when you create
more than one method with the same name. The Java compiler is able to
differentiate between the constructors that have been overloaded because the
constructors' arguments are different.

The following is a listing of the Employee class that has been modified to include
a new explicit default constructor and an overloaded constructor with three arguments.
Note that both constructors' names are the same as the class name:

```
//Class name: Employee.java
public class Employee {
  public String name;
  public double salary;
  public double hours;

  public Employee(){  //Default constructor
      name = "";       //Initialize name to empty string
      salary = 5.50;   //Initialize salary to the minimum wage
      hours = 0.0;
  }

  //Constructor that takes in three arguments for initializing
  public Employee(String name, double salary, int hours){
```

```
        this.name = name;
        this.salary = salary;
        this.hours = hours;
    }
}
```

Initializing the Constructors

The following example illustrates two examples of how to declare and initialize the data members listed in the two constructors of the `Employee` class:

```
//Create an object using the default constructor of the Employee data
//type. The object now contains the default value of the constructor
Employee emp1 = new Employee();

//Initialize the variables of the object
emp1.name = "John";   // Initialize value of name
emp1.hours = 40.0;    // Initialize value to 40 hours

//Create another object and initialize it with the three arguments
Employee emp2 = new Employee("Jill", 15.50, 25);
```

Using the this Keyword

If you look at the `Employee` constructor that has the three arguments, you will notice that it uses the keyword **this**. In the `Employee` constructor, the keyword **this** refers to the variable of the immediate object and removes the ambiguity between the member variables of the class and the arguments of the constructor:

```
public Employee(String name, double salary, int hours){
    this.name = name;
    this.salary = salary;
    this.hours = hours;
}
```

In the previous example, if you were to code the assignment of name = name, at compilation time, the compiler would not know which name identifier belongs to the argument and which name belongs to the member variable of the class. In this scenario, the use of the keyword **this** is mandatory to clearly differentiate the class members and the constructor arguments. You can avoid ambiguity and the use of the **this** keyword by using unique identifiers in the constructor arguments:

```
public Employee(String empName, double empSalary, int empHours){
    name = empName;
    salary = empSalary;
    hours = empHours;
}
```

Class Members

An *instance variable,* also called *instance field,* is created every time a new object of a class is instantiated. Conversely, a *class variable* is one where only one copy of the variable is created at runtime. Instance variables and class variables are collectively called *member variables.* In addition, the term *members of a class* refers collectively to the instance variables, class variables, and the methods of a class.

Class Variables and Class Methods

Use the **static** keyword to declare a class variable or a class method:

```
//A class variable
public static double minimumWage = 5.50;

//A class method
public static Employee WorkedMost(Employee emp1, Employee emp2){
   ...
   }
```

When you declare a class variable or a class method with the **static** keyword, there is only one copy of the variable or the method associated with the class, rather than many instances of the variable.

In the following example, the Employee class has been modified to include a class variable minimumWage and a class method WorkedMost(). The minimumWage variable is assigned the value of $5.50. The WorkedMost() method uses two employee objects as its input arguments, compares the number of hours of each employee object, and returns the Employee object that worked the most hours.

```
// Class name: Employee.java
public class Employee {
  public String name;
  public double salary;
  public double hours;

  // This creates a class variable
  public static final double minimumWage = 5.50;

  public Employee(){  //Default constructor
     name = "";        //Initialize name to empty string
     salary = minimumWage;  //Initialize salary to the minimum wage
     hours = 0.0;
  }

  // Constructor that takes in three arguments for initializing its
  // instance variables
```

```java
    public Employee(String name, double salary, int hours){
        this.name = name;
        this.salary = salary;
        this.hours = hours;
    }
    public void PrintPay(){
       System.out.println("The salary this week for " + name + " is $"
                            + salary*hours);
    }

    //This method is a Class method
    public static Employee WorkedMost(Employee emp1, Employee emp2){
       //Returns the employee who worked the most hours
       if (emp1.hours > emp2.hours)
          return emp1;
       else
          return emp2;
    }
}
```

You can access class variables and class methods through either the class name or an instance variable:

```java
//Create instances of the Employee class
Employee emp1 = new Employee("Jill", 15.50, 25);
Employee emp2 = new Employee("Mary", 27.00, 45);

//Access WorkedMost and minimumWage via class method and
//class variable
Employee.emp3 = WorkedMost(emp1, emp2);
System.out.println("The minimum wage is $" + Employee.minimumWage);

// Access the WorkedMost() method and the minimumWage variables
// through the declared variable emp2
Employee emp4 = emp2.WorkedMost(emp2, emp3);
System.out.println("The minimum wage is $" + emp4.minimumWage);
```

Constants

Use the **final** keyword to declare variables as constants. The variable must be initialized to a value when it is declared **final**. Once you declare a variable as **final**, it cannot be changed. Therefore, it makes sense for you to declare a **final** member variable as a class variable with the keyword **static**. If you do not, you will create a new copy of the variable or method every time a new object is created. In the Employee class, the minimumWage class variable is declared as a constant variable by using the keyword **final**:

```java
public static final float minimumWage = 5.50f;
```

The final Classes

If a class is declared as **final**, then the class cannot become a superclass of another class (see the "Creating Subclasses" section of this appendix). You can declare the Employee class as **final** if you do not wish this class to be subclassed:

```
final class Employee {
... //Method body omitted
}
```

Access Modifiers

The member variables and methods of the Employee class are all **public**. This means that all classes and packages have access to its members. However, this may yield some undesirable results. For example, if you created Employee objects with the salary information of the employees from a database. The programmers who use the class may not have the need to know the salary of the employees, or worse, have the privilege to change the salary. This information should be encapsulated and protected from the programmer. You could declare some of the member variables of the class with access modifiers so that they cannot be accessed by other classes or packages.

Java provides access modifiers as an encapsulation mechanism to protect classes and class members from being accessed. The access modifiers are placed at the beginning of variables and methods. The access modifiers use the keywords **private**, **protected**, and **public**. The fourth access protection is the "default package" access level, which does not have any access modifier.

Table B-2 shows the access protection level of each access modifier.

- **private** Member variables and methods are only visible within the class in which they are specified. The **private** members are not available to their subclasses or other packages. Other classes cannot access the **private** members of the class, even if they are within the same package.

- **protected** Member methods and variables of a class that are protected are only accessible from its class, subclasses, and the package that the class belongs to. In addition, the class members are available to its subclasses in other packages but not classes in other packages.

- **public** This modifier makes its members visible to all classes and packages.

- **default package** This modifier hides its members from other packages but classes in the same package have access to its members.

	Access Modifier			
				Default
	Public	**Protected**	**Private**	**Package**
Class	Yes	Yes	Yes	Yes
Subclass in same package	Yes	Yes	No	Yes
Subclass in different packages	Yes	Yes	No	No
Classes in different packages	Yes	No	No	No

TABLE B-2. *Access Protection and Visibility*

Method Return Types

Every method declared in Java requires a method return type. Methods must return an object of the method's declared return type. To return an object from a method, use the **return** keyword followed by a data type within the body of the method. When the **return** keyword is encountered, the immediate method stops execution and if the return type is not **void**, returns an object of the return type back to the method that called it. A method of return type **void** does not return anything. If the method return type is **void**, you have the option of not returning anything or simply use the **return** keyword by itself to stop execution of the method. Since the return type of WorkMost() method is the Employee class, it has to return an Employee object to the method that called it.

Creating Subclasses

Let us say that you want the Employee class to include two types of employees where some require a license for their occupation and some do not. The employees who have licenses get an extra 10 percent bonus. To store the license number as a string and print the weekly salary for these employees, an additional instance variable for the license number and another print method could have been added to the Employee class. Subclassing provides a more elegant way for you to add these additional features. This will permit you to use all the members of the Employee class method without having to make additional changes to the Employee class just for the employees who have licenses.

A subclass inherits all the **public** and **protected** members of its superclass (parent class). Use the keyword **extends** to define a subclass. The following class LicenseEmployee defines a subclass of its superclass Employee:

```java
//Class name: LicenseEmployeeloyee.java
public class LicenseEmployee extends Employee {
  public String license;  //License Number of the employee
  //10% extra pay for employee with license
  private static double bonus = 1.10;

  //Constructor method of the subclass
  public LicenseEmployee(String name, double salary, int hours,
                  String license){

     //Call the constructor of the super class
     super(name, salary, hours);
     this.license = license;
  }

  //A Method that overrides the PrintPay method in the Employee class
  public void  PrintPay(){
     System.out.println("The salary this week for " + name
                        + " is $" + salary*hours*bonus);
  }

  //A Method that is in the subclass but not the super class
  public void PrintSubclass(){
    System.out.print("License " + license + "; and ");
    super.PrintPay();
  }
}
```

A subclass can call its parent members. In this situation, the subclass can use the keyword **super** to explicitly invoke the superclass members. For example, the LicenseEmployee constructor from the LicenseEmployee class invokes its parent constructor to initialize its arguments and the PrintSubclass() method invokes its parent method to print the employee's salary.

Creating Packages

A *package* is a bundle or collection of related classes. The Sun JDK contains various packages for performing different functions. The JDK java.sql package, for example, contains the set of classes that defines the JDBC API. See Chapter 1 to learn more about the JDBC API.

You are not limited to the packages provided by Java; you can also create your own packages by following these rules:

- The optional **package** keyword must be the first statement at the beginning of your source code file.

- There can be only one **public** class in the file.

- The filename must have the `.java` extension.

The following code fragment shows an example of how to declare a package called `humanResource` for the `Employee` class:

```
package humanResource;
public class Employee {
  … //Class body omitted
}
```

Importing Classes and Packages

Use the **import** statement to make members of an entire class or package available to your program:

```
//Import all classes in the package by specifying the '*'
import java.sql.*;
//Import the ResultSet class
import java.sql.ResultSet;
```

Importing classes and packages saves you from having to type the fully qualified name of the class whenever it is used. For example, if you import the `java.sql` package, there is a class in this package called `ResultSet`. You can use `ResultSet` by itself instead of the fully qualified name of `java.sql.ResultSet` in your program.

Note that Java implicitly imports the classes of the `java.lang` package into your program, so you do not have to explicitly import this package.

Abstract Classes

Java provides the abstract class mechanism for representing abstract concepts. In the employee example, if you wanted to include the identification of an employee, you could not do it because you cannot instantiate the identification of an employee. It is an abstract concept. You can, however, instantiate the social security number of the employee as a string. Additionally, you can instantiate different types of identification numbers as strings or other data types.

Use the **abstract** keyword to declare a class as an abstract class. Within an abstract class, you can also have abstract method declarations without implementing the methods' body. The method bodies of an abstract class is implemented in the classes that extend them. The rules for abstract classes follow:

- Abstract classes cannot be instantiated.

- An abstract class can have abstract method declarations with no implementation of the method bodies.

- Abstract methods must be inside of an abstract class or interface.

- A subclass of an abstract class is abstract if it does not implement all abstract methods of the abstract class.

The following example, IDAbstract, is an abstract class that will return the identification number of its workers. The company hires permanent employees as well as independent contractors. Permanent employees use their social security number, and contractors use an Employee Identification Number (EIN) as their identification. The following example illustrates classes that use the IDAbstract abstract class to create two new classes, the Employee and Contractor classes. These two classes implement the abstract method ID() from the abstract class, with each class returning its own identification number.

```
public abstract class IDAbstract{
   public abstract String ID();
}

class Employee extends IDAbstract{
   protected String SSN;
   … //Other methods of the Employee class omitted
   public String ID(){ return SSN; }
}

class Contractor extends IDAbstract{
   protected String EIN;
   … //Other methods of the Contractor class omitted
   public String ID(){ return EIN; }
}
```

Interfaces

An **interface**, like an abstract class, defines a set of methods or constant declarations with no implementation of the method bodies. Unlike the abstract class, however, all the method declarations of the interface are automatically abstract and public. Any member variables declared in an interface are implicitly **static** and **final** (constant). In addition, a class can have multiple interfaces, whereas a class can only extend one abstract class.

An interface declaration is similar to a class declaration except that an interface uses the keyword **interface** instead of the **class** and **abstract** clauses. Methods of the interface are implicitly abstract even if the keyword **abstract** is not part of the method declaration. Use the **implements** clause on a new class to implement a declared interface. Every method of the interface must be implemented in the new class.

```
public interface Profile {
   public void PrintProfile();
}

class EmployeeProfile extends Employee implements Profile {
   public void PrintProfile(){
     //Must provide this class with a method body for the interface.
   }
}
```

In this example, the EmployeeProfile class is a subclass of the Employee class and it implements the Profile interface. For every method declaration in the Profile interface, in this example PrintProfile(), the EmployeeProfile class has to provide a method body.

Next, you will learn about Java applets.

Introduction to Java Applets

A *Java applet* is a program written in the Java programming language and is executed from a browser or an AppletViewer, a utility program for executing applets from Sun Microsystems. The browser invokes an applet's init() method to start program execution, the same way that the JVM invokes the application's main() method to run a Java application.

Once an applet is developed, the path to the applet code is added to an HTML page so that it can be run by a browser. An AppletViewer can also be used to run the applet from the command line.

The source code of a Java applet, as in the Java application, is stored in a file with the .java extension. The source code is compiled into a binary bytecode file with a .class extension. To create and run an applet:

1. Create a Java applet source code file with a .java extension, such as MyJavaAppletFromOracle8iBook.java.

2. Compile the source code that will generate the `.class` file.

3. Create a Web page with your favorite HTML editor.

4. Use the HTML `<APPLET>` tag to point to the `.class` file.

5. Run the applet in a browser or with the `AppletViewer` utility.

In this section, you will create the `MyJavaAppletFromOracle8iBook` applet, compile it, and learn the steps required to run it.

To create a Java applet, you must first import the necessary Java classes. When writing applet source code, you need to import at least two classes:

■ **`java.awt` (Abstract Windowing Toolkit) class**   Use this class to design the user interface (see "Brief Overview of the Java `AWT` Class" in this section).

■ **`java.applet.Applet` class**   Extend this class to create the functionality of the applet and to run it.

The following example illustrates how to import the necessary Java classes:

```
import java.awt.*;
import java.applet.Applet;
```

A Java applet is made up of at least one public class. The following declaration is used to create the applet class:

```
import java.awt.*;
import java.applet.Applet;
public class MyJavaAppletFromOracle8iBook extends Applet {
   ...
}
```

If you choose not to import the `java.applet.Applet` class, you can subclass it by using the fully qualified name of the class after the **extends** keyword:

```
import java.awt.*;
public MyJavaAppletFromOracle8iBook extends java.applet.Applet {
   ...
}
```

The class declaration defines the `MyJavaAppletFromOracle8iBook` class as **public**. The access modifier **public** indicates that the class can be extended and accessed by other Java classes and packages. The keyword **extends** causes the class to inherit all of the data members and methods of its superclass, the `Applet` class.

The `Applet` class is a subclass of the Java `AWT Panel` class. Consequently, both the Java `Applet` and the `MyJavaAppletFromOracle8iBook` class participate in the `AWT` event and drawing model of their superclasses. The `AWT` is the user interface toolkit that is provided as part of the Java language class library. Figure B-1 shows the inheritance hierarchy of the `Applet` class. This hierarchy determines the functionality of the applet class.

An applet uses the `Applet` API, which is a set of methods and interfaces that allows the applet to take advantage of the close relationship between applets and Web browsers. This API is provided by the `java.applet` package, specifically the `Applet` class and the `AppletContext` interface of the package.

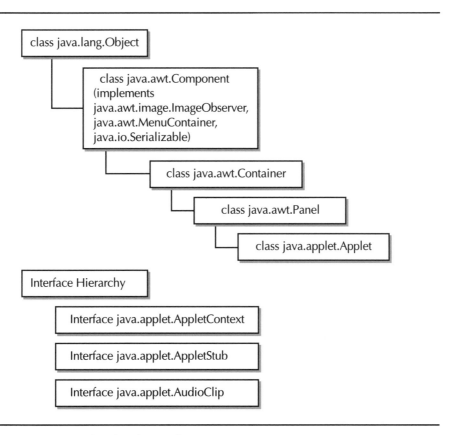

FIGURE B-1. *Applet class hierarchy*

The `Applet` API can do the following:

- Notify the API of the *milestone* methods: `init()`, `start()`, `stop()`, and `destroy()`.

- Display short status strings.

- Enable document display in a browser.

- Find other applets running on the same page.

- Play sounds.

- Get parameters from the `<APPLET>` tag.

In addition to the `Applet` API, an applet can use several other User Interface (UI) classes depending on the kind of information it needs to represent. Applets can play sounds, display videos, movies, documents, and so on.

There are four milestone methods from the `java.applet.Applet` class that allow applets to respond to major events:

- **The `init()` method**   Use this method to initialize the applet each time it is loaded. This is useful for any initialization that needs to be completed. Because it is similar to the Java constructor, include in the `init()` method where you would normally put in the constructor. Note that constructors should be avoided in an applet because the `init()` method must first run before the full environment becomes available to the applet. For quicker response, the `init()` method is a good place to have methods that load images.

- **The `start()` method**   Use this method to start program execution and use it to load or reload the applet.

- **The `stop()` method**   Use this method to stop program execution when the user leaves the applet page or quits the browser.

- **The `destroy()` method**   Use this method to clean up the environment and to free up any resources that the applet is holding.

The following example declares an `init()` method. This declaration tells the Java Virtual Machine (JVM) to override the `init()` method from the `Applet` class (see Chapter 1 for a discussion of JVM). A browser controls an applet's behavior by executing milestone methods.

```
import java.awt.*;
public class MyJavaAppletFromOracle8iBook extends java.applet.Applet {
```

```
public void init() {
    ...
}
...
}
```

In order for the applet to respond to events, it needs to override either some or all of the milestone methods. Your applet can override the `start()` method. This method performs the applet's work. Subsequently, if this method is overridden, the `stop()` method should also be overridden. The `stop()` method suspends the applet's execution so that it does not take up system resources when the user is not on the page where the applet is being executed. Furthermore, the `stop()` method does everything necessary to shut down the applet's thread of execution. Finally, applets do not need to override the `destroy()` method, particularly when the applets override the `stop()` method. Instead, use the `destroy()` method to release additional resources.

A Graphical User Interface is made up of elements called *components*. Components allow users to interact with programs regardless of whether the program is a Java applet or an application. In the `AWT` package, all the user interface components are instances of the class `Container` or of its subclass. These components must fit completely within the boundary of the container that holds them. In this example, the components are nested into the container and the result is a tree (Figure B-2) of elements, starting with the container as the root.

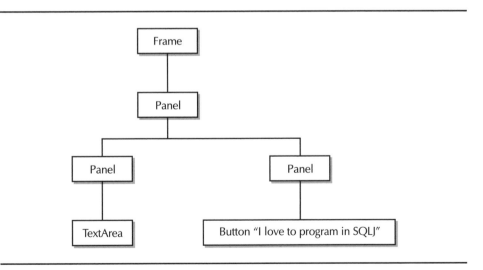

FIGURE B-2. *Component tree*

Because the `Applet` class inherits from the `AWT Container` class, it contains `Components` and other user interface objects such as buttons, labels, pop-up lists, and scrollbars (see the section "Brief Overview of the Java AWT Class"). In the following example, an instance of the `Button` class is created:

```
import java.awt.*;
public class MyJavaAppletFromOracle8iBook extends java.applet.Applet {
   public void init() {
      add( new Button("I love to program in SQLJ"));
      ...
   }
   ...
}
```

So far, you created an applet class with an inert user interface. In order to add more functionality to the `MyJavaAppletFromOracle8iBook` class, you need to understand the `AWT` package.

Brief Overview of the Java AWT Class

The Java `AWT` is a package of classes for building graphical user interfaces. It provides nine basic noncontainer component classes (Figure B-3). They are as follows: `Button`, `Canvas`, `Checkbox`, `Choice`, `Label`, `List`, `Scrollbar`, `TextArea`, and `TextField`. Additionally, there are four top-level display surfaces: the `Window`, the `Frame` and the `Dialog` that have borders and a title, and the `Panel` that is used to hold other components. You first create a container and then create components to place in it.

When building a user interface, first create an instance of the `Window` class or the `Frame` class. The frame, in the case of an applet, is the browser window. Since all applets subclass the `Panel` class, components can be added to instances of the `Applet` class itself.

Typically, a user interface has more than one container and component. To add components to a container, use the container's `add()` method. The code here adds a `Button` component to the `MyJavaAppletFromOracle8iBook` class:

```
add( new Button("I love to program in SQLJ"));
```

Note that the creation of the component is in the `init()` method and that this method is automatically invoked during the initialization of the applet. Therefore the buttons will be drawn and displayed as soon as the browser is notified by the `init()` milestone method.

In the previous statements, an object of type `Button` was created. You need to lay out the button after it is created. You can use the layout manager associated with the container to control the layout. In the `AWT` package, the layout manager classes implement the `LayoutManager` interface. The `AWT` provides five layout managers

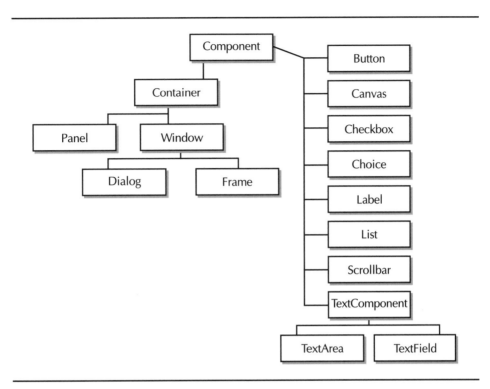

FIGURE B-3. *Java AWT package*

that are used to place components in a container. Each container has a default layout manager. The default layout manager for the `Panel` class is the `FlowLayout` manager. The `BorderLayout` manager is the default layout manager for both the `Frame` and the `Dialog` classes. Use the `BorderLayout` manager to adjust the placement of components within the regions `North`, `South`, `East`, `West`, and `Center`. Use the `FlowLayout` manager to arrange the components from left to right. Other layout managers provide additional layout flexibility.

```
import java.awt.*;
public class MyJavaAppletFromOracle8iBook extends java.applet.Applet {
    public void init() {
        // First create a variable of type Panel
        Panel aPanel;

        // Use the setLayout() method to use the BorderLayout Manager
        setLayout(new BorderLayout());

        // Instantiate your panel
```

```
        aPanel = new Panel();
      ...
        // add button to your applet
        add( new Button("I love to program in SQLJ"));
    }
    ...
}
```

You may wish to add a text area to the panel in your applet. This is accomplished by creating an instance of the `TextArea` class and adding it to the panel using the `add()` method from the `Panel` class.

```
import java.awt.*;
public class MyJavaAppletFromOracle8iBook extends java.applet.Applet {
    public void init() {
        Panel aPanel;
        // Use the setLayout method to use the BorderLayout Manager
        setLayout(new BorderLayout());

        // Instantiate your panel
        aPanel = new Panel();

        // Add a text area
        aPanel.add(new TextArea);

        // Place your text area in the south side of the panel
        add("South", aPanel);

        // add button to the applet
        add( new Button("I love to program in SQLJ"));
    }
    ...
}
```

So far you have an inert interface, that is, the applet does not do much. In order for the applet to do something, the user interface must take some action. This is accomplished through an event. Event handling is done by the `action()` method of the `Component` class and is beyond the scope of this book. To complete the applet, however, you will learn to handle at least one event through the `action()` method. The `Component` class is the superclass of the `Panel` class that handles events for basic components such as `Button`, `Checkbox`, `Choice`, and `TextField`. The `MyJavaAppletFromOracle8iBook` class overrides the `action()` method. This method has two objects as its arguments:

```
public boolean action (Event anEvent, Object anObject)
```

The anEvent parameter object describes the event that occurred, and the anObject parameter object contains different values depending on the type of event that occurred.

```
import java.awt.*;
public class MyJavaAppletFromOracle8iBook extends java.applet.Applet {
    TextArea aTextArea;
    public void init() {
        // Use the setLayout method to use the BorderLayout Manager
        setLayout(new BorderLayout());

        // Instantiate your panel
        Panel aPanel = new Panel();

        // Create a text area
        aTextArea = new TextArea();

        // Add a text area
        aPanel.add(aTextArea);

        // Place your text area in the south of the panel
        add("South", aPanel);

        // add a button to your applet
        add( new Button("I love to program in SQLJ"));
    }

    // Add an action() method to handle an event
    public boolean action (Event anEvent, Object anObject) {
        String aString = (String)anObject;

        // Use the method from the TextArea class to add a text
        aTextArea.appendText(aString + "\n");
        return false;
    }
}
```

Now that you have created the applet, it can be compiled. At the command line, type the following command:

```
javac MyJavaAppletFromOracle8iBook.java
```

Once the applet is compiled successfully, create an HTML file using your favorite editor to run the applet. The HTML file should be in the same directory as the compiled bytecode file MyJavaAppletFromOracle8iBook.class.

The applet may be customized with the many attributes of the <APPLET> tag. The following is an example of an HTML tag that tells the viewer or browser to load the applet with the initial size of the applet set to 500 pixels wide and 250 pixels high:

```
<APPLET code="MyJavaAppletFromOracle8iBook.class" width="500"
height="250"></APPLET>
```

To run an applet in a browser, a Java-enabled browser is needed such as Netscape 2.0 or greater, or Internet Explorer 3.0 or greater. You can also use the AppletViewer to run the applet.

When using a browser to view a page that contains an applet, the bytecode of the applet is downloaded to the browser and is executed on the client's computer. The applet is an independent program running within the browser. Web browsers execute the applet when the browser loads an HTML document that contains an applet tag.

The AppletViewer can also be used to run the applet:

```
AppletViewer MyJavaAppletFromOracle8iBook.html
```

In this appendix, you learned the basic features of the Java language such as variables, operators, expressions, classes, and objects through the investigation of a Java application and a Java applet. In Appendix C, you will learn about Java Database Connectivity (JDBC).

APPENDIX C

Introduction to Java Database Connectivity (JDBC)

JDBC application is a Java program that invokes SQL statements through the JDBC method calls to access relational databases. The communication between the program and the data server is done via the JDBC API (a set of Java interfaces, classes, and exceptions to support database connections) and multiple low-level drivers for connecting to different databases. See the "Basic JDBC Concepts" section in Chapter 1.

In this appendix, you will create the following JDBC programs to access a database:

- A JDBC application
- A JDBC applet that calls a PL/SQL stored procedure

You are referred to the *Oracle8i JDBC Developer's Guide and Reference* [38] and the *JDBC Database Access with Java* [21] for further information on how to program with JDBC.

Creating a JDBC Application

In this section, you will create a JDBC application to:

- Create a table, the DEPARTMENT_LIST, in a relational database
- Insert data into the DEPARTMENT_LIST table
- Query the DEPARTMENT_LIST table
- Display the query results via a JDBC ResultSet object

There is a standard organization to JDBC programs:

1. Import the JDBC API package, the java.sql package.

2. Load and register the JDBC driver. You can create connection objects after the driver has been registered.

3. Create a Connection object to connect to the database.

4. Create a Statement instance to send SQL statements to the database. This object can execute dynamic or static embedded SQL statements (see Chapter 1).

5. Use the JDBC Statement instance to execute database tasks as specified by the Statement class.

6. Use the JDBC `ResultSet` instance to store the results of a database query and retrieve the data via its `next()` method.

7. Close the `Statement` and the `ResultSet` instances.

8. Close the connection to the database.

Using the JDBC API, you will write `JdbcApplication`, an application to access, insert, and query data from an Oracle database:

```
// Program name: JdbcApplication.java

// Import packages necessary for the application
import java.sql.*;

class JdbcApplication {
    public static void main (String args []) throws SQLException {

        // Load and register the JDBC driver
        DriverManager.registerDriver(
                    new oracle.jdbc.driver.OracleDriver());

        // Connect to the database
        String anURL = "jdbc:oracle:thin:@data-i.com:1521:ORCL";
        Connection conn =
                DriverManager.getConnection(anURL, "scott", "tiger");

        // Create Statement Object
        Statement stmt = conn.createStatement ();

        // Create a table and Insert records into the table
        stmt.executeUpdate("CREATE TABLE DEPARTMENT_LIST(" +
                            "deptno NUMBER," +
                            "shortname VARCHAR2(8)," +
                            "longname  VARCHAR2(20))");
        stmt.executeUpdate("INSERT INTO DEPARTMENT_LIST " +
                            "VALUES(200, 'ACNT','Accounting')");
        stmt.executeUpdate("INSERT INTO DEPARTMENT_LIST " +
                            "VALUES(240, 'HR','Human Resource')");

        // Query the table
        ResultSet rset =
                stmt.executeQuery("SELECT * FROM DEPARTMENT_LIST");

        // Process the Result Set
        while (rset.next())
            System.out.println(rset.getInt(1)+ " " +
```

```
                        rset.getString("shortname") + " " + rset.getString(3));

        // Close the Result Set and Statement object
        rset.close();
        stmt.close();

        // Close connection to the database
        conn.close();
    }
}
```

1. Import the JDBC Package

Use the following syntax to make the JDBC class immediately available to
your program:

```
import java.sql.*;
```

Additionally, you may need to import vendor-specific driver packages for the
database that you wish to access. For example, you have to import the `oracle.sql`
package to access the Oracle types extension such as BLOB, DATE, and RAW.

2. Load and Register the JDBC Driver

You must tell the JDBC program how to manage driver communication with the
database. This is accomplished by loading the vendor-specific driver manager
and registering it with the `registerDriver()` method provided by the
`DriverManager` class of the JDBC API:

```
DriverManager.registerDriver (new oracle.jdbc.driver.OracleDriver());
```

The driver manager is responsible for connecting to the database with a
specified URL. It is also responsible for searching for an appropriate driver when
the `getConnection()` method from Step 3 is called.

Note that you need to register the driver once for each database that you wish to
access, regardless of the number of database connections that you wish to establish
to the same data server.

Alternatively, you can use the following syntax to load and register the
vendor's driver:

```
Class.forName("oracle.jdbc.driver.OracleDriver");
```

The `registerDriver()` method explicitly creates an instance of the
vendor-specific driver to register the driver, whereas the `forName()` method
implicitly does it for you. Note that the `forName()` method is valid only for
JDK-compliant Java Virtual Machines.

3. Create the Connection Object to Connect to the Database

Once the driver has been loaded, a Connection instance must be created in order for the program to connect to the database. A connection object from the java.sql. Connection class is instantiated through the getConnection() method of the DriverManager class. The Connection class contains methods to control connections to the database. The getConnection() method can be called with arguments specifying the database URL for the connection, the password, and the username. Other parameter signatures of this method accept different parameters. See Chapter 5 and the *Oracle 8i JDBC Developer's Guide and Reference* [38] to learn more about the getConnection() method and the various lists of its input arguments.

```
String anUrl = "jdbc:oracle:thin:@data-i.com:1521:ORCL";
Connection conn = DriverManager.getConnection(anURL, "scott", "tiger");
```

4. Create the Statement Instance to Perform Database Tasks

Now that you have established a database connection to the data-i database server, you need to instantiate objects to manage the SQL statements that will be executed against the database. Use the createStatement() method of the Connection class associated with a Connection object to create a statement object:

```
Statement stmt = conn.createStatement ();
```

5. Use the Statement Instance to Execute Database Tasks

The executeQuery() method of the Statement class is used to send query requests to a database, whereas the executeUpdate() method of the Statement class is used for sending SQL statements that modify the state of the database (DDL statements and DML statements such as INSERT, UPDATE, and DELETE). In the following example, create the table DEPARTMENT_LIST, and insert two rows of data into it.

```
stmt.executeUpdate("CREATE TABLE Department_list( " +
                                    "deptno NUMBER," +
                                    "shortname VARCHAR2(8)," +
                                    "longname  VARCHAR2(20))");
stmt.executeUpdate("INSERT INTO DEPARTMENT_LIST " +
                    "VALUES( 200, 'ACNT','Accounting')");
stmt.executeUpdate("INSERT INTO DEPARTMENT_LIST " +
                    "VALUES( 240, 'HR','Human Resource')");
```

6. Use the JDBC ResultSet Object

Use the `executeQuery()` method to retrieve the data and then store the results in a JDBC `Resultset` object:

```
ResultSet rset = stmt.executeQuery ("SELECT * FROM DEPARTMENT_LIST");
```

After you execute your query, use the `next()` method to get the values of the row. The `next()` method advances the `rset` object to successive rows of the JDBC `ResultSet`. This method returns a value of true while rows are still available or a value of false if there are no more rows (that is, when all table rows have been fetched from the result set). Use the `next()` method to iterate through the `ResultSet` object:

```
while (rset.next())
   System.out.println(rset.getInt(1)+ " " +
            rset.getString("shortname") + " " + rset.getString(3));
```

Use the various JDBC `getXXX methods such as the getString()` and the `getInt()` to retrieve column values from the current row of the result set. You can use either the table column name or the column index number as the input parameter to these methods. Note that the column index number refers to the position of the column of the result set and not the column of the database table.

In the `rset.getString("shortname")` statement, the parameter `shortname` is the column name of the result set, whereas in the `rset.getString(3)` is the relative position of the result set column. The 3 is the third column of the result set, which is the `longname` column.

7. Close the Statement Instances and the ResultSet

Use the `close()` method to close any `Statement` and `ResultSet` objects that you created. You should always explicitly close all `Statement` and `ResultSet` objects. If you do not explicitly close these objects, memory leaks may occur.

```
// Close the rset ResultSet and the stmt Statement objects
rset.close();
stmt.close();
```

8. Close the Connection to the Database

You must close your connection once you finish with the database connection. This is accomplished via the `close()` method of the `Connection` class:

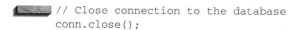
```
// Close connection to the database
conn.close();
```

Java Applet Calls a PL/SQL Stored Procedure

A *JDBC applet* is a Java applet that uses the JDBC API to access a database. See Appendix B to learn more about Java applets.

In this section, you will create a Java applet, the `JdbcApplet`. This applet calls a *PL/SQL* stored procedure to retrieve a list of vendors' names from the `VENDOR_LIST` table. Note that PL/SQL is an Oracle RDBMS procedural language extension to SQL. If you wish to access stored procedures from databases other than Oracle, you should consult your vendor's manual to learn how to create server-side stored procedures in your environment. See Appendix A to learn more about PL/SQL procedures, functions, and packages.

The `JdbcApplet` applet calls the Oracle PL/SQL `purchase_queries`. `SelectVendorName` stored procedure to select the name of the vendors from the `VENDOR_LIST` table and displays the results:

```
//Program Name: JdbcApplet.java

// Import Oracle jdbc driver
import oracle.jdbc.driver.*;

// Import the package necessary for the JDBC applet
import java.sql.*;

// Import the Java classes needed for the in applet
import java.awt.*;

public class JdbcApplet extends java.applet.Applet {
  // The button of the applet for executing the query
  Button execute_button;

  // The query displays its result in this text area
  TextArea output;

  // Use for connecting to the database
  Connection conn;

  // Create the User Interface
  public void init () {
    this.setLayout (new BorderLayout ());
    Panel p = new Panel ();
    p.setLayout (new FlowLayout (FlowLayout.LEFT));
    execute_button = new Button ("JDBC Applet");
```

```
    p.add (execute_button);
    this.add ("North", p);
    output = new TextArea (10, 60);
    this.add ("Center", output);
  }

  public boolean action (Event ev, Object arg) {
    if (ev.target == execute_button) {
      try {
        // Clear the output area
        output.setText (null);
          // Load the JDBC driver
        DriverManager.registerDriver(
                new oracle.jdbc.driver.OracleDriver());

        // Connect to the database
        conn = DriverManager.getConnection(
            "jdbc:oracle:thin:@data-i.com:1521:ORCL","scott", "tiger");
         // Create a callable statement object
        CallableStatement cstmt;  // (See Note 1.)
// Prepare the call
        cstmt = conn.prepareCall  // (See Note 2.)
            ( "{call purchase_queries.SelectVendorName(?)}" ) ;

        // Register the output parameter (See Note 3.)
        cstmt.registerOutParameter(1, OracleTypes.CURSOR);

        // Execute the callable statement
        cstmt.execute();            // (See Note 4.)

        // Get the results into an Oracle result set (See Note 5.)
OracleResultSet anOracleResultSet = (OracleResultSet)
                ((OracleCallableStatement)cstmt).getCursor (1);

        // Process the Oracle Result Set like you would process a
        // JDBC result set process the Result Set
        while (anOracleResultSet.next())
            output.appendText(anOracleResultSet.getString(1)+ "\n");

        // Close the Result Set
        anOracleResultSet.close();
        // Close connection to the database
        conn.close();
      }
      catch (Exception e) {
        output.appendText (e.getMessage() + "\n");
      }
      return true;
    }
```

```
    else
      return false;
  }
}
```

Notes on `JdbcApplet` applet:

1. To access a PL/SQL procedure from a Java program, you must create a callable statement object. This statement creates the `cstmt` object.

2. This statement prepares the call to the procedure. The procedure returns an Oracle object of type REF CURSOR. See Appendix A to learn about Oracle REF CURSOR.

3. The `registerOutParameter()` method registers the IN/OUT parameter.

4. This statement executes the procedure call.

5. This statement retrieves an object reference as an OUT parameter from a PL/SQL procedure, and you must cast your callable statement to an `OracleCallableStatement`.

Refer to Appendix B and the *Oracle8i JDBC Developer's Guide and Reference* [38] to learn more about Java applets and Java programs calling PL/SQL stored procedures.

In this appendix, you created two JDBC programs, an application and an applet where in each you used the JDBC API to connect to the database and execute dynamic SQL operations to manipulate the database. See Chapters 1 and 6 to learn more about dynamic SQL operations.

Appendix D presents a SQLJ quick reference guide.

APPENDIX
D

SQLJ Quick Reference Guide

n this appendix, you will learn about the following:

- Setting the SQLJ environment

- SQLJ declarations

- Java host expressions

- Executable statement clause

- Database connections

- Selected `sqlj.runtime` classes

- Supported types for host expressions

- Tools

Setting the SQLJ Environment

Developing SQLJ database applications requires the following:

- The *Java Development Kit* (JDK) version 1.1 or higher from JavaSoft or an equivalent Java interpreter and compiler. You can download the JavaSoft JDK from Sun Microsystems at http://java.sun.com/products/OV_jdkProduct.html. After downloading it, follow the instruction that comes with the JDK to install it.

  The Java JDK may already be on your system, especially if you are on a multi-user system such as UNIX or you have installed a Java Development Environment tool such as the Oracle JDeveloper or the Visual Café from Symantec. Test to see if the interpreter is installed on your system by typing at the command line:

  ```
  java -version
  ```

  If a version number of 1.1.*x* or greater is returned then you may not have to install a Java compiler and interpreter.

- A JDBC driver implementing the standard `java.sql` JDBC interfaces from Sun Microsystems. Note that if you are developing applications for an Oracle database (Oracle7 or higher), you should get the Oracle JDBC drivers.

NOTE
*Oracle SQLJ supports any standard-compliant JDBC
driver. Therefore, if you are connecting to a database
other than the Oracle data server then install the JDBC
API supplied by the database vendors.*

■ Oracle SQLJ. You can install the Oracle SQLJ by downloading it from
Oracle's Web site at http://www.oracle.com/java/sqlj or you can choose
to install it when you install the Oracle8*i* JServer. The installation includes
the class files for the SQLJ *translator*, SQLJ *profile customizer*, and SQLJ
runtime. These class files are available in the file `translator.zip` file.

Setting the CLASSPATH and PATH Environment Variables

Set the `CLASSPATH` environment variable after SQLJ has been installed on your
system. The `CLASSPATH` environment variable tells the Java compiler, the Java
interpreter, and the SQLJ translator where to search for Java class libraries. In
order to compile Java source codes, SQLJ source codes, or run Java programs, you
have to make sure that the `CLASSPATH` environment variable is set correctly. Do
the following, to set the `CLASSPATH`:

The two files that you need to set the `CLASSPATH` environment variable for
SQLJ are:

■ *classes[ver].zip* contains the JDBC API class files, where the *ver* is the
Oracle JDBC API version such as classes111.zip for use with JDK 1.1.*x*
and classes12.zip for use with JDK 1.2.

■ *translator.zip* has the class files for the SQLJ translator, the SQLJ profile
customizer, and the SQLJ runtime.

Do the following to set the `CLASSPATH` on the different operating system (note
that *jdbcdir* is the directory where you installed the JDBC drivers and *sqljdir* is the
directory where the `translator.zip` file resides):

■ On the Microsoft Windows 95/98 operating systems, type the following at
the command line:

```
SET CLASSPATH =
%CLASSPATH%;[jdbcdir]\lib\classes111.zip;[sqljdir]\lib\translator.zip;
```

If you do not want to type the class path every time you open an MS-DOS
window, you should include the `CLASSPATH` environment variable in the
`autoexec.bat` file.

■ On the Microsoft Windows NT, you can set the CLASSPATH variable each time you open an MS-DOS window with:

```
SET CLASSPATH =
%CLASSPATH%;[jdbcdir]\lib\classes111.zip;[sqljdir]\lib\translator.zip;
```

Alternatively, you can automatically set the CLASSPATH every time you open an MS-DOS window by setting it as a systems variable. To set the class path as a system variable, with an account that has Administrator privileges, do the following:

1. Go to the Control Panel and double-click on the System icon.

2. Choose the Environment tab and under System Variables choose CLASSPATH from the list. Append to the end of the line in the Values box:

```
[sqljdir]\lib\classes111.zip;[sqljdir]\lib\translator.zip;
```

■ On the UNIX operating system, you can set the CLASSPATH variable each time you open a sesssion using the following command:

```
setenv CLASSPATH
${CLASSPATH}:[sqljdir] /classes111.zip:[sqljdir]/translator.zip
```

If you do not want to type the class path every time you start a new UNIX session, you should include the CLASSPATH environment variable in a login file such as the .login file or the .cshrc file.

Note that SQLJ works with any standard-compliant JDBC driver. Therefore, if you are connecting to a database other than the Oracle data server then follow the instruction and include in your CLASSPATH the JDBC API supplied by the database vendors.

Setting the CLASSPATH can be very confusing and frustrating. If you run into trouble and need assistance, you can go to the SQLJ FAQ at the Oracle Web site http://www.oracle.com/java/sqlj/faq.html or the Oracle Technology Network (OTN) Web site at http://technet.oracle.com.

Set the PATH environment variable so that the operating system will know where to find the SQLJ executable files. The procedure to set the path is similar to the setting of the CLASSPATH environment variable previously discussed. Set the PATH by following the steps of setting the CLASSPATH and replacing instances of CLASSPATH with PATH. For example, set the PATH on the Microsoft operating systems:

```
SET PATH = %PATH%[Oracle Home]\bin;
```

Replace [Oracle Home] with your actual Oracle Home directory.

SQLJ Declarations

There are two types of SQLJ declarations: iterator and connection context declarations. A SQLJ declaration is made up of a #sql token, followed by a class declaration (see Chapters 1 and 3).

Iterator Declaration

A SQLJ iterator is similar to a Java ResultSet (see Appendix C) in that it is used to store query results from a database. There are two types of SQLJ iterators: *named* and *positional* (see Chapters 1, 2, and 3). The syntax is:

```
#sql <modifier> iterator Iterator_ClassName ( type declarations );
```

The modifier can be any standard Java class modifier such as **public**, **private**, **protected**, or the default package. SQLJ modifier rules correspond to the Java modifier rules (see Appendix B). The type declarations are separated by commas:

```
// A named iterator declaration
#sql public iterator Employee(int employeeno, String name);

// A positional iterator declaration
#sql public iterator Employee(int, String);
```

Connection Context Declaration

Use ConnectionContext class to establish database connections to schemas located on different data servers (see Chapters 3 and 5):

```
#sql <modifier> context Context_ClassName;
```

The modifier, as in an iterator declaration, can be any standard Java class modifier such as **public**, **private**, **protected**, or the default package. The SQLJ modifier rules correspond to the Java modifier rules (see Appendix B). In the following, LocalHostConnectionContext is a user-defined ConnectionContext class name:

```
#sql public context LocalHostConnectionContext;
```

implements Clause

You may use the Java **implements** clause with both the iterator and the connection context declaration types (see Chapters 3 and 5). The following declaration of the

`ConnectionContext` class, `Context_Classname`, specifies one or more interfaces to be implemented by the generated class:

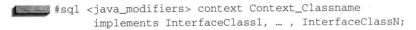

```
#sql <java_modifiers> context Context_Classname
     implements InterfaceClass1, … , InterfaceClassN;
```

The **implements** clause, `implements InterfaceClass1…InterfaceClassN`, derives one or more classes from a Java interface.

with Clause

The SQLJ **with** clause allows you to declare a SQLJ iterator or `ConnectionContext` class by specifying one or more constants that will be in the generated class (see Chapters 3 and 5). The generated constants will be **public static final**. The syntax follows:

```
// A connection context declaration and the with clause
#sql <java_modifiers> context Context_classname
     with (variable1=value1, …, variableN=valueN);

// An iterator declaration and the with clause
#sql <java_modifiers> iterator Iterator_classname
     with (var1=value1, …, varN=valueN) (type declarations);
```

Note that the **with** clause is unique to SQLJ and does not exist in Java. The following example demonstrates the use of a **with** clause in a named iterator declaration:

```
#sql public iterator Employee with (TYPECODE=OracleTypes.NUMBER)
     (int employeeno, String name);
```

The `Employee` iterator will define the **public static final** attribute `TYPECODE` and initialized to the value of the typecode for the `NUMBER` datatype, as defined in the Oracle JDBC `oracle.jdbc.driver.OracleTypes` class.

Java Host Expressions

SQLJ uses Java host expressions interspersed within the SQL statement to pass arguments between Java source code and SQL operations (see Chapter 3). A *host expression* is any legal Java variable or complex expression that is preceded by a colon (:) :

```
String emp;
int empNo = 1056;
…
```

```
// The following SQLJ statement uses the Java variables emp and empNo
// as host expressions. Note that a colon precedes the Java variables
// emp and empNo to make them host variables. In addition, variable
// emp maps SQL data to Java, and empno maps Java data to SQL.
#sql {SELECT lastname INTO :emp FROM EMPLOYEE_TABLE
            WHERE employeeno = :empNo };
```

Executable Statement Clause

A SQLJ executable statement clause is prefixed with the **#sql** token followed by an embedded SQL operation between curly braces and is terminated with a semicolon (see Chapters 3 and 5). The two types of executable clauses are the *statement* and the *assignment* clauses:

```
// A SQLJ statement clause produces no output
#sql {Embedded SQL operation};

// A SQLJ assignment clause is a clause that has a result expression.
// The following outputs the result into a predefined iterator iter
#sql iter = { embedded SQL operation };
```

The SQL Clause

The SQL clause is used in processing DML statements such as the standard SQL SELECT, UPDATE, INSERT, and DELETE (see Chapter 3):

```
#sql { INSERT INTO EMPLOYEE_LIST
          (employeeno, lastname, firstname, phone, departmentno )
            VALUES ( 1056, 'Jones', 'Rachel', '(305)555-0359', 15 ) };
```

The SELECT INTO Clause

The SELECT INTO clause is used to retrieve a single row of data into one or more host variables (see Chapter 3):

```
#sql { SELECT expression1,…, expressionN
          INTO :host_exp1,…, :host_expN
            FROM datasource [optional clauses] };
```

As in the example:

```
#sql { SELECT lastname, firstname,
          INTO :firstName, :lastName
            FROM EMPLOYEE_LIST
              WHERE employeeno = 1056 };
```

The FETCH INTO Clause

The FETCH INTO clause is used to retrieve multi-row data from positional iterators. The following example illustrates how to use the FETCH INTO clause (see Chapter 3):

```
//Declare the positional iterator EmployeeIter
#sql public iterator EmployeeIter (int, String, String);
...

// Then declare an iterator instance emps
EmployeeIter emps;
//Query to put data in the positional iterator 'emps'
#sql emps = { SELECT employeeno, lastname, firstname
                FROM employee_list };
...
String firstName;
String lastName;
int id;

while (true) {
  // Use FETCH INTO to retrieve data from the emps positional iterator
  #sql { FETCH :emps INTO :id, :firstName, :lastName };
  // Use the endFetch() method to determine the end.
  if (emps.endFetch()) break;    // This test must be AFTER fetch
  System.out.print("The Employee number: " + id);
  System.out.println( " and Name: " + firstName + " " + lastName );
}
emps.close();  // Close the iterator
...
}
```

The COMMIT and ROLLBACK Clauses

The COMMIT and ROLLBACK clauses are used for transaction control. You can use these transaction control statements if the auto-commit is set to false (see "Database Connections" in this appendix):

```
// USE COMMIT to commit any changes that have been executed since
// the last commit.
#sql { COMMIT };
// Use ROLLBACK to cancel any changes that have been executed since
// the last commit.
#sql { ROLLBACK };
```

NOTE
Do not use the COMMIT *or* ROLLBACK *clauses if the
auto-commit flag is enabled (see Chapter 9).*

The Procedure Clause

You can use the CALL token to call stored procedures from a database (see
Chapters 1 and 4):

```
#sql { CALL PROCEDURE_NAME(<PARAM_LIST>) };
```

As in the example:

```
// Assume that there is a PL/SQL stored procedure named
// InsertPurchaseOrder() in the database. Use CALL to access it.
int newOrderNbr;
...
#sql {CALL InsertPurchaseOrder ( :newOrderNbr ) };   // Procedure call
```

The Function Clause

You can use the VALUES token to call stored functions from a database. Because
functions have return values, you have to have a result expression in your SQLJ
executable statement (see Chapters 1 and 4):

```
#sql result = { VALUES(FUNCTION_NAME(<PARAM_LIST>)) };
```

As in the example:

```
...
// Assume that there is a stored function named InsertPurchaseOrder()
// in the database. Use VALUES to call it.
int empInsertSuccess;
#sql empInsertSuccess = { VALUES (InsertPurchaseOrder
                ( 1111, 'Smith', 'Michelle', '(305)555-0359', 15 ) };
```

The Assignment Clause (SET)

The *assignment* statement allows you to assign Java host variables values to the **SET**
token (see Chapter 3):

```
// SQLJ executable statements setting host variables
#sql { SET :hostvariable = expression };
```

The following example uses two stored functions to calculate the cost of an item and assign the results in the host variable `cost`:

```
double cost;
...
#sql { SET :cost = GetUnitPrice() * GetQuantity()};
```

PL/SQL Blocks

SQLJ allows you to include PL/SQL blocks as executable statements. The PL/SQL block is contained within the curly braces (see Chapters 1 and 2 and Appendix A):

```
// The <DECLARE ...> statement is optional for PL/SQL blocks
#sql { <DECLARE ...> BEGIN ... END; };
```

An example of a PL/SQL block:

```
// SQLJ executable statement using an Oracle PL/SQL block
// to create observation ids in the OceanicObservationList table
#sql {
    DECLARE
        incrementNo  NUMBER;
    BEGIN
        incrementNo := 1;
        WHILE incrementNo <= 100 LOOP
            INSERT INTO OceanicObservationList(obs_id)
                VALUES (2000 + incrementNo);
            incrementNo := incrementNo + 1;
        END LOOP;
    END;
};
```

Database Connections

In this section, you will find topics for connecting and controlling database connections (see Chapters 2 and 5):

- Connections with the `DefaultContext` class
- Connections with the `ConnectionContext` class
- Control SQL operations with the `ExecutionContext` class
- Connection properties file

The DefaultContext Class

Use an instance of the `DefaultContext` class or one of the methods of the `oracle.sqlj.runtime.Oracle` class, the `connect()` or the `getConnection()` methods, to establish database connections (see Chapter 5).

Single Connections

For single connections, you can use the `Oracle.connect()` method by specifying the URL, username, password, and the optional auto-commit flag or by specifying a `connect.properties` file (see the "Connection Properties File" section of this appendix and Chapters 2 and 5):

```
Oracle.connect(NameOfClass.class, "connect.properties");
```

The `NameOfClass.class` in the previous example is the name of your class. You can also use the `getClass()` method from `java.lang.Object` in lieu of specifying the name of your class:

```
Oracle.connect(getClass(), "connect.properties");
```

The following statement uses the Oracle thin driver and specifies a URL, username, and password, respectively. By default, the auto-commit flag is set to `false` (see Chapters 2 and 5):

```
Oracle.connect(
    "jdbc:oracle:thin:@data-i.com:1521:ORCL", "scott", "tiger");
```

You can also specify the setting of the auto-commit flag. The following statement uses the Oracle oci8 driver and specifies a URL, username, password and auto-commit flag, respectively:

```
Oracle.connect(
    "jdbc:oracle:oci8:@data-i.com:1521:ORCL", "scott", "tiger", true);
```

Multiple Connections

You can create multiple instances of the `DefaultContext` class to connect to one or more schemas. As with single connections, you can use the `oracle.getConnection()` method (see the "Selected `sqlj.runtime` Classes" section of this appendix and Chapter 5):

```
DefaultContext conn1 =
    Oracle.getConnection("jdbc:oracle:thin:@data-i.com:1521:ORCL1",
        "username1", "password1");
```

```
DefaultContext conn2 =
  Oracle.getConnection("jdbc:oracle:thin:@db:1521:ORCL2",
    "username2", "password2");
```

Use the `conn1` and the `conn2` objects with square braces to execute SQL operations in different schemas located on `data-i.com` and db, respectively.

```
#sql [conn1] { SQL operation };
#sql [conn2] { SQL operation };
```

Use the `setDefaultContext()` method of the `DefaultContext` class to switch the default connection from one schema to another:

```
// Set the default connection to conn2
DefaultContext.setDefaultContext(conn2);
#sql { SQL operation };  // This statement use conn2

// Set the default connection to conn1
DefaultContext.setDefaultContext(conn1);
 #sql { SQL operation }; // This statement use conn1
```

The ConnectionContext Class

You can also use a user-defined SQLJ declared `ConnectionContext` class to connect to a single database as well as to several databases (see the "SQLJ Declarations—Connection Context Declaration" section of this appendix and Chapter 5):

```
// A declared ConnectionContext class
#sql public context LocalHostConnContext;

// Syntax to instantiate a user-defined context class
LocalHostConnContext connDeclared = new LocalHostConnContext
    (url, username, password, autocommit);

//  For example,
LocalHostConnContext connDeclared = new LocalHostConnContext
  ("jdbc:oracle:thin:@localhost:1521:orcl", "scott", "tiger", true);

//  Associate the connection object with a SQL operation
#sql [connDeclared] { SQL operation };
```

The ExecutionContext Class

An *execution context* is an instance of the `sqlj.runtime.ExecutionContext` class (see the "Selected `sqlj.runtime` Classes" section of this appendix and Chapter 5). The `ExecutionContext` class contains methods to help you control the execution of your SQL operations. A SQLJ operation is always associated with an instance of the `ExecutionContext` class. If you do not associate an `ExecutionContext` object explicitly with your SQLJ clause, SQLJ will implicitly associate the default instance of this class with the clause:

```
// Create an instance of the ExecutionContext class from the
// default connection.
ExecutionContext anExecCtx = new ExecutionContext();

// Explicit association of an instance of a connection context class
// with an explicit instance of an instance of the ExecutionContext
// class
#sql [connDeclared, anExecCtx] emps =
    { SELECT lastname from EMPLOYEE_LIST};

// Implicit association of an instance of the default context class
// with an explicit instance of an instance of the ExecutionContext
// class
#sql [anExecCtx] emps = { SELECT lastname from EMPLOYEE_LIST};

// Use the following statement to retrieve the current instance of the
// ExecutionContext class that is associated with an instance of the
// DefaultContext class.
ExecutionContext anExecCtx =
    DefaultContext.getDefaultContext().getExecutionContext();

// Wait only 3 seconds for operations to complete
anExecCtx.setQueryTimeout(3);

// Select employees using the execution context of default connection
// context
#sql [anExecCtx] emps = { SELECT lastname from EMPLOYEE_LIST};

System.out.println("There are " + anExecCtx.getUpdateCount() +
                    " employees");
```

Connection Properties File

You can set the parameters of the `connect()` method in a properties file (see Chapters 2 and 5). You use the `connect()` method to establish a connection with the database:

```
# An example of a properties file called "connect.properties"

# Filename: connect.properties
# A line that begins with a '#' is a comment line.
# Users should uncomment one of the following URLs or add their own.
# This example uses the oracle thin driver to connect to the database
sqlj.url=jdbc:oracle:thin:@localhost:1521:ORCL
#sqlj.url=jdbc:oracle:oci8:@
#sqlj.url=jdbc:oracle:oci7:@
#
# In the following two lines, enter the username and password
sqlj.user=scott
sqlj.password=tiger
```

Selected sqlj.runtime Classes

This section lists the methods of the following classes:

- `sqlj.runtime.ref.DefaultContext`
- `sqlj.runtime.ExecutionContext`

The sqlj.runtime.ref.DefaultContext Class

The `DefaultContext` class provides a complete implementation of the `ConnectionContext` interface. This is the same class definition that would have been generated by the reference translator from the declaration:

```
#sql public context DefaultContext;
```

The `DefaultContext` class contains the following useful methods:

- **getConnection()** Gets the underlying JDBC Connection object. You can also use the `setAutoCommit()` method of the underlying JDBC Connection object to set the auto-commit flag for the connection.

- **setDefaultContext(DefaultContext ctx)** This is a static method that sets the default connection your application uses; it takes a `DefaultContext` instance as input. SQLJ executable statements that do not specify a connection context instance will use the default connection that you define using this method (or that you define using Oracle.connect()).

■ **getDefaultContext()** This is a static method that returns the DefaultContext instance currently defined as the default connection for your application (through the earlier use of the setDefaultContext() class method). The getDefaultContext() method returns null if setDefaultContext() was not previously called.

■ **getExecutionContext()** A method that returns the default ExecutionContext instance for this connection context instance.

■ **close(boolean** [CLOSE_CONNECTION/KEEP_CONNECTION]**)** Use this method to close a connection and release all resources.

The sqlj.runtime.ExecutionContext Class

The ExecutionContext class contains methods for execution control, execution status, and execution cancellation. This section lists the methods of the ExecutionContext class and categorizes them as:

■ Status methods.

■ Control methods.

■ Cancellation methods.

Status Methods

You can use the following methods to obtain status information about the most recent SQL operation:

■ **getWarnings()** Returns a java.sql.SQLWarning object containing the warnings reported by the last SQL operation that completed using this context, or returns a **null** if no warning occurred. The SQL Warning object ultimately represents all warnings generated during the execution of the SQL operation and the subsequent outputting of parameters to the output host expressions.

■ **getUpdateCount()** Returns the number of rows updated by the last SQL operation executed using this execution context instance. Zero (0) is returned if the last SQL operation was not a DML statement. The value of the constant QUERY_COUNT is returned if the last SQL operation produced an iterator or result set. The constant value of the EXCEPTION_COUNT is returned if the last SQL operation terminated before completing execution, or if no operation has yet been attempted using this execution context instance.

Control Methods

Use the following methods of an execution context instance to control the operation of future SQL operations executed using that instance (operations that have not yet started).

■ **getMaxFieldSize()** Returns an **int** specifying the maximum amount of data (in bytes) that would be returned from a SQL operation subsequently using this execution context. This applies only to columns of type BINARY, VARBINARY, LONGVARBINARY, CHAR, VARCHAR, or LONGVARCHAR (see tables in the "Supported Types for Host Expressions" section of this appendix). By default, this parameter is set to zero (0), meaning there is no size limit.

■ **setMaxFieldSize()** Takes an **int** as input to modify the field-size maximum.

■ **getMaxRows()** Returns an **int** specifying the maximum number of rows that can be contained by any SQLJ iterator or JDBC result set created using this execution context instance. If the limit is exceeded, the excess rows are silently dropped without any error report or warning. By default, this parameter is set to zero (0), meaning there is no row limit.

■ **setMaxRows()** Takes an **int** as input to modify the row maximum.

■ **getQueryTimeout()** Returns an **int** specifying the timeout limit, in seconds, for any SQL operation that uses this execution context instance. (This can be modified using the setQueryTimeout() method.) If a SQL operation exceeds this limit, a SQL exception is thrown. By default, this parameter is set to zero (0), meaning there is no query timeout limit.

■ **setQueryTimeout()** Takes an **int** as input to modify the query timeout limit.

Cancellation Method

The cancel() method can be used to cancel SQL operations in a multi-threading environment.

■ **cancel()** This method is used by one thread to cancel a SQL operation currently being executed by another thread. It cancels the most recent operation that has started but not completed using this execution context instance. This method has no effect if no statement is currently being executed using this execution context instance.

Supported Types for Host Expressions

In this section, you will find the supported SQLJ type host expressions:

- Standard JDBC types
- Java wrapper classes
- Oracle extensions
- SQLJ stream classes

Standard JDBC Types

Table D-1 summarizes the JDBC types that are supported by SQLJ.

Java Type	OracleTypes Definition	Oracle Data Type
boolean	BIT	NUMBER
byte	TINYINT	NUMBER
short	SMALLINT	NUMBER
int	INTEGER	NUMBER
long	BIGINT	NUMBER
float	REAL	NUMBER
double	FLOAT, DOUBLE	NUMBER
`java.lang.String`	CHAR	CHAR
`java.lang.String`	VARCHAR	VARCHAR2
`java.lang.String`	LONGVARCHAR	LONG
byte[]	BINARY	RAW
byte[]	VARBINARY	RAW
byte[]	LONGVARBINARY	LONGRAW

TABLE D-1. *Standard JDBC Types*

Java Type	OracleTypes Definition	Oracle Data Type
java.sql.Date	DATE	DATE
java.sql.Time	TIME	DATE
java.sql.Timestamp	TIMESTAMP	DATE
java.math.BigDecimal	NUMERIC	NUMBER
java.math.BigDecimal	DECIMAL	NUMBER

TABLE D-1. *Standard JDBC Types* (continued)

Java Wrapper Classes

Since Java primitive types cannot contain null values, you can use the Java wrapper classes (Table D-2) when the database may return a null value.

Oracle Extensions

The oracle.sql classes are wrappers for the SQL data and provide appropriate mappings and conversion methods to Java formats. Because data in an oracle.sql.* object remains in SQL format, no precision information is lost. When you use Java variables in your SQLJ program, the SQL output is converted to a corresponding Java data type (see Table D-3) and the SQL input is converted to a corresponding Oracle data type.

Java Type	OracleTypes Definition	Oracle Data Type
java.lang.Boolean	BIT	NUMBER
java.lang.Byte	TINYINT	NUMBER
java.lang.Short	SMALLINT	NUMBER
java.lang.Integer	INTEGER	NUMBER
java.lang.Long	BIGINT	NUMBER
java.lang.Float	REAL	NUMBER
java.lang.Double	FLOAT, DOUBLE	NUMBER

TABLE D-2. *Java Wrapper Classes*

Java Type	OracleTypes Definition	Oracle Data Type
oracle.sql.NUMBER	NUMBER	NUMBER
oracle.sql.CHAR	CHAR	CHAR
oracle.sql.RAW	RAW	RAW
oracle.sql.DATE	DATE	DATE
oracle.sql.ROWID	ROWID	ROWID
oracle.sql.BLOB	BLOB	BLOB
oracle.sql.CLOB	CLOB	CLOB
oracle.sql.BFILE	BFILE	BFILE
oracle.sql.STRUCT	STRUCT	STRUCT
oracle.sql.REF	REF	REF
oracle.sql.ARRAY	ARRAY	ARRAY

TABLE D-3. *Oracle Extensions*

NOTE
Numeric types in the Oracle database are stored as a NUMBER. When retrieving data from the Oracle database and converting to Java types, precision may be lost when using the Oracle JDBC drivers. Therefore, depending on the use, you may want to use the oracle.sql.NUMBER *to preserve the precision.*

SQLJ Stream Classes

Standard SQLJ provides Binary, ASCII, and Unicode classes (Table D-4), for convenient handling of long data in streams (see Chapter 6).

Java Type	OracleTypes Definition	Oracle Data type
sqlj.runtime.BinaryStream	LONGVARBINARY	LONG RAW
sqlj.runtime.AsciiStream	LONGVARCHAR	LONG
sqlj.runtime.UnicodeStream	LONGVARCHAR	LONG

TABLE D-4. *SQLJ Stream Classes*

Tools

This section discusses the SQLJ, EJB and CORBA tools:

- SQLJ Translator tool: `sqlj`
- Java Archive tool: `jar`
- JPublisher tool: `jpub`
- Load Java tool: `loadjava`
- Drop Java tool: `dropjava`
- Enterprise JavaBeans tool: `deployejb`
- Session Namespace tool: `publish`

SQLJ Translator Tool: sqlj

The Oracle `sqlj` tool is used for translating SQLJ source codes and invoking the Java compiler (see Chapter 2). The syntax for the `sqlj` tool at the command line is:

```
sqlj <option-list> file-list
```

The *option-list* is a list of SQLJ option settings separated by spaces (see Table D-5). The *file-list* is the list of files, `.sqlj`, `.java`, `.ser`, or `.jar`, separated by spaces. The * wildcard entry can be used in filenames.

Options	Descriptions	Default
-C <option>	Pass -<option> to javac compiler.	n/a
-classpath (command line only)	Option to specify CLASSPATH to Java VM and Java compiler (passed to javac).	None
-compile=false	Do not compile generated Java files.	True
-d=<directory>	Set output directory for generated `.ser` and `.class` binary files.	Empty

TABLE D-5. *sqlj Option List*

Options	Descriptions	Default
-dir	Option to set output directory for SQLJ-generated `.java` files.	Empty
-driver	Option to specify JDBC driver to register.	`oracle.jdbc.driver.OracleDriver`
-P<option>	Prefix that marks options to pass to SQLJ profile customizer.	n/a
Password=<password>	Option to set user password for database connection for online semantics checking.	None
-profile=false	Do not customize generated `*.ser` profile files.	True
-props	Option to specify properties file.	None
-ser2class	Convert generated `*.ser` files to `*.class` files.	False
-status, -v	Print status during translation.	False
-url=<url>	Specify URL for online checking.	jdbc:oracle:oci8:@
-user, -u	Enable online checking.	None (no online semantics checking)
-verbose (command-line only)	Passed to javac; enables status.	n/a
-warn	Comma-separated list of flags to enable or disable various warnings—individual flags are precision/noprecision, nulls/nonulls, portable/noportable, strict/nostrict, and verbose/noverbose; global flag is all/none.	precision nulls noportable strict noverbose

TABLE D-5.   *sqlj Option List* (continued)

The following example does not run the customize profile; it converts the `.ser` files to `.class` files, and sets the output directory for the `.class` files to "dist" (see Chapters 4 and 5):

```
sqlj -profile=false -ser2class -d=dist PIManager.sqlj
SqljInJavaApplet.java
```

Translator Properties File

You can supply a SQLJ properties file to the SQLJ translator instead of supplying options as arguments at the command line. When the SQLJ translator is invoked, it always searches for the *default* properties file `sqlj.properties`. The translator looks for this properties file in the following order: the Java home directory, the user home directory, and the current directory.

The `properties.file` rules and syntax follow:

- You cannot use the following options in the `sqlj.properties` files: -classpath, -help, -help-long, -help-alias, -C-help, -P-help, -J, -n, -passes, -props, -version, -version-long, and –vm.

- Each SQLJ option is prefixed by `sqlj`. For example:
  ```
  sqlj.warn=none
  sqlj.linemap=true
  ```

- Each Java compiler option is prefixed by *compile*, instead of -C-. For example:
  ```
  compile.verbose
  ```

- General profile customization options are prefixed by *profile*, instead of -P-. For example:
  ```
  profile.backup
  ```

The following is a sample `sqlj.properties` file that uses the default context:

```
# A line that begins with a '#' is a comment line.
# Set user/password and JDBC driver
sqlj.user=scott/tiger
sqlj.driver=oracle.jdbc.driver.OracleDriver
# Turn on the compiler verbose option
compile.verbose
```

Java Archive Tool: jar

The `jar` tool is an archive utility that combines (archives) multiple files into a single file with a `.jar` extension. This Java application tool is mainly used to facilitate the packaging of Java applets or applications into a single archive file. The following is the syntax for the SUN JDK jar utility:

```
jar {ctx}[vfm0M] [jar-file] [manifest-file] file1, file2, …
```

The options are:

Option	Description
-c	Create new archive.
-t	List table of contents for archive.
-x *filename*	Extract named (or all) files from archive.
-v	Generate verbose output on standard error.
-f	Specify archive filename.
-m	Include manifest information from specified manifest file.
-0	Store only; use no ZIP compression; jar file that can be put in your CLASSPATH.
-M	Do not create a manifest file for the entries.

The following example combines all the files containing `.class` and `.ser` extensions into an uncompressed jar archive file named `jarfile1.jar` (see Chapter 5):

```
jar -cvf0 jarfile1.jar *.class *.ser
```

The following example creates a jar archive file called `jarfile2.jar` and combines all the files of directory `dir1` and all the files with the extension of `.class` files from the directory `dir2`:

```
jar -cvf0 jarfile2.jar dir1 dir2/*.class
```

JPublisher Tool: jpub

The `jpub` tool is used for automatically generating custom Java classes (see Chapters 7 and 8). This tool connects to a database and retrieves the declarations of the SQL object types or PL/SQL packages that you specify on the command line or from an input file. The syntax for invoking the JPublisher tool is:

```
jpub <options>
```

Here's a list of options for the JPublisher tool:

Option	Description
-case=<case>	The Java identifiers that JPublisher generates. The <case> are `mixed`, `same`, `lower`, and `upper`; where the default is `mixed`.
-dir	The directory that holds generated packages.
-driver	The JDBC driver JPublisher uses to connect to the database. The default driver is `oracle.jdbc.driver.OracleDriver`.
-input	The file that lists the types and packages JPublisher translates.
-mapping	Specifies which object attribute type and method argument type mapping the generated methods support. The mapping types are `oracle`, `jdbc`, or `objectjdbc`. If no type is specified, then it assumes `objectjdbc`.
-methods	Determines whether JPublisher generates classes for PL/SQL packages and wrapper methods for methods in packages and object types. If `-methods=false`, JPublisher does not generate PL/SQL classes and methods. The default is `-methods=false`.
-omit_schema_names	Specifies whether all object type and package names generated by JPublisher include the schema name.
-package	The name of the Java package for which JPublisher is generating a Java wrapper.
-props=<filename>	Specifies a file that contains JPublisher options in addition to those listed on the command line.
-sql	Specifies object types and packages for which JPublisher will generate code.
-types	Specifies object types for which JPublisher will generate code. *Note:* The -types parameter is currently supported for compatibility, but deprecated in favor of -sql.
-url	Specifies the URL JPublisher uses to connect to the database. The default is `-url=jdbc:oracle:oci8:@`*sid*.
-user=<user/password>	An Oracle username and password. This must be supplied.

The following example causes JPublisher to connect to the database with username `scott` and password `tiger`. The `-mapping` option instructs JPublisher to map the object attribute types from the Oracle database into Java classes. With the `-package` option, JPublisher places the Java generated classes in the package `corp`. The `-dir` places all output in the `demo` directory:

```
jpub -user=scott/tiger -dir=demo -mapping=oracle -package=com.data-i
-types=PlatformType
```

JPublisher Properties File

Aside from passing command line parameters to the jpub tool, you can optionally use a properties file to specify parameters. This is accomplished by specifying the -props parameter with a text file:

```
jpub -props=jpublisher.properties
```

The following shows an example of the `jpublisher.properties` file:

```
# Filename: jpublisher.properties
# A line that begins with a '#' is a comment line.
jpub.user=scott/tiger
jpub.types=Employee
jpub.mapping=oracle
jpub.case=lower
jpub.package=corp
jpub.dir=demo
```

Using the previous `jpublisher.properties` file with the `jpub` tool is equivalent to the following:

```
jpub -user=scott/tiger -types=Employee -mapping=oracle -case=lower
-package=corp -dir=demo
```

Load Java Tool: loadjava

Use the `loadjava` tool to load resource files into the Oracle8*i* JServer. The `loadjava` tool creates schema objects from files and loads them into a schema (see Chapters 4, 5, and 8). You must have the CREATE PROCEDURE privilege to load files into your schema, and the CREATE ANY PROCEDURE privilege to load files into another schema. The syntax for the `loadjava` tool is:

```
loadjava [-user | -u] <user>/<password>[@<database>] [options]
    <file>.java | <file>.class | <file>.jar | <file>.zip |<file>.sqlj |
    <resourcefile> …
```

The options are listed here:

Option	Description
<filenames>	You can specify any number and combination of `.java`, `.class`, `.sqlj`, `.jar`, `.zip`, and resource filenames in any order. JAR and ZIP files must be uncompressed.
-andresolve	Directs `loadjava` to compile sources if they have been loaded and to resolve external references in each class as it is loaded. -andresolve and -resolve are mutually exclusive.
-debug	Directs the Java compiler to generate debug information.
-definer	By default, class schema objects run with the privileges of their invoker. This option confers definer privileges upon classes instead.
-grant <grants>	Grants the EXECUTE privilege on loaded classes to the listed users and/or roles. Any number and combination of user and role names can be specified, separated by commas but not spaces (-grant Bob,Betty not -grant Bob, Betty).
-oci8	Use the OCI JDBC driver. -oci8 and -thin are mutually exclusive; if neither is specified, -oci8 is used by default.
-oracleresolver	Use a resolver that requires all referred to classes to be found.
-resolve	Compiles (if necessary) and resolves external references in classes after all classes on the command line have been loaded. –andresolve and –resolve are mutually exclusive.
-resolver <resolver>	Use a resolver that requires all referred to classes to be found.
-schema	Designates the schema where schema objects are created. If not specified, the logon schema is used. To create a schema object in a schema that is not your own, you must have the CREATE PROCEDURE or CREATE ANY PROCEDURE privilege.

Option	Description
-synonym	Creates a PUBLIC synonym for loaded classes making them accessible outside the schema into which they are loaded. You must have the CREATE PUBLIC SYNONYM privilege.
-thin	Use the thin JDBC driver. -oci8 and -thin are mutually exclusive; if neither is specified, -oci8 is used by default.
-user, -u	Specifies a user, password, and database connect string. The argument has the form <username>/<password> [@<database>].
-verbose	Directs `loadjava` to emit detailed status messages while running.

The following example makes a connection to the default database with the default oci8 driver, loads the files contained in the `PurchaseItems.jar` file into the EMPLOYEE_LIST schema, and then resolves them:

```
loadjava -user scott/tiger -resolve
-schema EMPLOYEE_LIST PurchaseItems.jar
```

Next, connect with the thin driver and then load `TheSqljFile.sqlj` file, resolving it as it is loaded:

```
loadjava -thin -user scott/tiger@data-i.com:1521:ORCL
-resolve TheSqljFile.sqlj
```

Drop Java Tool: dropjava

Use the `dropjava` tool to remove Java schema objects from the data server (see Chapters 4 and 8 of this book and the *Oracle8i Enterprise JavaBeans and CORBA Developer's Guide*). This tool accomplishes the opposite of the `loadjava` tool. The syntax follows:

```
dropjava {-u | -user} <user>/<password>[@<database>] [options]
{<file>.java | <file>.class | file.sqlj | <file>.jar | <file>.zip |
<resourcefile>} …
```

Here is a list of the options of the dropjava tool:

Option	Description
-user	Specifies a user, password, and optional database connect string.
\<filenames\>	You can specify any number and combination of .java, .class, .sqlj, .jar, .zip, and resource filenames in any order. JAR and ZIP files must be uncompressed.
-oci8	Use the OCI JDBC driver. -oci8 and -thin are mutually exclusive; if neither is specified -oci8 is used by default.
-schema	Designates the schema from which schema objects are dropped. If not specified, the logon schema is used. To drop a schema object from a schema that is not your own, you need the DROP ANY PROCEDURE system privilege.
-thin	Use the thin JDBC driver. The -oci8 and -thin options are mutually exclusive; if neither is specified, then -oci8 is used by default.
-verbose	Directs dropjava to emit detailed status messages while running.

The following example removes the objects created by loading the TheSqljFile.sqlj file with the loadjava tool. The database connection is made through the default oci8 driver.

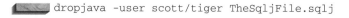

```
dropjava -user scott/tiger TheSqljFile.sqlj
```

If you translated your program on the client and loaded it using a .jar file containing the generated components, then use the same .jar file to remove the program:

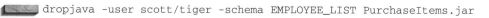

```
dropjava -user scott/tiger -schema EMPLOYEE_LIST PurchaseItems.jar
```

Enterprise JavaBeans Tool: deployejb

The deployejb tool reads the deployment descriptor and the bean .jar file containing interfaces and classes (see Chapter 8). The tool converts the text descriptor to a serialized object, generates and compiles classes that affect client-bean communication, loads compiled classes into the database. It also publishes the bean's home interface name in the session namespace so clients can look it up through JNDI.

```
deployejb -user <username> -password <password> -service <serviceURL>
-descriptor <file> -temp <dir> <beanjar> …
```

The options are as follows:

Option	Description
-user <username>	Username.
-password <password>	Specifies the password for <username>.
-service	URL identifying database in whose session namespace the EJB is to be published. The service URL has the form sess_iiop://<host>:<lport>:<sid>.
-descriptor	Specifies the text file containing the EJB deployment descriptor.
-temp	Specifies a temporary directory to hold intermediate files deployejb creates. Unless you specify -keep, deployejb removes the files and the directory upon completion.
-addclasspath <dirlist>	Lists table of contents for archive
-describe	Summarizes the tool's operation, and then exits.
-generated <clientjar>	Specifies the name of the output (generated) JAR file, which contains communication files bean clients need.
-help	Summarizes the tool's operation, and then exits.
-iiop	Connects to the target database with IIOP instead of the default session IIOP.
–keep	Do not remove the temporary files generated by the tool.
-republish	Replaces the published BeanHomeName attributes if it has already been published.
-role <role>	Specifies role to assume when connecting to the database; no default.
-ssl	Connects to the database with SSL authentication and encryption.
-verbose	Emits detailed status information while running.
-version	Shows the tool's version, and then exits.

The following example uses the `deployejb` tool to generate the `.jar` file to use on the client side to access the bean:

```
deployejb -republish -temp /temp -u obsschema -p obsschema
-service sess_iiop://data-i.com:1521:ORCL
-descriptor platform.ejb platform.jar
```

Session Namespace Tool: publish

The `publish` tool creates or replaces (republishes) a `PublishedObject` in a `PublishingContext` (see Chapter 8 and the *Oracle8i Enterprise JavaBeans and CORBA Developer's Guide*). Use the command-line `publish` tool to create (publish) `PublishedObjects`:

```
publish <name> <class> [<helper>] -user <username>
-password <password> -service <serviceURL> [options]
```

The options are as follows:

Option	Description
<name>	Name of the `PublishedObject` being created or republished; `PublishingContexts` are created if necessary.
<class>	Name of the class schema object that corresponds to <name>.
<helper>	Name of the Java class schema object that implements the narrow() method for <class>.
-user <username>	Username.
-password <password>	Specifies authenticating password for specified with <username>.
-service	URL identifying database whose session namespace is to be "opened" by sess_sh. The service URL has the form: sess_iiop://<host>:<lport>:<sid>.
-describe	Summarizes the tool's operation, and then exits.
-grant <schemas>	Grants read and execute rights to the list of schemas.
-help	Summarizes the tool's syntax, and then exits.
-iiop	Connects to the target database with IIOP instead of the default session IIOP.

Option	Description
-role	Role to assume while publishing; no default.
-republish	Republish if object already exists. If the `PublishedObject` does not exist, `publish` creates it.
-schema schema	The schema containing the Java \<class\> schema object.
-ssl	Connects to the database with SSL server authentication.
-version	Shows the tool's version, and then exits.

The following example publishes the CORBA server implementation vbjBankTestbank.AccountManagerImpl and its helper class as /test/bankMgr in the tool invoker's schema:

```
publish -republish -u obsschema -p obsschema -schema OBSSCHEMA
-service sess_iiop://data-i.com:1521:ORCL
/test/corbaPlatform platServer.PlatformImpl platform.PlatformHelper
```

Bibliography

1. *A Brief Overview of JDBC,* http://java.sun.com/products/jdbc/overview.html.

2. Albertson, Tom, *Best Practices in Distributed Object Application Development: RMI, CORBA and DCOM (Part 1 of 4),* http://www.developer.com/news/techfocus/022398_dist1.html, February 1998.

3. Albertson, Tom, *Distributed Object Application Development: The Java-RMI Solution (Part 2 of 4),* http://www.developer.com/news/techfocus/030298_dist2.html, March 1998.

4. Albertson, Tom, *Distributed Object Application Development: The Java-CORBA Solution (Part 3 of 4),* http://www.developer.com/news/techfocus/030998_dist3.html, March 1998.

5. Astrahan, M.M. et al, *System R: Relational Approach to Database Management,* ACM TODS 1, No. 2, June 1976.

6. Austin, Calvin and Monica Pawlan, *Writing Advanced Applications for the Java Platform,* http://developer.java.sun.com/developer/onlineTraining/Programming/DCBook/index.html#contents, August 1999.

7. Bauer, Mark, *Oracle8i Tuning, Release 8.1.5,* Oracle Corporation, 1999.

8. Burghart, Ted, *Distributed Computing Overview,* http://www.quoininc.com/quoininc/dist_comp.html, 1998.

9. *Cafe au Lait Java FAQs, News, and Resources,* http://metalab.unc.edu/javafaq.

10. Chen, Peter Pin-Shan, *The Entity-Relationship Model— Toward a Unified View of Data,* ACM TODS 1, No. 1, March 1976.

11. Coad, Peter, Mark Mayfield, and Jon Kern, *Java Design, Building Better Apps & Applets, Second Ed.,* Yourdon Press Computing Series, 1999.

12. Codd, E.F., *A Relational Model of Data for Large Shared Data Banks,* CACM 13, No. 6, June 1970.

13. *CORBA 2.2 Specification,* http://www.omg.org/corba/cichpter.html#idls&s, February 1998.

14. *Database Languages—SQL—Part 10: SQL/OLB (ANSI X3.135.10),* American National Standards Institute, 1998.

15. Date, C.J., *An Introduction to Database Systems, Sixth Ed.,* Addison-Wesley, 1995.

16. *Enterprise JavaBeans Tutorial: Building Your First Stateless Session Bean,* http://developer.java.sun.com/developer/onlineTraining/Beans/EJBTutorial/index.html.

17. Feldmann, Bronya and Jeff Stein, *Oracle8i ProC Manual,* Oracle Corporation, 1999.

18. Flanagan, David, *Java In A Nutshell,* O'Reilly, 1997.

19. Gosling, James, Bill Joy, and Guy Steele, *The Java Language Specification, Version 1.0,* http://asuwlink.uwyo.edu/sun-jws/, 1996.

20. Gray, Jim and Andreas Reuter, *Transaction Processing: Concepts and Techniques,* Morgan Kaufmann Publishers, 1993.

21. Hamilton, Graham, Rick Cattell, and Maydene Fisher, *JDBC Database Access with Java, A Tutorial and Annotated Reference,* Addison-Wesley, 1997.

22. Harold, Elliotte Rusty, *Java I/O,* O'Reilly, 1999.

23. Harris, Steven G., *Oracle8i Java Developer's Guide and Reference, Release 8.1.5,* A64682-01, Oracle Corporation, 1999.

24. Heller, Philip et al., *Java 1.1 Developer's Handbook,* Sybex, 1997.

25. *Java Naming Directory Interface (JNDI),* http://java.sun.com/products/jndi/.

26. *Java Remote Method Invocation Specification 1.50, JDK 1.2,* October 1998, http://java.sun.com/products/jdk/1.2/docs/guide/rmi/spec/rmiTOC.doc.html.

27. *JNDI 1.1 and 1.2 Documentation,* http://java.sun.com/products/jndi/docs.html#12.

28. Lorentz, Diana and Denise Oertel, *Oracle8i SQL Reference, Release 8.1.5,* Oracle Corporation, 1999.

29. McClanahan, David, *Oracle Developer's Guide,* Oracle Press, Osborne/McGraw-Hill, 1996.

30. Mohseni, Piroz, *Exploit Distributed Java Computing with RMI, NC World,* http://www.ncworldmag.com/ncw-01-1998/ncw-01-rmi.html, January 1998.

31. Mohseni, Piroz, *Exploit Distributed Java Computing with RMI, Part II, NC World,* http://www.ncworldmag.com/ncw-02-1998/ncw-02-rmi2.html, February 1998.

32. Momplaisir, Gerald, *Design of a Financial Administrative System Using the Semantic Binary Model,* Master's thesis, School of Computer Sciences, Florida International University, 1997.

33. Monson-Haefel, Richard, *Enterprise JavaBeans,* O'Reilly & Associates, Inc., June 1999.

34. Morisseau-Leroy, Nirva, *Atmospheric Observations, Analyses, and the World Wide Web Using a Semantic Database,* Master's thesis, School of Computer Sciences, Florida International University, 1997.

35. Orfali, Robert, and Dan Harkey, *Client/Server Programming with Java and CORBA, Second Ed.,* John Wiley & Sons, 1998.

36. Orfali, Robert, et al., *Instant CORBA,* John Wiley & Sons, 1997.

37. *Part 1—The Stored Procedure Specification, Part 2—The Stored Java Class Specification,* http://www.oracle.com/java/sqlj/standards.html.

38. Pfaeffle, Thomas, *Oracle8i JDBC Developer's Guide and Reference, Release 8.1.5,* Oracle Corporation, 1999.

39. Portfolio, Tom, *Oracle8i Java Stored Procedures and Developer's Guide, Release 8.1.5,* Oracle Corporation, 1999.

40. Portfolio, Tom, *PL/SLQ User's Guide and Reference, Release 8.1.5,* Oracle Corporation, 1999.

41. Raphaely, Denis and Susan Kotsovolos, *Oracle8i Application Developer's Guide—Large Objects (LOBs), Release 8.1.5,* Oracle Corporation, 1999.

42. Raphaely, Denis, *Oracle8i Application Developer's Guide—Fundamentals, Release 8.1.5,* Oracle Corporation, 1999.

43. *RMI over IIOP,* http://java.sun.com/products/rmi-iiop/, June 1999.

44. Schlicher, Bob, *Applying CORBA in the Enterprise,* http://developer.netscape.com/viewsource/schlicher_corba.html, February 1998.

45. Schlicher, Bob, *CORBA in the Enterprise, Part 2: Prerequisites and Analysis,* http://developer.netscape.com/viewsource/schlicher_corba2/schlicher_corba2.html.

46. Schlicher, Bob, *CORBA in the Enterprise, Part 3: Object-Oriented System Design,* http://developer.netscape.com/viewsource/schlicher_corba3.html.

47. Schlicher, Bob, *CORBA in the Enterprise, Part 4: Applying Object-Oriented and Component Design,* http://developer.netscape.com/viewsource/schlicher_corba4/schlicher_corba4.html.

48. Shah, Rawn, *Bean Basics: Enterprise JavaBeans Fundamentals, NC World,* http://www.ncworldmag.com/ncw-04-1998/ncw-04-ejbprog2.html, April 1998.

49. Shah, Rawn, *Bean Basics: Enterprise JavaBeans Programming, NC World,* http://www.ncworldmag.com/ncworld/ncw-03-1998/ncw-03-ejbprog.html, March 1998.

50. Shah, Rawn, *Enterprise JavaBeans: Industrial-Strength Java, NC World,* http://www.ncworldmag.com/ncworld/ncw-01-1998/ncw-01-ejbeans.html, January 1998.

51. Siple, Matthew, *The Complete Guide to Java Database Programming, JDBC, ODBC, and SQL,* Computing McGraw-Hill, 1998.

52. Smith, Tim and Bill Courington, *Enterprise JavaBeans and CORBA Developer's Guide, Release 8.1.5,* Oracle Corporation, 1999.

53. *SQLJ Availability in DB2 for OS/390,* http://www.software.ibm.com/data/db2/os390/sqlj.html .

54. *SQLJ,* http://www.sqlj.org/.

55. Stonebraker, Michael, Eugene Wong, Peter Kreps, and Gerald Held, *The Design and Implementation of INGRES,* ACM TODS 1, No. 3, September 1976.

56. *Sun Microsystems Enterprise JavaBeans Specification 1.0,* http://java.sun.com/products/ejb/docs10.html, March 1998.

57. *Sun Microsystems Glossary,* http://www.sun.com/glossary/glossary.html.

58. *Sun Microsystems JavaBeans Specification 1.01,* http://java.sun.com/beans/spec.html, December 1996.

59. *Unicode Consortium,* http://www.unicode.net.

60. Urman, Scott, *Oracle8 PL/SQL Programming,* Oracle Press, Osborne/McGraw-Hill, 1997.

61. Valesky, Tom, *Enterprise JavaBeans, Developing Component-Based Distributed Applications,* Addison-Wesley, 1999.

62. Wang, Paul S., *Java with Object-Oriented Programming and World Wide Web Applications,* Brooks/Cole Publishing, 1999.

63. Wright, Brian, *Oracle8i SQLJ Developer's Guide and Reference, Release 8.1.5,* A64684-01, Oracle Corporation, 1999.

Index